Rev. Wm. E. Caldwell.
from Young Ladies Circle of
Whitinsville Cong'l Soc. 1876.

BAPTISM

TESTED BY

SCRIPTURE AND HISTORY

OR

THE TEACHING OF THE HOLY SCRIPTURES, AND THE PRACTICE AND TEACHING OF THE CHRISTIAN CHURCH IN EVERY AGE SUCCEEDING THE APOSTOLIC, COMPARED IN RELATION TO THE SUBJECTS AND MODES OF BAPTISM

BY

WILLIAM HODGES, D. D.

RECTOR OF CHRIST CHURCH, WEST RIVER, MARYLAND

Third Edition, Revised and Improved

"Prove all things: hold fast that which is good." — ST. PAUL

NEW YORK
E. P. DUTTON AND COMPANY
713 BROADWAY
1875

Riverside, Cambridge:
Stereotyped and Printed by
H. O. Houghton and Company.

PREFACE.

THIS third edition of BAPTISM TESTED BY HOLY SCRIPTURE AND HISTORY, comes before the public revised with much care; its authorities all reëxamined; portions re-written; some parts condensed, and others amplified. It may be presumed, therefore, that it is relieved of defects in former editions, and advanced to more perfect knowledge on points at issue.

The general plan of the book is the same; the witness of the Church on the *subjects* and *modes* of Baptism traced through the Fathers up to the fountain head of Holy Writ; and the proof-texts of Scripture carefully and minutely analyzed. In connection with which, is examined the relation of Circumcision to Baptism; the *rites* and *usages* of the Jewish Church; also the use and acceptation of terms applied to little children in the NEW TESTAMENT, compared with their use and application in the next age after it was written. Thus uniting evidence *positive*, *historical*, and *circumstantial* to elicit the true interpretation of God's word.

In tracing the mode or modes of Baptism, and the meaning of the terms βαπτίζω and βαπτισμός, about which so much has been written, the following pages will show, that since words so often depart from their primary meaning, and are used in a different sense in one age from what they are in another, that it is more important to ascertain what was the *meaning or usage of these terms in the times of Christ and his Apostles*, than to know their root or origin; for all critical scholars will admit that, "A word may come to enlarge its meaning so as to lose sight of its origin," — and that, "USE IS THE SOLE ARBITER OF LANGUAGE."

Therefore, instead of confining our inquiries to the primary meaning of βαπτίζω, and its use in former ages, the author of this work proceeds to show what was its USAGE in the age and country in which the NEW TESTAMENT was written — and especially in the pages of that book itself. And instead of a SPECIFIC term embracing "only one mode of action," the attentive reader will find that it is GENERIC, and applicable to various modes. And further, that during the whole history of the Church, whatever was the prevailing mode at any particular period, other modes were allowed also, and practised when circumstances rendered it expedient.

Having devoted much time to these subjects, and sought instruction from every source within his reach, of which he supposed light could be obtained, without regard to names or shades of faith, the author has used the information thus acquired in the way which he supposed would develop most fully, and enforce most successfully the truth. And in his citations from authors, ancient and modern, he has not hesitated, irrespective of Shibboleths, to give in full and without partiality the name and testimony as far as the evidence is pertinent to the question in point — and always credited the proper authority when conscious of using his words, or of expressing himself in similar language.

The *Effects* of Baptism, he has not regarded as coming necessarily within the range of his present work; and being desirous to free as much as possible the legitimate inquiries of the "Subjects and Modes" of Baptism from whatever might complicate and incumber his undertaking, he has endeavored to avoid all *mooted points* among the members of his own Church, and between them and others who practise Infant Baptism as well.

And he now submits the following pages to his brethren in Christ, and to all earnest seekers for the truth; humbly trusting that the Giver of all Grace will make them instrumental in leading inquirers to the knowledge and obedience of his will, and to the building up of the Redeemer's Kingdom!

At the suggestion of friends, an abridgment of the present work for the use of Bible classes and Sunday-schools is contemplated.

Rectory of Christ Church,
West River, Md.

CONTENTS.

CHAPTER I.

ARE LITTLE CHILDREN EMBRACED IN THE TERMS OF THE CHRISTIAN COVENANT?

CHAPTER II.

HISTORICAL TESTIMONY, CONTINUED.

CHAPTER III.

HISTORICAL TESTIMONY, CONTINUED.

CHAPTER IV.

TESTIMONY HISTORICAL AND CIRCUMSTANTIAL.

CHAPTER V.

RELATION OF BAPTISM TO CIRCUMCISION.

CHAPTER VI.

RELATION OF CIRCUMCISION AND BAPTISM, CONCLUDED.

CHAPTER VII.

TESTIMONY OF THE HOLY SCRIPTURES.

CHAPTER VIII.

TESTIMONY OF THE HOLY SCRIPTURES, CONCLUDED.

CHAPTER IX.

MODE OR MODES OF BAPTISM.

CHAPTER X.

EXAMINATION OF THE MEANING AND MODES OF BAPTISM, CONTINUED

CHAPTER XI.

BAPTISM BY DIFFERENT MODES VALID IN EVERY AGE OF THE CHURCH.

CHAPTER XII.

THE ORIGIN OF ANTIPÆDOBAPTISM, AND THE CLAIMS OF BAPTISTS EXAMINED.

BAPTISM

TESTED BY SCRIPTURE AND HISTORY.

CHAPTER I.

ARE LITTLE CHILDREN EMBRACED IN THE TERMS OF THE CHRISTIAN COVENANT ?

Preliminary Remarks. — Nature of the Testimony. — Removal of Extraneous Matter. — State of the Question. — Point at Issue. — Principles of Interpretation.— Practice of all Ancient Churches. — Origin of Antipædobaptists. — Infant Baptism traced. — Constantly referred to in the Pelagian Controversy. — Admitted to be the Rule of the Universal Church by Pelagius and Celestius. — Council of Carthage, Two Hundred and Fourteen Bishops present. — Council of Milevium. — Synodical Letter from Africa.

§ 1. THE ruling desire of every heart should be, to embrace *the truth*, *only the truth*, *and the whole truth* contained in the system of Religion taught by our Lord Jesus Christ. No man has the right to erect for himself a standard lower than this ; nor to reject any means, within his reach, that will aid him in the attainment of Gospel truth. The Holy Scriptures being our RULE OF FAITH, our first duty is to endeavor to understand them.

When *two* opposing doctrines are drawn from their holy pages, it is certain that one is wrong. Both cannot be right. Truth calls for an investigation of the claims of each. The principles of interpretation on which they depend should be examined, and their true meaning earnestly sought out.

How do men proceed in such cases with other *Ancient writings?* All readers of the ancient classics know, that in order to ascertain the entire meaning of passages found on almost every page of such writings, we must make ourselves acquainted with the customs, laws, and various institutions of the country and age of the writer. And when called on to decide between the opposing interpretations of Annotators, we bring to our aid *all the light* that can be obtained *from every source*. Shall we observe less care and diligence in the interpretation of the ancient records of the Holy Scriptures? Is it more important to ascertain the full meaning of the ancient classics, than the true intent of the teaching of the Bible? Surely this will not be admitted. What then? Shall we take for granted there is nothing in the Scriptures "hard to be understood" — nothing but what is plain to the most illiterate reader, and about which all men may easily agree? The *Divine record itself*, as well as *facts numerous*, testify to the contrary.

Many take up the New Testament, read over the English translation in a cursory manner, interpret it without any regard to the *circumstances* under which the events and teaching therein recorded took place, and not finding, for instance, Infant Baptism, the Divinity of Christ, or any other doctrine, taught in the way which they had marked out in their own imagination, they discard them as unworthy of belief, and refuse to hear anything more about them.

In this way *half* of the doctrines of our holy religion may be rejected — ay, the *whole Scriptures* of both the Old and New Testaments — hence, the whole of our religious faith! Some even go so far as to *prescribe* "*a plain, positive precept or example*," as necessary to their reception of any doctrine! Such presumption need not be noticed here, however, further than to ask — "Who hath known the mind of the Lord, or who hath been his counsellor?" Is it not *His* to command, and *ours* to obey?

2. A *clearly implied duty* is as binding, as one made known in any other way. Our business in such cases, is to *examine testimony*, not to *prescribe what kind* it shall be. Be it *express* or *implied*, *direct* or *circumstantial*, we must hear it, and give it the authority to which it is entitled. God, our Supreme Lawgiver, has the right to teach us in any way that he pleases; and if any truth or duty be *clearly implied* in his holy word, it is at our *peril*, that we reject or neglect it. We are not permitted to dictate the *mode*, in which He shall teach us. But must thankfully receive his instructions *in whatever way* he may choose to give them. Thousands split on this rock. They *prescribe the way beforehand* in which Infant Baptism must be made known; not remembering that the Church was planted before the New Testament Scriptures were written; that it was only necessary to *allude* to many things because well known to all at the time; and that the Evangelical record is a very concise statement of the sayings and doings of Christ and his Apostles, preserving merely the *seeds*, for the future use of the Church, — we say, not *bearing in mind these things*, they do not govern their expectations accordingly, and hence not finding Infant Baptism set forth in that *bold relief* which they anticipated, they reject it without *examining the question properly*. In the same way the Jews rejected the Saviour! They had pictured in imagination, a royal personage in pomp and splendor, to which the meek and lowly Jesus did not cor-

respond when he came; and before examining sufficiently to discover that He was the *promised Messiah*, they rejected him! as others now do many of his doctrines!

3. Another obstacle that stands in the way of an impartial examination of this question is, the want of *clear and definite ideas* of what is embraced in the inquiry. Many associate with Infant Baptism the *mode* of baptizing; supposing the *mode* to be included in the question at issue; as if young children could not be baptized in *any way*, that you may baptize an adult. Again, certain abuses, that have been witnessed in the baptizing of children are often associated with the ordinance as a necessary part of the question itself; but what institution may not be abused?

In order to enter upon an impartial examination of this question, all these obstacles must be removed. The examiner should endeavor to free his mind from all previous bias *for* or *against* Infant Baptism; lay aside all preconceived notions as to the *kind* and *degree* of evidence; remove from the question itself all extraneous matter, and place before him the simple inquiry — "Is Infant Baptism a Divine Institution, or is it not?

4. Bearing in mind these preliminaries, and thus relieving the question of much unnecessary incumbrance, we may next inquire into the *state* of the controversy; for Infant Baptism is not a question which has just begun to be controverted, — it has been in the field of theological polemics more than three centuries; and the subject of occasional debate more than six!

During the last century Antipædobaptists[1] have labored with great zeal and energy to spread their

[1] Now generally called Baptists.

principles in newly settled countries; but they are yet few in number, compared with those who baptize children. All the ANCIENT CHURCHES now in existence, without an exception, still baptize Infants, and contend that the Apostles and their successors did the same. And more than *seven-eighths* of those bearing more modern names adhere to the same rite; for which they claim the authority of Scripture and History; and we challenge the proof of a single sect (which baptized at all), that did not baptize little children during the first thousand years of Christianity.

To all which, Antipædobaptists reply, — that although it was the general custom of Christians to baptize Infants for a long series of years, it had its beginning after the death of the Apostles, — yet they admit that they do not know in what way or at what particular time it was introduced.

5. Such being the state of the case, we ask how shall this controversy be settled? It will perhaps be replied, — "Let both parties go to the Holy Scriptures." This they have done, but differ in their interpretations on this point. Various passages are pointed out, one party saying, — "Here it is commanded" — "there it is again implied" — "that passage takes for granted the church-membership of little children" — "this alludes to the same thing," — and so on. But the other denying, construes them all differently.

Must they always continue in this state of opposition to each other? Shall the Church of Christ be thus rent in twain, and a schism perpetuated to the end of time, notwithstanding the Saviour himself prayed the Father, that his followers might "all be one, as he and his Father were one?" And when the Apostle Paul also, with so much earnestness enjoins it on Christians that there should be no divisons among them? saying, "*Now I beseech you, brethren, by the name of our Lord Jesus Christ, that ye all speak the same thing, and that there be no divisions among you; but that ye be perfectly joined together in the same mind and in the same judgment.*"[1] Surely, if we desire to obey the injunctions of Divine writ, we must desire to see this controversy brought to a close. And if we love truth, if we love peace, if we love our Lord Jesus Christ, we will avail ourselves of all lawful means to find truth, preserve peace, and honor our blessed Redeemer.

6. Now there are principles of interpretation received and applied to other ANCIENT WRITINGS, and likewise to other portions of THE HOLY SCRIPTURES, which, if applied to these disputed passages, may show on which side the truth lies. There are also the writings of early Christian authors, who wrote in the next and following age after the Apostles, that may aid us in this matter, — writers who were members of the Church, and who devoted their lives to the cause of Christ; suffering some of them, even unto death in defence of the Gospel. Shall we hesitate to consult them on this point, — whether so notable a thing as Infant Baptism was practised in their day? whether a public ordinance of the Church, about which they could not be deceived, was then observed? *surely not.* They had eyes as well as we; they had memories too. And if pious, conscientious men, why refuse their testimony to that which is the object of the senses and of public notoriety? If they speak of the baptizing of young children in their writings, why

[1] 1 Cor. i. 10.

not believe they speak the truth in this, as in other things? Is it to be presumed, they would refer to a thing that had no existence? And if we cannot trust their testimony on a point of this kind, how can we trust it in regard to the different books of the New Testament? To whose writings do we now appeal in support of the genuineness of each book?[1] The same which we now propose as witnesses to Infant Baptism. And what inducement could they have had to deceive us in regard to an *ordinance* of our religion, that did not operate in regard to *the books* of the same? They were as well qualified — even better, we may suppose — to testify to a public practice like Infant Baptism, than to the *authenticity* of the different manuscripts sent to the various churches. And therefore, consistency, as well as love for the truth require, that if we receive their testimony to the one, we should to the other also. We cannot reject it as to the Holy Scriptures: how then can we reject it as to Infant Baptism?

And here we remark for such as have not for themselves drawn the distinction — that there is a wide *difference between the testimony* of early Christians to *facts*, and their mere opinion as to *doctrines*. We may receive the former and give it all the credit of a qualified witness, whilst the latter should be received as we receive the *opinion* of other Christians, making due allowance for the advantages of time, place, and other circumstances.[2] Respect is due the opin-

[1] To this question the attention of the reader will be more particularly called in another place.

[2] On this point a living author remarks as follows: "Another remark which I would here offer is, that we draw a wide distinction between the value of the testimony of the Fathers as to doctrines and the oral teaching of the Apostles, and their testimony as to those matters of fact, that came under their immediate cognizance. It is important to keep this in

ions and commentaries of early Christians, because their nearness to the Apostles gave them many facilities of ascertaining their teachings which we have not. But the testimony of the Fathers as to *facts* must be regarded as something more than the mere *opinions* of good men; must be received as *valid testimony* to the truth to which they depose; just as we regard the testimony of Christians in this day concerning the *practices* of their respective Churches.

Will any one say, that some hundreds of years hence, the writings of the Bishops and other ministers of Christian Churches must not be consulted, when trying to find out the rites and religious services of the respective Churches to which they belonged? If, for instance, there should be found at that time, in the writings of the ministers of the Lutheran, Presbyterian, Methodist, and other Christian bodies, accounts of the baptizing of young children, shall it be objected: "Such testimony cannot be received concerning the practice of those Christians?" No one will say this. Why then object to testimony of the same kind, on the same subject in the earlier days of Christianity? When such writings have been examined and believed to be genuine,[1] and are received as testimony on other points, we must receive them on this likewise. And when all men shall be brought to take an enlightened and correct

view, because the value of human testimony is very different in one of those cases to what it is in the other. The value of a man's testimony to a fact that takes place under his own eye, or to a matter that is the object of the senses, is very different to that of his report of an oral statement, especially with respect to matters of doctrine." — *Goode's Divine Rule of Faith and Practice.*

[1] Only those writings, and portions of writings, the authenticity of which has borne the test of sound criticism, and received the approval of scholars generally, will be introduced as authority in this work.

view of this question, and shall search after truth from a love of it, they will doubtless avail themselves of all the aid that such testimony affords. They will rightly examine also *the principles of interpretation* which they adopt, and omit nothing that will throw light on the subject of their inquiry.

7. The *state of the controversy*, *the point at issue*, and *nature of the evidence* being now considered; let us proceed to the examination of the question, — "*Is Infant Baptism of Divine authority, or is it an innovation brought into the Church since the death of the Apostles?*" In conducting this investigation it must be remembered, we are not to bring this question and place it in the midst of the customs and institutions of our own age, and examine it under their colorings and shadows; but transfer ourselves in imagination to the Apostolic age, and there in the midst of the *institutions* and *customs* that surrounded the Apostles, conduct this examination. Thus we shall correct an error into which many fall, who seem not to remember that we are many centuries after the time of the Apostles; that the USAGES, LAWS, and HABITS of this age, differ *widely* from those of that age; and hence in looking at this question through the medium of any other than its own age and institutions, we may view it in very different colors from its true one.

To comprehend fully the meaning of any writer, it is necessary to know the circumstances that affected his mind at the time he wrote. Therefore, in order to understand as correctly as possible the meaning of the writings of the Apostles, we should endeavor to place ourselves in the same age, amidst the same customs, surrounded by the same circumstances, and read as if a contemporary with them.

8. Guided by these preliminaries, we will take up the practice of baptizing young children, as we find it now among us, and trace it back through the different ages of the Church, to ascertain when it commenced — or whether there be any period between this and the *Apostolic age*, when it was not known in the Church? And if we find it in all the intervening ages, we will then take up THE HOLY SCRIPTURES, and having made ourselves acquainted (so far as we shall be able) with the laws, customs, and influences likely to have affected the Apostles, examine *their writings* on this point — bearing in mind those influences under which they wrote.

§ 2. Beginning then at the present time (a little beyond the middle of the nineteenth century), we find that all the *Ancient Churches* known to us, *The Greek Church*, *Syrian Church*, *Latin or Roman Church*, *Nestorians*, *Armenians*, *Copts*, *Abyssinians*, and all the sects of *Monophysites*, *baptize Infants*. And so, likewise, nine-tenths of those bearing more modern names, — *Protestant Episcopalians*, *Moravians*, *Lutherans*, *Presbyterians*, *Congregationalists*, *Methodists*, and numerous others, all baptize Infants.

1. On the other hand, the Antipædobaptists [1] form a large and respectable body of Christians, and are found in various parts of the religious world. They are known in history by several different names,— "Anabaptists — Mennonites or Minnists, — Baptists," and some others. But they prefer now, with few exceptions, the name of Baptists. And though

[1] Antipædobaptists — this term embraces all those who are opposed particularly to the baptism of children (ἀντὶ, against; παῖς, παιδός, child; βαπτίζω, to baptize.

differing among themselves on many other points, are united in their opposition to the baptism of young children, — that is, are all Antipædobaptists.

But however respectable in numbers, at the present time, before we travel back more than three centuries, they dwindle into a few scattered sects, confined chiefly to Holland, Upper Germany, and countries contiguous to the Alps.

About A. D. 1536, their system was first reduced into consistency and moderation.[1]

2. Continuing our march some four centuries farther, we come to the period when their principles as Antipædobaptists, are first brought to light in the history of the Church. It seems that Pierre de Bruys, a native of Toulouse, about A. D. 1110, began first to preach publicly against the baptism of young children, — denying that they could be saved! He continued his career some twenty years, and collected a considerable number of followers, but was arrested in A. D. 1130, by the Papal authority, burnt to death, and his followers dispersed![2]

On this point we shall dwell more at large in another place, in connection with the history of the Waldenses. It is only necessary to glance at these centuries in our march, for history has made them familiar to every reader. No one doubts the fact that Infant Baptism was the prevailing practice of Christians during this period, and it would be a work of supererogation to swell this volume with citations of the proof.

3. Passing on through the *eleventh*, *tenth*, and

[1] See Mosheim, *Encyclopedia of Religious Knowledge* (a Baptist work), and others.

[2] See Mosheim — Waddington and Wall.

ninth centuries, we find it *universal* — *practised everywhere, and by all.* No one called it in question who baptized at all. There were some who rejected water baptism altogether — but no record (so far as we can learn) tells of any baptizing sect that rejected Infants. Indeed, nearly the whole Church, in those countries where Christianity had been introduced at an early period, was composed of members baptized in their infancy. Adult baptism was comparatively a rare thing except in places more recently converted to the Christian faith, and in those regions where missionaries were at work. In all the *National Churches* Infant Baptism was not only universally practised, but almost the only baptism, because family baptism had been handed down from past generations.[1]

4. And so with the *eight*, *seventh*, *sixth*, and *fifth* centuries; Infant Baptism had no one to oppose it except those who opposed all baptism. Its *universality* is virtually admitted by the concession even of Mr. Tombs, a celebrated Antipædobaptist writer, who says, " It was carried *almost without controul*," during this period. Wall objects to his use of the word "*almost*" — and says, Tombs puts in the word "*almost*" as if some, though few, did oppose it: there is on the contrary, not one saying, quotation, or example that makes against it, produced or pretended, but that has been clearly shown to be a *mistake*. As in the first four hundred years (of Christianity) there is none but one Tertullian, who advised it to be delayed till the age of reason; and one Nazianzen until three years of age, in case of no danger of death: So in the following six hundred years there is no account or report of any one man that opposed it at all."[2]

1 See W. Wall's *History of Infant Baptism.*

2 Wall's *History of Infant Baptism*, Third London Edition, vol. ii. c. vii.

This question called forth much research and great labor about the close of the seventeenth, and beginning of the eighteenth centuries. And among others, as Wall informs us, a Mr. Danvers, an Antipædobaptist writer of those times, found as he supposed various passages in the writings of authors of the first thousand years of Christianity that *did imply* opposition to Infant Baptism, but Wills and Baxter, who followed him on the other side, discovered and exposed his many mistakes and errors. "There wants nothing but looking into the books themselves (continues Wall) to see they are nothing to the purpose. Mr. Danvers created to Mr. Wills and Mr. Baxter a great deal of trouble in sending them from one book to another, to discover his mistakes and misrepresentations of several authors within this space; but withal a great deal of discredit to himself, for there is not one of his quotations that seemed material enough to need searching, but proved to be such"[1] (i. e. mistakes or nothing to the purpose).

5. Since the time of these writers historical evidence is much less appealed to by the opponents of Infant Baptism, they confining themselves chiefly to certain controverted passages, and to their own interpretation of the Holy Scriptures.

In some of their publications, however, the errors just referred to are to be found; to which we shall recur in the progress of our investigation, and particularly to a passage taken from a defective copy of the works of the venerated Bede.

The universality of the baptism of little children at that period being so well known to all students of ecclesiastical history, and conceded by so high au-

[1] Third edition, London, vol. ii. c. 7, p. 213.

thority on the other side, we might pass on to the next century nearer to the apostolic age; but before doing so let us glance at the *high authority* yielded to Infant Baptism, and with what confidence its claims were appealed to, during the "Pelagian Controversy," which arose in the beginning of the fifth century, and agitated East and West the Christian world.

It was the doctrine of the Church then as now, that by the *fall of Adam, the original state of man was lost;* and that all his posterity partake of the infirmities and depravity of his fallen condition; that his descendants are born with a corrupt, sin-stained nature, which inclines them to evil. Some were of opinion that the *guilt*, as well as *stain and pollution* of Adam's sin, passed to his posterity; and the effect upon his race, whatever it be, they called "*Original Sin.*"

Pelagius, a monk, born in Britain, and now living at Rome; and Celestius, another monk, of Irish birth, his friend, denied *Original Sin*, and taught that the posterity of Adam are born in the same state that he was before his fall —*free from sin.* This new doctrine, in connection with some others, spread rapidly and was embraced by men of notoriety holding prominent places in the Church in various portions of Christendom, by whom were aroused bishops and men of learning on the other side. Among them was Augustine, Bishop of Hippo, a man of great ability and energy, who acted a very prominent part in this controversy. Holding very decided, perhaps extreme views of the effects of *Original Sin*, he took up the doctrines of Pelagius and Celestius, and discussed them in every phase in which they were presented, and charged upon them, — especially upon

Pelagius, — that he made void the Baptism of Infants. If they have no *Original Sin*, and have committed no *actual* sins of their own; for the remission of what sins, he asked, are they baptized?

Pelagius would not admit that his doctrines came in conflict with the authority of Infant Baptism; but enumerated other benefits conferred by it, other reasons for its administration than that of *Original Sin.*

Augustine contended that he thus changed the chief object for which Baptism was given, and made two baptisms; that his theory subverted *all true Baptism.* Both admitted the authority of Infant Baptism, — that was placed beyond all doubt. Hence Augustine used it to disprove Pelagius' theory of the moral state of man at his birth.

§ 3. Instead of rejecting Infant Baptism, Pelagius declared that, "He never heard of even an *impious heretic* who would avow such a thing." And to correct the many misrepresentations in circulation, both Pelagius and Celestius drew up articles of their belief and sent them to the Bishop of Rome. In which Pelagius, when he comes to Baptism, says: —

LIBELLUS FIDEI.

"We hold one baptism which we affirm must be administered with the same sacramental words to infants with which it is to elder persons." [1]

He thus acknowledges his faith in Infant Baptism, but evades the doctrine of original sin, and also cuts off the charge of two baptisms, by saying, the "same sacramental words" are to be used in all cases.

He sent likewise with his "confession of faith" an accompanying letter, parts of which are quoted by

[1] "Baptisma unum tenemus, quod iisdem sacramenti verbis in infantibus quibus etiam in majoribus asserimus esse celebrandum."

Augustine, in order to make his animadversions upon them. In one place Augustine quotes him, saying: —

"He is slandered by men, as if he denied the sacrament of baptism to young children, and did promise the Kingdom of Heaven to any, without the redemption of Christ." [1]

After some remarks on this, Augustine quotes him as next saying: —

"He never heard even of any impious heretic who would avow such a thing in regard to little children: for who is there so ignorant of Gospel reading (*Evangelicæ lectionis*) that he would — not to say, venture to affirm this — but even in a heedless way say, or indeed think such a thing? In a word, who can be so impious as to wish little children not to be sharers in the Kingdom of Heaven, and so forbid them to be baptized and regenerated in Christ?" [2]

Again, —

"Who is there so impious as to interdict the common redemption of mankind to any age whatever?" [3]

Augustine, commenting on these passages and others of like import, charges Pelagius with evasions and ambiguity. That he keeps away from the main point at issue. That the question was not whether Infants *ought* to be baptized, but if they have no original sin, why are they baptized? And when did they sin? Or, if they have no sin at all, what is their condition before Baptism?

1 "Se ab hominibus infamari quòd neget parvulis baptismi sacramentum, et absque redemptione Christi aliquibus regna cœlorum promittat." — *Augustin. de Peccato Originali,* c. 17, 18.

2 "Nunquam se vel impium aliquem Hereticum audisse, qui hoc quod proposuit de parvulis, diceret: Quis enim ita Evangelicæ lectionis ignarus est, qui hoc non modo affirmare conetur, sed qui vel leviter dicere aut etiam sentire possit? Denique quis tam impius, qui parvulos exortes regni cœlorum esse velit, dum eos baptizari et in Christo renasci vetat." — *Ibid.*

3 "Quis ille tam impius est, qui cujuslibet ætatis parvulo interdicat communem humani generis redemptionem." — *Ibid.*

Here we would remark that we have nothing to do with the subjects of controversy that may be brought up in connection with the question before us. Our only business is to find out, at each successive step, whether Infant Baptism is still the practice of Christians?

Whatever doctrines may be advocated or opposed, it forms no part of our present plan to defend one side or the other, or to stop to show that Infant Baptism is not answerable for men's fancies. The simple fact, "Is Infant Baptism the practice of the Church, or is it not?" is all with which we have to do at the present time.

§ 4. Celestius, in his confession of faith (*Libellus fidei*) is more open and explicit on original sin. As recited by Augustine, he says: —

AUGUSTIN. DE PECCATO ORIGINALI, C. 5.

"We acknowledge that Infants ought to be baptized for the remission of sins, according to the rule of the Universal Church, and according to the meaning of the Gospel. For the Lord has ordained that the kingdom of Heaven is not to be conferred on persons unless they are baptized [referring to St. John, iii. 5], which, because the power of nature cannot give, it is necessary to confer through the liberty of grace. But we do not therefore say that Infants are to be baptized for the remission of sins, that we may seem to confirm the opinion of the propagation of sin, which is a thing far from the Catholic sense. For sin is not born with a man which is afterwards committed by him. Because it is not the fault of NATURE, but of the WILL, as may be demonstrated. It is, therefore, proper to confess the former, lest we seem to make divers kinds of baptism; and also necessary to guard against the latter, lest by means of this mystery, it be to the reproach of the Creator said, that sin was conveyed through nature to man before it was acted out by man." [1]

[1] "Infantes autem debere baptizari remissionem peccatorum secundum regulam universalis Ecclesiæ, et secundum Evangelii sententiam confite-

In this passage Celestius not only shows that he did not oppose Infant Baptism, but tells us that it is the "rule of the universal Church," and doctrine of the Gospel (*Evangelii sententiam*). Pelagius said he had never heard even of any impious heretic who denied it (meaning among those who baptized at all), and asks, who is so ignorant of gospel reading (*Evangelicæ lectionis*) as even to think such a thing much less affirm it.

The testimony of these two men is the more important on this point, because of the great advantages they had enjoyed for knowing the custom of the Church in different parts of the world. They were born and bred, the one in England and the other in Ireland, came to Rome early in the fifth century, and resided there till the invasion of the Goths, A. D. 410. They both went thence to Carthage, in Africa, at which place Celestius remained some time, and attempted to gain admittance as a Presbyter into the Church; but being disappointed, afterwards travelled over Greece and various portions of Asia, visiting all the most noted Eastern Churches of Europe and Asia. Pelagius settled in Jerusalem.

Both of them, who had enjoyed such opportunities of knowing by personal observation the practice of all the most noted churches in Christendom, sent in

mur; quia Dominus statuit regnum Cœlorum non nisi baptizatis posse conferri: quod quia vires naturæ non habent, conferre necesse est per gratiæ libertatem. In remissionem autem peccatorum baptizandos infantes non idcirco diximus, ut peccatum ex traduce firmare videamur; quod longè à Catholico sensu alienum est. Quia peccatum non cum homine nascitur, quod postmodùm exercitur ab homine; Quia non naturæ delictum, sed voluntatis esse demonstratur. Et illud ergo confiteri congruum, ne diversa baptismatis genera facere videamur: et hoc præmunire necessarium est, ne per mysterii occasionem, ad Creatoris injuriam, malum antequam fiat ab homine tradi dicatur homini per naturam."

See Wall's *History*, vol. i. c. xix.

written declarations of their faith in A. D. 417, one saying, "Infant Baptism is the rule of the Universal Church," — the other, he had "never heard of even an impious heretic that denied Baptism to Infants."

§ 5. The following year a council was held at Carthage, in which all the provinces of Africa were represented, — two hundred and fourteen Bishops were present, and eight canons passed against the Pelagian tenets. In the second canon Infant Baptism is referred to, and two errors condemned, — one against the doctrine of Pelagius and Celestius in regard to original sin, — the other against the opinion of some who thought Baptism ought to be delayed until the eighth day after birth — the time of circumcision.

That which regards Infant Baptism, is as follows: —

CONCILII CARTHAG. ANNO 418, CANON SECUNDUS.

"Resolved also, that whosoever denies that Infants may be baptized fresh from their mothers' womb, or says that they are indeed baptized for the remission of sins, but yet they derive no original sin from Adam, which is expiated by the laver of regeneration (whence it follows that in them, not the true form of baptism for the remission of sins is understood, but a false one), let him be Anathema. For what the Apostle says — 'by one man sin entered into the world, and death by sin; and so death passed upon all men, for that all have sinned,' can in no otherwise be understood but in the way the Catholic [1] Church extended everywhere has always understood it. For by this rule of faith also the LITTLE ONES, who cannot as yet have committed any sin in themselves are truly baptized for the remission of sins, that what they derive by generation may be cleansed by regeneration." [2]

[1] "Universal," not "*Roman*" Catholic.

[2] "Item placuit ut quicumque parvulos recentes ab uteris matrum baptizandos negat; aut dicit in remissionem quidem peccatorum eos baptizari, sed nihil ex Adam trahere originalis peccati quod lavacro regenerationis expietur (unde sit consequens ut in eis forma baptismatis in remissionem peccatorum non vera sed falsa intelligatur) Anathema sit. Quoniam non aliter intelligendum est, quod ait Apostolus, Per unum hominem peccatum

Further testimony could add nothing to the *certainty of the fact that Infant Baptism was the doctrine and practice* of the Church in this century. If a council of two hundred and fourteen Bishops pronounced an Anathema on any one "who shall deny original sin, and that Infants are baptized that what they derive by generation may be cleansed by regeneration;" and Pelagius, a Briton, who had lived in Rome, then in Carthage, and settled finally in Jerusalem, tells us he had "never heard of even an impious heretic that denied Baptism to Infants," — and Celestius, who had travelled far and near, and visited the most noted churches in Europe and Asia, proclaims it to be "the rule of the Universal Church;" nothing more can be needed to satisfy the most skeptical inquirer. We pass on, therefore, to a period before the *rise of Pelagianism.*

NOTE. Much has been written concerning the effect of Adam's sin on his posterity; and exclamations of horror often expressed at the idea of little children suffering for the sin of another. But it should be borne in mind that whatever be the effect of Adam's sin on his descendants, whether they only lost the primeval state of man, or whether born with a sinful corrupt nature, or whether involved in his guilt; provision was made for their loss before it came. Where sin abounded grace superabounded. Before the foundation of the world Christ devised the plan of their redemption. And though God cannot look upon *any shade* of sin, we may charitably hope that no child is actually damned eternally for original sin. Christ has redeemed all from the curse of original sin, Infants, Idiots, and every one not responsible for actual sin, and will save them with every *penitent* for his actual sins. Only those who commit *actual sins of their own, continue impenitent, and reject the terms of redemption,* are excepted. And if actual transgressors on repentance receive the *seal* of the remission of all sin, much more the little ones who have committed no actual sin, the *seal* of the remission of *original sin.*

---

intravit in mundum et per peccatum mors, et ita in omnes homines pertransit, in quo omnes peccaverunt: Nisi quemadmodum Ecclesia Catholica ubique diffusa semper intellexit. Propter hanc enim regulam fidei, etiam parvuli, qui nihil peccatorum in seipsis adhuc committere potuerunt, ideo in peccatorum remissionem veraciter baptizantur, ut in eis regeneratione mundetur quod generatione traxerant." — *Cited by Wall.*

CHAPTER II.

HISTORICAL TESTIMONY CONTINUED.

Testimony of Council of Carthage. — Aurelius. — Donatists. — Chrysostom. — Baptism and Christian Circumcision. — Original Sin. — Benefits of Baptism. — Jerome. — Augustine. — Ambrose. — Optatus. — Gregory Nazianzen. — Basil. — Council of Eliberis.— Council of Carthage, Sixty-six Bishops present, Cyprian presiding. — Tertullian.

§ 1. ABOUT A. D. 400, or 300 from the Apostolic Age,[1] a question was proposed in a Council at Carthage, which shows the prevalence of Infant Baptism at that time. It was the case of certain persons carried away captives, in their infancy, into barbarian countries, who after a lapse of years had been found and ransomed by their friends. But when brought back none of their relatives, then alive, could testify whether or not they had been baptized before they were carried off. They being little children when their parents were captured, were of course too young to remember anything about it, and their friends were in doubt what to do. They would by no means have so important a thing neglected, and yet they were afraid of desecrating the sacrament by re-baptism. The case was laid before the Fifth Council at Carthage, and the following is its decision: —

[1] The last book of the Holy Scriptures was written about A. D. 96 and St. John died A. D. 102. Therefore inspired men were continued in the Church to supervise and preserve it from serious error until the end of the first century. This period constitutes what is called the "*Apostolic Age.*" In reckoning from the close of this age, will be used in this volume "A. Apos." for "*After the Apostles*" — Apostolic Age.

CONCILII CARTHAGINIENSIS QUINTI, CANON 6.

"It is resolved CONCERNING INFANTS, when positive witnesses cannot be found, who will testify that they have been baptized without doubt, and they, by reason of their age, are not able to answer as to the administration of the sacrament to them; that they be baptized without any scruple; lest that scruple do cause them to go without the benefit of the sacrament. For our brethren sent from the Mauritanians, have asked our advice on this point." [1]

This not only proves that they practised Infant Baptism, but that it was so rigidly observed, they hesitated to baptize a person who had been carried away in early infancy, fearing they would be guilty of re-baptism, so great was the probability that such, however young when carried off, were previously baptized.

§ 2. In a preceding council held three years before at the same place, in regard to the promotion of persons to *offices* in the Church who had once belonged to schismatic bodies, a canon was issued which incidentally testifies to the prevailing custom of Infant Baptism. Aurelius, the Bishop, remarks: —

CANONUM CODEX ECCLESIÆ AFRICANÆ, CAN. 57.

"In a former council it was resolved, you remember, that they who were baptized in their INFANCY among the Donatists before they were able to understand the mischief of that error, and when afterward they had come to the age of understanding, — the truth being acknowledged by them. . . . they were received by us. . . . such, without doubt, ought to be promoted to Church offices, especially in times of so great need, as all must concede.

"Some of the teachers of the same sect, would come over with

1 "Placuit de infantibus quoties non inveniuntur certissimi testes qui eos baptizatos esse sine dubitatione testentur, neque ipsi sunt per ætatem idonei de traditis sibi sacramentis respondere; absque ullo scrupulo eos esse baptizandos. Ne ista trepidatio eos faciat sacramentorum purgatione privari. Hinc enim legati Maurorum fratres nostri consuluerunt," etc. — *Cited by Wall.*

their congregations, if they might continue in their offices with their honors among us; but this I leave to the further consideration of the brethren, only that they consent to our determination, . . . that those baptized in Infancy be admitted to orders."[1]

Infant Baptism is here mentioned as a thing common and well known, and the points at issue, are, whether those baptized among the Donatists in infancy are not less to be blamed than those received among them at adult age? And whether such ought to be debarred from holding offices in the Church, if they return to it, as soon as they come to years of discretion?

§ 3. The following resolution had been passed in council on this subject: —

CONCILII CARTHAG. TERTII, CAN. 48.

"In reference to the Donatists, resolved that we consult our brethren and fellow Bishops, Siricius and Simplicianus, concerning only those who are baptized in INFANCY, among them — that when they have been converted to the Church by the wholesome purpose of God, whether that which they have not done by their own judgment, but was the error of their parents, shall hinder them, that they shall not be promoted to Ministers of the holy altar?"[2]

[1] "Superiori consilio statutum esse mecum recognoscit unanimitas vestra ut hi qui apud Donatistas parvuli baptizati sunt nondum scire valentes erroris eorum interitum, et postea quam ad ætatem rationis capacem pervenerunt, agnita veritate, ... recepti sunt . . . . sine dubio ad officium clericatus tales esse applicandos, et maxime in tanta rerum necessitate nullus est qui non concedat.

"Quanquam nonnulli ejusdem sectæ clerici cum plebibus atque honoribus suis ad nos transire desiderent,. . . . Sed hoc majori fratrum supradictorum considerationi dimittendum censeo. Tantum de his qui Infantes baptizati sunt satagimus, ut nostræ, si placet, in iisdem ordinandis consentiat voluntati." — *Can.* 57, *Ibid.*

[2] "De Donatistis, placuit ut consulamus fratres et consacerdotes nostros Siricium et Simplicianum, de solis infantibus qui baptizantur penes eosdem, ne quod suo non fecerunt judicio, cum ad Ecclesiam Dei salubri proposito fuerint conversi, parentum illos error impediat, ne provehantur sacri altaris ministri."

From this resolution and the words of Aurelius, we see that the Donatists, a schismatical body, baptized young children, as well as the great body of the Church; and yet some opponents of Infant Baptism tell us that they themselves are descendants of the Donatists!

We need nothing plainer or more conclusive, — as it regards the Church of Carthage at this time. Let us pass on some twenty years nearer the Apostles and see what was the practice in other places?

§ 4. JOHN CHRYSOSTOM was a native of Antioch, called the "golden mouthed" on account of his eloquence, — was a voluminous writer,[1] and finally made patriarch of Constantinople. In one of his homilies on Genesis, he speaks of the pain and suffering of circumcision, and the advantages of Baptism over it, in the following manner: —

HOM. 40 IN GENESIN.

"But our Circumcision, I mean the *grace of baptism*, gives cure without pain, and procures for us a thousand benefits, and fills us with the grace of the Spirit. And it has no determinate time as that had; but it is lawful to any one in the very BEGINNING OF HIS AGE, or in the middle of it, or in old age, to receive this circumcision made without hands. In which there is no trouble to be undergone, but to throw off the load of sins and receive pardon for all foregoing offences."[2]

1 We quote only from those books that are generally acknowledged to be authentic, or such portions as are received by Protestants and Romanists.

2 'Η δὲ ἡμετέρα περιτομὴ, ἡ τοῦ βαπτίσματος, λέγω, χάρις, ἀνωδύνον ἔχει τὴν ἰατρείαν καὶ μυρίων ἀγαθῶν προξεντος γίνεται ἡμῖν, καὶ τῆς τοῦ Πνεύματος ἡμᾶς ἐμπίπλησι χάριτος. Καὶ οὐδέ ὡρισμένον ἔχει χαιρὸν καθᾶπερ ἐκεῖ ἀλλ' ἔξεστι καὶ ἐν ἀώρῳ ἡλίκια καὶ ἐν μέσῃ, καὶ ἐν αὐτῷ τῷ γήρα γενόμενον τινα ταύτην δέξασθαι τήν ἀχειροποίητον περὶτομὴν ἐν ᾗ οὐκ εστι πόνον πὑμεῖναι, ἀλλ' ἁμαρτημάτων φορτία ἀποθέται καὶ τῶν ἐν παντὶ χρόνῳ πλημμελημάτων συγχώρησιν ἐυρέθαι. — *Savil. Edit.*, vol. i.

Chrysostom here calls Baptism the Christian's Circumcision, and says, it is confined to no particular age as was Jewish Circumcision. Instead of the eighth day after birth, we may receive it in the very beginning of age (ἐν ἀώρῃ ἡλίκια) or in the middle of it, or in old age. Meaning at any time when in the providence of God the sacrament can be administered.

That he means by "the beginning of age" the *first stages of infancy*, is obvious both from the sense, and from his use of the same phrase in another place concerning Circumcision; where he says, "Circumcision was appointed on the eighth day, because the cutting off the flesh is more easily borne 'in the beginning of age'" (ἐν ἀώρῃ ἡλίκια), *i. e.*, when very young, the infant is not so sensible of the pain.

§ 5. In another of his homilies, he condemns a heathenish and superstitious practice of some mothers in rubbing a certain kind of mud on the forehead of a newly born child, to keep it from being bewitched; and asks them how they can bring such children to the priest to be baptized. His words are: —

HOM. 12, IN 1 EPIST. AD CORINTHIOS.

"He that anoints an infant so with mud, how can he think but that he makes it abominable? How can he bring it to the priest? Tell me, how can you think it is fitting for the minister to make the sign on his forehead, when you have besmeared it with that mud."[1]

By the "sign," he refers to the sign of the cross then made on the forehead in Baptism, and seems to think that the child is rendered unfit to receive Baptism, and have *that sign* made on the same

[1] Ὁ Βορβόρῳ χρίων πῶς οὐχὶ καὶ βδελυκτὸν ποιεῖ τὸ παιδίον; πῶς γάρ αὐτὸ προσάγει ταῖς χερσὶ τοῦ ἱερέως; εἶπέ μοι, πῶς ἀξιοῖς επὶ τοῦ μετώπου σφραγίδα ἐπιτιτεθῆναι παρὰ τῆς τοῦ πρεσβυτέρα χειρὸς ἔνθα τὸν Βόρβορον ἐπεχεισὰς;

place, which had been defiled by such a superstitious rite.

§ 6. There is still another passage taken from a Homily of Chrysostom, not extant in the Greek, but cited by both Julian and Augustine on opposite sides, in their controversy on Original Sin, the one in Latin and the other in Greek. Julian's citation in Latin is as follows [1]: —

"Blessed be God, who only does wonders; who has created and ordered all things. Lo! they do enjoy the serenity of freedom who but even now were held in captivity; they are become Citizens of the Church, who were in the vagabond state of Aliens; and they are entered into the lot of the righteous, who were under the confusion of sin. For they are not only free, but saints; nor saints only, but justified; and not only justified, but sons; and not only sons, but heirs; not only heirs, but brothers in Christ; not only His brethren, but co-heirs; not only co-heirs, but members of Him; not members only, but His temple; and not His temple only, but organs of His spirit. You see how many are the benefits of Baptism. And yet some think that the heavenly grace consists only in the forgiveness of sins; but I have reckoned up *ten* advantages of it. For this cause we *baptize Infants also, though they are not defiled with sin*, that there may be superadded to them saintship, righteousness, adoption, inheritance, a brotherhood with Christ, and to be made members of Him."

Augustine admits the correctness of this translation, except the last clause of the sentence, "For this cause, we baptize Infants also, although they are not defiled by sin." He objects to the rendering, "*not defiled by sin*," and cites the Greek; rendering it, "*although they have no sins*." In the first case, "*not defiled by sin*," would seem to teach freedom from any infection of Adam's or Original Sin. And in the other, "*have no sins*," may be understood,

[1] Wall's *History*, vol. i., chap. 14.

"sins of their own;" not referring to original or sin derived from Adam, but of their own personal acts.

Whatever views he entertained in regard to Adam's sin, the passage shows beyond doubt that Infant Baptism was the rule of the Church in Antioch in Syria, as well as in Carthage in Africa.

We pass next to Rome, a place of resort at that time from every part of the world, to see whether this practice prevailed there also.

§ 7. JEROME, who was educated at Rome, and now residing there again after having spent some years in Syria, was highly esteemed and much courted for his literary attainments. In writing to a lady of great distinction, and endeavoring to impress on her mind her responsibility in training up her young daughter, he tells her that the sins of children are laid to the charge of the parents till they arrive at the age of discretion; and specifies among others the neglect of their Baptism as a sin of the parent, and not of the child. Supposing her to object in the language of Ezekiel, — "The sins of the father are not imputed to the children, nor those of the children to the father, but the soul that sinneth, it shall die," he answers: —

HIERON. AD LETAM DE INSTITU. FILIÆ.

"This is said of those that are able to understand; of such as he was, of whom it is written in the Gospel, 'He is of age, let him speak for himself.' But he that is a child, and thinks as a child (until he come to years of discretion, and the letter Y of Pythagoras brings him to the place where the road parts into two), his good deeds as well as his evil deeds are imputed to his parents.

"Unless you suppose the children of Christians, if they do not receive baptism, are themselves accountable for the sin, and the wickedness not imputed to those who would not give it to them, particularly at the time they ought to receive it, and could not have made any opposition to receiving it." [1]

Here again we see Infant Baptism spoken of as the practice of Christians, and in a way that declares it to be a sin in parents to neglect it. But that which is most important to our purpose is, that it is *incidentally* referred to, not brought up as a question of doubt. And we wish the reader to observe that in all the places in which it has yet been introduced, it was brought in for the purpose of sustaining, or illustrating in some way, other questions at issue. And it will be further seen, if we mistake not, that Infant Baptism itself *never was called in question* during the earlier ages of Christianity. Whenever referred to, its *Divine authority* is always taken for granted.

We have now seen that *before* the rise of the Pelagian controversy as well as *after* it, Infant Baptism was the practice of the Church in each of the then known quarters of the globe. But as it has been alleged that Augustine never alluded to Infant Baptism till after the rise of the Pelagian controversy, we will cite one more passage from him, written in the earlier part of his life, and not far from the time we are now considering. And we do so for the twofold object of showing, both the *universality* of the practice, and his opinion as to its Divine authority.

§ 8. The DONATISTS were a body of Christians

[1] "Hoc de his dicitur qui possunt sapere, de quibus in Evangelio scriptum est; ætatem habet, loquatur pro se. Qui autem parvulus est et sapit ut parvulus, donec ad annos sapientiæ veniat, et Pythagoræ litera Y eum perducat ad bivium; tam bona ejus quam mala parentibus imputantur. Nisi forte existimas Christianorum filios, si baptisma non receperint, ipsos tantum reos esse peccati; et non etiam scelus referri ad eos qui dare, noluerint; maximè eo tempore quo contradicere non poterant qui accepturi erant." — *Epistle* vii.

that had separated from the Church Catholic, or universal, in consequence of certain objections to Cecilianus, who was made Bishop of Carthage in A. D. 311, or 211 after the Apostles. They objected to Cecilianus both on account of his own previous conduct, and on account of the life of one of his Consecrators. They called themselves the "*true Church*," and required all that had been baptized in the Church under Cecilianus, when they came over to them, to be re-baptized, on the ground that a Church that permitted such an officer to perform its functions was corrupt and in error, and its ordinances therefore invalid.

Augustine made issue with them on this point, and took the position, that error in the head or heart of an officer, did not annul the authority of his office; that the validity of Baptism was not destroyed by error of the life, or of the judgment of the administrator while acting under proper authority. Nor even in the case of a person *receiving* Baptism, would error in judgment, or the want of the right faith, necessarily make void his Baptism. In defence of this position, he adduced the practice of the Church in giving Baptism to young children, who could not as yet exercise faith. The following are his words: —

AUGUST. DE BAPTISMO CONTRA DONATISTIS.

"Which sentiment the whole body of the Church holds as handed down to them, when little Infants are baptized. Who certainly cannot yet believe with the heart unto righteousness or confess with the mouth unto salvation, as the thief could: [who by NECESSITY was saved without baptism,] nay, by their crying and noise while the sacrament is administered to them, they hinder from being heard the mystical words. And yet no Christian will say they are baptized to no purpose.

"And if any one should seek Divine authority in this thing:

although that which the UNIVERSAL Church holds, and not instituted by councils, but was ever in use and most rightly believed to be handed down by none other than Apostolic authority; nevertheless, we can make a probable estimate of what the sacrament of baptism avails to young children, by the circumcision of the flesh, which God's former people received." [1]

After this he goes on to show the similarity between circumcision and baptism, — but we have enough for our present purpose. The most learned man of ancient times here informs us *that Infant Baptism is a doctrine held by the whole body of the Church, and not instituted by councils, but ordained by nothing less, as all believed, than the authority of the Apostles.*

§ 9. We next visit the Church of Milan, and find the Bishop, Ambrose, in commenting on the history of Abraham, led to speak of the *Circumcision of Infants;* and he gives as a reason for it, that "as *the disease is from Infancy, so is the remedy.*" And in applying the same principle to *Baptism*, cites St. John, iii. 5, to enforce its necessity: —

AMBROSIUS DE ABRAHAM PATRIARCHA.

"*For unless any person be born again of the water, and of the Holy Spirit, he cannot enter into the Kingdom of God.*" [2] You see (he adds) he excepts no person; not an Infant, not one that

1 "Quod traditum tenet universitas ecclesiæ cùm parvuli infantes baptizantur; qui certè nondum possunt corde credere ad justitiam et ore confiteri ad salutem, quod latro potuit: Quinetian flendo et vagiendo cùm in eis Mysterium celebratur, ipsis mysticis vocibus obstrepunt. Et tamen nullus Christianorum dixerit eos inaniter baptizari.

"Et si quisquam in hâc re Divinam auctoritatem quærat; Quanquam quod universa tenet Ecclesia, nec Conciliis institutum sed semper retentum est, non nisi auctoritate apostolicâ traditum rectissime creditur; Tamen veraciter conjicere possumus quid valeat in parvulis baptismi Sacramentum ex circumcisione carnis quam prior populus accepit." —*Lib.* 4, *chap.* 15. *Cited by Wall.*

2 *i. e.*, There is no other prescribed mode but that.

is hindered by any unavoidable accident. And even if such have freedom from punishment, I know not that they shall have the honor of the Kingdom." [1]

He regarded Baptism not only as generally necessary to *every one*, young or old, or as a law which all are bound to obey; but would not take on himself the responsibility of saying, that even those who missed of Baptism by accident or by no fault of their own, would *certainly* have the *honor of Heaven*, although they might escape any positive punishment.

We cannot here discuss the extreme nature of his views, but more unequivocal testimony to the doctrine of Infant Baptism in the Church of Milan at that time could not be given.

§ 10. Passing on thirty years nearer to the Apostles, we come to the time when Optatus, Bishop of Milevis, wrote. In comparing the Christian's putting on Christ in Baptism, to the putting on of a garment, he says: —

LIB. 5. DE SCHISMATE DONATISTARUM.

"But lest any one should say I speak irreverently in calling the Son of God a garment; let him read what the Apostle says: 'As many of you as have been baptized in the name of Christ, have put on Christ.' O! what a garment is this, — always one, and innumerable; that decently fits all ages and all shapes; neither too big for INFANTS nor too little for men, and without any alteration fits women." [2]

This is too plain to need comment. The garment

[1] "Nisi enim quis renatus fuerit ex aquâ et Spiritu Sancto, non potest introire in regnum Dei. Utique nullum excipit: Non infantem, non aliquâ preventum necessitate. Habeant tamen illam opertam penarum immunitatem, nescio an habeant regni honorem." — Lib. 2, ch. 11.

[2] "Sed ne quis dicat, temerè à me Filium Dei vestem esse dictum; legat Apostolum dicentem: Quotquot in nomine Christi baptizati estis, Christum

of Baptism "fits *all ages and all shapes*, not too *big for Infants*, nor too *little for men*."

§ 11. Let us turn next to Gregory Nazianzen, who wrote about the same time with Optatus, but in a different part of the world; was born in Cappadocia and educated in Athens. In reference to Baptism, he often uses the terms, "*Laver of regeneration*," "the *seal*," the "*grace*," the "*anointing*," to be "*sanctified*," and some others. Finding that there were those among his hearers who were almost persuaded to be Christians, but who then, as is too often the case now, could not make up their minds fully to unite themselves with the Church — some of them having been catechumens for a long time, (*i. e.*, receiving a course of instruction to prepare them for baptism) yet delayed to come forward, he admonishes them, that Satan "*Sets on all ages and must be resisted by all. Art thou a youth? fight against pleasures and passions with this auxiliary strength; enlist thyself in God's army. . . . Art thou old? let thy gray hairs strengthen thee: strengthen thy old age with baptism*."

ORATIO DE BAPTISMO, 40.

"Have you an Infant? Let not wickedness have the advantage of time: from his INFANCY let him be *sanctified*; from the cradle let him be *consecrated* by the Spirit. You fear the *seal* on account of the weakness of nature: how faint-hearted a mother and of little faith! Hannah, even before Samuel was born, promised him to God, and consecrated him immediately after his birth, and brought him up in the priestly dress, not fearing any human infirmity, but trusting to God."[1]

induistis. O tunica semper una, et innumerabilis; quæ decenter vestiat et omnes ætates et formas: nec infantibus rugatur nec in juvenibus tenditur, nec in fœminis mutatur." — *Cited by Wall.*

[1] Νήπιόν ἐστι σοὶ; μὴ λαβέτω καιρὸν ἡ κακία, ἐκ βρέφους ἁγιασθήτω, ἐξ ὀνύχων

Gregory here urges that no time be lost, — that Infants be "sanctified" and receive the "seal" (baptism) from the cradle; and rebukes faint-hearted mothers who sometimes delay the Baptism of their children on account of their weakness, — pointing them to Hannah's faith.

But afterwards, in a different part of his address, he recommends three years as a suitable age, where weakness or disease did not endanger the life of the child. When that was the case, however, he would allow no time to elapse before Baptism. But either case admits the principle involved in the question of Infant Baptism, and shows that this was then the usage of the Church. In the latter case he was reproving certain candidates for baptism, who seemed more concerned in making outward preparation than inward, — telling them that a preparation of heart, and an earnest desire for it, was the acceptable thing to God,[1] — but lest some might suppose that what he had said conflicted with an established doctrine of the Church, he adds: —

> "Some may say, 'suppose this to hold in the case of those who *can* desire baptism; what say you as concerning those who are as yet Infants, and are not sensible of its loss or of its grace, shall we baptize them too?' By all means, if any danger make it requisite. For it is better that they be SANCTIFIED [baptized] without their own sense of it, than that they should die UNSEALED and UNINITIATED. And a ground of this to us is Circumcision, which was given on the eighth day, and was a TYPI-

να ἱερωθήτω τῷ Πνεύματι. Σὺ δέδοικας τὴν σφράγιδα διὰ τὸ φύσεως ἀθενὲς ὡς μικρόψυχος ἡ μήτηρ καὶ ὀλιγόπιστος. Ἡ Ἄννα δὲ καὶ πρὶν ἢ γεννηθῆναι τὸν Σαμουὴλ καθυπέρκετο τῷ Θεῷ, καὶ γεννηθέντα ἱερὸν εὐθὺς ποιεῖ, καὶ τῇ ἱερατικῇ στολῇ συνανέθρεψεν, οὐ τὸ ἀνθρώπινον φοβηθεῖσα, τῳ δέ Θεῷ πιστεύσασα.

[1] The error that Grotius fell into in this passage has been so often exposed that it is unnecessary to examine it here.

CAL SEAL, and was practised on those who had no reason; as also, the anointing of the door posts, which preserved the first-born by things which had no sense. As for others, I give MY OPINION, that they should stay three years or thereabouts, when they are capable to hear and answer some of the holy words: and though they do not perfectly understand them, yet they form them; and that you then seem to sanctify them in soul and body with the great sacrament of initiation."[1]

It seems rather strange that this passage was ever referred to in behalf of Antipædobaptism. Nothing can be more manifest than its *recognition* of the doctrine of Infant Baptism. Every one who thinks at all, must know that three years of age is not the "age of *discretion*," which is the lowest limit that Antipædobaptism will allow. Gregory gives it merely as *his* "*own opinion*," (not the doctrine of the Church), that in such cases it will be well to delay it until about that age. But his longest limit admits Infant Baptism, much more his answer in regard to the weak and sickly. Baptism at any age before the stage of moral responsibility, is virtually *Infant Baptism*.

2. It would be difficult, perhaps, to reconcile the teaching of this Father, when at one time he exhorts persons procrastinating duty to avail themselves of this "auxiliary strength," and not to permit "wickedness to have the advantage of time with their chil-

1 Ἔστω ταῦτα, φησὶ, πἔρι τῶν ἐπιζητούντων τὸ βάπτισμα, τὶ δ' ἂν εἴποις περὶ τῶν ἔτι νηπίων, καὶ μήτε τῆς ζημίας ἐπαισθανομένων, μήτε τῆς χάριτος; ἢ καὶ ταῦτα βαπτίσομεν; πάνυγε, εἴπερ τὶς ἐπείγῃ, κίνδυνος. Χρεῖωον γὰρ ἀναισθήτως, ἁγιασθῆναι, ἢ ἀπελθεῖν ἀσφραγίστα, καὶ ἀτέλεστα. Καὶ τούτου λόγος ἡμῖν ἡ ὀκτάημερος περιτομὴ, τυπική τις οὖσα σφραγίς, καὶ ἀλογίστοις ἔτι προσαγομενή, ὡς δὲ καὶ ἡ τῶν φλιῶν, χρίσις διὰ τῶν ἀναισθήτων φυλάττουσα τὰ προτότοκα. Περὶ δὲ τῶν ἄλλων δίδωμι γνώμην, τὴν τριετίαν ἀναμένοντας, ἢ μικρὸν ἐντός τούτου, ἤπερ τούτου, ἡνίκα καὶ ἀκοῦσαι τὶ μυσικὸν καὶ ἄποκρίνεθαι δύνανται, εἰ καὶ μὴ συνίεντα τελείως ἀλλ' οὖν τυπόυμενα, οὕτως ἁγιάζειν καὶ ψυχὰς καὶ σώματα τῷ μεγάλῳ μυστηρίω τῆς τελειώσεως.— *Oratio de Baptismo*, 40.

dren, but *consecrate* and *seal* them from the cradle;" and at another, advises delay until "three years of age, unless danger make it requisite." — It is, however, not unusual for men in the warmth of feeling to push a favorite theory too far, and then stretch other principles beyond their lawful bounds to harmonize with it.

He was very justly reproving those who were more anxious to have one high in office to baptize them, and to avoid the poor and have the rich their fellow-recipients, than they were about their own fitness for the sacrament; and hence in admonishing them that a due preparation of heart — a right spirit — a "*heart inflamed with the desire for it*," were things more important than *all external* prerequisites and appendages. But to apply, what was true of all capable of *desiring* it and needing such preparation, to little children who were incapable of the "inflamed desire," and deferring Baptism in their case to a time when they might at least *seem to desire* it by *pronouncing* the words expressive of the feeling, is stretching his principle beyond its powers of application. His reply, however, to the simple question — "Shall Infants be baptized, too?" "*Yes, by all means, if danger make it requisite; for it is better that they be sanctified without their own sense of it, than that they should die unsealed and uninitiated*" — settles the question as to his views of the lawfulness and importance of Infant Baptism.

In connection with this we will notice another writer of this age, whose testimony has been brought forward to produce the impression that Infant Baptism was not the universal practice of the Church at this time; and then pass on to that which is more explicit on the subject.

§ 12. BASIL, a contemporary of Gregory Nazianzen, and Bishop of Cæsarea, in an exhortation to catechumens, uses language which seems to imply, as some think, that young children were not baptized by him. He reminds some of his auditors that "they *had been catechised from childhood*, and still put off their baptism." This is brought forward, as if proof positive that Infant Baptism was not then universal. But every one at all familiar with Church history knows, that as early as the close of the second century, so great was the influx of uninformed persons into the Church, that it was found necessary to adopt measures by which applicants for Baptism should be instructed. Pouring into it, from every class, and of different nations, and bringing with them, as we may suppose, every variety of opinion; many of them knowing but little more of the doctrines of Christianity than the great truths of Christ's death and resurrection; it was expedient that all such should be more thoroughly instructed before they were admitted to Baptism.

And for this purpose, they were first formed into classes and taught by questions and answers; afterwards schools and teachers in different places were provided for them. They who chose, brought also their children with them to these schools. At that time, only the children of baptized persons were baptized, except such as were *adopted* by Christians, or for whom Christians stood as *sureties* for their thorough religious training; and this system soon suggested the idea to pious parents of availing themselves of a similar method for the instruction also of their baptized children; and by and by, classes of these were likewise formed.

2. As it appears, some of those who had entered the catechetical school under Basil became careless and lukewarm in regard to their baptism, and put it off till they had now grown old, and some of their children had grown up to manhood, who were brought with them when very young. These were not baptized during their minority, because their parents themselves were not, and now they were old enough to receive the *sacrament* on their own responsibility, they were following the example of their parents in *putting it off*. Basil, in a public address, thus speaks to this latter class of persons: —

ORATIO EXHORTATORIA AD BAPTISMUM.

"Do you procrastinate, and deliberate, and put it off? Having been catechised from a little child in the word, have you not yet learned the truth? Always hearing it, and not yet come to the knowledge of it. A trier all your life long; a considerer till you are old. When will you become a Christian? When shall we see you become one of us?"[1]

This passage has been cited by the opponents of Infant Baptism to prove that it was not universal in the time of Basil. Had it been, they urge, there would not have been among his catechumens persons unbaptized, who had been "catechised from early childhood." It should be remembered, however, that in these schools heathen candidates for Baptism took their children to be instructed at the same time with themselves, even as young as seven years of age, and

[1] 'Οκνεῖς καὶ βουλεύῃ καὶ διαμέλλεις; ἐκ νηπίου τὸν λόγον κατηχούμενος οὔπω συνέθου τῇ ἀληθείᾳ; πάντοτε μανθάνων οὐδέπω ἦκθες πρὸς τὴν ἐπίγνωσιν; πειραστὴς διὰ βίου, κατάσκοπος μέχρι γήρως; πότε γενήσῃ χριστιανὸς; πότε γνωρίσωμέν σε ὡς ἡμέτερον."

sometimes younger;[1] and in imminent danger of death, such were allowed clinic baptism.[2] The children of Christian parents were baptized in their infancy. Basil tells us himself *that Baptism was not confined to any age*. Referring to the words of Solomon, that there is a "time for everything," he adds: —

1. "There is, therefore, the proper season for several things — a time peculiar for sleep, and one peculiar for watching; a time for war, and a time for peace. But the whole life of men, (or any time of one's life) is proper for Baptism."[3]

§ 13. Passing on to a Council of Eliberis, held a little more than 200 years from the age of the Apos-

NOTE. — There is another passage of Basil's — also one from Jerome — that are sometimes introduced into this controversy. But they are not deemed of sufficient importance to be given a place in the body of this evidence. A mere glance at their import will show that they have no bearing on the question before us. The passage of Basil referred to was introduced in an argument with the Eunomians, who denied the Divinity of the Son and Holy Ghost. He argued that in thus acting they renounced their baptism — for that was in the name of all three persons in the Trinity, hence into the faith of the Divinity of each. And as the faith into which they were baptized is prior to the act of baptism, a renunciation of that faith was a renunciation of their baptism. This is the substance of the passage and argument. But what pædobaptist, if he should choose to adopt the same kind of reasoning, might not say the same thing? That all rightly baptized are baptized into the faith of the Trinity — that an adult must believe and be baptized in the name of the Father, Son, and Holy Ghost — Infants are baptized likewise in the same faith, and taught to believe, and are brought up in the same doctrine. In Baptism, as it was in circumcision, faith is prior in the purport of the design, but not in the execution of the artist — not necessarily prior in point of time in its application to its subjects. Nor does Basil mean anything more than this, as is evident both from the passage and nature of the argument which he used.

In the case of Jerome, he was commenting on the commission "to teach and baptize all nations," in which he shows the necessity of instructing

---

1 Bingham's *Antiquities*, book x., sec. 4. 2 Ibid., sec. 5.

3 Καιρὸς μὲν οὖν ἄλλοις, ἄλλος ἐπιτήδειος ἴδιος ὕπνου, καὶ ἴδιος γρηγορήσεως, ἴδιος πολέμου καὶ ἴδιος εἰρήνης. Καιρὸς δὲ βαπτίσματος ἅπας ὁ τῶν ἀνθρωπων βίος. — *Exort. ad Baptismum*, § 2.

tles, we find a canon passed, containing regulations in regard to schism, and the conditions on which those who had been guilty of that sin should be received back into the church when application was made by them.

CONCIL. ELIBERITANUM. CAN. 22.

"If any one go over from the Church Catholic to any heresy (or sect) and again return to the Church: Resolved, that repentance be not denied to such an one, inasmuch as he has acknowledged his fault. Let him be in a state of repentance for ten years, and after ten years be admitted to the communion.

"But if they were *Infants* when they were carried over, inasmuch as it was not their own fault that they erred; they ought to be admitted without delay."[1]

From this we learn again that infants were made members of schismatical sects, as well as of the Church Catholic, or great body of Christians. This canon was passed on account of schism, and the conditions made in regard to such as had gone over from the Church, or were carried over (*transducti*), which implies that all such were members of the Church before they were carried over. And the manner in which infants are referred to very clearly shows what was the common practice of the age.

nations before we baptize them. To which every pædobaptist will agree, and according to which every one acts. Whenever sent to a heathen land, no one ever dreams of baptizing before he has convinced the people of the truth of his message, and instructed them to some extent in the great principles of Christianity. But as soon as this is done, and parents who have children believe, and are baptized, he also baptizes their young children. Just as we believe the Apostles acted under the same commission. Jerome, as has been already seen, expressly declares it to be a sin in parents to neglect the Baptism of their children. It is, therefore, loss of time to dwell on this passage.

1 "Si quis de Catholicâ Ecclesiâ ad heresim transitum fecerit, rursusque ad ecclesiam recurrerit: placuit huic penitentiam non esse denegandam, eo quod cognoverit peccatum suum: qui etiam decem annis agat penitentiam; cui post decem annos præstari communio debet. Si vero infantes fuerint transducti; quod non suo vitio peccaverint, incunctanter recipi debent." — *Wall*, vol. i. ch. vii.

§ 14. Fifty years still nearer to the Apostles, a Council was held at Carthage, in which, among the questions brought before that body for their deliberation, was one which brings out very clearly the practice of the Church, and the opinion of the Council in regard to Infant Baptism. The question proposed was, whether it would not be better to delay the Baptism of Infants till the eighth day after their birth, than to continue baptizing them so young as two and three days old, as was at that time the custom? It was then likewise usual to give the "holy kiss" to all who were baptized. Fidus, who sent up this question to the Council, gives among other reasons for its delay till the *eighth* day, that this was the time when circumcision was administered, and that it would be more pleasant to give them the holy kiss at that age, than when only two or three days' old. His proposed change and reasons being considered in a Council of sixty-six bishops, a synodical letter was written in reply to him, of which the following are extracts: —

CYPRIANI EPIST. 64 AD. FIDUM.

"We read your letter, most dear brother. . . . So much as pertains to the case of *Infants*, who you think ought not to be baptized within the second or third day from their birth; and that the ancient law of circumcision should be observed, so that none should be baptized and sanctified before the eighth day after birth; it seemed to all in our Council far otherwise. For as for what you proposed to be done, there was *not one* of your opinion. But on the contrary, it was our unanimous judgment that the grace and mercy of God should not be denied to any one born of men. . . . And whereas, you say that an infant in the first days after its birth is unclean, so that one dislikes to kiss it; we do not think that it ought to be any impediment to giving it the heavenly grace." [1]

[1] "Legimus literas tuas, frater carissime. . . . Quantum vero ad causam

There are several things for the reader to observe in this place.

First, That this testimony is like all the other heretofore given, incidental. The right of infants to Baptism is taken for granted, and a secondary question implying its previous existence discussed; *i. e.*, the mere appendage of a few days' delay.

Secondly, That the reasons assigned for its delay till the eighth day, instead of affecting its divine authority, were offered, because, in the first place, circumcision was given formerly on the eighth day; and in the second, when children were so young it was unpleasant to give them the holy kiss, which was the common practice of that age.

And thirdly, That we have now arrived within about one hundred and fifty years of the Apostolic age, and may presume that most of these bishops living so near that time had abundant means of ascertaining whether this thing was of divine authority, or not. And further, that of so large a number as sixty-six, it is not unreasonable to suppose that some of them were old men, whose memories would carry them back half the intervening time, and only leave them some sixty or seventy years to trace it to the Apostles. For which, family tradition coming through only the father and grandfather, would be sufficient: and which

infantium pertinet, quos dixisti intra secundum vel tertium diem, quo nati sunt, constitutos baptizari non oportere et considerandum esse legem circumcisionis antiquæ: ut intra octavum diem, eum qui natus est baptizandum et sanctificandum non putares, longe aliud in Concilio nostro omnibus visum est. In hoc enim quod tu putabos esse faciendum nemo consensit. sed universi potius judicavimus nulli hominum nato misericordiam Dei et gratiam denegandam. . . . Nam et quod vestigium infantis in primis partus sui diebus constituti mundum non esse dixisti, quod unusquisque nostrum horreat exosculari: nec hoc putamus ad cœlestem gratiam dandam impedimento esse oportere. — *Oxford Edition Epist.* 64. See also *Ante-Nicene Christian Library*, vol. viii.; Cyprian, vol. i., Epist. 58.

is a kind of tradition few will hesitate to receive, when in the line of their own ancestors. Further be it observed that the *whole number* without a dissenting voice decided against even the *secondary* question of a few days' delay.

Thus far the way is open and clear before us. Other testimony could have been introduced, but was deemed unnecessary, and therefore omitted. As we draw nearer to the apostolic age the number of writers must be less, because the nearer to the beginning, the smaller the number of members. And the few writers among them were chiefly occupied in opposing *heresies* and combating *new doctrines*. Infant Baptism not being one of these, is introduced in connection with other subjects, with which it is more or less intimately connected.

Tertullian, to whom allusion has been several times made in these pages, was the first and only man during the first thousand years of Christianity that did oppose Infant Baptism, so far as we can learn, unless we regard Nazianzen's advice to "delay it *until three years* of age *in case of no danger*," opposition to it. Even Tertullian's advice to delay it is limited by *immediate danger of death*, as we shall presently see.

Tertullian was born, according to the estimates now generally received, about A. D. 150; embraced Christianity 185; adopted the opinions of Montanus about 199, and died 220.

1. He laid much stress on the *authority* and *effects* of Baptism. Introduces his Treatise on that subject in the following strain: "Happy is the sacrament of our water, in that, by washing away the sins of our early blindness, we are set free into eternal life."

[1] Intro. c. i.

2. In his work against Marcion he ascribes to Baptism the spiritual blessings of remission of sins, deliverance from death, regeneration, and participation in the Holy Spirit.[1]

3. In regard to Adam's transgression, and its effects on his race, he teaches that the effect of his transgression has been to make his offspring the heirs of his condemnation: to entail upon them a corruption of nature, from which no man born into the world is exempt, and for which there is no other remedy than to be born again by water and the Holy Spirit.[2]

4. Again, "every soul is reckoned in Adam, until it is enrolled anew in Christ; and so long unclean till it be so enrolled, and sinful, because unclean." [3]

5. And yet again, "*the prescript* is laid down that without Baptism salvation is attainable by none" (grounded chiefly on that declaration of the Lord, who says, "*unless one be born of the water he hath not life*") John iii. 5.[4]

Now, one may well ask, if this man taught that all of Adam's descendants inherit a corrupt condemned state in consequence of his trangression, for which there is no other remedy than to be born again of the water and the spirit; that every soul is reckoned in Adam until enrolled anew in Christ; that through Baptism is obtained remission of sins, deliverance from death, regeneration, and participation in the Holy Spirit; and that the *prescript is laid down, that without Baptism salvation is attained by none*, for unless one be born of water he hath not life (John iii. 5) —

[1] Lib. i. c. 28.

[2] De Anima, c. 3; De Baptismo, c. 5; De Jejuniis, c. 3, cited in Bishop of Bristol's *Eccl. Hist.*, pp. 325-328.

[3] De Anima, c. 40.

[4] De Baptismo, c. 12.

if these be his doctrines, whether they be *true* or *false*, how could *he* advise the *delay of Infant Baptism*?

Let these preliminaries aid us in *interpreting the passage*, so often referred to in his writings, to prove that "he opposed Infant Baptism" (?) which is as follows: —

TERTULLIANUS DE BAPTISMO, C. XVIII.

6. "Therefore according to the circumstances and disposition, and even age, of every one, the delay of Baptism is the more profitable: especially in the case of little children. For what need is there (unless absolutely necessary) [imminent danger of death] that sponsors also be thrust into danger; since they both by reason of mortality, may themselves fail to fulfil their promises; and may be disappointed by the development of an evil disposition [in the children for whom they become sureties]. The Lord does indeed say, '*Forbid them not to come unto me.*' Let them '*come*' then when they are growing up, let them '*come*' while they are learning, while they are taught whither they are to '*come*;' let them become Christians when they are able to know Christ.

"Why does the innocent period of life hasten to the remission of sins? Men will act more cautiously in worldly matters; so that to one to whom no earthly substance is committed, that which is Divine is committed! Let them know how to 'ask' for salvation, that you may seem [at least] 'to have given to him that asketh.' For no less cause must the unmarried also be deferred — in whom is the preparation for temptation; alike in virgins by reason of maturity; as in the widowed, by their vacation [of married life] — until they either marry or else be confirmed in continency. If any understand the weight of Baptism, they will fear its reception more than its delay. Faith unimpaired is secure of salvation."[1]

1 "Itaque pro cujusque personæ conditione ac dispositione, etiam ætate cunctatio baptismi utilior est; præcipuè tamen circa parvulos. Quid enim necesse est (si non tam necesse) sponsores etiam periculo ingeri? quia et ipsi per mortalitatem destituere promissiones suas possunt et provent malæ indolis falli. Sit quidem Dominus Nolite illos prohibere ad me venire. Veniant ergo dum adolescunt, veniant dum discunt, dum quo veniant docentur; fiant Christiani qum Christum nosse potuerint; Quid festinat innocens ætas ad remissionem peccatorum? Cautius agitur in secularibus: ut cui substantia terrena non creditur Divina credatur. Norint petere

This passage clearly advises the delay of Baptism to all persons who are likely to be subjected to strong temptation after it; young men, maidens, widows, and especially little children: *the young of all classes.*

7. The reader very naturally asks, Why? Is not the grace of God sufficient for all classes? No doubt Tertullian's peculiar views of "*sin after Baptism*," and the rigid rule of the Church at that time; which did not allow members who had fallen into sin after their Baptism, to be received back into its fold till after long and the most thorough *repentance*,[1] and then *but once*, was the ground work of this advice. And perhaps he then held *privately* the doctrine to which he gave utterance and adopted soon after embracing Montanism: namely, that only sins of a venial character, committed after Baptism, could be forgiven at all. For those of deeper dye, such as homicide, adultery, fornication, blasphemy, denial of Christ, idolatry, and fraud committed after Baptism, he says "There is no remission; and that even Christ will not intercede for those who commit them."[2]

But before his open avowal of Montanism, and in the same treatise on Baptism, from which the extract under consideration is taken, he wrote: "There is to us *one*, and but *one*, Baptism; as well according to the Lord's gospel, as according to the Apostle's letter." (Eph. iv. 4, 5, 6.) .... "We enter the font *once*; *once* our sins are washed away, because they ought never to be repeated"[3]

salutem, ut petenti dedisse videaris. Non minori de causa innupti quoque procrastinandi, in quibus tentatio præparata est: tam virginibus per maturitatem, quam riduis per vacationem donec aut nubant aut continentia corroborentur. Fides integra secura est de salute."

1 De Pœnitentia, c. vii. Also Bingham, *Antiquities*, book xix. c. 12.

2 De Pudicitia, c. xix. Also *Eccl. Hist.*, Bishop of Bristol.

3 De Baptismo, c. xv.

8. Again, in his tract on Repentance written before or soon after his treatise on Baptism, he warns such as had lapsed after their Baptism, against trampling on God's mercy ; as if the "*redundance of celestial clemency constituted a license for human temerity.*" *Repeated sin* "*will find an end of escaping, when it shall not find one of sinning.*"[1]

He expresses much admiration of the reverence of those who "are unwilling a second time to be a burden to the Divine mercy"—who "fear even to seem to trample on the benefits which they had attained;" for such having been received and overcome once by the machinations of Satan, "God foreseeing his poisons, *although the gate of forgiveness has been shut and fastened up with the bar of Baptism*, has permitted it still to stand somewhat ajar. In the vestibule He has *stationed repentance the second*, to open to such as knock; but *now once for all*, because *now for the second time, but nevermore*; because the last time it had been [open] in vain. Is not even *this once enough*, You have what you deserved not, for you had lost what you had received. If the Lord's indulgence grants you the means of restoring what you had lost, be thankful for the benefit renewed, not to say amplified; for *restoring* is a greater thing than *giving*, inasmuch as *having lost* is more miserable than never having *received* at all."[2]

These extracts, though not remarkable for perspicuity, explain clearly enough why Tertullian advised the delay of Baptism to such as would probably be exposed to temptation above others after it. According to his views there was much less hope of forgiveness of sins *after*, than *before it.* Baptism washed away all past sins, but "*shut and fastened up the gate of*

[1] De Pœnitentia, c. vii. [2] Ibid.

forgiveness as with a bar," in such a way that mercy could extend forgiveness only in exceptional cases; such as sins of ignorance and those of less vicious nature when not too *frequently* indulged; "but only *once for all*, because, now for the second time; *but never more*, because the last time it had been in vain."

9. He could not have meant at the close of the passage, that "faith unimpaired is secure of salvation" to the *neglect* of Baptism; because he had more than once repeated directly the opposite doctrine. In the thirteenth chapter of his "Treatise on Baptism," in reply to the objection, "Baptism is not necessary for them to whom faith is sufficient; for withal Abraham pleased God by a sacrament of *no water*, *but of faith;*" he said, [" True;] but in all cases it is the *later* things which have a conclusive force, and the *subsequent* that prevail over the *antecedent*. Grant that in days gone by, there was salvation by means of *bare faith*, before the *passion and resurrection* of the Lord; but now that faith has been enlarged, and is become a faith which believes in his *nativity*, *passion*, and *resurrection;* there has been an amplification added to the sacrament, [namely] the *sealing act of baptism;* the clothing, in a certain sense, of the faith which was before bare, and which cannot exist now without its proper law. For *the law of baptizing* has been *imposed*, and the *formula prescribed*: '*Go*,' (saith He,) "*teach the nations, baptizing them into the name of the Father, and of the Son and of the Holy Spirit.*" This law in unison with that limitation — "unless a man have been reborn of water and the spirit, he cannot enter into the kingdom of Heaven," *hath bound down faith to the necessity of Baptism.*[1]

Tertullian, therefore, could not have meant that

[1] De Baptismo, c. xiii.

faith without Baptism, *where it could be had*, was sufficient for salvation; but that a faith unimpaired by neglect or by unjustifiable motives sufficed for delay in Baptism, wherein one's best interest (as he supposed) might require delay.

10. And so when he advised the delay of Baptism to little children, he could not have meant that Baptism to them was of no avail, conferred no benefit, and hence no need for their sponsors to assume responsibilites which they might not be able to fulfil; he meant as he said "*more profitable*" (*utilior est*) to delay it unless in *great danger*. His views of *sins after Baptism*, to which we have just adverted, no doubt led him to advise the delay of it to *all* most likely to be drawn into such sins, *except in cases threatened with immediate death*. For in cases of "*necessity*" [danger of death] he had urged in the *preceding chapter* [1] that even a *layman must baptize* sooner than let one die unbaptized; or he would be guilty of a *great loss* to such an one by refraining from doing what he had power to do.

He was at the time treating of the "authority *to administer Baptism*," and wrote as follows: —

De Baptismo, chap. xvii.

11. "Of giving it [Baptism] the Chief Priest (who is the bishop) has the right; in the next place, the Presbyters and Deacons, yet not without the Bishop's authority on account of the honor of the Church, which being preserved, peace is preserved. Besides these, even laymen have the right; for what is equally received can be equally given. And unless bishops or presbyters or deacons be on the spot, laymen are called." [After some remarks on submission to superiors, he continues:] "The most holy apostle has said: 'all things are lawful, but not all things expedient;' let it suffice assuredly, in *cases of necessity*, to avail yourself of that power, [to baptize] if at any time circumstance

1 De Baptismo, c. xvii.

either of place or time or person compels you; for then the steadfast courage of the succorer, where the *case of the endangered* one *is urgent*, is admissible : inasmuch as he will be guilty of a human creature's great loss, if he shall refrain from bestowing what he is able to bestow." [1]

This explains what Tertullian means by delaying the Baptism of little children — "si non tam necesse" — "*if no great necessity*," or, "*if not absolutely necessary*" — meaning *no immediate danger of dissolution.* In such cases we see, as just cited in the chapter before us (written before that containing this passage) *the rule laid down that none must be permitted to die without Baptism. Even* a *layman*, *in the absence of those* higher in authority, must baptize in the hour of *extreme necessity*, or he will be guilty of great injury to the dying, by refraining from doing for him what he had the power to do. Some would construe "si non tam necesse," as if referring to Baptism and not to the *subjects* of Baptism. "For why is it necessary — if Baptism be not so indispensably necessary [2]

[1] See *Library of the Fathers* by members of the English Church, Oxford, vol. i., p. 275. *Ante-Nicene Library*, vol. xi.; Tertullian, vol. i. chap. xvii.

[2] We were surprised to find that the translator in the Ante-Nicene Christian Library has adopted this construction, and that he gives us a reason for it, that "Tertullian allows (in chap. xvi. De Baptismo) that Baptism is not indispensably necessary to salvation." From which it is obvious that he has misapprehended the purport of that chapter and meaning of Tertullian's words, whose object was not to *lessen*, by any means, the great importance of Christian Baptism, but to give a *still higher* importance *to Baptism in one's own blood*. As the Saviour after his Baptism referred to his *sufferings on the cross* as another Baptism (Luke xii. 50) that he must receive, which of course was of much greater importance than that already received, because upon that the other was dependent for its power; so Tertullian regarded martyrdom or Baptism in one's own blood (which he calls a "second Baptism") as bearing a similar relation to Christian Baptism, and therefore sufficient to "supply the place of the fontal washing when it has not been received, and to restore it when lost." —c. xvii.

Tertullian and his contemporaries generally held the necessity of Baptism to salvation (when it could he had) chiefly, on the words of the Saviour — "He that believeth and is baptized shall be saved" and "Except a man

— that sponsors be thrust into the danger" of not fulfilling their promises, etc.?

But such a construction would involve Tertullian in self contradiction, and inexcusable inconsistency. For in divers places he lays great stress on the *importance and necessity of Baptism*, as we have already shown. He ascribes to it *the power of washing away sin and setting us free into eternal life*;[1] says it is the *prescribed remedy for the corruption of Adam's sin, from which none are exempt*;"[2] the only rule laid down by which salvation is attainable by any one (John iii. 5);[3] that nothing can supply its place except the *Baptism of martyrdom*, which is *Baptism in one's own blood*, and which he calls a second Baptism;[4] — and that even a layman must give it, if the danger to life be great, or great loss may be the consequence.[5]

Having thus expressed his views of the *necessity* of Baptism in these and various other places, how could he consistently teach in this that Baptism is not of sufficient importance to endanger the risk of sponsors' not fulfilling their promises made at the Baptism of a little child? Such a construction is in *direct contradiction to his teaching*, wheresoever he has expressed himself on the subject of Baptism. And but for his peculiar views *of sin after Baptism*, and the rigor exercised in receiving back lapsed members into the Church, he

be *born of the water and of the spirit*, he cannot enter into the kingdom of God." But for extraordinary cases they made exceptions such as *martyrdom*; and where *no fault could be attached to the subjects*, supposing the *invisible Baptism of the spirit* in such cases supplied the want of the external element of water. See Bingham's *Antiquities*, book 10, p. 442.

1 De Baptismo, Intro. c. 1.

2 De Anima, c.iii.

3 De Baptismo, c. xii.

4 c. xvi.

5 c. xvii.

would never have suggested the delay of Baptism to little children, however *free from danger they might* have been.

A consistent interpretation, therefore, of the writings of Tertullian, and justice to his religious character, show him to be *not the opposer of Infant Baptism*, but its *earnest advocate in time of danger and a decided witness to its practice in his day.*

12. The *practice of the Church* is what we wish to know; and the manner in which he alludes to it, and the mode of reasoning pursued by him in regard to it, prove the *existence* of Infant Baptism at the time. For he refers to the Baptism of young children in no otherwise than he refers to other classes of persons usually baptized, and argues the point in a way that proves beyond all doubt that Infant Baptism was then the usage of the Church. "What need is there," he asks, "that their *sponsors* (god-fathers) be brought into danger?" This shows not only that young children were at the time baptized, but that SPONSORS also were then used at their Baptism. Why should he refer to such things if they did not exist?

He also attempts to reconcile with his new theory a passage of Scripture which was regarded by himself as authority for bringing young children into Christ's kingdom. "Our Saviour (he admits) does indeed say, 'do not forbid them to come to me,' but let them come when they are growing up — let them come when they learn, when they are taught whither they are to come." By introducing this passage, he shows what was the age of the children (parvulos) to whom he referred; and also how the passage was generally understood in that early age of the Church. He was evidently speaking of the same class of little children that were brought to our Saviour, and which He took up in his arms and blessed, saying: "Of such is the kingdom of God" (Mark x. 14). Their infantile state is further manifest by his speaking of them as so young that their "disposition was not yet unfolded" — that they did not "know whither they were coming" — were unable to ask for themselves, and being of an innocent "guiltless age."

But be it observed that he does not appeal to the *usage of the Church* at that time, nor to any *previous period* between that and the days of the Apostles to sustain his opinion. He does not say that it is not the uniform practice of the Church, or a new thing brought into the Church, nor intimate anything of the kind. How easily might he have *put down* this practice, and established his own theory by an appeal of this kind, had there been any ground for it. And how natural is it for men to appeal to the strongest known authority when anxious to establish any point. The absence of all such reasoning is of itself strong presumptive proof that Tertullian had no example to sustain his theory. For we cannot suppose a man of his acquirements could not trace back a public usage of the Church a little over one hundred years, which would bring him to the Apostolic age. The whole of his reasoning shows that he was trying to introduce a new custom in the Church, which he placed entirely on grounds of expediency. Nor does it appear that the Church or the Montanists with whom he afterwards united, followed his advice on this point.

13. "He was endowed (says Mosheim) with a great genius, but seemed deficient in point of judgment. His piety was warm and vigorous, but at the

same time, melancholy and austere. His learning was extensive and profound; and yet his credulity and superstition were such as might have been expected from the darkest ignorance. And with respect to his reasoning, it had more of that subtlety that dazzles the imagination, than of that solidity that brings light and conviction to the mind."

14. "The very advice to delay (says another), or if you will, the condemnation of Baptism in infancy (though these two are far from being the same, and the former alone properly belongs to Tertullian), is conclusive evidence of the previous existence of the practice. This is the point. The opinion is nothing to the purpose. It has no authority. His simple proposition to delay it when there is no danger, not only proves its previous existence, it proves *more*. It proves that it was no innovation. When a man condemns a practice, he is naturally desirous to support his peculiar views by the strongest arguments. Could Tertullian therefore have shown that the practice was of recent origin; that it had been introduced in his own day, or even at any time subsequent to the lives of the Apostles, we have every reason to believe he would have availed himself of a ground so obvious and so conclusive. It proves further, that the Baptism of Infants was the general practice of the Church in Tertullian's time. His opinion is his own. It is that of a dissentient from the universal body of professing Christians. He never pretends to say that any part of the Church had held or acted upon it. Of his *opinion* and *advice* then, we may say, *Valeant quantum valere possunt.* But the total absence of any attempt to support and recommend them by appeal to the practice of the Church in Apostolic times, or of

any part of the Church at any intervening period between those times and his own, certainly goes far to prove the matter of fact with which alone we have to do — that "*Infant Baptism was the original and universal practice.*" [1]

Such is the authority of Tertullian; his *testimony* proves, that it was then the *usage* of the Church to baptize Infants; his *advice* shows that he reasoned from *false premises.*

Had he embraced correct views of Baptism in the first place, and instead of applying it only to past sins, regarded it as the seal of a covenant co-extensive with the existence of the parties, we should never have heard of Tertullian as an opposer — or rather as the advocate for the postponement of all Baptism till late in life, or just before death!

We have dwelt the longer on the testimony of this Father, because his name is so often quoted by persons who never take the trouble to examine his writings. As to the *usage* of the Church in his time, that is placed beyond all doubt by contemporaneous authority. It does not admit of controversy. The evidence on this point will be adduced in the next chapter, with other proof that Infant Baptism was the doctrine and practice of the Church in the first century after the Apostles, and before Tertullian was born.

1 Wardlaw *On Inf. Bap.*, edit. 2, p. 138.

CHAPTER III.

HISTORICAL TESTIMONY CONTINUED.

Origen born of Christian Parents. — His Piety, Learning, and Travels. — His Declaration that Infant Baptism is the Usage of the whole Church, handed down by the Apostles. — Care of Early Christians to preserve the True Faith. — Irenæus, Hearer of Polycarp, the Pupil of St. John. — His Zeal for Apostolic Usage. — Use of the Term Regeneration, and Testimony to the Baptism of all Ages. — Agreement of Various Sects on this Point. — Interpretation of St. John iii. 5, and Titus iii. 5.

§ 12. ORIGEN was a cotemporary of Tertullian — born about eighty-five years after the death of St. John, of Christian parents, baptized in infancy — and the most learned man of his day. "His works," says Waddington, "exhibit the operation of a bold and comprehensive mind, burning with religious warmth, unrestrained by any low prejudices or interests, and sincerely bent on the attainment of truth."

In his commentary on the Epistle to the Romans, he is led to speak of the inherent corruption of every one born into the world, and refers to David as teaching the same doctrine in the fifty-first Psalm: "In sin did my mother conceive me." Concerning which he says, "there is in the history no account of any particular sin that his mother had committed," and adds: —

COMMENT. IN EPIST. AD ROMANOS, LIB. 5.

"For this also it was, that the Church had from the Apostles the tradition (or injunction) to give Baptism to young children. For they, to whom the Divine mysteries were committed, knew that there is in all persons the natural pollution of sin, which must be done away by water and the Spirit, on account of which the body itself is also called the *body of sin*.[1]

In this passage, we see that Origen appeals to Infant Baptism as the usage of the Church, not only at that time, but as handed down from the Apostles. Nor does he seem to add the latter clause of the sentence to give authority for the usage, but merely refers to it as an acknowledged and undisputed truth, believed by all; adduced, as he would adduce any other acknowledged truth, to bear on the point before him — namely, the corrupt nature of every one that is born into the world. "Tradition" was a term at that early period used for what was written as well as delivered orally,[2] and was regarded as including the written words of the Apostles, as well as those unwritten. The Apostle Paul uses the term in the same way — "Hold the traditions which you have been taught, whether by word or our epistle" (2 Thess. ii. 15). Although this term has been variously

[1] "Pro hoc et Ecclesia ab apostolis traditionem suscepit etiam parvulis baptismum dare. Sciebant enim illi quibus mysteriorum secreta commissa sunt Divinorum, quia essent in omnibus genuinæ sordes peccati, quæ per aquam et spiritum ablui deberent; propter quas etiam corpus ipsum, corpus peccati, nominatur." — *Epist. ad Romanus*, lib. 5.

[2] The term traditio — παράδοσις, "tradition," as used by the ancient Fathers, signifies good and credible evidence delivered by one person to another, either written or by speaking; and is applied even to the Gospels, which were called (Suicer, *Thesaur.*, tom. ii.) Εὐαγγελικαὶ παράδοσεις. "traditionary gospels." — *C. Taylor*.

Gregory Nazianzen calls the books of the New Testament — "The Evangelical and Apostolical traditions" (Εὐαγγελικαῖς τὲ καὶ ἀποστολικαῖς).

Tertullian, referring to portions of the New Testament, exhorts their opposers to "believe what is delivered" (Crede quod traditum est).

Hippolytus, the Martyr, quoting certain passages of the New Testament, calls on his brethren, saying, "Let us believe, dear brethren, according to the tradition of the Apostles" (κατὰ τὴν παράδοσιν τῶν ἀπόστολων. — *Goode's Divine Rule of Faith and Practice*, vol. i. p. 18, *and following*.

used since that time, and made the cloak of many errors, it was at that early period of binding authority, and doubtless referred to by Origen as such. Which shows the antiquity and authority of Infant Baptism at that time.

ORIGEN was a warm advocate of innate corruption; his mind is said to have been tinctured with the Platonic philosophy, but that does not affect his testimony as a witness to what was the daily practice of the Church. He could not be deceived in regard to a fact that was constantly occurring before his eyes. And his theory of natural corruption led him to refer oftener to the Baptism of Infants than he would otherwise have done, because *this* he regarded as acknowledged authority for the *depravity* of every one born into the world. In a Homily on a part of Leviticus, he refers also to the same words of David just noticed, saying: —

HOMILIA 8 IN LEVIT., C. 12.

"Hear David speaking: 'In iniquities I was conceived,' says he, 'and in sins did my mother bring me forth:' showing that every soul born in the flesh is polluted with the filth of sin and iniquity; and that on this account *that* was said, which we mentioned before: 'No one is clean from pollution, though his life is but the length of one day.'

"Besides all this, let it be considered, since the Baptism of the Church is given for the remission of sins; why, according to the *usage* of the Church it is likewise given to little children: whereas, if there was nothing in little children that needed remission and mercy, the grace of Baptism would be superfluous to them."[1]

Here he introduces again the *usage and authority* of

[1] "Audi David dicentem; In iniquitatibus inquit, conceptus sum et in peccatis peperit me mater mea: ostendens quod quæcunque anima in carne nascatur, iniquitatis et peccati sorde polluitur, et propterea dictum esse illud quod jam superius memoravimus; quia nemo mundus a sorde, nec si unius diei fuerit vita ejus. Addi his etiam illud potest, ut requiratur quid causæ sit, cum Baptisma ecclesiæ in remissionem peccatorum de-

Infant Baptism to confirm the doctrine of original sin, or natural corruption, and argues that if Infants were free from a sinful nature, *the rite of the washing away sin* would be superfluous to them.

Such was the *acknowledged authority* of Infant Baptism in that early period of the Church, that it was frequently introduced by this writer to elucidate and enforce his view of such passages of Holy Scripture or doctrines as seemed to him to imply the infection of Adam's sin.

In his commentary on St. Luke's gospel, he again uses the same kind of argument, and testifies as unequivocally to the practice of Infant Baptism.

HOMIL. IN LUCAM 14.

"Little children are baptized for the forgiveness of sins. Of what sins? Or when did they commit them? Or how can any reason be given for baptizing them, but only according to that sense which we mentioned a little before: 'None is free from pollution, though this life be but the length of one day upon the earth.' And for that reason infants are baptized, because by the sacrament of Baptism, the pollution of our birth is taken away." [1]

To these might be added yet other passages from the writings of ORIGEN to the same effect, were it necessary. Let it now be remarked, first — that Infant Baptism was not of itself a matter of dispute, but introduced in connection with other questions; second — that it is appealed to in this place, as if a thing, the

tur, secundum ecclesiæ observantiam etiam parvulis baptismum dari: cum relique si nihil esset in parvulis quod ad remissionem deberet et indulgentiam pertinere gratia Baptismi superflua videretur." — *Homil.* 8 *in Levit. c.* 12.

[1] "Parvuli baptizantur in remissionem peccatorum. Quorum peccatorum? Vel quo tempore peccaverunt? Aut quomodo potest ulla lavacri in parvulis ratio subsistere, nisi juxta illum sensum de quo paulo ante diximus: Nullus mundus a sorde, nec si unius diei quidem fuerit vita ejus super terram? Et quia per baptismi sacramentum nativitatis sordes deponuntur, propterea baptizantur et parvuli." — *Homil. in Lucam* 14.

authority of which no one doubted. So certain was Origen that all would admit the authority of this sacrament, that he based his reasoning on the foundation that a denial of natural corruption would come in conflict with the apostolic rite of Infant Baptism. For (says he) it was for this reason that the "Church had from the Apostles the tradition to give Baptism to young children." Infant Baptism is therefore brought in incidentally, and in such a way as to prove that it was the established, honored, and universally acknowledged doctrine of the Church at that time.

As to the authority of these passages — it so happened that two different writers made translations of the writings of Origen in the next century after he wrote, and they belonging to opposite parties on many points of which he treats, but in both of which the doctrine of Infant Baptism is fully set forth, which makes his testimony even more certain than if found only in the original works purporting to be his own. The passages already adduced are from both translators — two from RUFINUS and one from JEROME.

§ 13. Before we proceed, however, to the next witness, we will consider the many advantages possessed by ORIGEN, to know whether this "USAGE of the Church was handed down from the Apostles" and universal. In regard to his learning and piety, as has been already remarked, the Church in that age did not possess his equal. "He was a man (says Mosheim) of vast and uncommon abilities, and the greatest luminary of the Christian world that his age exhibited to view. Had the soundness of his judgment been equal to the immensity of his genius, the fervor of his piety, his indefatigable patience, his extensive erudition, and his other eminent and superior talents, all encomiums must have fallen short of his merit. Yet, such as he was, his virtues and his labors deserve the admiration of all ages: and his name will be transmitted with honor through the annals of time as long as learning and genius shall be esteemed among men."

Added to which he had enjoyed peculiar advantages to qualify him to speak on this subject. EUSEBIUS informs us, that he was born and bred in Alexandria; lived some time in Greece and in Rome; visited Cappadocia and Arabia in his travels, spending some time in each; and passed the greater part of his life in Syria and Palestine, the seat of the first Churches. [1]

Thus, in addition to the other means which men of learning possess for knowing the doctrines of their Church, ORIGEN could speak from *personal observation* in regard to Infant Baptism, in all these portions of the world — Alexandria, Greece, Rome, Cappadocia, Arabia, Syria, and Palestine. We must bear in mind also that a man born only eighty-five years from the Apostles' times, of Christian parents, baptized and taught the Scriptures from infancy, remarkable for his piety in boyhood, in mature manhood the "brightest luminary of his day," having visited all these portions of the world — appeals in his written works to Infant Baptism, as a PUBLIC RITE of the Church, handed down by the Apostles, and as such received and observed by all—and merely referred to in elucidating other doctrines.

Now can we suppose that such a writer as this would appeal in argument to a *rite* and that *frequently*

[1] Eusebius, liber 6.

concerning which, there was any doubt? Would a man whose fame had spread over Christendom, risk his reputation and his cause by making such appeals, without giving reasons in support of that to which he appealed, had there been any question about its Divine authority? On the contrary ORIGEN by referring to Infant Baptism in support of other doctrines, and taking for granted its Divine authority, and Tertullian, by referring to it because in some measure conflicting with a favorite theory, and yet not calling in question its Divine authority, establish beyond all doubt both the *prevalence* and antiquity of the rite.

These two writers lived in different parts of the world. Tertullian wrote the earlier of the two, but being born of heathen parents was converted to Christianity in adult age, while Origen enjoyed the privilege of descending from Christian parents, and of being taught the Christian doctrine from childhood.

To doubt whether these two men could trace back a public rite in the Church, the short time intervening between them and the Apostolic age, is to deny all that the learned have said in regard to their mental endowments. Tertullian, at the time he wrote, need go no farther than to ask the old men then living, whether their own fathers practised it. Origen's ancestors being Christians from the middle of the Apostolic age, he need not have gone out of his family to inquire; for his biographer informs us that "the Christian doctrine was conveyed to him by his forefathers."[1] RUFINUS translates it, "grandfathers and great-grandfathers," which would reach back into the middle of the Apostolic age. Origen's own father practised it; and if his father before him did the same (and no one

[1] Eusebius.

called it in question), this was as far as he need go. For this would reach the days of the Apostles, and if administered under, and sanctioned by them, we need no higher authority.

They were the authorized agents of Christ, "endued with power from on High," and set apart for the express work of building up his Kingdom on earth. The Saviour did not himself baptize, nor did the Gospel Church assume any definite form or structure while He was on earth. But He prepared the way and made ready all that was necessary, and then committed to his Apostles the duty of executing and consummating what He had taught them concerning his Kingdom.

They were commissioned "to disciple all nations, baptizing them in the name of the Father, and of the Son, and of the Holy Ghost; teaching them to observe all things whatsoever (He) had commanded them:" with the promise, "Lo I am with you alway, even unto the end of the world." (Matt. xxviii. 19-20.) And after his resurrection, he continued with them forty days longer, instructing them,[1] — "speaking of the things pertaining to the kingdom of God."[2]

He also commanded them to tarry at Jerusalem after his ascension, until they were baptized by the Holy Ghost, which would complete their qualification for the great work to which He had assigned them, And on the day of Pentecost the Holy Ghost was accordingly poured out upon them, and miraculous gifts conferred — and then it was, the *New Dispensation proper* began.

The thousands soon converted,[3] called forth the application of principles that gave the visible form,

[1] St. Luke xxiv. 1-51. [2] Acts i. 3. [3] Acts ii. 41-47.

and resulted in the organization, peculiar to the Christian Church.

The inspired Apostles being appointed agents of Christ, and qualified by the Holy Ghost for this work, whatever they sanctioned and practised as *essential elements* in the Christian Church has an authority to which we must all submit. In a matter *so fundamental* as the *subjects of Baptism*, there can be no appeal from their teaching and practice. If they sanctioned Infant Baptism, the question as to *its authority* is settled. We need nothing more on that point.

The Apostle John lived, according to our best chronologists, beyond the close of the first century, and wrote his "General Epistle" as late as A. D. 91 or 92. The object of which was to refute the prevailing errors of that period. And had Infant Baptism been one of them, he would have referred to it as such, beyond all doubt. But it is *not* included among those errors, and therefore, if in use at that time it was with his approbation and has all the authority we should ask.

Nor ought the teaching and influence of the Apostles to be confined to the age in which they lived. "To commit to faithful men, able to teach others also," the charge of the Churches, was their anxious concern.[1] And of these "faithful men," there were some *we know*, who did not fail to fulfil all that was expected of them — all that their responsible position demanded.

Polycarp, for instance, who lived through the greater portion of time between the death of St. John and birth of Origen, has the attestation of the Holy Spirit to *his faithfulness* to his charge. He is *commended by Him* who is the "First and the Last," as the

[1] 2 Tim. ii. 2.

"Angel (Bishop) of the Church of Smyrna." (Rev. ii. 8–10.) — "*He always taught the thing which he had learned from the Apostles, and which the Church had handed down, and which only are true*," writes a contemporary.[1] "*He was remarkable for his vigilance and strict adherence to the one only true faith which had been taught him by the Apostles*,"— adds Eusebius.[2]

Under such a man as this, it should require some evidence of the fact to induce one to believe that an innovation on the most public and well known usage of the Church was introduced, and neither he nor any other taught by the Apostles, raised his voice against it. Yet we have never read or heard of even *an allusion* to such an innovation or complaint in his day.

And as to the *means* and *ability* of Origen to ascertain whether this rite was in use among the Apostles, there can be no controversy. He it was that made the first catalogue of the different books that compose the New Testament canon. For as yet the *whole* of the writings of the New Testament had not been collected together and put into the possession of all the churches. Nor had it been determined how many of those claiming inspired authority should be received into our present canon. And to no one member of the primitive Church are we more indebted for his labors, nor to whom did the Church pay greater deference in settling this question, than to this Father: who not only tells us that Infant Baptism is the *usage* of the Church, handed down by the Apostles,[3] but from this *usage* argues the infection of original sin.

Shall we then admit the authority of his testimony

1 Irenæus, lib. 3, chap. viii. 2 Lib. 4, chap. xiv. 15.
3 *Comment. in Epist. ad Romanos*, lib. 5.

in regard to the books of the New Testament, but reject it in regard to Infant Baptism? Admit the greater, but deny the less?

Can we reject the authority of such a man as this, and believe without *one word of evidence*, that this "great innovation, the source of so many evils," according to some Baptist writers and declaimers, was palmed on the Christian Church with the connivance of the most vigilant and faithful guardians through whose hands it has ever passed, and who for its preservation and the defence of the truth, suffered martyrdom at the stake and in the amphitheatre?

We are to decide, not between two *new doctrines*, which of them to adopt? but whether we will denounce and cast out of the Church that which we find to be its doctrine and practice in every age since the Apostles; and always believed to be *practised by them*, and no evidence to the contrary. Shall we then adopt the "*surmise*" (for that is all), and exclude little children from God's covenanted blessings, a privilege which they have enjoyed ever since God has had a visible people on earth, because forsooth, Infant Baptism is not taught in the New Testament in the way which some men choose to prescribe to the HOLY SPIRIT? Remember, whether you have children of your own, or not, by uniting with those who proscribe the Baptism of children, you thereby unite in excluding from the covenanted blessings of the Gospel all the little ones of present and coming generations!

First, let the inquiry be well pondered: If the rejecters of Infant Baptism cannot show *when* or *how* it began, and it has been the practice of Christians in every age since the Apostles, and received by them as the doctrine and practice of the Apostles — on what ground is it now resisted? Is there anything in the Bible that excludes them from the *New Covenant?* To which we answer unhesitatingly, *not one word*, that does not apply with equal force to the *Old Covenant* into which they *were always received.*

The commission under the New, makes no exception to little children, but on the contrary St. Peter declares, that the promises are "*to the children*," as well as to their parents [1] — the Saviour took the *little children* up into his arms and blessed them — saying, "*Of such* is the kingdom of God.[2] *Family Baptisms* are recorded as a common thing.[3] And among the saints in the Epistles addressed to the Churches, children are numbered, and instructions given *to them*, and *concerning them.*[4]

But lest we anticipate too much, we return to the Historical branch of evidence, and examine further — first, *the testimony of Irenæus.*

§ 14. IRENÆUS was a native of Asia Minor, and in his youth enjoyed the instructions of Polycarp, a disciple of the Apostle John. Through this link passed to him the spirit of St. John, and apostolic doctrine. "What I heard from him," he says, "that wrote I not on paper, but in my heart, and by the grace of God, I constantly bring it fresh to mind." In the true spirit of St. John, commenting on the multiform theories of the Gnostics, he writes, "*The way to God is love.* It is better to be willing to know nothing but Jesus Christ, the crucified, than to fall into ungodliness through over-curious questions and paltry subtilties."

[1] Acts ii. 38, 39. [2] Matt. xix. 14, 15 ; Mark x. 13-16.
[3] Acts xvi. 13-15, 33.
[4] Ephes. v. 1-4 ; Col. iii. 20.

He was an enemy to all schism, and an uncompromising defender of *Apostolic usage*. In A. D. 178, or seventy-eight years after the Apostolic age, he was made Bishop of Lyons, and labored by tongue and pen for the spread of Christianity; and with great success in confuting heretical doctrines, and establishing "the one only true faith."

His great work, "Against Heresies," in five books, is doubtless one of the most remarkable productions of the second century, and generally admitted "one of the most precious remains of early Christian Antiquity."[1]

In the writings of IRENÆUS, "*Baptism*" is frequently referred to, or implied under the term "*regeneration:*" such phrases as "*regeneration to God; regenerated through water; the washing; laver of regeneration;*" are generally applied by him to *Christian Baptism*. Indeed, this was the *common usage* of his times. The continuation, with variations, perhaps, of St. Paul's phraseology — "The washing (laver) of regeneration." (Titus iii. 5.)

2. JUSTIN MARTYR, for instance, describing the mode of receiving members from heathenism into the Church, says, — "Then they are brought by us where there is water, and are *regenerated* in the same way of *regeneration* by which we were ourselves *regenerated*.[2] For in the name of God, the Father and Lord of the universe, and of our Saviour Jesus Christ, and of the Holy Spirit, they are washed with water (or, receive the washing with water). For Christ also said, "Except ye be born again [regenerated] ye shall not enter into the kingdom of heaven."[3] (St. John iii. 5.)

[1] *Ante-Nicene C. Library, Intro.* [2] Italics our own.
[3] *Apol.*, i. ch. 61; *Ante-Nicene C. Library*, vol. ii. p. 59.

In this passage it must be plain to every reader that *Justin* alludes to and implies *Baptism* under the terms — "*regeneration*" and "*regenerated.*" "They are brought by us where *there is water*, and they are *regenerated* in the same way of *regeneration*, by which we were ourselves *regenerated*. . . . *They are washed with water:*" [baptized].

3. In the "DIALOGUE WITH TRYPHO," Noah having saved his family by means of the Ark from the Deluge, is pointed out as a type of Christ saving his people by water, faith, and the cross. JUSTIN writes: "For Christ being the first of every creature, became the chief of another race *regenerated* by himself through water [Baptism] and faith, and wood, containing the mystery of the cross: even as Noah was saved by wood [ark] when he rode over the waters with his household.[1]

"Regeneration through water," in the connection in which it here stands, of course, refers to *Baptism*. After his resurrection Christ became the head of a people saved by him through *Baptism with water*, and faith in the mystery of the cross: even as Noah after the flood, having saved his family in the ark by water, became the head of the race who repeopled the earth afterwards.

4. CLEMENT OF ALEXANDRIA, head of the Catechetical school at that place in the latter part of the second century, exposing the pretentions of a sect of Valentinians, in his work called "Pædagogus," uses *baptism and regeneration interchangeably* through several successive pages. The Valentinians claimed for their Baptism greater perfection than that of the great body of Christians, because, as they said, they

[1] *Dialogue*, ch. cxxxviii.

baptized into a power higher than that of Jesus — into Him that descended on Jesus at his Baptism, and who is first of all. Besides which they had added ceremonies which (as they believed) made more complete their redemption.

CLEMENT argues, "None can be superior to the WORD, or teacher of the only Teacher." His Baptism is perfect, because it is in the name of Him who is perfect, and needs nothing beyond what He commanded, to put one into a complete state of redemption." Straitway on our *regeneration* [Baptism] we attained that perfection after which we aspired. . . For the moment of the Lord's Baptism there sounded a voice from heaven as a testimony to the beloved — "Thou art my beloved son," etc.

"Let us then ask of these wise men, is the Christ, 'begotten to-day,' already perfect, or — what were most monstrous — imperfect ?" [1]

After explaining that the *perfect one* was baptized — not because He needed anything as to his Divine nature, but to fulfill the profession that pertained to humanity — he says, "He was perfected by the washing — of Baptism — alone, and sanctified by the descent of the Holy Ghost. . . . . The same also takes place in our case, whose exemplar Christ became. . . . . He who is only regenerated, as the name is or means, and enlightened, is delivered forthwith from darkness, and instantly receives the light." [2]

[1] "It is not clear from the text whether this passage refers to the prophetic declaration in Psalm ii. 7, of Christ's sonship and perfections; or to his Baptism by John. Wall refers it to the latter, and renders it "Let us ask of these wise men, was Christ as soon as he was regenerated, [baptized] perfect? or will they be so absurd as to say, He still wanted anything?" Σήμερον ἀναγεννηθεὶς, admits the construction — "as soon as *regenerated*," as well as "the begotten to-day."

[2] Lib. 1, ch. vi.; also *Ante-Nicene C. Library*, vol. iv. p. 151.

Towards the end of the book he makes the following summary: "The view I take is, that He (Christ) himself formed man of the dust, and regenerated him by water; and made him grow by his spirit; and trained him by his word to adoption and salvation, directing him by his sacred precepts; in order that transforming earth-born man into a holy and heavenly being by his advent, He might fulfill to the utmost that Divine utterance, 'Let us make man in our own image and likeness.'"[1]

CLEMENT uses *washing*, *regeneration*, *baptism*, and *illumination*, in the same or similar sense.

5. IN perfect accordance with the *usage* of his contemporaries, and concerning this same sect of Valentinians, IRENÆUS writes: "When we come to refute them, we shall show in its proper place that these men have been instigated by Satan to a denial of that *Baptism which is regeneration to God;* and thus the renunciation of the whole faith."[2]

"Baptism, which is regeneration to God," implies at least, that "regeneration to God" and "baptism" are, to a certain extent, *one* and the *same thing*. According to such language the one may be given as a *popular definition* of the other. And that IRENÆUS means *Christian Baptism* in this passage is obvious, because the Valentinians had set up a Baptism, which in his opinion was the work of Satan to supersede or overthrow Christian Baptism, — which he was proceeding to defend. Therefore, "*it is Christian Baptism*," which he says "*is regeneration to God.*" And such the sense in which "regeneration to God" is used by him in the following passages.

[1] Lib. 1, ch. xii; Gen. i. 26.

[2] Irenæus, *Adv. Hæres.*, lib. 1, ch. xxi. ***Ante-Nicene C. Library*, vol. v.** p. 81.

6. Commending the compassion of Christ in submitting to all the inconveniences of humanity — that He evaded no age or condition of life, nor set aside any law which he had appointed for the human race; but passed himself through the different stages of life to sanctify them all — he says: —

IRENÆUS ADV. HÆRES., LIB. II. CH. XXII.

"He came to save all through means of Himself—all, I say, who through Him are *regenerated to God* — infants, and little children, and boys, and youths, and elder persons. Therefore He passed through every age; for infants made an infant, sanctifying infants; a child for little children, sanctifying them of that age, at the same time being to them an example of piety, righteousness and dutifulness: a youth to youths; becoming an example to youths, and thus sanctifying them for the Lord."[1]

So likewise of adult age, etc.

IRENÆUS entertained views peculiar to himself in regard to the number of years Christ remained on the earth; but they do not pertain to our present inquiry. We see in the passage just cited, that every age, from the earliest stage of infancy to perfect manhood, is enumerated among the "*regenerated to God*" — infants or babes, little children, boys, youths and older persons — all of every age. And the following passage explains what is the meaning of the "power of regeneration to God:" —

LIB. III. CH. XVII.

"*Giving to His disciples the power of regeneration to God*, He said to them: 'Go and teach all nations,

[1] "Omnes enim venit per semel ipsum salvare: Omnes, inquam, qui per eum renascuntur in Deum; infantes, et parvulos, et pueros et juvenes et seniores. Ideo per omnem venit ætatem; et infantibus infans factus, sanctificans infantes: in parvulis parvulus, sanctificans hanc ipsam habentes ætatem; simul et exemplum illis pietatis effectus, et justitiæ, et subjectionis: in juvenibus juvenis," etc. — Lib. ii. ch. 39, Oxford edit. Lib. ii. ch. 22, *Ante-Nicene C. L.*, vol. iv. p. 200.

baptizing them in the name of the Father, and of the Son, and of the Holy Ghost.' "[1]

His translator, in the "Ante-Nicene Christian Library," comparing these words, "regeneration to God" (renascuntur in Deum), in their application to infants in the preceding passage, with their exposition in this, says, "*The reference in these words is doubtless to Baptism*, as clearly appears from book iii. 17, 1."

Wall remarks on the same passage (lib. 2, ch. xxii.): "We have here the statement of a valuable fact as to the Baptism of Infants in the primitive Church." Whitby, Neander, and most others familiar with the writings of the primitive Christian fathers, agree in the same construction. And we may here ask: In what other way could the Apostles regenerate infants and little children to God, under their commission, but by Baptism?

7. We have now seen that Justin Martyr and Clement of Alexandria — one writing a few years sooner, and the other a few years later than Irenæus — both use "regeneration" to denote or imply "Baptism;" which may be shown to be also a *common usage* of the second and several succeeding centuries.

Tertullian, Gregory Nazianzen, Jerome, Ambrose, Augustine and others, used it in like manner, which has been continued from time to time to the present day.

And not only "regeneration," but other terms were adopted for like purpose. Baptism was sometimes called "*illumination, spiritual circumcision, grace, the washing, seal, symbol of redemption, and perfection.*"

But to these terms were not always attached the same shade of meaning. It was generally believed

[1] Compare lib. 3, ch. xvii. with lib. 2 ch. xxii.

that Baptism secured the *forgiveness of sin* and *communication of the Holy Spirit.* Some held that it washed away sin only that was past, and then followed the descent of the Holy Ghost after the order of Christ's Baptism.[1] Others, that it washed away all sin, *original* and *actual*, and the subject became instantaneously illuminated by the indwelling of the Holy Spirit.[2] Others, again, arguing from St. John iii. 5, held that Baptism was *essential to salvation;* to which the exceptions of the "bloody Baptism of martyrdom," and "unavoidable omission," gradually obtained.[3] That Baptism rightly received, delivered from past condemnation, and put one in a state of salvation, with the grace and means, or gift of a new regenerating power to holiness, was perhaps the prevailing doctrine of *Ante-Nicene* Christians. Hence the use of the terms "regeneration," "illumination," "spiritual circumcision," and such like, to express its name and objects.[4]

1 Tertullian. 2 Clement of Alex.

3 Clement Romanus and Justin Martyr.

4 The phraseology of the Apostle Paul (often varied), "The washing (laver) of regeneration" (Titus iii. 5), was much in vogue in the primitive age of the Church, and its exposition very similar to that of some of the best commentators of our own times. For instance, Dr. Whitby paraphrases the passage just referred to: "Not by works of righteousness which we have done, but according to his mercy He saved us by the washing of regeneration (in Baptism), and (by the) renewing of the Holy Ghost (given then to the baptized)." To which Dr. Bloomfield consents, and adds: "The best expositors are agreed that the sense is — 'hath put into a state of salvation.' . . . It must, however, likewise import deliverance from the consequences of former sins, negligences, and ignorances, by having the means of true knowledge and virtue communicated. . . . The ancient expositors almost universally, and all the most eminent modern commentators are agreed that by the 'washing,' or 'laver of regeneration' (Διὰ λουτροῦ παλιγγενεσίας) is meant *baptismal regeneration.* And that this is the doctrine of our Church is certain from its 27th Article. (See Bishop Marsh and Dr. Whitby)."— In regard to the renewing of the Holy Ghost (ἀνακαινώσεως Πνεύματος ἁγίου), he says: "Must, of course, be

It does not, however, as before remarked, come within the range of our present task to defend the *opinions* or peculiar doctrines of the Ancient Fathers of the church, nor do we give them any higher authority than we would to any other class of uninspired men who had enjoyed the same advantages of character, time, and place, to learn the doctrines of Christ and his Apostles; and even then, we must take into consideration the *genuineness* of the text, and *faithfulness* of the translations where the texts have perished.

8. To a *public fact* — the *existence of* a *notable public custom*, or *sacrament* of the Church in their own day, they are competent witnesses; but their *private opinions* and *teaching* as to the *meaning* and *effects* of such a custom, of course have not always the same weight of authority. The *one is a fact* witnessed by their own eyes, oftentimes the subject of frequent remark among friends, and questions connected with it frequently discussed. The other an *inference* or *opinion* formed, it may be, according to the peculiar mental perception or idiosyncrasy of each mind.

Having settled the authority of the writings of any Father of the Church, the next thing is to look to his *usage* of language; and any peculiarity of meaning, or the sense of *words* or *phrases* used by him, may be ascertained by comparing them in the different places in which they occur.

Such is the course that we have pursued with the

primarily understood of the renovation proceeding from the regenerating grace of Baptism; though it must not be confined to that; but understood of that moral renovation begun in Baptism, but requiring the aid of the Holy Spirit throughout the whole life." — See Greek Testament, Titus iii. 5.

writings of Irenæus, and found, by comparing the different passages in which the words "regeneration to God" occur, that he means thereby *Christian Baptism;* and these words being applied by him to little children and persons of all ages,[1] he bears testimony to Infant Baptism in the first age after the Apostles.

But this is not his only testimony to Infant Baptism in his own times. By another and different line of argument we gather from his writings that Infant Baptism was the practice of the Church from its earliest missionary condition.

In his work "Against Heresies," he begins with the first sect that sprung up in the times of the Apostles, and takes them up one by one in the order of time at which they arose, giving their tenets and history down to the time at which his work closes. That is, he collected their *peculiar doctrines, usages, and whatever* did not conform to the teaching and usage of the Apostles, from the time of Simon, the Magician, down to nearly the end of the next century after the Apostles.

These are his own words: —

"*Since then there is manifold evidence against all the sects, and that my purpose is to confute each of them according to their several tenets, I think it proper to recount from what fountain and original they sprung.*"[2]

He therefore made it his business to expose their errors and trace them to their sources. And began with the first sect that arose in the days of the Apostles, and continued his catalogue several years beyond the time of Origen's birth. Who, as we have seen, records it as the practice in his day to baptize

[1] Lib. ii. ch. 22. [2] See Wall, vol. i. c. xxi. § 2.

Infants, and that the "usage was handed down by the Apostles."

Now if there was any difference in opinion or in practice on the point of Infant Baptism, between these sects and the Church (or great body of Christians), he would of course have mentioned it. But what is the fact? He begins with Simon, the Magician, and Menander as the first, — points out their designs and errors. Next takes up Saturninus and Basilides, and specifies their error. Then Carpocrates and Cerinthus, and enters into their peculiar doctrines. And so on with the Ebionites, Nicolaitans, Encratites, Caians, Marcionites, Valentinians, and others, down to between eighty and ninety years after the Apostles, at which time we have already seen that the great body of the Church everywhere baptized young children. He enumerates their different tenets, — shows in what particulars they differed from the Church, and so far as Baptism is concerned, speaks of some who used no Baptism at all; of others who mixed oil and water together to pour on the head; of others, who baptized persons lately dead; and of the addition of various ceremonies in connection with Baptism; but says not one word of the rejection or adoption of Infant Baptism as the peculiarity of a single sect.

Although he enters into the minutiæ of their practices and doctrines, Infant Baptism, as a point of difference, is not mentioned in a single case. What is the inevitable inference? Unquestionably that they did not differ from the Church on this point. If any of them had differed in this particular, would Irenæus have noticed such things as the above and passed over this? Who, that knows anything of the controversy that has continued to agitate the Church ever since the Divine authority of Infant Baptism was first called in question in the twelfth century, can believe its introduction would have been passed over unnoticed in an age, when the least deviation of opinion or of practice from the Church was called heresy? The legitimate conclusion is, that the Church and all the sects that baptized at all, were agreed in the Baptism of their young children, or else none baptized them. But that it *was the usage* of the Church, at the time Irenæus wrote, to baptize Infants, there can be no doubt. Apart from his own declaration, the testimony of Origen settles that point, for he was born and baptized in *infancy* during the same period. Seventeen years after, his father, Leonides, suffered martyrdom, and the following year (A. Apos. 103), and next after the death of Irenæus, Origen was appointed the President of the Catechetical School of Alexandria. Thus he was contemporary with Irenæus in the latter part of his life, who, in early life, was the contemporary and friend of Polycarp, the pupil of St. John. And hence of the old men of his times who had heard and known those who had been taught and trained by Apostles, and particularly through his father and family, could be obtained all necessary information in regard to the usages of the Church under the Apostles.

For this end Irenæus enjoyed still greater advantages, for he was *personally* acquainted with those who had been taught by Apostles. His friend, Polycarp, was the contemporary of St. John some twenty years, and was not only instructed by Apostles and had conversed with many who had seen Christ, but was also by Apostles in Asia appointed Bishop of

Smyrna.[1] "The things which he learned from Apostles, and which the Church has handed down, and which alone are true" — are the tests, as Irenæus informs us, to which he brought the tenets and practices of the heretical sects, and pointed out what had been added to or taken from Apostolic usage.

And, whereas, there was no difference on this question between them and this STANDARD, down to the period when Irenæus was writing, at which time, *we know*, the Baptism of Infants was the usage of the Church, it follows that the Apostles, the baptizing sects, and the primitive Church, all baptized little children.

Four other writers, Epiphanius, Philastrius, Augustine and Theodoret, continued this parallel, each in his turn, till it comes down long beyond the time when the universality of Infant Baptism is as well known as the existence of the Church itself. Thus indorsing the faithfulness of Irenæus as a witness, and by a negative train of concurrent testimony, corroborating what has been proved by evidence both *positive* and *circumstantial* — i. e., *That Infant Baptism was the usage of the primitive Church, practised and "handed down from the Apostles."*

Wherefore the venerated Irenæus, who was taught by the disciple and personal friend of St. John, and who, in his latter days, said he remembered what his teacher, Polycarp, said and did better than the occurrences of the then present period,[2] and who was as anxious to adhere to "*the only true faith*" as his teacher, testifies to the Divine authority of Infant Baptism in two ways — first, by the *Baptism of all ages*

[1] Irenæus, vol. i., book iii., c. 3, *Ante-Nicene C. L.*

[2] Irenæus, vol. ii. p. 158, *Ante-Nicene C. L.*, vol. ix.

—"*Infants*, and *little ones*, and *children*, and *youths*, and *elder persons*." Second, by the *perfect unanimity of the baptizing sects with the primitive Church on this point, in the first and second centuries.*

As some minds are slow in comprehending how it is that the absence of controversy can ever prove the existence and unity of practice, let them suppose three parallel columns; and in the first the Church, under the Apostles; in the second the Church, after the Apostles; and in the third, the doctrines and practices of the various sects during both periods. Then select one who was born and had grown up to manhood among those who had been eye-witnesses of the doings of Apostles, and had been taught and trained by a disciple of one of their number, and let him mark all things in each column that differ from either of the other two; and then suppose the eye to pass over the things in which they differed; and then to see that Infant Baptism, though only implied in *two of them,* is written in distinct characters in the third, yet not *noted as a point of difference* from them, and what does he infer from it? Obviously, that it was *approved and in harmony with all*, as no mark of disapproval or objection was made against it. It was embraced in general terms in the others, but brought out in specific language in the latter.

Things are often taken as granted, and referred to in general terms in one place, but specified by name in another. Harmony in sentiment and action but seldom calls forth an expression of opinion in regard to the thing in hand.

Further, let four others in the next and succeeding generations review the same, and continue the parallel to successive periods, and still this perfect agreement is manifest, while the practice of Infant Baptism is as common and well known as the public worship of Christians, and a new doctrine seeming to conflict with Infant Baptism subjected its advocate to trial, and the declaration that he "*never heard of even an impious heretic that denied Baptism to little children.*"

We pass on to another witness, born about the close of the Apostolic age.

CHAPTER IV.

TESTIMONY HISTORICAL AND CIRCUMSTANTIAL.

Testimony of Justin Martyr, born at the Close of the Apostolic Age, in the Midst of Christians. — Many baptized in Childhood. — Gentile Christians received Circumcision in Baptism. — Interpretation of Col. ii. 11, 12. — Clemens Romanus. — All Ages corrupt, and Remedy provided before born, or Necessity of putting all into a New State. — Hermas. — Necessity of Baptism to all. — Infants, and those who continue Infants without Malice most honorable of all. — Interpretation of John iii. 5. — Christian Church organized before New Testament written. — Infant Baptism before New Testament Canon settled. — Universal in the next Age after the Apostles. — Improbability of so notable an Innovation without Opposition in that Period. — The Adherence to "the One Only Faith" by Polycarp, Irenæus, and Christians immediately succeeding the Apostles. — Summary of Historical and Circumstantial Evidence.

§ 15. JUSTIN MARTYR, whose name is held sacred by those familiar with his history, was born near the end of the first century in Flavia Neapolis, a city of Samaria, where he passed the earlier part of his life, and consequently was acquainted with the common or spoken Greek of Palestine. He was also well versed in the literature and philosophic systems of that age; and suffered martyrdom in the reign of Marcus Aurelius.

1. In an Apology, addressed to Antoninus Pius and the Roman Senate, in defence of Christians who were falsely accused by their enemies of teaching pernicious doctrines and indulging in gross immoralities, he cites largely from the written teaching of Christ Himself, to show the *purity* of morals inculcated by Him, and the superiority of his doctrines over those of their

accusers — in that He forbids not only the *overt acts* of lust, but also the *hidden thought and desire.* And then appeals to examples — to living witnesses of the influence and fruits of such teaching — and especially to the *purity* of those whose *whole life, from childhood to old age*, had been under Christian training: of whom, he writes, "*there are many.*" His words are as follows: —

JUSTIN MARTYR AD ANTONINUM PIUM.

"And many, both men and women, sixty and seventy years of age, who have been made disciples to Christ from childhood, continue pure." [1]

From this passage it appears that many then among them were baptized in their *childhood* in the *apostolic age.* Justin was writing some forty-seven or eight years after the death of St. John; some think earlier;[2] and seventy years from that time would carry us twenty years and more into the Apostolic age, when *Divine Inspiration* guided and controlled the rulers of the Church, and whilst St. John, St. Philip, St. Jude, also Timothy and Titus were still alive.

2. Objection has been made that the term (παίδων) "children" is not confined to little children, but embraces all the stages of childhood up to full grown youth; which is true, but it extends to little infants also, and is the same word applied by St. Matthew (chap. ii. 16) to the little children "two years old and under," slain "in Bethlehem, and in all the coasts

[1] "Καὶ πολλοί τινες καὶ πολλαὶ ἑξηκοντοῦται καὶ ἑβδομηκοντοῦται, οἱ ἐκ παίδων ἐμαθητεύθησαν τῳ Χριστῷ, ἄφθοροι διαμενουσι." *Apol.*, i. chap. xv. See also *Ante-Nicene C. L.*, vol. ii. page 18.

[2] Chronologists differ in regard to the date of this Apology. Wall dates it A. D. 140, or forty years after the Apostolic age. Schaff, thirty-nine. Burton, forty-eight. Palmer, fifty. In former editions the author followed Wall, but in this, he adopts Burton.

thereof," by the order of Herod. And Justin is here speaking of a *large class of persons*, πολλοί τινες καὶ πολλαὶ, "*many of both sexes*," and we may suppose that children of *all the ages of childhood* would be found with the *many parents* converted to Christianity in those times; and to *embrace them all*, it was necessary to use a term that would include *all the ages* of childhood, just as Justin has done. Had he referred to a few isolated cases of a particular stage in childhood, then we may suppose he would have used a more *specific term* expressive of *that stage;* but he tells us there were "*many*," and adds in the next sentence to the passage cited, "and I boast that I could produce such of every race of men." [1] Hence the inference that children of different ages and of different countries were taken into the Church in the Apostolic age, as they were afterwards, and are at the present day.

3. This interpretation is in agreement with the closing part of the passage, which tells us that these persons who were made disciples to Christ (ἐκ) "out of" their childhood "*continued pure*," or uncorrupt to old age. They were a class taken into the Church, as it seems, before they had become defiled by evil thoughts and lustful desires; and under Christian training the innocence and purity of their childhood had been "*continued*." And Justin having added that he could "produce such of every race of men;" turns immediately to another class, and adds, as if asking a question — "What shall I say too of the *countless multitude* of those who have reformed intemperate habits and learned these things?" [2] This was a much larger body, an "immense multitude." He

[1] *Apol.*, i. ch. xviii. [2] Ibidem.

did not refer therefore to a few *outlaws*, but to the great body of the Church who were converted from the error of their ways.

The first class had "*continued pure*;" the other had "*reformed*" their evil habits and "learned" to do well.

Now the natural inference from all which is, that those so young as not to have indulged evil thoughts and unlawful desires, had not reached the age of moral accountability, and therefore could not have been baptized on their own responsibility; and any Baptism under that age is *Infant Baptism* in its ordinary and true acceptation.

4. But some have gone so far as to doubt whether these "disciples" had been baptized. Such a doubt is scarcely deserving serious consideration. JUSTIN would hardly appeal to the lives of men *out* of the Christian Church, in defence of those *within* its pale. Would he write to the Emperor and Roman Senate, commending the characters of men "ever learning and never able to come to the knowledge of the truth," in defence of that truth?

The members of the Christian Church were called "disciples" till after the spread of the Gospel in Antioch, when they began to be called "Christians" (Acts xi. 26). After which "disciples" and "Christians" became synonymous terms, in reference to church-membership. And JUSTIN, no doubt, used words in their ordinary acceptation when he appealed to the characters of those made "disciples to Christ" in childhood, in vindication of Christian teaching and morals. And as President Dwight justly remarks, "There never was any other mode of making *disciples* from childhood except by *Baptism*."

Therefore the natural and no doubt correct construction of the passage is, that there were, at the time JUSTIN was writing, many old members of the Church baptized in the Apostolic Age, in different stages of childhood, as in our own and other ages.

It is of little importance, however, how this passage is construed, so far as the practice of Infant Baptism is concerned during the time of the writer. The testimony of IRENÆUS, who lived through the whole period in which JUSTIN wrote, and who had better opportunities of knowing what had been the *usage* of the Church from the beginning, has *established* that fact beyond doubt. We may lay aside JUSTIN altogether, and the truth *on that point* remains unshaken. Yet it is important for the confirmation of any truth to have the corroborative testimony of such a man, which we obtain also from his teaching on the relation of Baptism to *Circumcision*; likewise the *hereditary* or consequent effect of Adam's sin on his posterity.

Having informed Trypho that circumcision and offering of sacrifices ended in HIM who was born of a virgin of the family of Abraham, and of the tribe of Judah, he then adds: —

DIALOG. CUM TRYPHO.

"And we who have approached God through HIM have received not carnal, but spiritual circumcision, which Enoch and those like him had. And we have received it by *Baptism*, through God's mercy, for we were indeed sinners; and all men may receive it in like manner." [1]

[1] Καὶ ἡμεῖς οἱ διὰ τούτου προχωρήσατες τῳ Θεῷ, οὐ τάυτήν την κατὰ σάρκα παρελάβομην περιτομὴν, ἀλλὰ πνευματικὴν, ἣν Ἐνὼχ καὶ οἱ ὅμοιοι ἐφύλαξαν. Ἡμεῖς δὲ διὰ βαπτίσματος αὐτην, ἐπειδὰν ἁμαρτωλοὶ ἐγεγόνειμεν, διὰ τὸ ἐλὲος τὸ παρὰ τοῦ Θεοῦ ἐλάβομεν καὶ πᾶσιν ἐφετὸν ὁμοίως λαμβάνειν. Ed. Steph., page 59. See also *Ante-Nicene C. L.*, vol. ii. p. 140.

The teaching of this passage is, that the spiritual Circumcision which Enoch and those like him had (which was symbolized by the circumcision of the flesh until the new dispensation under Christ began), is now by his mercy obtained by *Baptism*. Not *absolutely*, but *ritually* (as we may suppose), in the same sense in which Circumcision was the sign, seal, and instrument of spiritual blessings ; so Baptism obtains the same or like blessings, through the mercy of Christ, without the painful rite of the circumcision of the flesh.

5. The same doctrine is taught in the "Replies to the Orthodox," ascribed to Justin, but written by a later hand : —

> "QUESTION. Why if Circumcision be a good thing, do not we (Gentiles) use it as well as the Jews?
>
> "ANSWER. We are circumcised by Baptism; by Christ's Circumcision (Col. ii. 11, 12). 'In whom also ye are Circumcised with the Circumcision made without hands, in putting off the body of the sins of the flesh by the *Circumcision of Christ;* buried with him by Baptism.'"[1]

The words of the Apostle Paul we see, are here appealed to as teaching the same doctrine; which is in perfect accordance with the dialogue with Trypho, to wit: that under the new or Christian dispensation, we receive Spiritual Circumcision, not by carnal Circumcision as formerly, but by *Baptism*. This doctrine was generally held by the fathers of the primitive Church.

Now as Circumcision was given to little children, Baptism having superseded it and taken its place, it follows that Baptism should also be given to little children; no exception being made by the law-giver in their case.

[1] Cited by Wall, vol. i. ch. 2.

6. Again, the infection of Adam's sin on his posterity, and their consequent bondage and sin-stained nature, were subjects of frequent comment before and after the close of the Apostolic age. Whence it was inferred by many that Baptism was given to infants to wash away the *pollution of original sin:* although other blessings were likewise conferred by it. And sometimes its *necessity* implied and enforced, when not mentioned by name, by dwelling on original sin and the *corrupt nature* of little children, *apart* from *personal transgression.* For instance, JUSTIN tells us that Christ suffered for *all mankind as fallen from Adam*, as well as for the *personal transgression* of all who sin. He says: —

> "Now, we know that He did not go to the river because He stood in need of Baptism, or of the descent of the Spirit like a dove; even as He submitted to be born and to be crucified; not because He needed such things, but because of the human race, which by *Adam* was fallen under the *power of death* and the *guile of the serpent;* and also each one of them who had committed *personal transgression.*" [1]

This passage teaches that the *whole human race is in a fallen state and under the guile of the serpent through Adam, for which hereditary infection and loss, Christ suffered; as well as for the personal sins of each transgressor.* And we have introduced it to show that JUSTIN'S views on the infection of Adam's sin accord with the views of those, who infer from it the necessity of Infant Baptism; also as a *set off to the inference*, which some would draw from the fact that infants are not mentioned in Justin's description of the manner in which *converts from heathenism* were received into the Church, who of course were adults;

[1] Dialog. cum Trypho, *Ante-Nicene C. L.*, vol. ii. ch. lxxxviii.

for the Church being yet in a missionary state, the parents must be converted before their children are reached.

But as he teaches the *fallen state* of all mankind in consequence of Adam's fall, which his contemporaries believed made *necessary* the Baptism of Infants; and as he held the opinion that Baptism superseded Circumcision, which carried with it the right of Infants to Baptism, we may presume that he did not depart from his *doctrines* in reducing them to practice.

§ 16. We pass on to two more writers who *lived* and *wrote* in *the time of the Apostles*. Contentions and divisions having again sprung up in the Church in Corinth, similar to those that called for the first Epistle of St. Paul to that Church,[1] CLEMENT OF ROME addressed to them an epistle, in an earnest, pious strain, containing many excellent sentiments, in which he recommends more *humility*, and the imitation of the lives of holy men of old; citing, among others, the teaching and example of Job and David. He writes: —

CLEMENS ROMANUS, EPIST. AD CORINTHIOS.

1. "No one is free from pollution; no, not though his life be but of one day."

This is taken from the Septuagint Greek, but not stronger than our own translation for his purpose:

"Who can bring a clean thing out of an unclean? Not one." Job xiv. 4.[2]

In the following chapter he quotes from David: —

"Behold I was shapen in iniquity; and in sin did my mother conceive me." Ps. li.[3]

[1] 1 Cor. ch. i.

[2] Archbishop Wake, chap. xvii., p. 50. See also *Ante-Nicene C. L.*, ch. xvii.

[3] Archbishop Wake, chap. xviii. *Ante-Nicene C. L.*, ch. 18.

Thus teaching *humility* through these men, and the low estimation every man ought to set upon himself on account of the corrupt nature with which he was born. He then goes on to speak of various doctrines and duties, and urges upon them peace and union of effort, that all of them may be saved in Jesus Christ. "Let none grow proud of any spiritual attainment over his corrupt nature, knowing that he received it from another." And in the latter part of the Epistle, he continues: —

"Let us consider, therefore, brethren, whereof we are made; who and what kind of persons we came into this world, as it were out of a sepulchre and from utter darkness. He that made us, and formed us, brought us into his own world, having prepared for us *his benefits*, even *before we were born*. Wherefore, having received all these things from Him, we ought, in everything, to give thanks unto Him, to whom be glory for ever and ever, Amen."[1]

The true meaning of which is: Notwithstanding our mysterious formation and entrance into this world, in a dependent state, and with a corrupt nature, He who made and formed us provided for us all that we need before we were born. For which we ought, in everything, to give Him thanks. That is, though we have all come into this world under the sentence of condemnation, in consequence of the fall of the one man, Adam, by the grace of God *redemption* and *greater benefits* have been obtained for us, through the one man, Jesus Christ. "Therefore, as by the offence of *One* judgment came upon all men to condemnation, even so by the righteousness of *One* the free gift came upon all men unto justification of

[1] Archbishop Wake, chap. xxxviii., p. 59. *Ante-Nicene C. L.*, chap. 38, p. 34. The "Apostolic Fathers" are so familiar to Christian students, and easy of access, the original text need not here be *added*.

life. For as by one man's disobedience many were made sinners, so by the obedience of one shall many be made righteous." (Rom. v. 18, 19.) "And not as it was by *one* that sinned, so is the gift: for the judgment was by one (offence) to condemnation, but the free gift is of many offences to justification. (Rom. v. 16.) Where sin abounded, grace did much more abound." [1] (Verse 20.) Through Christ, as "the lamb slain from the foundation of the world," provision is made for all the ills of Adam's sin.

> "In HIM the tribes of Adam boast
> More blessings than their father lost."

2. As to the extent of Adam's sin upon his race, there is difference of opinion among theologians; but all, who are not Pelagians, admit that its consequences are such that all his descendants have become involved in it; they come into this world with a nature so corrupt that it will, left to itself, certainly lead to sin every one that reaches the age of moral development.[2] And as all shades of sin are offensive to God, whether we hold to the "*imputation of guilt*," or only to the "*loss of the moral image of our Maker*, and a defiled nature through Adam,"—either theory would exclude from the kingdom of holiness all his race, had no remedy been provided. But *propitiation for sin having been made*, only those who reject their redemption and refuse to *repent* of their *own transgressions*, and to conform to the conditions of forgiving mercy, shall be excluded from the Kingdom of the Saints in glory. *Infants*, *Idiots*, and *all others* not personally responsible for sin, have been redeemed by the shedding

[1] The transposition of these verses is to bring their meaning more clearly before the mind, while it does not affect the sense.

[2] Stuart *On Romans*.

of Christ's blood on the cross, as well as *penitent believers.*

3. The course prescribed for all who have committed *wilful sin* is, to *repent* and *be baptized* in the name of their Redeemer, and *follow Him.* Acts ii. 38: "Repent and be baptized, every one of you, in the name of Jesus Christ, for the remission of sins, and ye shall receive the gift of the Holy Ghost," saith St. Peter. Acts xxii. 16: "Arise and be baptized, and wash away thy sins, calling on the name of the Lord," saith Ananias to the penitent Saul of Tarsus. Titus iii. 5: "Not by righteousness which we have done; but according to his mercy He saved us, by the *washing of regeneration* and the renewing of the Holy Ghost," writes St. Paul to Titus.

Such is the course marked out for penitent believers to secure a covenant right and title to the redemption wrought out by Christ Jesus unto eternal life. *Infants* and others not guilty of sins of their own to *repent of*, have the same claim to the seal of their Redemption; *i. e.*, Baptism and its benefits; but are dependent on the faithfulness of others to secure to them their *rights* in this as in other things. And as the *penitent believer* is not lost, if from no fault of his own he fails of Baptism, as in the case of the thief on the cross; so *Infants*, whatever may be the nature of the sin inherited, or consequent on the fall of Adam, if they fail of Baptism to "wash away its pollution," we may charitably hope they shall not be deprived of their purchased Redemption by Christ; because it was no fault of their own, and the sin of omission of duty on the part of others must rest where it belongs.

But though they *lose* not their *inheritance* in the

Kingdom of Glory, if they *die* in Infancy, we know not how great may be their loss in other respects, particularly if they *grow up to man and womanhood;* and therefore no efforts should be spared to secure to them all the benefits of this sacrament. Its loss, however, does not *necessarily* involve the loss of salvation beyond the grave (so far as we can learn), and we *hope* and *believe* that the eternal "damnation of Infants" has no existence outside the brain of theorists.[1]

Among the redeemed, Infants being included, they have all the rights of the redeemed, so far as they can be appropriated; consequently, the blessings and privileges conferred by Baptism. How many and great these may be, we are not informed; but our Saviour *commanded* his people to be baptized, and obedience to his command is our duty. Why should the blessings of this sacrament be withheld from little children until they superadd sins of *their own transgression* to *original sin*, "to repent of," before they shall receive the seal of their Redemption? In the mean time, many die and *never* receive it!

§ 17. We turn to HERMAS, surnamed the PASTOR, who lived and wrote about the same time that did CLEMENT OF ROME. In several of his similitudes he alludes to Baptism, and considers it of very great importance — even *necessary* to enter the kingdom of God, and calls it *a* "*seal.*"

SIMILITUDE IX., CHAP. XVI.

"For before any one receives the name of the Son of God, he is ordained unto death; but when he receives that *seal*, he is

1 For a critical examination of the effects of Adam's fall upon his race, see, among modern writers, the works of the late Moses Stuart, of Andover, and Charles Hodge, of Princeton.

delivered from death and assigned unto life. Now that *seal* is the *water of Baptism*, into which persons go down liable to death, but come up assigned to life." [1]

He regards Baptism as a *seal*, certifying and securing to baptized persons their deliverance from condemnation, and *title* to eternal life, through the redemption of Christ. And what he says of *the necessity* of this seal to that end is in accordance with the general interpretation, more or less modified, of the ancient Fathers of these words of our Lord to Nicodemus: [2] "Except one (ἐὰν μή τις), '*any one*' be born of the water and of the spirit, he can not enter into the kingdom of God." John iii. 5.

Therefore, the *teaching* of these men of Apostolic times, and the *Interpretation* of the words of our Saviour by *primitive Christians*, show that they understood Baptism to be *necessary to all*— to every one— (ἐὰν μή τις) *any one:* not necessary in that absolute sense that knows no exception, but as a law that *binds all*, and cannot be laid aside by men.

Both of these writers lived and wrote whilst inspired Apostles were still on the earth, and their writings were *reckoned* by many as *books of the Holy Scriptures*, and *read* in many of the churches as such; according to Eusebius.[3]

Thus, before the canon of the New Testament had been settled, *Practice, Doctrine, and the received Interpretation* of the words of Christ, and of his Apostles,

1 Archbishop Wake. Ante-Nicene C. Library.

2 WALL says: "Our Saviour's said words to Nicodemus do so stand in the original, and are so understood by all the ANCIENTS, as to include all persons, men, women, and children. . . And that by the *Kingdom of God* there is meant the *Kingdom of Glory*, is proved from the plain words of the context, and from the sense of all *Ancient* Interpreters." — *Infant Baptism*, vol. ii., p. 451.

3 *Eccl. Hist.*, lib. 3, c. 3.

ALL *unite in corroborating the Divine authority of the Baptism of Infants.*

And had any doctrine been advocated in the first ages of the Church, militating *directly* or *indirectly* against it, much more, doubtless, would have been written concerning it, as in the case of original sin.

But questions of other kinds arose in those days to occupy the attention of the Church, such as the Divinity and humanity of Christ, the paschal feast, and various forms of Gnosticism. When, however, any question did arise affecting or calling forth any allusion to Infant Baptism, we find it mentioned or alluded to as often as any other well-known and established rite should be, in similar circumstances; and its authority *never questioned.*[1]

1. Again, it is a fact not known, perhaps, to some who oppose Infant Baptism, that the same authority which settled and handed down the New Testament canon, did, at the same time, practise and hand down the Baptism of little children. In other words, the Primitive Church at the time it was determining what books should be received as its rule of faith, or the men who acted a conspicuous part in the settlement of that question, recognized Infant Baptism as the authoritative teaching of those Scriptures which they received. For that the Baptism of little children was the settled practice of the Church, before the New Testament canon was a settled question, is beyond all controversy. This no student of Ecclesiastical Literature will doubt.

Let us enter a little into detail. We know that the

[1] It is unnecessary to repeat here the proof that Tertullian did not deny the *authority* of Infant Baptism, but only advised its delay, except in certain cases.

Christian Church was founded before the books of the New Testament were written, and that it had been planted in places wide and far apart, before important portions of that canon had been committed to paper.[1] We know also that these writings were sent, some of them to the Church in one place, and some of them to it in another. They were not deposited in the same congregation, or in the same city, but written at different times by different men, in different places, and sent to different portions of the world. During the same time, and soon after, epistles and writings were circulated from pens that were not inspired. Some of these bore the genuine names of their authors, others were spurious and ascribed to Apostles and writers who never saw them.

Of course the good must be selected from the bad, and the manuscripts or copies from all these points, collected together and decided upon by competent authority, before the canon of the New Testament could be closed. This was a work of time and great care.

Many Christians have fallen into the mistake of supposing that the New Testament was given to us as a constitution, *prescribing* the organization and order of the Christian Church. But not so. The Church was organized, or had passed into the Christian Dispensation before *any part* of the New Testament was written. And instead of *minute directions* and *specifications* on every point, many things are taken for granted, and only so much committed to writing and deposited among the faithful, as was deemed necessary by the Head of all, to *preserve* and *perfect* what was already begun. All the essential doctrines of salvation,

[1] See dates of the Epistles, and the opinions of Horne and other learned men on the subject.

and whatever was requisite for the defence of the Church against the " Gates of Hell," and to secure its success in the earth, were committed to its care and keeping, in a way that should be handed down to the latest posterity. Much, therefore, is *implied*, that would require *express precept* in a formal constitution.

The Holy Scriptures contain the words of eternal life, and make up the standard of our faith and practice. They are the touchstone to which everything *new* must be brought, and to which everything must conform. But before the different writings that compose the New Testament had been collected together, and the present canon adopted, we find by reference to the early Christian writers, that Infant Baptism was beyond doubt the established usage of the Church, and received as the doctrine and practice of the Apostles.

2. Origen, who acted a very important part in sifting out and testing the authority of the various manuscripts, who gives us the *first regular Catalogue* of all the books of the New Testament,[1] and who by reading, travel, and a long residence in Palestine, enjoyed many advantages to be well informed in regard to the received doctrines and public rites of the various portions of the Christian Church, refers to the usage of Infant Baptism, as we have seen in his Homilies both on Leviticus and the Gospel of St. Luke, also in his Commentary on the Epistle to the Romans, and in the latter tells us: *It is handed down from the Apostles.*

And if he is high authority in regard to the canon of the Holy Scriptures, why not in regard to a received

[1] Even he omitted St. James and St. Jude, but quotes them in other places.

doctrine and public rite of the Church at the same time? If he was competent to judge and aid in the decision of the *external* and *internal* evidences of the different books of the New Testament, should we not conclude that he ought to know whether Infant Baptism was inconsistent with their teaching?

Among those before him who are cited as authority, and who were instrumental in establishing the claims of no small portion of the Inspired Writings — the *most prominent of them* have referred in their writings to the *usage* of Infant Baptism. We have seen that Justin, who wrote between forty and fifty years after the death of St. John, and Irenæus, who was taught by Polycarp, the friend and disciple of St. John, and likewise Tertullian, *confirm the same usage.*

And of those who came after him (among whom full catalogues became numerous), the brightest lights of their day have also left their undoubted testimony to the authority and universality of Infant Baptism. See Jerome and Augustine among others. But in the time of Origen, the canon of the New Testament may be regarded as virtually settled, although doubts and differences of opinion at times prevailed in portions of the Church, respecting some of the books received, and others rejected, which were not finally put to rest till the Council of Laodicea.[1]

3. There are undoubtedly *internal* as well as *external* evidences of the Divine authority of the New Testament. But these are not all evident to the Christian reader of the present day, and hence our indebtedness to the primitive Church for settling the authenticity of these books; and we now receive them as the gen-

[1] For a full exposition of the question of the genuineness and authenticity of the New Testament, the reader is referred to Horne and Lardner.

uine works of their authors, chiefly because they have been handed down to us by the Church from its purest days, and when it enjoyed advantages which we do not for so important a decision. We have still means and tests, however, by which we can verify much that was then done for us, but in the rejection of some books, and the reception of others, we should find ourselves quite unable, at the present time, to make a satisfactory decision without the aid of primitive Christians. For instance, what is there in the character and style of the Epistles of Clement and Barnabas, which were read as authoritative writings in some of the churches for a time, by which we could determine they are of less authority than the Epistles of St. John or that of St. James? Yet we reject the former and receive the latter. Why? not upon the authority of our own independent investigation alone, but by the aid and decision of the primitive Church, or competent authority in that Church.

And shall we admit that the authority which was able to decide between the genuine and spurious books first read in the churches, was incompetent to decide at the same time whether Infant Baptism was of Apostolic origin? Will we as Christians consent that before the New Testament Canon was settled as the law and rule of faith in the Christian Church, one of its most public and important rites was perverted and applied to a class of people never intended? and that there was not wisdom enough in the Church to detect this error, and hence it was practised and handed down by the very authority that handed down the Scriptures? and this too the Church established by inspired Apostles, to be "committed to faithful men who shall be able to teach others" also? concerning which the Saviour said, the "Gates of Hell shall not prevail against it"— and to its founders made the promise, "Lo, I am with you alway, even unto the end of the world?" And yet before the next generation had passed away — aye, whilst the persons and teaching of several of its founders were fresh in the memories of many, its most public and well known ordinance was by universal consent perverted, and the foundation of the whole structure sapped? "Tell it not in Gath, publish it not in the streets of Askelon"— lest the enemy of our holy religion triumph over us!

If before one generation after the Apostles had passed away, our religion became *fundamentally corrupt*, and there was neither the ability to detect nor the spirit to oppose the error, what confidence can we have in it now? What new power has been communicated to the present age, that was not then given? If we admit the Church to have been so corrupt and ignorant in the beginning, how shall we defend it against the attacks of Infidelity? Or if we admit that the writings of the Fathers have been so much interpolated, and so much fraud practised in the name of the primitive Church, that, after all efforts to separate the genuine from the spurious, *no reliance* can be placed on their testimony, how shall we defend the authenticity and purity of the Holy Scriptures? Can we lay aside *all antiquity* and prove that a single book in the New Testament was written by its reputed author, or that every book has not been corrupted since, and its teachings altered? No — we must receive the *aid* of such testimony, or the key of the arch remains loose, and the whole structure will fall. Not that we are dependent upon it exclusively, but as important testimony to be cautiously received in confirmation of the high claims of the Gospel of Christ. It is not by *one train* of proof, or a *single* argument, that the Divine authority of Christianity can be sustained at the present time; there are *opposing* reasons and difficulties that are sufficient to annul the force, or hold in abeyance any *one kind of proof*, unless corroborated and supported by others. Neither the *internal evidence alone*, nor the *historical*, nor the *fulfillment of prophecy*, nor *miracles*, nor any other independent proof of itself, would overcome all the objections of the natural heart. But these all united and corroborating each other — interwoven by a thousand circumstances, and all pointing to the same centre — intrench our common Christianity within a bulwark that all the battering rams of an infidel world can never shake to the end of time. And in this magnificent structure, the aid of the primitive Church and the testimony of the early Christian Fathers form a part — the whole would not be complete without them.

If primitive Christians could testify to the genuineness of a manuscript read in the churches, they could testify to the practice of a public rite in the same churches. And if we receive their testimony in regard to some of the churches, we must receive it in regard to all; they having by travel and reading enjoyed the advantages necessary to such knowledge. And since we have their testimony to the fact that Infant Baptism was the usage of the *whole Church*, handed down from the Apostles, we have *legitimate proof* of the *universal practice of Infant Baptism in the primitive Church.* For "*what has been received everywhere, always, by all*" (quod ubique, quod semper, quod ab omnibus creditum est), is authority which every one should respect in the history of *the Christian Church.*

Reject this, and admit that whilst Apostles were yet fresh in the memories of many, the *initiatory sacrament* of the Church had been perverted to a use never intended, and *one fraught with the direst of evils*, according to Baptist writers, and that this evil had spread throughout the Christian world, before even the code of laws left for the preservation and guidance of the Church could be collected together, and that no man was found to protest against it as unauthorized — no one discovered its invalidity for a thousand years afterwards — in consequence of which the Church was, during all that time, filled with invalid baptisms, or with persons not baptized at all! Admit all this, and how ridiculous do we appear in the eyes of an infidel world! In what endless absurdities do we involve ourselves!

4. Consider further the *improbabilities*, that such an innovation in a *public rite*, could have gained foothold among the next generation after the Apostles, without opposition.

It must be remembered that it was the care of the Apostles, "to commit to faithful men who shall be able to teach others also" (2 Tim. ii. 3), the charge of the churches. And we may suppose that these "faithful men," selected and instructed by the Apostles themselves, would very probably continue the doctrine of their instructors during their own lives. Now St. Jude, St. Philip, St. Thomas, also St. Luke, all lived, according to our best authorities, beyond A. D. 70, some of them beyond A. D. 80, and St. John died, as has been before remarked, about the close of the first century; Timothy and Titus a few years before. Polycarp, the friend and disciple of St. John, and who also, if "the angel (bishop) of the Church of Smyrna," is highly commended by the Head of us all (Rev. ii.), lived till about sixty-five years beyond the death of St. John. And Irenæus, the friend and disciple of Polycarp, lived beyond the end of the second century, — at which time few who have accompanied us thus far in the examination of the question will doubt whether it was then the custom of the Christian Church to baptize Infants.

If Infant Baptism is an innovation, it was brought into the Church during the lives of Polycarp and Irenæus.[1] And although we have seen, from the testimony, both direct and indirect, of Irenæus and Justin Martyr, that Infant Baptism was the practice of the Church during that period and before it, we will, nevertheless, consider the *probabilities* of the introduction of a thing of the kind under them without open opposition on their part to such an innovation.

5. St. John spent the last years of his life at Ephesus, and was instrumental in making his friend Polycarp bishop of the Church of Smyrna. Between these places and Alexandria, the intercourse by sea was direct, and from Alexandria to Crete almost daily. With the customs of the churches of Alexandria, Crete, and others along the Mediterranean, he therefore could not have been ignorant. His General Epistle to the churches, the main object of which was to confute the prevailing errors of that time, and

1 Polycarp was instructed by *Apostles*, and Irenæus by Polycarp. One suffered martyrdom A. D. 167; the other A. D. 202.

guard Christians against false teachers, was written about A. D. 91 or 92, according to Mill and Le Clerc, and as late as the close of that century, according to Du Pin, L'Enfant, Beausobre, and Townsend. But among those errors Infant Baptism is not alluded to as one; hence if then practised, it was not an error. He wrote the Apocalypse, or book of "Revelation," as is generally believed, after his General Epistle, and very shortly before his death: in which he specifies particularly the errors and "things wanting" in the churches of Asia Minor (Rev. ii. and iii.), and as the Baptism of young children is not alluded to among these errors and "things wanting," it was, of course, not one of them; because under the influence of the Spirit by which he was directed to write, he specifies the different things which were disapproved: "Unto the Angel of the Church of Smyrna write. . . . I know thy works, and tribulations, and poverty (but thou art rich), and I know the blasphemy of them which say they are Jews, and are not, but are of the synagogue of Satan. Fear none of these things which thou shalt suffer: behold, the devil shall cast some of you into prison, that ye may be tried; and ye shall have tribulation ten days. Be thou faithful unto death, and I will give thee a crown of life" (Rev. ii. 8, 10).

In the Church of Smyrna, therefore, over which Polycarp was the bishop, or angel thus addressed, and who continued a zealous defender of the faith and of Apostolic doctrine through a long life, we must infer no error of this kind prevailed; for this and the Church of Philadelphia, are the only two out of the seven against which charges are not brought, and received the unqualified commendation of the Spirit.

For these, then, we have the testimony of the Spirit, to their freedom as yet from innovation.

The errors of the others being particularly specified, is equally conclusive against the existence of all other errors not specified. Infant Baptism, therefore, if practised in these churches at this time, has the seal of the Spirit's approval. If not in practice, it was introduced under Polycarp; the probabilities of which we will now examine with reference to his *known character* and *vigilance*, as a steward of the heavenly mysteries.

5. He sealed his conviction of the truth of what he taught and practised, by his own life's blood A. D. 167, or sixty-five years after the death of St. John — during the persecution of Marcus Antoninus. When the persecution began to rage with great violence, Polycarp, through the persuasion of his friends, retired to a farm, not far distant from the city, and there continued in constant prayer in behalf of the churches. But on hearing that some of his friends were put to the torture, to make them betray him, he could remain no longer concealed. "The will of the Lord be done," was his pious ejaculation, and he then came forward and surrendered himself to his enemies. When brought to the place of execution, the pro-consul, beholding his extreme age and venerable person, used many efforts to induce him to renounce Christ, that he might release him. To which he replied, "Eighty and six years have I served Him, during all of which time He never did me an injury; how then can I blaspheme my king and Saviour?" When still further urged, his answer was, "I am a Christian." He was then fastened to the stake, and expired amidst surrounding flames.[1]

[1] See Eusebius, lib. iv. cap. xv. See also *Ante-Nicene Christian Library* — Martyrdom of Polycarp, cap. ix.

This man, says Irenæus also, "had been instructed by Apostles, and had familiar intercourse with many that had seen Christ; he had also been appointed bishop by Apostles in Asia, in the Church of Smyrna, whom we have also seen in our younger days, for he lived a long time, and to a very advanced age, when, after a glorious and most distinguished martyrdom, he departed this life. He always taught the things which he had learned from the Apostles, which the Church has handed down, and which alone are true. . . . . . The same Polycarp, coming to Rome under the Episcopate of Anicetus, turned many of the aforesaid heretics to the Church of God, proclaiming the one and only true faith which he had received from the Apostles — to wit: that which was delivered by the Church."[1]

Now how much probability is there that a man, who had been the intimate friend of the Apostle John, who "always taught the things which he had received from the Apostles, and which alone are true," would permit an entirely unauthorized error, utterly opposed to what had always been the doctrine and practice of the Apostles (as Infant Baptism would have been, if a new thing), and not have raised his voice against it, as he did against all other errors? Who can for a moment entertain the surmise, when he sees how conscientious, firm, and vigilant was this man for Apostolic doctrine — sealing with his own life's blood his faith in the same — that *he* would encourage or permit so radical a change to be made in the doctrine which he had been taught?[2]

[1] Eusebius, lib. iv. cap. xiv.; *Ante-Nicene Christian Library*, vol. v. — Irenæus, vol. i. lib. iii. c. 3.

[2] If the Christian life of Polycarp, which at the time of his martyrdom, he said was "eighty and six years" included his whole life from infancy, as is generally supposed, he must have been baptized in infancy more than twenty years before the end of the Apostolic age, while the Church

6. To this consideration now add also the character and influence of IRENÆUS, who was a friend and hearer of Polycarp more than twenty years; whom all historians unite in praising for the elevation of his character, loftiness of his feelings, and value of his writings. His name was the praise of martyrs in his own day, and has been handed down with veneration ever since. He lived nearly through the whole of the second century, was a strenuous advocate of Apostolic Usage, and the most successful of all the opposers of heresies during his time. He wrote and preached against all the errors and new doctrines advocated in his day. An extract from his own writings will show what his character was in this respect, and what probability there is that he would receive an error of this kind.

Writing to Florimus, who had lapsed into Valentinianism, he says: "These doctrines were never delivered to thee by the Presbyters before us, those who were the immediate disciples of the Apostles. For, when I was yet a boy, I saw thee in Lower Asia, with Polycarp, moving in great splendor at court, and endeavoring by all means to gain his esteem. I remember the events of those times much better than those of more recent occurrence (inasmuch as the studies of our youth growing with the mind unite with it the more firmly). I can describe the very place where the blessed Polycarp was accustomed to sit and discourse — his going out and coming in — his general mode of life, and the form of his body, and his conversations with the people, and his familiar

was under *the rule of inspired men*. This fact alone would establish the Authority of Infant Baptism. So our opponents may lay hold of either horn of the altar — the great improbability of so great an innovation under Polycarp and Irenæus: or admit that the religious and natural life of Polycarp were nearly of equal length of time.

intercourse with John, as he was accustomed to narrate; as also his familiarity with the rest of those that had seen the LORD. How also he used to repeat their discourses, and what things he had heard from them concerning the LORD. Also concerning his miracles, and his doctrines — all were recounted by Polycarp in consistency with the Holy Scriptures, as he had received them from the eye-witnesses of the Word of Life. These things, by the mercy of God, and the opportunity then afforded me, I attentively heard, noting them down, not on paper, but in my heart; and these same facts I am continually in the habit, by the grace of God, of revolving faithfully in my mind. And I can bear witness in the sight of God, that if that blessed and Apostolic Presbyter had heard any such thing as this, he would have exclaimed, and stopped his ears, and according to his custom, would have said: 'O good God, unto what times hast thou reserved me, that I should tolerate these things!' He would have fled from the place in which he sat or stood, hearing doctrines like these. From his epistles, also, which he wrote to the neighboring churches, in order to confirm them, or to some of the brethren, to encourage or admonish them, the same thing may be clearly shown." [1]

This shows how anxious Irenæus was to adhere to the doctrines of the Apostles, with his father in the Lord, Polycarp, and also what advantages he had for knowing their doctrines. He remembered what was said and done by Polycarp better than the things that were then occurring in more advanced life, which is the experience of all old men in regard to what has occurred in youth and early manhood.

[1] Eusebius, lib. v. cap. xx. See also *Ante-Nicene Library*, vol. ix. — Irenæus, vol. ii. pp. 158, 159.

7. Now, how much probability is there that an entire new practice, diametrically opposed to what Baptists contend is the only true faith, could have been introduced under this man and Polycarp? — the one, teaching the "*things which alone are true*," which he had received from Apostles and men who had seen Christ; the other, what he had heard from the former, and old men who were his contemporaries. The piety of Irenæus is acknowledged to be of the highest character — whose love and zeal for truth led him to oppose with great earnestness the least departure from Apostolic Usage — even writing out in order, one by one, everything which he regarded as opposed to, or wanting Apostolic authority.

The character of these two men alone, ought to be sufficient refutation of a groundless suspicion like that alleged against Infant Baptism. For it has not a vestige of testimony to sustain it, save a contracted method of interpreting the Scriptures, which is utterly at variance with the spirit and design of their Author.

If this controversy were concerning the introduction and establishing of a *new thing in the Church*, there might be some apology for hesitating to adopt it. But it is about a sacrament, found in the Church in its earliest and purest days, practised in every place where the Church was planted, and regarded as of Divine authority, from the first time that it is alluded to. Hence the question to be settled is, shall the application to Infants of this ancient, universal rite, so highly prized by primitive Christians, handed down with and sustained by the Holy Scriptures (as the majority of Christians in every age have interpreted them), be cast out of the Church as an innovation? or shall it be continued?

8. To Polycarp and Irenæus may be added Justin Martyr, who, though not born of Christian parents, was born in Palestine, in the midst of Christians, about the close of the Apostolic age; studied in the schools of philosophy in Alexandria; wrote his celebrated apology for Christians between forty and fifty years after the death of St. John; preached the Gospel in Italy, Asia Minor, and Egypt; passed the latter part of his life at Rome, and finally suffered martyrdom for his religion, about the year after the Apostles, 65.

Is it probable that this man, who boldly taught the superiority of Christian doctrine over all the philosophy of his age, advocated Christianity in the face of persecuting emperors, and gave his own life in defence of the truth, would countenance a public innovation of this character?

We may here appeal to the candor of every reader who can comprehend the very plainest kind of reasoning, to say whether there is the least ground for supposing that a new public rite, like that of Infant Baptism, could have been introduced into the Church during the lives of these men — or that it could have spread over Christendom and become the established practice of churches extending thousands of miles (as the testimony of Origen shows it had), and not one word be uttered against it? not one man found to rise up and oppose such an innovation on the sacred usages of his fathers and the Apostles? Is the mere surmise that because Infant Baptism is not commanded in the Holy Scriptures in such terms as some have unwarrantably prescribed for it, sufficient of itself to establish the point that it was introduced under these men, in the face of all this to the contrary?

Does not the manner in which Infant Baptism is

first mentioned, after the Apostolic age, indicate its antiquity as well as prevalence? It is never referred to as something new, or as that about which there was any doubt, but *incidentally* mentioned as occasion required, and as a thing well known to all; and its authority questioned by none. Just as any other rite would be referred to, concerning which there was no dispute, when other questions called it forth. How can we account for this but on the principle that it was the practice of the *Apostles?*

Thus evidence positive and negative, from different sources, and in various ways accumulates, and with united strength scatters as chaff before the wind the objections urged against the validity of Infant Baptism.

§ 18. We have now seen, by tracing its history, that Infant Baptism has been the practice of the Church *in every age since the Apostles.* We have followed it in a continuous line from the present time — first, to the time of the great Pelagian controversy which agitated the Church throughout the Christian world; when —

A. D. 417 or A. A. 317. AUGUSTINE, the most learned man of that age, then declared, "The Baptism of little infants is held by the Universal Church, and not instituted by Councils, but ever in use, handed down by none other than Apostolical authority." When —

A. A. 317. CELESTIUS admitted, "Infants ought to be baptized according to the *Rule of the Universal Church and meaning of the Gospel.*" And,

PELAGIUS said, "He never heard even of an impious heretic that would deny Baptism to little children." And when, A. A. 317.

In a Council held in Carthage, about the same time, it was "*Resolved*, Whosoever says Infants are baptized for the remission of sins, but yet they derive no original sin from Adam, which is expiated by the *laver of regeneration*, let him be anathema." A. A. 318.

Advancing onward we come to another Council, in which, in cases of doubt in regard to the Baptism of little children who had been captured and taken off by the enemy before they were old enough to remember, and afterwards recovered, it was "*Resolved*, That such be baptized without any scruple; lest that scruple do cause them to go without the cleansing of the sacraments." A. A. 300.

A few years nearer to the Apostles, a Canon was passed at Carthage concerning such as had come into the Church from some of the schismatical sects, which gave to little children an advantage in regard to *Church offices* over those who acted on their own responsibility when they united with the Donatists;

It was "*Resolved*, That they who were baptized in their Infancy among the Donatists, before they were old enough to understand the mischief of that error, ought to be promoted to Church offices, especially in times of so great need." The case of the others was deferred to another time. A. A. 297.

A. A. 280. CHRYSOSTOM writes, "Our Circumcision —I mean the Grace of Baptism — gives cure without pain, and has no determinate time as that had (the eighth day), but it is lawful to one at the beginning of life (first day of his birth), or in the middle of it, or in old age, to receive this circumcision, made without hands." He also enumerates the benefits of Baptism, and adds, "For this cause we baptize infants also, though they be not defiled by sin" — of their own.

A. A. 278. JEROME, the author of the Latin translation of the Holy Scriptures, called the Vulgate, writing to a lady of distinction says: "The good and evil deeds of the child are imputed to his parent; unless you suppose the children of Christians, if they do not receive Baptism, are themselves accountable for the sin; and the wickedness not imputed to those who would not give it to them, particularly at the time they ought to receive it, and could make no opposition to receiving it."

A. A. 274. AMBROSE, bishop of Milan, writes: "No man comes to the kingdom of Heaven but by the sacrament of Baptism."[1] For which he quotes our Saviour's words to Nicodemus, "Unless any one be born again of water and of the Spirit, he cannot enter the kingdom of Heaven"— and then makes this comment: "You see (He Christ) excepts no

[1] *i. e.*, no other prescribed mode for any.

person — not an Infant, not one that is hindered by any unavoidable accident."[1]

OPTATUS, bishop of Milevis, calls Bap- A. A. 260.
tism "the putting on a garment that fits all ages — not too big for Infants nor too small for men."

GREGORY NAZIANZEN was of opinion A. A. 260.
that "Baptism to Intants might be delayed till three years of age, or thereabouts, unless danger made it necessary sooner. And in such cases it must not be postponed."

BASIL, bishop of Cæsarea, specifying the A. A. 205.
proper time for various things, remarked, "The whole of one's life is proper for Baptism." That is, from infancy up to old age, or until received.

A Council in Eliberis decided that those A. A. 205.
baptized in infancy by schismatical sects, might be received into the Church without the same delay that was imposed on such as were grown up when baptized by them."

A Council in Carthage, to whom was re- A. A. 150.
ferred the question whether it would not be better to delay Baptism to the eighth day after birth than to give it to children so young as two or three days old, decided in the negative, "lest by such delay some might die without it," and added, "As far as in us lies, no soul, if possible, is to be lost."

ORIGEN, who was himself baptized in in-

[1] Such, he thought, would not suffer positive punishment, but he could not say would certainly enter the kingdom of heaven.

Wrote A. A. 110. Born A. A. 85.

fancy, and whose father and grandfather were Christians before him, concerning "the sinful nature of every one born into the world," remarks: "It is for this reason the Church had from the Apostles the injunction to give Baptism to little children." Again, "No one is free from pollution, though his life is but the length of one day. . . . Therefore, according to the *usage* of the Church, Baptism is given to little children."

Wrote A. A. 100. Born A. A. 60.

TERTULLIAN, confining Baptism to the washing away of past sins, advised its delay to all young persons, virgins, and those in widowhood, and all such as were likely to fall into sin after Baptism; and, of course included young children. He asks, "What need is there that their sponsors be brought into danger, for they may fail in their promises by their own death, or by the child's proving of a wicked disposition."[1] Which shows that Infant Baptism was the usage of the Church at that time, or he could not have referred to it and its connection with sponsors.

Born soon after the end of the Apostolic Age. Lived beyond the end of the 2d century.

IRENÆUS, who was born about twenty years after the Apostolic age, and lived beyond the end of the second century, writes: "Christ came to save all who are through Him regenerated (baptized) unto God — Infants, and little ones, and children, and

[1] Which proves that sponsors were then used by Christians as they were among the Jews.

youths, and elder persons;" [1] hence, all ages.

JUSTIN MARTYR was born in the times of the Apostles, and wrote between forty and fifty years after St. John's death. In his Apology for Christians, he says: "*I know many of both sexes, sixty and seventy years old, who were made disciples to Christ from childhood.*" Hence they were baptized in childhood, in the middle of the Apostolic age proper, as there can be no other way to make children disciples of Christ but by Baptism.[2] He also tells us that "Christians receive their Circumcision in Baptism" — and calls Baptism "Christ's Circumcision." By which he teaches that Baptism has superseded Circumcision as the initiatory rite of the New Covenant under the Christian dispensation; and he is supported by Origen, Chrysostom, Basil, Augustine, and others of the most noted of the Christian Fathers. Thus testifying — first, to the Baptism of many in childhood in Apostolic times, — and second, to the right of little children to Baptism by virtue of their right to Circumcision.

Born in Apos. Age. Wrote A. A. 40—50.

Born in the days of the Apostles.

POLYCARP, the disciple of St. John, who "*always taught the one only true faith,*" lived more than twenty years beyond the

Born in the time of the Apostles and taught by St. John.

1 Neander admits, "this passage, without doubt, points to Infant Baptism." *Ante-Nicene C. Library* says: "The reference of these words is doubtless to Baptism, as clearly appears from comparing Book iii. 17, 1, with Book ii. 22, 4."

2 Baptism at any age before one is capable of acting as a moral agent, is virtually Infant Baptism.

time when Justin wrote this Apology, whose character is a guarantee that he would have sanctioned *no innovation* in his day.

Born and wrote while the Apostles were yet living.

CLEMENT and HERMAS wrote, both of them, during the lives of the Apostles, and their writings were read in some of the churches for a time as of Divine authority. And like all others who had received and submitted to the teaching of St. Paul, they held that *the pollution of original sin needed cleansing* as well as that of *actual sin.*

Clement writes, "Infants as well as others are corrupt. . . . *None is free from pollution, though his life be but one day on the earth.*" Afterwards, "He that brought us into this world hath prepared for us his benefits."

HERMAS says: "*Baptism is necessary to all* — and whosoever shall *continue as Infants is more honorable than all, for Infants are esteemed by our Lord as first of all.*"

Cotemporaries of the Apostles.

Now after tracing Infant Baptism up to the days of the Apostles, add what these cotemporaries of the Apostles say about *original sin — the necessity of Baptism to all — the estimation in which Infants are held,* and how could *circumstantial and positive proof* more perfectly unite and sustain each other? And remember that about the same time, the Baptism of whole families by the Apostles, is recorded in the Holy Scriptures as a common thing; children are called "*Saints*" in the letters of the Apostles, and directions given to their parents for their "training and nurture in the Lord."

Again, that Baptism has superseded Circumcision (as we shall further prove), holds the same place in the same Church, while the law for Infant membership has never been repealed.

And yet again, that Infant Baptism was the doctrine and practice of the UNIVERSAL CHURCH *before the New Testament Canon was even settled* — was always referred to, as a thing well known and acknowledged by all — and has the *consentient testimony of antiquity to its authority.* Quod ubique, quod semper, quod ab omnibus creditum est.

§ 19. Whenever history and the testimony of the ancient Fathers are appealed to in controverted questions of the present day, it is the custom of many to reply, "O! this is the way by which the claims of Romanism are established." Not so, but exactly the reverse. This is the way to divest Rome of all her groundless claims. Whatever was the doctrine and practice of Christians "*always, everywhere, by all,*" in the primitive Church, if an essential doctrine, should be continued. And whatever Rome can gain by that rule let her have — nor should we abandon it, *because she has it.* But bring her to the test of the Holy Scriptures interpreted by the universal practice and teaching of the primitive Church, and you strip her of all claims and pretensions beyond what belonged to the other churches established by the Apostles. And this can be done without making our Holy religion the sport of infidels,[1] or admitting any writing that will not bear the test of sound criticism.

Trace back the unauthorized dogmas of the Romish Church as we have traced the history of Infant Baptism, and how many of them will you find in the primitive Church, immediately after the death of the Apostles? How far do you trace back the "Infallibility of the Pope?" "Immaculate Conception?" How far Transubstantiation? The Worship of the Host? Can Rome trace back the doctrine of Indulgences — or the worship of the Virgin Mary, or the practice of praying to departed Saints, or Purgatory, or any *authority* in the bishop of Rome over his fellow bishops, to the next century after the Apostles? No. Such doctrines and such authority were unknown to the Christian Church in that age. And what ignorance to call Infant Baptism a "Relic of Popery!" What tyro does not know that Infant Baptism was long in the Church before Popery began?

If you would expose the fallacies of the Roman Church, trace them back to their origin, and show when and how they began, and their inconsistency with the teaching of the Holy Scriptures, and early practice of the Church. This was the way the English Reformation was conducted, and this is the only way to take our stand on a basis that the combined powers of Infidelity and Romanism can never shake.

Thus, we can show that Infant communion, which is so often lugged in to detract from the authority of Infant Baptism, is never spoken of before the time of Cyprian, and never became universal in the Church. As to customs unimportant in their nature, such as

[1] As does the rejection of all antiquity.

chrism, the holy kiss, the washing of feet — partly social and partly religious, which may be continued or omitted without affecting the essential character of the Church, let those continue them who may choose to do so. But a rite *fundamental in the organization of the visible Church*, like that of Infant Baptism, which involves the validity of the Baptism of generations, and places our little children in a relation to God, and to ourselves, with claims to the care and sacred training of parents and Christian friends, that few appreciate, and fewer still discharge — such a rite is of vital import to the nature of the Church, and to the character of its membership. It is one of those things that cannot be left to our own choice, and laid aside. It has an authority that knows no distinction between "DIVINE" and "APOSTOLIC." Whatever was ordered by the Apostles, of like nature, is as binding as that instituted by the Saviour in person. They were his appointed agents, divinely inspired; and what they established as an essential element in the visible Church of Christ cannot be discarded and laid aside by Christians. Those who have been so much influenced by the ridicule of "baby sprinkling" that they cannot rest contented with *pouring* the water on the infant, ought to have it baptized by *dipping* it into the water. For they cannot omit the Baptism of their children altogether, without injury to the child, and the sin of violating the order of the Church of God. Nor can those who have no children of their own unite with those who exclude little children without incurring like condemnation.

THIS TABLE REPRESENTS INFANT MEMBERSHIP EXISTING IN THE CHURCH OF GOD AT THE BIRTH OF CHRIST, AND AS TRACED BY A CHANNEL THROUGH THE FIRST FOUR CENTURIES OF CHRISTIANITY.

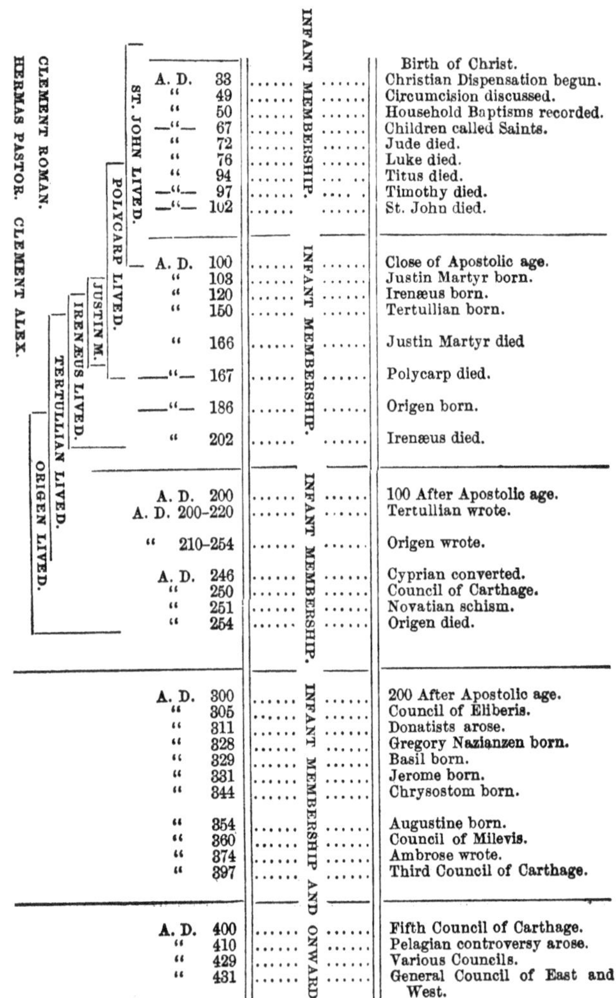

	INFANT MEMBERSHIP.	Birth of Christ.
A. D. 33		Christian Dispensation begun.
" 49		Circumcision discussed.
" 50		Household Baptisms recorded.
" 67		Children called Saints.
" 72		Jude died.
" 76		Luke died.
" 94		Titus died.
" 97		Timothy died.
" 102		St. John died.
A. D. 100	INFANT MEMBERSHIP.	Close of Apostolic age.
" 103		Justin Martyr born.
" 120		Irenæus born.
" 150		Tertullian born.
" 166		Justin Martyr died
" 167		Polycarp died.
" 186		Origen born.
" 202		Irenæus died.
A. D. 200	INFANT MEMBERSHIP.	100 After Apostolic age.
A. D. 200-220		Tertullian wrote.
" 210-254		Origen wrote.
A. D. 246		Cyprian converted.
" 250		Council of Carthage.
" 251		Novatian schism.
" 254		Origen died.
A. D. 300	INFANT MEMBERSHIP AND ONWARD.	200 After Apostolic age.
" 305		Council of Eliberis.
" 311		Donatists arose.
" 328		Gregory Nazianzen born.
" 329		Basil born.
" 331		Jerome born.
" 344		Chrysostom born.
" 354		Augustine born.
" 360		Council of Milevis.
" 374		Ambrose wrote.
" 397		Third Council of Carthage.
A. D. 400		Fifth Council of Carthage.
" 410		Pelagian controversy arose.
" 429		Various Councils.
" 431		General Council of East and West.

CHAPTER V.

RELATION OF BAPTISM TO CIRCUMCISION.

A Church on Earth when Christ came. — The Temple and Synagogue Services. — Preceded by the Tabernacle, with its Altar, Mercy Seat, and consecrated Ministers. — Preceded by the Abrahamic and Patriarchal Dispensations. — Circumcision the Outward Token of the Abrahamic Covenant, sealing spiritual and temporal Promises. — Abraham made the Father of a Spiritual Seed, in virtue of being at the Head of a Covenant bearing the Seal of the Righteousness of Faith. — This Covenant perpetual. — Mosaic Dispensation added to it. — Circumcision continued to the Coming of Christ, "the Promised Seed." — The Change of the Seal from Circumcision to Baptism did not affect the Right of Infants. — The Law for their Membership not having been repealed, they have the same spiritual claims to Baptism that they had to Circumcision. — Baptism called by St. Paul, "the Circumcision of Christ," and by Primitive Christians, "Christian Circumcision." — Holds the same Place in the same Church while Circumcision has passed away.

§ 19. We shall now proceed to examine more closely the connection between Baptism and Circumcision. For if Justin Martyr and the Ancient Fathers of the Church are right in calling Baptism "Christian Circumcision," and in teaching that Baptism has taken the place of Circumcision under the Christian Covenant, then we have another separate and distinct line of proof, full and independent of all others, leading to the same result.

1. In the first place, we must admit that the early Fathers of the Church had as good, and even better opportunities to learn what was a doctrine of the Apostles than we have; for Justin had the instruction of those who had seen and heard the Apostles,

to aid him in the interpretation of their writings. And if Circumcision under the Old has been succeeded by Baptism under the New Covenant, it follows that infant children must be baptized; for we all know they were circumcised by *express law*. And unless that law has been repealed, it of course covers the substitute as it did the rite in the place of which it stands, and therefore binds Christians to the duty of continuing infant membership and family religion under the New Administration. Changing merely the "seal" of a covenant, contract, or deed of gift, does not affect or change the covenant itself. The new seal covers what the old one did at the time the change was made. So little children have the same religious privileges under the seal of Baptism which they had under Circumcision.

But has the seal of Circumcision been changed into that of Baptism? or does Baptism occupy the same place as a religious rite under the Gospel Dispensation that Circumcision did under the Jewish? And is the Church of Christ a continuation, in its *essentials*, of the Ancient Church or Covenant into which God's former people were received and trained? When the "Redeemer came to Zion,"[1] did He find no church, no temple, no synagogue, no religious organization, in the public worship of which He and his Apostles could unite on the Sabbath day? (Luke iv. 16, Acts xiii. 14.) Or did He destroy that "kingdom" which He compared to a "vineyard," and forewarned the Jews that it would "be taken from them and given to a people bringing forth the fruits thereof?" (Matth. xxi. 43.) Or was it merely *transferred* into the hands of other husbandmen, as

[1] Isaiah lix.

He said it would be? and under its new administration improved and enlarged by more efficient culture and better regulations?

Now we know that our Saviour did find such a Church, and that He and his Apostles did recognize the Divine authority of its ordinances and worship — and that it was "their custom" to attend and unite in the services of the temple and synagogues.[1] And we know, also, that in this Church were trained the prophets and holy men of old, who spake as they were moved by the Holy Ghost; and that to "Israel" were "committed the oracles of God" (Rom. iii. 2); and that to them as the Church of God, "*pertained the adoption, and the glory, and the covenants, and the giving of the law, and the service of God, and the promises*" (Rom. ix. 4, 5); and that this temple succeeded to the *tabernacle*, with its altar and mercy seat, its consecrated ministers, and prescribed services, all fashioned and modelled according to God's own appointment (Exod. xxv. 40), called the "Church in the Wilderness" (Acts vii. 38), — not a promiscuous assembly, as Ἐκκλησῖα sometimes denotes, but a regular ecclesiastical organization, denominated by St. Paul "a house," in which Moses acted as a "servant," and afterward Christ as a "son," and adds, "*Whose house are we.*" (Heb. iii. 5, 6.)

2. And further we know, that in this Church in which Moses was faithful as a "servant," and which is called by the various names of "House," "Israel," "Zion," "Vineyard of the Lord,"[2] were taught and practised the worship of the true God, and the duties

1 Luke iv. 16; Acts xiii. 14; xv. 21; xvi. 13.

2 Isaiah v. 1–7.

of the true religion.[1] And for the preservation and continuance of this religion and worship, Moses was raised up, and commanded to conduct this people into a land to themselves." [2] They having become seriously affected with idolatry and the sins of the Egyptians, during their sojourn among, and their oppression by that nation; in order to deliver them from this oppression, and reform their religion, Moses was appointed to remove them to a land favorable to this work, and to give them a system of laws, rites, and ceremonies adapted to this end; and for the transmission of this religion to the dawning forth of a brighter day, whose rising sun would reveal with perfect clearness its glorious beauties now so dimly seen under a darker dispensation.[3]

Hence the Apostle Paul tells us, "The law (Mosaic Dispensation) *was added* because of transgression till the seed (Christ) should come." (Gal. iii. 19.) The corrupt state of the world, and the sins and idolatry with which Israel had become infected, made it necessary to add, to the Covenant of Grace under which they lived, the Dispensation of Moses, as subservient to the preservation and continuance of the doctrines and truths of their religion to the coming of Christ with his brighter light and perfect dispensation.

The Jews had long been in covenant relations with God, chosen by Him for his select people, to whom He promised the special doctrines and duties of religion, and whom He had brought into a Church state for the purpose of preserving and handing down the

[1] Exod. iii., xviii., xix.; Leviticus; Deut.; Acts vii. 34–38.
[2] Exod. iii. 12; ix. 1; xx.; Joshua xxiv. 2–14.
[3] Gal. iii. 19; Heb. x. 1.

worship of the true God, and the promises connected with a coming Saviour.

This solemn covenant had been ratified by an outward and visible sign and symbol of a new heart,[1] and had been in existence from the time of Abraham, bearing the sign of Circumcision — "*a seal of the righteousness of faith*," that its blessings "*might be of grace*."[2] And it was declared by God to be an "everlasting covenant."[3]

Afterwards when sin and idolatry had multiplied, "the law," or Dispensation of Moses was added to it, to subserve in promoting the great ends for which it had been established among men. Hence the Saviour teaches, "Circumcision is not of Moses but of the Fathers" (John vii. 22), — and it was continued by Him for the perpetuation of the original covenant to which it belonged, and to which the Mosaic Dispensation was added for special reasons.

3. Thus we trace back the visible Church of God on earth to Abraham's day. Before that period, God had not given to his people a peculiar badge or visible sign, by which they were to be distinguished from others. He had included all under a course of discipline, by which a people who were infants in knowledge would perhaps be sooner taught his dislike to sin, from its public punishment. Instead of collecting the better portion of mankind into one body, by calling them out from among the wicked, — his plan was to drive out the wicked from among them, and thus preserve them from the contagion of evil, while at the same time his displeasure at sin would be manifest to all. Cain, in his wickedness, was

1 Rom. iv. 11 Rom. ii. 29. 2 Rom. iv. 16.
3 Gen. xvii. 7.

driven away, and he and his descendants not permitted to dwell with the righteous branch of Abel in the presence of the shekinah.[1] And when the two races came together afterwards and the "sons of God" intermarried with the wicked, and sin, as a consequence, greatly multiplied, a deluge swept off the ungodly, leaving only righteous Noah and his family on the earth.[2] And when his descendants fell into idolatry and various other sins, then Abram was called out into a different land from them, to form a separate and distinct people for the Lord. And now God changes his mode of administration, but not the principles upon which it is founded. Up to this time He had manifested his displeasure against sin by driving out and punishing the wicked. Now and hereafter He will exhibit rather his love of virtue by calling out the righteous from among the wicked, and forming them into a separate people under covenanted privileges, thereby granting high and peculiar favors to those who shall love Him and keep his commandments. The great principles of his government, and the end to be secured, are the same under both methods, and ever must be the same. For God is ever the same, and cannot change. But He applies those principles in the way best adapted to the age and condition of the people who are to be affected by them. Therefore his outward and visible "Covenant of Grace," embracing present and future blessings to the faithful, begins with Abraham.

4. It was instituted under the following circumstances.

The descendants of Noah, although they worshipped

[1] Gen. iv. [2] Gen. vi.

the true God, had now converted created objects into deities, and the sun and moon, stars and winds, rocks and rivers had become objects of worship ; and these demanding no morality in conduct, the practice of virtue and the knowledge and worship of the true God were fast disappearing from among them. And for the purpose of preserving and transmitting the religion and worship of the One only true God, with kindred subjects,[1] Abram, a man of faith and of the right spirit, was selected and commanded by the Lord to leave his country and kindred and go into a land which He would show unto him; adding — " And I will make of thee a great nation, and I will bless thee, and make thy name great; and thou shalt be a blessing ; and I will bless them that bless thee, and curse them that curse thee, and in thee shall all the families of the earth be blessed." (Gen. xii. 1–3.)

Abram obeyed and " went out, not knowing whither he went." (Heb. xi. 8.) And when he came to the land of Canaan, " the Lord appeared unto him and said, Unto thy seed will I give this land ; and there builded he an altar unto the Lord who appeared unto him." (Gen. xii. 7.) And when his faith and obedience had been more fully tested, and Abram was was now ninety and nine years old, God ratified under the form of a visible seal, all that He had promised unto him, under the solemn injunction — " *I am the Almighty God : walk before me, and be thou perfect.* And I will make my covenant between me and thee." (Gen. xvii. 1, 2.) Abram fell upon his face, and God in a summary manner reiterated his former promises. All of which may be considered as briefly comprehended in the 7th verse: " *I will establish my*

[1] Gen. xii; Joshua xxiv. 2–14.

coveuant between me and thee, and thy seed after thee, in their generations, for an everlasting covenant; to be a God unto thee and thy seed after thee." To be a God unto us and our descendants, is all that we need and all we should desire in any covenant with Him. Such a covenant embraces all that is good for all ages and all countries.

And to this Abram gladly gave his consent, by submitting to a religious rite affixed as the seal of this covenant, in which his name was changed to Abraham, because to him was sealed the promise of an innumerable seed, and he was thus made the father of all that believe — The First and Head of the Visible Covenant of Grace embracing a promised Saviour."[1]

As to the nature and character of this covenant, none, we presume, can explain it better than an inspired Apostle. And no interpretation will be received of higher authority than that of the Apostle Paul. He tells us, first, that a promised Saviour was thereby covenanted. "Now, to Abraham and his seed were the promises made. He saith not, And to seeds, as of many; but as of One, And *to thy seed, which is Christ.*" (Gal. iii. 16.) This he further explains in the next verse (17,) and calls it "*the covenant that was confirmed before of God in Christ.*" The promised Saviour, was therefore the grand feature in this compact, or Deed of Gift. The Apostle next informs us that it is a *Covenant of Grace* in which men are justified by faith. "Abraham believed God, and it was counted unto him for righteousness." (Rom. iv. 3.) And in the 16th verse, he adds, "Therefore it is *of faith* that it *might be by grace ;* to the end that the promise might be sure to all the seed: not to that

[1] Rom. iv. 11-13.

only which is of the law, but to that also which is of the faith of Abraham, who is the father of us all." So justification by faith is another feature in that covenant.

Further, the same Apostle informs us that Abraham, Isaac, and Jacob, regarded the land of Canaan as merely a type of the Heavenly Canaan, and that they "sojourned in the land of promise as in a strange country, looking forward to a city which hath foundations, whose builder and maker is God;" and that they and multitudes of their descendants, "all died in faith, not having received the promises, but having seen them afar off, and were persuaded of them, and embraced them, and confessed that they were strangers and pilgrims on the earth. For they that say such things, declare plainly that they seek a country. And truly if they had been mindful of that country from whence they came out, they might have had opportunity to have returned. But now they desire a better country, that is, an heavenly. Wherefore God is not ashamed to be called their God; for He hath prepared for them a city." (Heb. xi. 9–16.)

Thus we see the great end and efforts of the members of the Abrahamic covenant, were to reach the heavenly city. They lived by faith, looking forward to that spiritual Jerusalem, whose builder and maker is God; which He has prepared for all "Abraham's seed and heirs according to the promise." (Gal. iii. 29.) Nor were they disappointed; for God is not ashamed of those who thus fulfil his covenant. Hence the Abrahamic covenant vouchsafed to its faithful members a *promised Saviour*, *justification by faith, and the final possession of heaven.*

And is not this the same which the Gospel covenant

now proposes — the promised Saviour (having come) and fulfilled for those who look back — precisely what He did for those who looked forward to his coming? And does not the Apostle Paul expressly teach that the Christian covenant is *the continuation of this same covenant formed with Abraham?* — that Christ redeemed us from the curse of the law, that the blessing of Abraham might come upon the Gentiles through Jesus Christ? (Gal. iii. 13, 14), —and that, if we are Christ's, then are we Abraham's seed and heirs according to the promise. For neither the law, nor any other power could annul the covenant made with Abraham. (Gal. iii. 15–17.) Read the third chapter of the Epistle to the Galatians.

5. See first, the declaration that the Gospel was preached unto Abraham: "And the Scripture foreseeing that God would justify the heathen through faith, *preached before the Gospel unto Abraham*, saying, In thee shall all nations be blessed. So then, they which be of faith are blessed with faithful Abraham." (Gal. iii. 8, 9.)

See next, that Christ has redeemed us, that the blessing of Abraham might come upon the Gentiles through Jesus Christ. "Christ hath redeemed us from the curse of the law, being made a curse for us: for it is written, Cursed is every one that hangeth on a tree: that the *blessing of Abraham* might come on the Gentiles through Jesus Christ; that we might receive the promise of the Spirit through faith." (Gal. iii. 14, 15.)

Now mark, that this covenant, by which "they who are of faith, the same are the children of Abraham,"[1] the Apostle affirms has not been annulled,

[1] Gal. iii. 7.

and cannot be annulled. "Brethren, I speak after the manner of men; though it be but a man's covenant, yet if it be *confirmed*, no *man disannulleth or addeth thereto.* Now, to Abraham and his seed were the promises made. He saith not, And to seeds, as of many; but as of one, And to thy seed, which is Christ. And this *I say, that the covenant that was confirmed before of God in Christ, the law, which was four hundred and thirty years after, cannot disannul, that it should make the promise of none effect.*" (Gal. iii. 15, 16, 17.) More explicit evidence of the perpetuation of the Abrahamic covenant could not be given. Apostolic declaration is supported by Apostolic argument to show that that covenant is still in force.

Four hundred and thirty years after the calling of Abraham, the "Law" was given at Mount Sinai, and the Mosaic Dispensation then commenced. Some might suppose the Abrahamic Covenant was then *annulled*, and superseded by the Mosaic. Not so, says the Apostle. The Law was *added* in subserviency to the ends for which the covenant with Abraham was instituted. It was grafted on the Abrahamic Covenant for a specific object. "Added (to it), because of transgressions till the seed (Christ) should come, to whom (or concerning whom) the promise was made." (Gal. iii. 19.) That is, the Dispensation of Moses was *added* to the Covenant of Abraham, to serve in counteracting the influence of sin, and in preserving the knowledge and worship of the true God until the coming of Christ. It shadowed forth and prepared the way for the coming Saviour and his more spiritual administration. But when the promised Seed came, its work was done. Its term of office expired; having "waxed old" it "vanished away," leaving the Abrahamic Covenant as it found it — *in full force.*

The Saviour came like the rising sun, lighting up into perfect day the dim twilight spread over this Covenant, and revealed to view the beauty and glory of much that had remained unperceived and hence unappreciated. He himself was the grand object in the foreground of the picture; in Him was fulfilled, and through and by Him are being fulfilled all that it promised, and all that will be needed to its perfect fulfilment to the end of time.

The fuller development of its principles was followed by some change in *externals*, and the mode of its application to a more enlightened age; but no change in the *principles themselves.* Circumcision has been superseded by the more comprehensive rite of Baptism; and the seventh day Sabbath by the Lord's day, which embraces the *completion of the Redemption* also with the *Creation* of the world.

The Gospel Covenant being therefore a *continuation of the Abrahamic Covenant*, more enlarged in its mode of application to our fallen race, and little children circumcised and made its members by law, it follows that they must by authority of the same law be now baptized; their right to membership having never been repealed, the change of the Seal cannot deprive them of it. This will be admitted by those who admit that the Abrahamic and the Christian is one and the *same Covenant.* And *that must be admitted* by all who will apply themselves to the question until they properly understand it.

6. As to the objection sometimes urged, that Circumcision only embraced temporal blessings and the lin-

eage of Abraham — one must have read his Bible to little profit, who can seriously entertain it. Are there no spiritual blessings embraced in the following language? "And he (Abraham) received the sign of circumcision, a seal of the righteousness of the faith which he had yet being uncircumcised; that he might be the father of all them that believe, though they be not circumcised, that righteousness might be imputed to them also; and the father of circumcision to them who are not of the circumcision only, but who also walk in the steps of that faith of our father Abraham, which he had, being yet uncircumcised." (Rom. iv. 11, 12.)

Are not the things here specially pointed out *spiritual?* Did Abraham receive the *seal* of merely *temporal promises* for a *temporary* end? Or did he receive "the *seal of the righteousness of faith,*" that he might be the *spiritual father* also of true believers, whether they were circumcised or uncircumcised? Did not the Apostle introduce these passages for the special object of showing that *Circumcision* was the *seal* of a covenant of grace, by which all true believers should be regarded as the *spiritual seed* of Abraham? And what does "the righteousness of faith" mean, but *justification by faith?* And if Abraham received the *seal of justification by faith,* could he have received the seal of a higher and greater spiritual blessing? Again, "The promise was not to Abraham or to his seed through the law, but through the righteousness of faith." (Rom. iv. 13.)

The thing is too plain to dwell upon, and the more intelligent, in order to escape the legitimate sequences, resort to the alternative of making Circumcision mean *one thing to Abraham*, and another and different thing to his posterity. To Abraham, say they, "it was a seal of the righteousness of his faith; but to his posterity, not of faith but of a certain covenant."

Wonderful discovery! A sign of one thing to Abraham, and of *another to every one else!* Was it ever heard that, when a grant was made to certain persons, and the *authoritative seal* of the State affixed to the instrument, it did not confirm to all alike according to the specifications? God said, "I will establish my covenant between me and thee and *thy seed* after thee. And with *Abraham*, *his seed* stands connected in every specification made in the grant;[1] and the same *seal* or *token* is applied to every one of the party. If it was a seal of justification by faith, when applied to Abraham, it was therefore the same when applied to Infants.

Abraham and his seed are made members of the *same covenant*, signed with the *same seal*, confirming to each the *same things*. Who has the power to distribute to each *contrary* to the terms of the grant?

But here refuge is again sought in the attempt to draw a distinction between the "seal" and "token" of a covenant. "Circumcision," say they, "was the 'token' or 'mark' of the covenant with Abraham's seed — not a '*seal*' *to them*, but only to *him*."

Let us analyze this distinction. Suppose you call it a "token," or a "mark," or whatever you please. Was it not the *sign* of God's covenant with them? And if a *sign*, was it not an *authoritative sign* — *appointed by God?* And if an *authoritative sign* of the covenant, what is that but *a seal?* What is the seal of a promise or contract but the *mark* of an *appointed sign?*

[1] Genesis xvii. 7, 14.

And now if God appointed, as the "token" or "sign" of this covenant, the "seal of the righteousness of faith," and ordered it to be applied to Abraham and his posterity alike, did not the sign of itself indicate the *nature* of the covenant, and *include* all the parties under it, and remind young and old that they must "walk in the steps of that faith of their father Abraham which he had being yet uncircumcised?" (Rom. iv. 12.) And does it not still proclaim to Jew and Gentile the *power of faith* and the *way* of becoming the true spiritual children of Abraham?

But here a third effort to escape is made under the shelter of "faith." "Abraham's *faith only* (say they), made him the father of all believers." Not so — writes the Apostle Paul — "Abraham believed God and it was accounted unto him for righteousness. . . . And he received the sign of Circumcision, a seal of the righteousness of the faith which he had yet being uncircumcised, that he might be the father of all them that believe." (Rom. iv. 3, 11.)

Mark, he "received the sign of circumcision that he might be the father of all them that believe." The Apostle is specific in giving the reason why Circumcision was added. Faith alone, did not make Abraham the "father of the faithful," but the sign of Circumcision was ordered, "that he might be the father of all them that believe." His faith publicly attested by God, with the sign and seal of the righteousness of faith, made him the father of future believers.

Abraham's faith before his Circumcision brought to him *justification*, but the *power* of that faith was made known through Circumcision. His faith was the groundwork, but the Divine attestation of a visible sign and seal placed him at the head of a Covenant, by means of which the righteousness of faith is proclaimed to men, and he made the father of all who believe. That is, Circumcision pointed him out as an example and made him the first in the visible line of God's people on earth. He thus became the head and father of a visible Covenant of Grace; by virtue of which he is called by the Apostle "The father of us all."

Were it not for Circumcision, Enoch and Noah, and others, would each more properly be called the prototype and father of the faithful. For they lived before Abraham, and "had the testimony that they pleased God." (Heb. xi. 5, 6, 7.)

But Circumcision was a notable and significant sign — the seal of a Covenant embracing things temporal and spiritual, promising to Abraham an innumerable seed — in which the Apostle informs us a spiritual as well as a natural seed is included,[1] and thus he is made the father of all true Christians.

7. Hence by virtue of this Covenant Abraham is called the "father of the faithful," although Enoch, and Noah, and Abel lived before him. To their faith the Holy Ghost hath testified, as well as unto Abraham's, but with them that visible Covenant of Grace had not been formed, of which Abraham is made the head, and through which all true Christians are called "his children," and into which fathers, and mothers, and their little children have been received some four thousand years.

It is true that Circumcision did include temporal with spiritual blessings, but it was administered *to all* who united themselves with the people of God. Ishmael and his descendants, who never inherited any

[1] Rom. iv. 9, 12.

portion of the land of Canaan, and those purchased for servants, and the *thousands of other nations* who from time to time became Jews, were all alike circumcised. The land of Canaan, as a type and pledge of the Heavenly Canaan, was included; and for the purpose of preserving and transmitting the worship of the true God, it was important that they should have a separate and distinct country to themselves at that period. But this and all things of a temporary character, with the Legal Dispensation of Moses added, were subsidiary to the higher and spiritual ends of a promised Saviour, and justification by faith, of which Circumcision was the *sign and seal.*

And when that which is temporary and limited in a covenant expires by its own nature or limitation, that does not affect the validity of the remaining portion. All that is permanent and unlimited in its character, continues as firmly secured, and the covenant as binding, as if no part had run out. In the words of another, "A covenant, considered as a contract, or deed of gift, or a promise showing the purpose and plan of the author, may be made to-day, the items increased to-morrow, and the seal not applied until the third day, or some subsequent period; and yet whenever it is affixed, it covers *all* the items embraced in the covenant.

"Some of these items may be temporary in their nature, and expire by their own limitation, while the covenant remains in force; others may be permanent, and have no end; still, the *seal* covers with its sanction all the various provisions, just so long as by their nature or the original appointment they continue in force.

"Again, the *seal may be changed*, without touching the covenant itself. Lawful authority may decide that the old seal shall no longer be used, and ordain that another shall take its place, transferring all its legal force to the substitute. And when this appointment goes into effect, the new seal ratifies the covenant precisely as the old one did, at the time of the transfer. If any part of the covenant had from any cause expired, if any part terminated at the very moment the transfer was made, then the new seal covers and continues just what the old one would have done had it been continued afterwards."

Thus Circumcision covered all that was contemplated and promised from the calling of Abraham to the time the covenant was closed and the *seal affixed.* And when the temporary items terminated, as in the case of the land of Canaan; the spiritual Canaan typified, and other blessings embraced, still remained as secure as before.

So when Christ, the promised seed, came in the flesh, he went on to fulfil the duties implied and necessary to the perfection of a covenant of grace, securing to men salvation through faith. And every fulfilment that thus takes place, should inspire us with greater confidence in that which is yet to come — confidence in the promise that "He will be our God," and make us all the spiritual "children of Abraham," who "walk in the steps of the faith of Abraham," and bless us with the realization of all that was expected from a promised Saviour and an inheritance of the Heavenly Canaan.

And when the seal of Circumcision was changed for that of Baptism, then Baptism sanctioned all that Circumcision would have secured had it been continued.

Therefore, the membership of Infants under the *New* is as valid and binding as it was under the Old.

No change was made in their case at the time of the abrogation of the old seal; there is nothing in the nature of the new, or in the terms of the covenant, by which it could be terminated; and who will dare assume the responsibility to take from them a right which they have so long possessed?

8. It has been objected that Baptism did not take the place of Circumcision because they were both practised together for some time after the Gospel Dispensation had begun. We might as well contend that the Lord's Day did not take the place of the Jewish Sabbath, because both days were kept by Jewish believers for some years after the Gospel was preached and embraced among them. Jewish Christians for a long period continued Circumcision and the Jewish Sabbath and other rites of their old religion, after they embraced Christianity.[1] They supposed that the Christian religion was something to be superadded to what they already possessed, to perfect their own system of religion. And therefore they added the Lord's day to their own Sabbath, and Baptism as an additional rite to their other ceremonies. And the continuance of Circumcision itself proves that they regarded their little children as embraced in the Gospel Church. For they could not have added a system which excluded little children to one that embraced them, supposing the two to harmonize and make one whole, had they been informed that little children could no longer be continued in God's Church with their believing parents. And that Circumcision was generally regarded as a religious, not merely a national rite, is placed beyond all question by the fact that it was urged by Jewish Christians upon Gentile converts as necessary to their salvation:

[1] Acts xv., xxi.; Irenæus, i. 26; Euseb., iii. 32.

"Except ye be circumcised after the manner of Moses, ye cannot be saved." (Acts xv. 1.)

This happened some sixteen years [1] after the Gospel Dispensation had been in successful operation, which proves that they still circumcised their children, and supposed it to be a rite necessary to salvation. But had infants been refused Baptism, the nature of Circumcision must have been discussed and defined long before this, instead of which a Council of the Church was held at this time in Jerusalem to decide on the authority of Circumcision in the Christian Church, and whether it should be imposed on Gentile converts.[2] Now if they had been taught that little children could not be received into the new Covenant, and that the Circumcision which they had continued among them so long in the Christian Church, was only a national badge, how could such a difficulty have then arisen? We call upon the opposers of Infant Baptism to reply. The thing is obvious. Infant membership had been continued; the Jews were permitted to circumcise and to baptize; and as long as Jewish ceremonies were made subordinate to those more strictly Christian, they were not proscribed, because they were not in their spirit opposed to the Christian system. But now that undue importance is given to them, and Circumcision supposed to be an essential part of the religion of Christ, it is time for the Church in Council to declare that it is not necessary to the Gospel Dispensation. These Gentile converts had been baptized, and as baptism was a public profession of Christ and the initiatory rite into his Church, this was sufficient.

So Jewish Christians long kept both the Lord's day

[1] See best chronologers — Hales, Townsend, and others.

[2] This question will be more fully discussed under the Scriptural texts for Infant Membership. Acts xv. and xxi.

and the Jewish Sabbath; but Gentile believers, and those who accepted the Gospel of Christ in its simplicity, kept only the "Lord's day," and observed only Baptism as the seal of the Christian Dispensation. Baptism and the Lord's day could not be said in point of fact to take the place of Circumcision and of the Jewish Sabbath for those who united the two Dispensations; but to all, then and now, who receive the Gospel, and practise only its own ordinances, the Lord's day is *instead* of the Jewish Sabbath, and Baptism the initiatory rite of religion instead of Circumcision. And whether we choose to call one the substitute of the other or not, Baptism has succeeded Circumcision, as the Lord's day has succeeded the Jewish Sabbath, and answers *all the spiritual purposes*, *holds the same place in the same Church*, while Circumcision has passed away.

Circumcision was the door of admission into the Church of God under the Patriarchal and Mosaic Dispensations. (Gen. xvii. 10; Ex. xii. 48.)

Baptism is the door of admission under the Christian Dispensation. (Matt. xxviii. 19.)

Circumcision was the token of God's covenant with his ancient people. (Gen. xvii. 11.)

Baptism is the same with his people of the present day. (Mark xvi. 16.)

Circumcision of the flesh was symbolical of the circumcision of the heart in the spirit. (Rom. ii. 29.)

So Baptism is symbolical of the cleansing and renewing of the heart by the same spirit. (Acts. xxii. 16.)

Circumcision was the seal of the righteousness of faith. (Rom. iv. 11.)

And "as many as have been baptized into Christ

have put on Christ. There is neither Jew nor Greek, there is neither bond nor free, there is neither male nor female ; for ye are all one in Christ Jesus. And if ye be Christ's, then are ye Abraham's seed, and heirs according to the promise." (Gal. iii. 27, 29.)

And accordingly St. Paul calls *Baptism* "the *Circumcision of Christ*"—"In whom also ye are circumcised with the Circumcision made without hands, in putting off the body of the sins of the flesh by *the Circumcision of Christ;* buried with him in Baptism:" (Col. ii. 11, 12.)

Hence the ancient Fathers, adopting the same language, were in the habit of calling Baptism the "Circumcision made without hands," and "the circumcision of Christ."[1] Justin Martyr, who lived when many were yet upon the earth, who, as before remarked, had seen and heard the Apostles with their own eyes and ears tells us that Christians put off the body of the sins of the flesh by Christian Circumcision, *i. e.*, Baptism. "*We have not received that Circumcision which is according to the flesh, but that which is spiritual. . . . . . And we have received it in Baptism.*"[2] *Again,* "*We are circumcised by Baptism, by Christ's Circumcision.*"[3]

Origen says, "*Christ gives us Circumcision by Baptism.*"[4] Fidus hesitated to baptize children before the eighth day after their birth, the time at which Circumcision was always administered. And Cyprian, to whom the question was referred, and sixty-six bishops in council, gave as their judgment that it might be administered before; especially in time of danger to the child's life.[5] Such a question would never have arisen

1 Justin, Basil, Chrysostom, Augustine, and others.

2 *Dialog. cum Tryph.*, page 59.

3 Quest. ad Orthodox.

4 Hom. v.

5 Cypriani Epis. 64.

had it not been that Baptism was regarded as having superseded Circumcision. Chrysostom says, "*There was pain and trouble in the practice of Circumcision, but our Circumcision, I mean the Grace of Baptism, gives cure without pain . . . . and has no determinate time as that had, but in the very beginning of age, or the middle of it, or any other time one may receive this Circumcision made without hands.*"[1]

Basil writes, "*And dost thou put off the Circumcision made without hands* in the putting off the flesh *which is performed in Baptism,* when thou hearest our Lord himself say: 'Verily, verily I say unto you, except one be born of the water and the Spirit, he shall not enter into the kingdom of God?'"[2]

10. We need hardly add others, to satisfy any reasonable mind that the early fathers in the Church believed, and so understood St. Paul to teach, that Baptism in spiritual things, had taken the place of Circumcision. We will, however, cite one more witness to show not only the relation of the two rites to each other, but what was the teaching of the brightest luminary of the ancient Church in regard to this whole subject. The celebrated Augustine, Bishop of Hippo, after stating that "Infant Baptism was the practice of the whole Church, *not instituted by councils, but ever in use* by Apostolic authority,"[3] speaks of its importance in the following terms: "We may make a true estimate how much the sacrament of Baptism does avail Infants, by the Circumcision which God's former people received. For Abraham was justified before he received that; as Cornelius was

[1] Hom. xl.

[2] Oratio exhortatoria ad Baptismum.

[3] Augustine *De Baptismo contra Donatistas,* lib. iv. chap. 15.

indued with the Holy Spirit before he received Baptism. And yet the Apostle says of Abraham that he received the sign of circumcision, a seal of the righteousness of the faith, by which he had in heart believed, and it had been counted to him for righteousness. Why then was he commanded to circumcise all his male infants on the eighth day, when they could not yet believe with the heart, that it might be counted to them for righteousness, but for this reason, because the sacrament itself is of itself of great import? Therefore, as in Abraham the righteousness of faith went before; and Circumcision, the seal of the righteousness of faith, came after; so in Cornelius the spiritual sanctification by the gift of the Holy Spirit went before; and the sacrament of regeneration by the laver of Baptism came after. And as in Isaac, who was circumcised the eighth day, the seal of the righteousness of faith went before, and (as he was a follower of his father's faith) the righteousness itself, the seal whereof had gone before in his infancy, came after; so in infants baptized, the sacrament of regeneration goes before, and (if they put in practice the Christian religion) conversion of the heart, the mystery whereof went before in their body, comes after." [1]

Such is a summary of the whole matter as received in Augustine's day.

First, That Infant Baptism was the practice of the universal Church, and admitted by all to be of Apostolical authority.

Second, That it conveyed all the spiritual blessings of Circumcision, and was therefore of great import.

[1] Augustine *Contra Donatistas*, lib. iv. c. 15.

And third, That it is the seal of the sanctification of the spirit, or of justification by faith, as was Circumcision. And as Circumcision was given to children before they could believe, so Baptism is given to children before they can believe. Where then is the force of the objection, Little children must not be baptized because they cannot believe? Could the children of Abraham believe? and yet did they not receive the sign of circumcision, a seal of the righteousness of faith and symbol of the circumcision of the heart? How then can the reader of the preceding pages exclude little children from Baptism on such a plea as this? And need we prolong this chapter to prove that Baptism has superseded Circumcision and secures to Christians and to their little children all the spiritual blessings of the first seal? We can do so, but surely no intelligent reader will deem it necessary. But we write for all.

CHAPTER VI.

RELATION OF CIRCUMCISION AND BAPTISM, CONCLUDED.

St. Paul's Definition of Circumcision. — Exposition of the Moral Law under Moses. — Old Testament appealed to by Christ and his Apostles. — Transfer of the Kingdom. — Branches of the Wild Olive grafted into the Good Olive Tree. — Strangers and Foreigners made Fellow-citizens with the Saints. — New and Better Covenant. — New and Old, Comparative Terms. — Basis of the Christian Church. — Gentiles brought in with Jews. — Faith of Parents avails for their Children. — Hannah. — Nobleman. — Woman of Canaan. — Religion always a Family Thing. — Baptism on the Faith of the Parent. — Practice of all the *Ancient* Churches.

§ 20. It is truly painful to witness the reckless manner in which partisan writers often treat and speak of Circumcision and the Patriarchal and Mosaic Dispensations. "Circumcision (say they) was a mere national badge by which Abraham's descendants were to be distinguished from the rest of the world, and to remind them of the promise of the land of Canaan. And the Mosaic Dispensation was a religio-political commonwealth instituted for a specific end, and temporary in its nature."

1. Will such permit inspired Apostles and God's own Son to explain the character and objects of these institutions? Does St. Paul say that Circumcision was a mere national badge implying only temporary blessings? Hear him: "For he is not a Jew, which is one outwardly; *neither is that Circumcision which is outward in the flesh. But he is a Jew which is one inwardly: and Circumcision is that of the heart, in*

the Spirit, and not in the letter ; whose praise is not of men but of God." (Rom. ii. 28, 29.)

Can language teach more plainly that Circumcision pointed to things spiritual as well as temporal? Does not the Apostle in these words, beyond all controversy, teach that Circumcision is an outward visible sign of an inward spiritual grace, — to wit, the circumcision of the heart, which is necessary to make us the true children of Abraham?

And did our Saviour regard that as a mere national institution, to the members of which he said — "Many shall come from the east and from the west, and shall sit down with Abraham, Isaac, and Jacob in the kingdom of heaven, but the *children of the kingdom shall be cast out?*" (Matt. viii. 11, 12.)

"Children of what kingdom?" and what connection had it with "Abraham, Isaac, and Jacob in the kingdom of heaven," but as the visible part of a kingdom begun here on earth to prepare men for its perfect state in heaven, into which Abraham, and Isaac, and Jacob had already entered? The Jews were members of this kingdom on earth, and the Saviour thus warns them of the danger of being excluded, for the want of fitness, from its perfect state and blessings in heaven.

Is it more reasonable to conclude, that God called out Abraham into the land of Canaan to bestow on him and his descendants merely temporal blessings, and to point out the lineage of our Saviour through the flesh some two thousand years before he came, than for the higher purpose of preserving the true religion,[1] and establishing a visible covenant that

[1] Joshua xxiv.; Exodus; Romans; Galatians.

should be a witness to the grace of God, and of the fulfilment of his promises to faith and obedience, as well as in regard to the lineage of Christ? thus encouraging works of piety and fitting men for the kingdom of heaven; while at the same time proofs of the fulfilment of his promises, and of the claims of the Saviour would be accumulating?

2. Strange that a covenant which testifies to justification by faith, and points out Abraham as the father of a spiritual as well as of a natural seed, and the members of which are held up as patterns to Christians of the present day, should ever have been supposed by any one, to be a mere national institution.

And the more so from the fact, that to avoid the idolatry and sin of his people and to fulfil the great duties of religion, constituted the grand object for which Abram was called out from among his people.[1] And even as a preliminary to the confirmation of that covenant the command was issued, "*Walk before me, and be thou perfect;*"[2] and he was *commended* afterwards for his faithfulness in training his children in the way of the Lord. "For I know him that he will command his children and his household after him, that *they shall keep the way of the Lord, to do justice and judgment;* that the Lord may bring upon Abraham that which he hath spoken of him."[3] And his faith and devotion were yet more highly approved in the offering up of his son Isaac, in obedience to Divine command.[4]

Further, for the purpose of carrying out the spirit and end for which this covenant was established, Moses was also raised up, and additional laws and

[1] Joshua xxiv. [2] Gen. xvii. 1. [3] Gen. xviii. 19. [4] Gen. xxii

ceremonies appointed,[1] by which to develop more clearly its character and to combat more successfully the influences of wickedness from within and without. The moral law which had been written in the hearts of men from the beginning, and which lies at the bottom of true religion and all duty, becoming less intelligible and perhaps almost erased from the minds of some, God commanded to be written on stone, and kept among them: a more imposing ritual and outward form of public worship was adopted, and such rules and regulations, civil and religious, as circumstances called for, were introduced by Divine authority. And not only did he give them the law, the spiritual nature of which we presume no one will call in question, but God also called them "*A holy people unto himself.*" "For thou art an holy people unto the Lord thy God, and *the Lord hath chosen thee to be a peculiar people unto Himself above all the nations that are upon the earth.*" And he enjoined duties accordingly. "Hear, O Israel, the Lord our God is one Lord. And *thou shalt love the Lord thy God with all thine heart, and with all thy soul, and with all thy might.* And these words which I command thee this day shall be *in thine heart; and thou shalt teach them diligently unto thy children, and thou shalt talk of them when thou sittest in thine house, and when thou walkest by the way, and when thou liest down, and when thou risest up.*" (Deut. vi. 4, 5, 6.) Are these duties of merely a national character, or are they strictly spiritual? "*Ye shall be holy, for I the Lord your God am holy.*" (Levit. xix. 1.) Yet again, "*Sanctify yourselves therefore, and be ye holy; for I am the Lord your God.*" (Levit. xx. 7.)

[1] Gal. iii. 19.

Such are specimens of the doctrines and duties inculcated under this so-called "Religio-political commonwealth." God its founder and the only object to be worshipped — they, his peculiar people, who must love him with all the heart, soul, and strength; and diligently teach their children his statutes, and seek to be holy, for their God is holy.

Now if the moral law, or ten commandments, with such expositions as these, do not inculcate a spiritual religion, will some one tell us what a spiritual religion is? If the religion of Christ be more spiritual, please point out the difference, and show in what that difference consists? In a word, did not Moses and the prophets teach the *very law* which Christ came to fulfil? and in rendering to it the duty due from sinful men, open up to them the way of justification by faith, by which Abraham and all his spiritual seed become the heirs of righteousness?

3. The addition of a civil polity to regulate the civil and social relations of the Jews, did not destroy the spiritual character of their Church. The Apostle tells us in specific terms, as before referred to, that the law which was four hundred and thirty years after, could not annul the covenant made with Abraham; and therefore neither the addition nor removal of the Mosaic Economy — its civil nor religious institutions — destroyed the spiritual principles and life which underlay the superstructure, and from which the Mosaic Economy derived all its strength and efficacy.

And notwithstanding the mixed character of civil and religious regulations in the polity of the Patriarchal and Mosaic Dispensations of the Church, it must be remembered that under that polity were trained the prophets and holy men of old, who spake and wrote "as they were moved by the Holy Ghost;" that to it as the keeper of the truth were committed the sacred oracles of God; and that from it we receive the canonical Scriptures of the Old Testament as the inspired word of God.

And to these writings did Christ and his Apostles constantly appeal in support of their own teaching. In the worship of that Church did they regularly unite. And to the members of that Church who would not accept the Saviour as their Messiah, he said, "The kingdom of God shall be taken from you, and given to a nation bringing forth the fruits thereof." What fruits did He mean, but those "of righteousness and peace?" and what kingdom but the Church of which "He is the Head?"[1]

Again, to the members of the Jewish Church he said, "Other sheep I have, which are not of this fold; them also must I bring, and they shall hear my voice, and there shall be one fold and one shepherd."[2] What "*fold*" was this to which he referred but the Jewish Church, and what "other sheep" but converts among the Gentiles? And did He not teach the sufficiency of that dispensation for the salvation of men, in the parable of the rich man and Lazarus, when He informed the rich man in hell that Moses and the Prophets were sufficient to save his brethren in this world from coming to the same place? The rich man, when informed that Lazarus could not come to him to mitigate his sufferings, besought Abraham, "I pray thee, father, that thou wouldst send him to my father's house, for I have five brethren, that he may testify unto them, lest they also come

[1] Col. i. 18. [2] John x. 16.

into this place of torment. Abraham saith unto him, They have Moses and the Prophets; let them hear them. And he said, Nay father Abraham, but if one rose from the dead they will repent. And he said unto him, If they hear not Moses and the Prophets, neither will they be persuaded though one rose from the dead." [1]

Now did Christ, in this parable, overrate the value of Moses and the Prophets? and if not, did he not teach the sufficiency of the Mosaic Dispensation for the salvation of the people for whom it was provided? And does he not speak of this same Dispensation (including with it of course the stock into which it is grafted) under the figure of a "vineyard," and point to the Jewish nation as the husbandmen, who, because of their unfaithfulness and wickedness in killing the son of the Lord of the vineyard (Christ), should therefore be driven out, and the vineyard let out to other husbandmen? (Matt. xxi. 33-41.) And does He not call this same vineyard, "the kingdom of God," and say unto the Jews, "Therefore the kingdom of God shall be taken from you and given to a nation bringing forth the fruits thereof?" [2]

Was then this "vineyard" and "kingdom of God" destroyed in passing into other hands, or was it continued and improved under the management of more faithful rulers?

Hear St. Paul describe the cause and manner of the transfer. Some of the Jews were continued in it, but the great majority excluded. In describing the process, he uses the figure of an "olive tree and its branches." The Jews, he calls the "natural branches;" the Gentile believers, the "branches of

[1] Luke xvi. 27-31. [2] Matt. xxi. 43.

a wild olive tree." And he cautions the Gentile believers against boasting, and the danger of being broken off also, saying, "If some of the branches be broken off, and thou being a wild olive tree wert grafted in among them, and with them partakest of the root and fatness of the olive tree; boast not against the branches: but if thou boast, thou bearest not the root, but the root thee. . . . And they also (the Jews), if they abide not still in unbelief, shall be grafted in: for God is able to graft them in again. For if thou (Gentile) wert cut out of the olive tree which is wild by nature, and wert grafted contrary to nature into a good olive tree; how much more shall these which be the natural branches be grafted into their own olive tree?" (Rom. xi. 17, 18-23, 24.)

Now how can the Jews be called the "natural branches," and the Christian Church "their own olive tree," from which they had been "broken off because of unbelief," if it be not a continuation of their Church which was under Moses and Abraham? Remember, St. Paul is addressing the members of the Christian Church at Rome — Gentile believers into whose hands chiefly the "kingdom" had now passed. And he calls the children of Abraham its "natural branches" — the Christian Church "their own olive tree," from which they had been "broken off," and Gentile believers, the "branches of a wild olive tree" grafted into it.

If the covenant with Abraham had now ended, and the Christian Church were an entire new Church, how could Jewish believers be "grafted *again*" (πάλιν ἐγεντρίσαι) into that to which they had never belonged? and on what ground could it be called "their own olive tree" from which they had been "broken off," either as a nation or individuals?

If the Abrahamic tree was dead and rooted up, how would you graft its "natural branches" into it again, or what "fatness" would Gentiles grafted into it, derive from its dead "roots?" Do men graft living scions into dead stocks, or can the branches live if the stock be dead?

4. What does the Apostle mean, then, when he calls the Christian Church the "olive tree" from which unbelieving Jews were "broken off," and believing Christians are "grafted" into it, and tells us that the Jews, its "natural branches," if they abide not in unbelief, shall be "grafted into it again?" What but the *tree* planted in the days of Abraham, rooted in the promise of Christ Jesus, nourished by patriarchs and prophets, and continuing to live and to grow; and which is now waving its branches over every part of Christendom, ready to receive returning Israel and every other people desiring to partake of its inexhaustible fatness in a Covenanted Saviour? And were not little children grafted into this tree from the beginning?

We could hardly frame testimony more full and clear to certify that the Christian Church is a continuation of the Abrahamic Covenant; and hence, the continuation of infant membership.

It is unnecessary to attempt to prove more clearly to the intelligent reader, that the Christian scheme is the continuation of the religion of the Old Testament more fully developed and clearly understood. But, for those who need line upon line, additional proof of the same will be found in the fact, that the Gentiles were called by the Apostles "aliens and strangers;" and the Jews "saints," and "Israel," and the 'household of God." St. Paul writes to the Ephesian converts, "Therefore ye are no more strangers and foreigners; but fellow-citizens with the saints, and of the household of God."

Now, why were the terms "aliens" and "strangers" applied to the Gentiles, and the Jews called "saints," and the "household of God," with whom the Gentile strangers were made "fellow-citizens,"[1] but because of the fact, that Gentile Christians were brought into the kingdom of the Jews, which was continued under the Christian dispensation, and under the increased purifying light of which unbelieving Israel was excluded and "broken off," and believing Gentiles brought in and grafted into their places?

And for this end, the Apostle tells us, the "middle wall of partition" between Jews and Gentiles was broken down, that they who were without, might be brought in, by the blood of Christ. For "in time past," he writes to Gentile Christians, "Ye were without Christ, being aliens from the commonwealth of Israel, and strangers to the covenants of promise, having no hope, and without God in the world; but now, in Christ Jesus, ye who sometime were far off, are made nigh by the blood of Christ.. For He is our peace, who hath made both one, and hath broken down the middle wall of partition between us; having abolished in his flesh the enmity, the law of commandments contained in ordinances; for to make in Himself of twain one new man, so making peace." (Ephes. ii. 11–15.) That is, the law and ordinances, by which were secured to the Jews superior privileges over other nations, are now deprived of their exclusive power, and set at naught, and the way opened to *all* to come in and enjoy equal favors with them. So

[1] Read the whole chapter, Ephes. ii.

that the faithful of other nations, uniting with the faithful of the Jews, might make "*one new man*" in Christ Jesus. Not by the Jews going out to the Gentiles, but by the Gentiles coming in to the Jews, and taking their stand with them on the basis of the covenant of grace formed with their father Abraham. Therefore the "new man" formed in Christ, does not mean a new and independent Church in an absolute sense then begun, but a union of the faithful of other nations with the faithful of Israel in their covenant privileges, to be trained under the teachings of apostles and prophets.

5. And that such was the basis of union, and order of process in the organization of the Christian Church, is a historical fact as well as a divine doctrine. Not only to the Jews "*pertained the adoption, and the glory, and the covenants, and the giving of the law, and the services of God, and the promises*"[1] — but among them, and of them, was formed the first Christian Church — and while they still regarded themselves members of the Jewish Church, they received Christ as their promised Messiah, who had come to fulfil and perfect what was begun under their fathers.[2] And when Gentile converts were brought in among them and it became generally known that they were to enjoy equal privileges with them under Christ, it was an unsettled point whether they should observe the peculiar rites of the Jewish, as well as of the Christian Church.[3] This of itself proves, that these "aliens" were carried into the "household" of the Jews; and the branches of the wild olive tree hence grafted among the branches of "the good olive tree."[4] For as yet they did not understand that the "new

[1] Rom. ix. 4. [2] Acts ii. and iii. [3] Acts xiii., xv., xxi. [4] Acts xv.

and better covenant" of the Gospel was to supersede that of Moses which had now served its purpose, and having "waxed old was ready to vanish away"[1]—leaving only the Abrahamic covenant upon which to graft the "new." And in this there shall be neither Jew nor Greek, and instead of circumcision Baptism shall certify outwardly "Abraham's spiritual seed and heirs, according to the promise."[2] For, writes the Apostle Paul, "as many of you as have been baptized into Christ, have put on Christ. There is neither Jew nor Greek, there is neither bond nor free, there is neither male nor female,[3] for ye are all one in Christ Jesus. And if ye be Christ's, then are ye Abraham's seed, and heirs according to the promise." (Gal. iii. 27, 28, 29.)

After reading this it could hardly have been a matter of doubt among the Galatians, whether the Christian dispensation was to supersede that of Moses, and was designed to carry out and perfect the promise made to Abraham; and that by Baptism, instead of Circumcision, we put on Christ, through whom all are made the children of Abraham, without regard to nation or condition of race.

Thus history and doctrine explain each other, and unite their strength in testifying to the perpetuation of the Abrahamic covenant, and infant membership under the Gospel.

As to the objection made on the ground that the Gospel covenant is called a "new and better cove-

[1] Heb. viii. 13. [2] Gal. iii. 27-29.

[3] To females were secured the blessings and promises of nation and race, by obedience to the laws of matrimony, and living in harmony with the regulations of the covenant of circumcision. And further following the faith of Abraham, they secured the blessings and title of his spiritual seed.

nant," and therefore different from the "old," the reader need only refer to the passages in both the Old and New Testaments, to convince him that the comparison is made between the Mosaic and Christian covenants — not between the Christian and Abrahamic. "Behold the days come, saith the Lord, when I will make a new covenant with the house of Israel and with the house of Judah; not according to that I made with their fathers in the day when I took them by the hand to lead them out of the land of Egypt." (Heb. viii. 8, 9.)[1] The time, when they were "led out of the land of Egypt" was the period at which Moses was called to act, some four hundred and thirty years after the calling of Abraham. And hence the Gospel is called a "new and better covenant" in comparison with that made with Moses. The terms "new" and "old" are often used in a comparative sense. For instance, the Corinthian Church is exhorted to "purge out the old leaven" that it may be a "new lump"[2] — not to go to work and found a new Church, but to cleanse and purify the old one. Purge it of offending members and erroneous doctrines, and then it would be reformed into a "new body" or "lump"— as an altered or amended constitution of a state is called a "new constitution;" or a kingdom to which new domains have been added, and in which new laws are introduced and other changes made, is by liberty of speech called a "new kingdom." So the Gospel Dispensation is called a "new" and a "better covenant, which was established on better promises" than Moses, "who served unto the *example* and *shadow* of heavenly things."

The same principle applies to the use of the term

[1] Jeremiah xxxi. 32. [2] 1 Cor. v. 7.

"build," and other forms of speech. As when the Apostle Paul tells the Ephesian elders the word of God's grace is able to "build" them up. (Acts. xx. 32.) By which he does not necessarily imply the beginning, but rather the continuing, of that which had been already begun. So when our Saviour said to Peter, "Upon this rock I will build my church,"[1] — found the Christian Dispensation, — He did not necessarily imply the beginning of everything pertaining to church organization — that He would originate an entirely new thing, never before known — but build up a new dispensation under which the Church, which had been in existence many centuries, must now be guided and ruled. He will now set up a kingdom (or government) that shall never be destroyed. "The gates of hell shall not prevail against it."[2] "It shall stand forever."[3] The day has dawned in which "the Gentiles shall come to her light, and kings to the brightness of her rising" — and "The forces of the Gentiles shall come as a cloud, and as doves to her windows, and shall know the Lord, her Saviour and Redeemer, the mighty one of Jacob."[4]

Thus through the shadow of good things to come, the voice of Prophecy unites with that of Christ and his Apostles in proclaiming, instead of the destruction of Zion and a new and distinct Church in her place, that her Redeemer would come to her assistance and revive *her;* that he would enlarge her borders, and exalt her grandeur beyond that of her first glory.

And in accordance with her enlarged sphere and more fully developed character, means of grace and

[1] Matt. xvi. 18. [2] Matt. xvi. 18.
[3] Daniel ii. 44. [4] Isaiah ch. lx.

aids to faith are adopted. The services of Moses have been changed into a more simple and spiritual worship, and the bloody rite of Circumcision into Christian Baptism, which can be applied without distinction to male and female, to Jew and Gentile, to all classes — even to infants in the beginning of life. And the sooner they are brought into the nursery of the Church, and the more diligently they are trained in its duties and doctrines, as the foster children of Christ, and thus truly "brought up in the nurture and admonition of the Lord," the better for them, and for the cause of our common Christianity.

Religion always has been and always should be, a family matter; and to deny to little children Baptism because they cannot *believe*, is to object to the wisdom of God's government of his people in all past ages. For they ever have been included with their parents in covenanted blessings with Him, and need as much the nurture of the Church under the Gospel as they did under the Law. And the very same reasons assigned for excluding them from the one would have excluded them from the other. Infants could not of themselves have entered into covenant relations under Abraham, nor were they capable of exercising the faith and inward graces of Circumcision as a covenant, any more than they are those of Baptism.

6. Both rites were based alike on faith. Circumcision was not only the mark of nation and race, but the symbol of the circumcision of the heart — the badge of God's people — the sign and seal of the righteousness of faith. And yet it was given to little children only eight days old. Baptism can mean no more, and yet it is denied to little children by some because they cannot believe! And the oft-repeated

quotation — as oft *abused* as quoted in such a connection — is made, " They which are of faith, the same are the children of Abraham,"[1] as if any one now doubted that by faith, Gentiles as well as Jews are "blessed with faithful Abraham." But does this exclude their children from being blessed likewise with Abraham's, and annul the doctrine so frequently taught in the Holy Scriptures, that God will show mercy upon the children of those who love Him, "even upon children's children of such as keep his commandments?"[2]

We would ask of those who suppose the father's faith imparts no benefit to his child — if they have never read what the faith of Hannah did for Samuel? and the faith of the nobleman in the Gospel for his son at the point of death? and the faith of the woman of Canaan for her daughter vexed with the devil, and other like examples? If so, why try to deprive little children of all the advantages thus secured to them under Gospel grace?

From Circumcision alone, are derived the following arguments in favor of Infant Baptism: —

1. The analogy of the office of Baptism and Circumcision. Baptism, as an initiatory rite, holds the same place under the new, which Circumcision did under the old.

2. The perpetuity of the Abrahamic covenant, proves that Baptism holds the same place, in the same Church, and fulfils the same spiritual ends, while Circumcision has passed away.

3. The writings of the most celebrated of the ancient fathers teach, that in things spiritual, Baptism

[1] Gal. iii. 7–9.
[2] Exod. xx., Deut. x., xxx.; Ps. ciii., cxii.; Rom. xi.

was regarded by primitive Christians as having taken the place of Circumcision.[1]

4. In point of *fact*, Baptism did supersede Circumcision in the progress of the Christian Church. For both being practised together for some time by Jewish Christians, it was decided by a council of Apostles, elders, and brethren in Jerusalem (Acts xv.), that Circumcision was not necessary under the Christian Dispensation, and it gradually ceased, and only Baptism was continued.

Now, in addition to this independent line of proof, remember that we have traced through history the practice of baptizing infants up to the Apostolic age — and then to the *middle of that age;* when family baptisms are recorded as if as much a *matter of course* as individual baptisms; when during a missionary visit of the Apostle Paul with some brethren to Philippi, we read that two families were baptized — and these only; *Lydia and her household, the Jailer and all his*; no names are given, nor the faith of any specified, except of the head of each family. If all the members of these families were baptized on their own profession of faith, it would be very remarkable, in the first place, that *every member* of them should be suddenly converted and baptized, and no others in the town; and in the second place, if each one was baptized on his own individual faith, that the names of none should be recorded but those of the head of each family. But admit that these family baptisms were composed of minors and little children with their parents, then all is plain, and just what we might anticipate.[2] And another fact is also ex-

[1] See Justin Martyr, Origen, Chrysostom, Augustine, and others.

[2] These cases will be more fully examined under the head of "Scriptural Testimony."

plained, why in *all places* where the Apostles and their successors planted churches — in every country of whatever language, *all the Ancient Churches, however widely separated, by whatever name called, Greek, Syrian, Roman, Armenian, Coptic, Nestorian, Eutychian,* and others, EVER HAVE, AND DO STILL BAPTIZE LITTLE CHILDREN.

CHAPTER VII.

TESTIMONY OF THE HOLY SCRIPTURES.

The Grand Commission to the Apostles to Baptize all Nations. — True Principles of Interpretation. — Infants had been always Members of the Church, and no Restriction now made in Regard to Them. — Jewish Practice with Proselytes. — Talmud and Mishna. — Objection to Baptizing before Teaching, answered. — The Church a School. — Objection to the Want of Faith in Little Children, answered. — Christ's Treatment of Little Children shows they were not to be regarded as "Aliens and Strangers" to his Kingdom. — True Rendering of the Text, "Of such is the Kingdom of God." — The Promise to Children repeated in the First Sermon under the Gospel Commission. — Family Baptisms — Lydia and her Children, the Jailer and all his, and the Family of Stephanus. — Meaning of Οἶκος, "House." — In the Absence of Demonstration, the GREATER PROBABILITY, the Law of Action. — Claims of Duty between an Old Established Rite, and Supposed Error.

§ 21. HAVING traced the practice of baptizing the infant children of believers up into the Apostolic age, and shown from the history and teaching of the Primitive Church, that in the first generation after the Apostles, Christians baptized infant children; and having shown that Baptism has taken the place of Circumcision, hence Infant Baptism the place of Infant Circumcision; let us now see whether the Holy Scriptures confirm our conclusions by more direct teaching? And we will begin with the first recorded authority for baptizing in the name of Christ, in the sacred record.

1. On a mountain in Galilee were met together the eleven disciples of our Lord, by his own appointment, made after his resurrection. "And Jesus came and

spake unto them, saying, All power is given unto me in heaven and in earth."

MATT. xxviii. 19, 20. — "*Go ye therefore and teach (disciple) all nations, baptizing them in the name of the Father, and of the Son, and of the Holy Ghost; teaching them to observe all things whatsoever I have commanded you: and lo, I am with you alway, even unto the end of the world.*"

This is the Grand Commission under which the Apostles were to act in planting the Christian Church. They were to tarry in Jerusalem until baptized by the Holy Ghost, and then commence in that same city the momentous work herein assigned them. But how did they understand their commission? This is the point for us to settle. The language in which it is couched seems to this age rather general; but to them, no doubt, was sufficiently definite. Why more definite to them than to us? Because of previous instruction, and their acquaintance with circumstances of which we are ignorant. We say ignorant, unless we will examine and learn the usages, manners, and laws of the Jews at that time, together with the peculiar circumstances under which this commission was issued.

This brings us to that most important of all laws in the interpretation of the Holy Scriptures, or of any other ancient writing, and to which we have before alluded: that is, to make ourselves acquainted, as far as possible, with all the circumstances and influences under which everything was said and done — to study the manners, customs, and peculiarities of the people, and endeavor to place ourselves in the midst of the same age, and collect around us all the "circumstances and influences" by which the writer or speaker was at the time affected.

In this commission no exception is made to nation, person, age, or sex. "Go ye, therefore, and disciple all nations, baptizing them in the name of the Father, and of the Son, and of the Holy Ghost." But inasmuch as no age is specified, the question has been raised whether he intended to include the young children or not. The command to "disciple all nations" (μαθητεύσατε πάντα τὰ ἔθνη), translated in our version, "teach all nations," seems not to be sufficiently definite to satisfy the minds of many that young children are included. Before entering on a philological inquiry, however, let us first try this passage by the principle of interpretation to which we have just alluded, and see how, according to that plain and obvious rule, the Apostles must have understood their commission.

In giving directions or issuing a command, certain things are always taken for granted as being well known, and we only aim to be explicit enough to be clearly understood. For instance, a messenger is sent to the post-office; the order issued is, "Go and bring my papers," or simply "Go to the post-office." The messenger goes and brings letters, newspapers, and pamphlets; and he acts in accordance with the intention of him who sent him; although, perhaps, he simply told him "to bring his papers," or merely to "go to the post-office." Again, the merchant tells his clerk to collect certain debts, but does not tell him to carry with him the accounts or give receipts: these are taken for granted as known to be embraced, and necessary to the execution of his orders. And thus we might cite numerous examples, in which much is generally taken for granted in all kinds of commissions and orders.

Now put a novice, unaccustomed to either of the above duties, in the place of one or both of these individuals, and he would not execute the orders thus given. Why not? Because things are taken for granted in which he has never been instructed. And so, many things are often implied in one age, that are not known to following ages; and orders and instructions then given, or allusions made, are not understood, or are misapprehended in following years, because things then taken for granted, or the circumstances under which they were spoken, are unknown.

And hence it is, we find many things in Latin and Greek authors, and in the Holy Scriptures likewise, which are perfectly unintelligible to us, till we learn that certain usages and laws prevailed in those countries during that age. For instance, it is recorded by the Evangelists (Matt. ix. 17, Mark ii. 22, and Luke v. 37, 38), "that if we put new wine into *old* bottles, the bottles will break and the wine run out, but if we put it into *new* bottles both will be preserved." How shall we interpret this passage without some knowledge of the nature of the bottles used in the Apostolic age? So far as the bottles of this age are concerned, those that have been proved by use are more to be depended on than new ones. But so soon as we learn that the bottles used in those days were made of the skins of animals, and that when those skins became dry and old they lost their elasticity, and would not distend sufficiently to allow for the fermentation of their new wines, we see at once the force and beauty of the illustration.

Again, it is recorded that when (Matt. v. 13) "salt has lost his savor, it is thenceforth good for nothing, but to be cast out and trodden under foot of men." Now we know that the muriate of soda, which is the common salt used in this country, must entirely evaporate before it can lose its saltness; so obscurity hangs over this passage till it is known that the rock salt of Judea, used in the time of the Saviour, was dug from the earth, and found mixed with a white earthy substance, which, when the salt had evaporated by exposure to the weather, was good for nothing but to be scattered along walks and such like places. Now, the darkness is dissipated, and the beauty of the illustration appreciated.

Various other passages might be adduced, and some of a much stronger character, but these are selected because simple and plain, and sufficiently illustrate the principle, that some knowledge of the age and its usages in which the Apostles wrote, is indispensably necessary to a clear understanding of the Holy Scriptures.

Let us then take a case that shows the application of this principle to the passage under consideration. Suppose some one of the Christian denominations in our land were about to send eleven missionaries to one of the Pacific Isles, and should say to them in nearly the words of the Saviour: "Go ye, therefore, and disciple all the people, baptizing them in the name of the Father, and of the Son, and of the Holy Ghost." Would they not construe these words according to the former practice of the Church to which they belonged, and act in regard to the young children as they and their people with whom they were associated had always acted? Most assuredly. If sent out by the Methodists, or Presbyterians, or Lutherans, or any other denomination among whom young children are baptized, they would understand their commission to include young children with their parents, and would baptize them. Wherefore? Because they had always been accustomed to receive young children, and knew that those who sent them did the same, and therefore it was not necessary to specify more minutely in the charge given them. But suppose this same number of men had been sent out by the Baptist denomination, how would they understand the charge? Why, that children are not included. And for the same reasons given in the case of the others, — they were not accustomed to the Baptism of little children, and knew that those who sent them were opposed to it; and therefore there was no necessity for them to be more specific in regard to young children. Both equally sincere — both acting in accordance with the intention of the charge given them, and yet acting in direct opposition on this point.

In both cases there was no necessity for being more explicit, and yet so much is taken for granted, that a third party in a different country would not be able to understand such a commission, until they had made themselves acquainted with the rites and practices of those by whom the commission was given. Here, then, we see the absolute necessity of going back to the days of the Apostles, and endeavoring to make ourselves acquainted with the usages of the Jews, and the peculiar circumstances under which this commission was issued. We have seen how those who immediately succeeded the Apostles understood it; let us, then, in the next place, examine the rites and usages to which the Apostles had been accustomed, and the circumstances under which they received it, and see if we can learn how they acted under it.

2. Now these very men unto whom this "commission" was given, had been themselves made members of the Jewish Church in their infancy. They had been accustomed all their lives to regard young and old of the same family as members together of the same Church — all alike included in the same covenant — entitled to the same religious privileges, heirs together of the same Divine promises. With such training and ideas of Church organization, how would they probably interpret a commission that made no exception to young children? As Infants had always been received into the Church up to that time, is it at all probable that they would now exclude them without specific instructions so to do?

No one doubts whether it was the custom of the Jews to confer the initiatory rite of their religion on their children in early infancy, and that their children were regarded as capable of covenanted privileges, and recognized throughout the Old Testament Dispensation as members of the Church with their parents. And when to men, who had been thus associated all their lives, is given a "commission" broad enough to include little children — ay, expressed in the very terms commonly applied to Jewish members (μαθηταί, μαθητεύσατε) "disciples and make disciples" (St. John ix. 28), [1] how must they have construed it in regard to infants, no exception being made to them? When commanded to disciple all nations, would they not suppose all were included, little ones as well as their parents?

Suppose Circumcision to be put in the place of Baptism, and their commission had run "Go ye and disciple all nations, circumcising them in the name of the

[1] See Talmud.

Father, and of the Son, and of the Holy Ghost;" doubt ye that they would have hesitated a moment about circumcising the children of their converts? You cannot, since you know that this was continued for a long time, together with Baptism.[1] And if children were no longer considered capable of covenanted blessings, we ask again, why was it not made known, instead of permitting them to be circumcised by members of the Christian Church? If the Messiah intended to curtail the religious privileges which little children had enjoyed with their fathers ever since God had established a visible Church for his people, is it not reasonable to suppose some specification would be made in this commission, or in his teaching, otherwise? But instead of any intimation of that kind, He had on the contrary declared that "of such is the kingdom of God:" had commanded little children to be brought to Him to receive his blessing, and had shown by word and gesture they were not to be treated as "aliens" in his Church.

Further, these men had been already ordained to preach" (Mark iii. 13, 14; Matt. x. 5, 7), and had preached to and worshipped with Jews, recognizing them and their little children as fellow-members of the same Church; but now the "middle wall of partition is broken down"— Christ has tasted death for every man, and risen from the dead; all power is given unto him, and he commissions them to "go into all the world, and preach the Gospel to every creature"; their commission is enlarged, not diminished; Gentiles are included with Israel. Restrictions are removed instead of being imposed — parents

[1] Acts xv., xxi.

and children of other nations are to be baptized in the name of the Father, Son, and Holy Ghost.

3. Again, at the time our Saviour delivered this commission, it was, and had been for many centuries, as we shall show, the custom of the Jews to baptize all their proselytes from other nations, both parents and children. Their rule was first to circumcise, then baptize, and then offer for them a sacrifice. Circumcision brought them under the Abrahamic Covenant, Baptism brought them under the Mosaic. The offering of the sacrifice was in obedience to the ritual law. And they referred to Numbers xv. 15, for thus acting with proselytes, which reads: "One ordinance shall be both for you of the congregation, and also for the stranger that sojourneth with you, an ordinance forever in your generations: as ye are, so shall the stranger be before the Lord." By stranger, all of other nations were included, whether young children found in an exposed state and taken home, or parents with their children who joined their religion, or even those who became servants to them.[1]

Maimonides, the great interpreter of the Jewish law, says: —

> "And so in all ages, when an Ethnic is willing to enter into covenant and gather himself under the wings of the Majesty of God, and take upon him the yoke of the law; he must be circumcised and baptized, and bring a sacrifice. As it is written, 'As you are, so shall the stranger be.' How are you? By circumcision, and Baptism, and bringing of a sacrifice. So likewise the stranger (or proselyte) through all generations; by circumcision, and Baptism, and bringing of a sacrifice."[2]

Baptism was administered to all the children who were born before the parents' Baptism, but not to

[1] See Lightfoot and Wootten. [2] Isuri Bia. c. 13, cited by Wall.

those born after it, because these were by birth inheritors of the ceremonial privileges obtained by it. This was in conformity also to the above rule: for their forefathers were all of them Jews, baptized unto Moses in the cloud and in the sea — men, women, and children; but those born afterwards were by birth inheritors of the privileges of Baptism, and only circumcision and sacrifice were necessary for them. "The sons of proselytes (says Lightfoot) in the following generations were circumcised, but not baptized, as being already Israelites." Maimonides says, "A proselyte under age, they are wont to baptize on the knowledge of the house of judgment [the court], because this is for his good."[1] That is, when orphans were baptized the court or consistory acted as parents for them.

Concerning the age of the child to be baptized they had this rule. "Any male child, a proselyte, that is under the age of thirteen years and a day, and females that are under twelve years and a day, must be baptized as infants, at the request and by the assent of the father, or the authority of the Court, because such an one is not yet the son of assent"— that is, not old enough to be baptized on his own responsibility.

The Jerusalem Mishna says that if a girl, born of heathen parents, be made a proselyte after she be three years and a day old, she is not to have such and such privileges. And the Babylonian edition reads, if she be made a proselyte before that age, she *shall* enjoy such privileges.[2] From which it must be obvious to

[1] See Wall, vol. i., Intro. sec. 3.

[2] *Ibidem.*

This shows that the objection raised against Maimonides as not ancient enough, is of no force, since the Mishna [the text] of both the Jerusalem and Babylonish Talmuds, contains regulations for children made proselytes under and beyond three years of age. The Mishna was com-

every reader, that children, however young, were made proselytes.

Thus we see that Infant Baptism itself was practised from time to time before John the Baptist came preaching the Baptism of Repentance. Hence it was the people manifested no surprise at Baptism itself, but that John should baptize, as sanctifying the people for some great personage, and new dispensation, when he acknowledged himself not to be the Christ nor Elias, nor that prophet which was to come. "Why baptizest thou then,"[1] was their inquiry, "if thou be none of these"? Why this extra ablution and preparation of Jews, if not for their promised Messiah, and his dispensation, or for some prophet that is to come? Which corroborates the Talmud, that Baptism, or purification by water, was a thing in use and well known before the coming of John.

Now what can be more obvious than that men, who were Jews, acquainted with the usages of their nation, who possessed the feelings of Jews — who had always been accustomed to have their children in the Church with them, and familiar with the practice of both circumcising and baptizing children, would construe this commission precisely as the missionaries who were accustomed to the Baptism of children, unless ex-

piled at so early a date, that no one will accuse the Jews of borrowing this practice from Christians, or if they do, they admit the point at issue, which is that the Apostles practised it. According to Dr. Prideaux, the Jerusalem Mishna was compiled in the Apostolic age, just after the destruction of the Temple, and by the almost unanimous consent of critics, admitted to be completed in the second century. And if Jehuda the Holy, who was engaged forty years in digesting these laws, did not collect this concerning "young proselytes" from among the old customs of his nation in use before the coming of Christ, then it was borrowed from or suggested by the practice of Christians at a period so early, that it is as fatal to the cause of Antipædobaptism as would be the admission of its previous existence.

[1] St. John i. 25.

pressly instructed to the contrary? How could they restrict it to certain ages, when they had never known any age excepted before? and when their commission was as broad as language could make it — "Go ye, therefore, and disciple or proselyte all nations"?

"The Anabaptists object," says Lightfoot, "that it is not commanded to baptize infants, therefore they are not to be baptized. To whom I answer: It is not forbidden to baptize infants, therefore they are to be baptized. And the reason is plain. For when Pædobaptism, in the Jewish Church, was so known, usual, and frequent in the admission of proselytes, that scarcely anything was more known, usual, and frequent, there was no need to strengthen it with any precept when Baptism was now passed into an evangelical sacrament. For Christ took Baptism into his hands, and into an evangelical use as he found it — this only added, that he might promote it to a worthier end and a more extensive use.

"The whole nation knew well enough that little children used to be baptized. There was no need of a precept for that which had ever by common use prevailed. . . . .

"On the other hand, there was need of a plain and open prohibition, that infants and little children should not be baptized, if our Saviour would not have them baptized. For since it was most common in all foregoing ages that little children should be baptized, if Christ had wished to have that custom abolished, he would openly have forbidden it. Therefore, his silence and the silence of Scripture in this matter, confirms Infant Baptism, and continueth it unto all ages." [1]

When the Saviour came, all male proselytes were

[1] *Hor. Hebr.* on Matt. iii.

admitted into the Jewish Church by Circumcision, Baptism, and sacrifice — the female by Baptism and sacrifice. He abolished, in his death, circumcision and sacrifice, and only Baptism was left as a sign of the covenant, or profession of religion, and this He directed to be given to all, in the name of the Holy Trinity, as indicative of the new dispensation.[1] Or if any one prefers it, for the sake of illustration say, He abolished all former ordinances, and selected Baptism, because common to both sexes, less burdensome, and more expressive of the new dispensation, and hence made it the initiatory rite of the Church under this dispensation. In either case, how would men accustomed to see this rite applied to children, understand the commission "to disciple," and apply it to "all nations?" Would they not suppose that young children were included also? If the boy sent to the post-office must infer letters and pamphlets were included with the "newspapers," and the missionaries of the Lutheran and other Pædobaptist Christians, that young children were included in this commission, so must the Apostles have understood children included in theirs. We ask the opposers of Infant Baptism to pause and consider this case, and candidly to say if in these circumstances this commission can be rightly construed in any other way? We

[1] Some have concluded from Jewish Baptism that it is unnecessary to continue Baptism among a people whose forefathers have all been baptized. But they should remember that God's people have always had some badge or mark of profession — that although among the Jews, and the proselytes to their religion, Baptism was not given to succeeding generations, yet circumcision was, and sacrifice offered. But these are abolished under the Christian dispensation, and Baptism only remains, which must be given to every one, as a mark or seal of the new covenant, as circumcision was under the former dispensation. This is plainly taught in Colossians ii. 11, 12. But as the opposers of Infant Baptism, as well as its advocates, admit Baptism is to be given to every disciple, there is no need for discussing that question in this place.

may even lay aside all the influence the sacrament itself would exert, and adopt any other ceremony of admitting members into the Christian Church, and the construction would be the same. For these men were all Jews, educated Jews possessing the feelings of Jews, loved their children, and had always seen such received into the Church, and whatever religious rite had been instituted as the door into the visible Church, they would have admitted the children with their proselyted parents — unless instructed expressly to the contrary — and have justified themselves for it on principles of duty and reason, as well as of education and usage. For God was the same God He ever had been. He had not changed, and could not change. The great principles of his religion and the foundation of his Church were the same now as in the days of Abraham. The relation between parent and child were still the same. He was about to change his dispensation in the government of his people, but not the essentials of his Church. Rituals and ordinances were to be changed, means of grace and helps to faith instituted better adapted to the state of the world, while the inward righteousness and essence of the Church must ever remain the same, because founded on the immutable principles of the nature of the great Jehovah Himself. These being the same before these rituals were first ordained, and while they were in force, and after their abolition; were, and are, and ever must be still the same. And if children were fit to be members at one time, why not fit at any other time? If God commanded that they should be received with their fathers, and the seal or mark of his covenant be given them from the first moment He began to mark out for Himself a select visible people, and has never since, by word or deed, forbidden them this privilege; who will dare to prohibit them simply because that badge is changed for another?

Again, in the language of another, — "Not only do circumstances at the time, and usages before a command is given, enable others at a later period the more clearly to understand it, but the state of things that follow afterwards often throw much light on it."[1] Suppose, for instance, in the case of the missionaries referred to, some fifty or a hundred years after their death, we were to visit those isles, and find their successors practising Infant Baptism, and were to ask them by what authority they did this, and they were to inform us that the "first missionaries, their apostles, practised and ordered it;" should we not infer that one of those Christian bodies that practised Infant Baptism sent those missionaries? And should we not give credit to their answers, when we found that they were conscientious, pious men? ay, intelligent as well as pious, and surrounded by those who had known and conversed with intimate acquaintances and friends of their first missionaries?

Now this is precisely the state of the question before us. The churches of Greece, Rome, Alexandria, Cappadocia, Syria, Arabia, and Palestine, spread over thousands of miles, separated, some of them so far from others that there had been probably little or no communication between them, are all found in the practice of Infant Baptism, as we have seen, in the next century after the Apostles, and no one ever calling in question its lawfulness.

Considering the whole evidence in the case, the custom of the Jews at the time this commission was

[1] Knapp's *Theology*.

given, the language itself, and the state of things found in the Churches soon afterwards, the fact is as fully established, according to fixed laws of interpretation, that the commission given to the Apostles for organizing the Christian Church embraces Infant Baptism, as that water should be used in the administration of the ordinance.

§ 22. Let us now consider some of the objections that have been urged against this interpretation. First, it is said the Apostles were commanded to "teach," and then baptize: therefore, the persons to be baptized, were only such as could first be taught. In reply to which, we remark, the word in the first part of the commission (μαθητεύσατε), translated in our version "teach," is an entirely different word from that in the latter part [διδάσκοντες,] translated "teaching." The former means to "disciple" or "proselyte"—while the latter means imparting instruction as by a master to his pupil. The better rendering of the whole passage (as every reader of the original well knows) is, "Go ye, therefore, and disciple [make learners of] all nations, baptizing them in the name of the Father, and of the Son, and of the Holy Ghost; teaching them to observe all things whatsoever I have commanded you:" which means, "Go and bring into my kingdom every nation, initiating them by Baptism, and teaching or training them up in all the doctrines and precepts which I have commanded you."

Now, as kingdoms of the world are confined to no age or sex, so the kingdom of Christ on earth, which He chose to represent under the same name, is confined to none, but designed to embrace all ages and nations. To convert nations to any faith, we must of course in the beginning work chiefly among the responsible portion of the nation, we must first convert the parents before we can expect them to permit us to bring their children under the influences of our principles. So in the kingdom of Christ, his ambassadors were sent forth to address and convince the parents — the responsible portions of the community, who must be converted before they could reach their children. But when these were converted they would bring their children with them of their own accord. Or as St. Peter did on the day of Pentecost, when multitudes were made to cry out — " Men and brethren, what shall we do ? " tell them the " promise is to you and to your children." (Acts ii. 37, 39.) And as in the case of the jailer and others, whose children were present when the parents believed, baptize them all. (Acts xvi. 15–33.)

Instead of the term μαθητεύειν [1] "to disciple or proselyte," militating against young children, it is of itself when rightly construed, proof positive that they are included. For it is as applicable to children as to adults, and we have not the slightest intimation that it is used here in a limited sense. On the contrary, it seems to be given in its widest possible application —" disciple all nations "— hence all that compose nations of every age and sex. Μαθητεύσατε is from μαθητής

[1] The μαθητεύειν, says Alford, consists of two parts — the *initiatory* admissory rite, and the *subsequent teaching*. It must be regretted that the rendering of μαθητεύσατε, " teach, " has in our Bibles clouded the meaning of these important words. It will be observed that in our Lord's words, as in the Church, the process of ordinary discipleship is *from Baptism to instruction*, *i. e.*, admission in infancy to the covenant, and growing up into τηρεῖν πάντα, κ. τ. λ. — the exceptions being, what circumstances rendered so frequent in the early Church, instruction before Baptism, in the case of adults On this we may also remark that Baptism, as known to the Jews, included just as it does in Acts xvi. 15–33, whole households — wives and children."—*Alford on St. Matt.* xxviii. 19.

a "disciple," which is from μανθανω, to "learn." Therefore "a disciple" is a learner, and to "make disciples" is to make learners. The Church in all ages has been a school for teaching the things of God and training its members in the way of holiness. Of the father of Circumcision, God said, "Seeing that Abraham . . . . will command his children and his household after him, and they shall keep the way of the Lord, to do justice and judgment; that the Lord may bring upon Abraham that which He hath spoken of him." (Gen. xviii. 18, 19.) Moses was instructed to teach Israel, "And these words which I command thee this day, shall be in thy heart: And thou shalt *teach them diligently to thy children*, and shalt talk of them when thou sittest in thy house, and when thou walkest by the way, and when thou liest down, and when thou risest up. And thou shalt bind them for a sign upon thy hand, and they shall be as frontlets between thine eyes. And thou shalt write them upon the posts of thy house, and on thy gates." (Deut. vi. 6, 9.)

Such was the character of the Church for teaching and training its members from earliest childhood under the Old Testament Dispensation. Under the New, precisely the same is to be retained. "Go ye, therefore, and teach (make disciples — learners) of all nations, baptizing them in the name of the Father, and of the Son, and of the Holy Ghost; teaching them to observe all things whatsoever I have commanded you; and lo, I am with you alway, even unto the end of the world" (Matt. xxviii. 19, 20), was the commission of the Saviour himself.

1. Now a school must have different grades of learners, or else there must be many schools. Christ

has but one school for all — and this school wonderfully adapted to every age. It has instructions for the first impression the youngest mind can receive. And the first impression made on the infant mind ought to be of Christ's teaching. "As the twig is bent, the tree 's inclined." And as a learner, whose name is simply enrolled, is called a pupil or scholar before he commences to learn, so in the case of a disciple; whoever is received into the Christian covenant to be trained in the school of Christ, is called a disciple from his Baptism; just as all the males of the Kohathites, from a month old and upwards, are called "keepers of the charge of the sanctuary" — infants as well as adults; because belonging to the body and designed for that office: or as the little ones recorded in the book of Deuteronomy (xxix. 11, 12), are said to "enter into covenant with the Lord," although too young to know what the term covenant meant. "Little proselytes," a phrase of the same import with "disciples," was in familiar use among the Jews in the days of our Saviour. Children, however young, whether received with their proselyted parents, or brought under the Jewish faith in any other way, were called "young proselytes." The Mishna of the Jewish Talmud, both of Babylon and Jerusalem, speaks of such proselytes, and as already cited, defines the privileges which may be enjoyed by those born of heathen parents, and made "proselytes" after *three years and a day old*, and of such as shall be made proselytes *before that age.*

Justin Martyr, as has been already remarked, applies the very same word which is used in this commission to children in general, saying that he knew many of both sexes made disciples (ἐμαθητεύθησαν) to Christ from childhood.

2. It is also objected that this commission, as recorded by another Evangelist, requires faith before Baptism. Mark xvi. 15, 16: "Go ye into all the world and preach the Gospel to every creature — he that believeth and is baptized shall be saved, but he that believeth not shall be damned." The commission is here embraced in the first verse, "Go ye into all the world and preach the Gospel to every creature." The next merely affirms what will be the consequence of receiving or rejecting their mission — "He that believeth and is baptized shall be saved, but he that believeth not shall be damned." Now if this passage is to be arrayed against children to keep them from Baptism, it must also keep them from salvation, for it expressly says, "he that believeth not shall be damned." But who will apply it to children, and dare affirm that all who cannot believe shall be damned? No one. By what authority then can we apply one clause of a sentence to children to keep them from Baptism, and then exclude them from the next part of the sentence, when there is evidently no change of subject matter in the mind of the author? [1] The true state of the case is, the Evangelist simply records the broad and universal character of the commission, and then states what will be the result to those who receive or reject the offer of salvation under it. Those who will hear shall live, but those who will not hear shall die.

The spread of the Gospel, of course, depended on the reception it met with among the acting, thinking portion of the community. If this class of persons

[1] The reason given by the first sect who rejected Infant Baptism, as we have seen, was that infants could not believe, therefore they could not be saved. But that was in the Dark Ages, and their followers have since changed their ground.

received it, its blessings would by their consent be given to minors and children. But if they rejected it, much that might be conveyed to others would be lost to such as were in part dependent on them. To this class of persons alone then, so far as faith is concerned, do those words of St. Mark apply.

3. *Repentance*, as well as *faith*, are generally made prerequisites for Baptism, but not in the case of infants. It is said (Acts ii. 38), "Repent and be baptized every one of you, in the name of Jesus Christ, for the remission of sins." Again, Philip said unto the Eunuch (Acts viii. 37), "If thou believest with all thy heart, thou mayest" [be baptized]. But these are replies made to those who had proposed particular questions. The very same would in this day be said by any orthodox missionary under similar circumstances, whether an advocate for the Baptism of children or not. For every sound divine requires repentance and faith on the part of adults. But it does not follow that the same must be required of little children. The covenant made with Abraham was based on faith; nevertheless children were embraced in it who could not believe. "Abraham believed God, and it was counted unto him for righteousness." . . . . "And he received the sign of circumcision, a seal of the righteousness of the faith which he had, yet being uncircumcised;"[1] but to Ishmael, thirteen years old, and to Isaac, eight days old, and to all infant male descendants afterwards, as we have already seen, was this sign and seal given, which brought them into the same covenant, although they were incapable of faith. Abraham was "justified by faith," and commanded to "walk

[1] Rom. iv. 3, 11.

before the Lord and be perfect." (Gen. xvii.) The covenant therefore made with him was based as much on faith in God, and obedience to his commands, as is the covenant now under Christ. Indeed, the Christian covenant, as we have already seen, is the continuation of the Abrahamic covenant more fully developed, and under a more advanced dispensation, into which children were received from the first, and continued up to the time of Christ. Why should their incapacity to "believe and obey," exclude them after the coming of Christ, if it did not before?

And though the Christian were one entire new covenant, it would be no more a covenant of *faith* than that of Abraham. And if the inability of little children to exercise faith did not exclude them from the latter, why should it from the former? If none can be baptized but those who can believe according to such an interpretation of that passage, then consistency requires it to be interpreted that none can be saved who cannot believe; for the only alternative then allowed, is damnation to those who do not believe! Shall we accept such a construction, or rather suppose that the passage does not refer to little children except through their parents and representatives, and that as they were involved in the sin of the first Adam, without their own personal acts, so they can be made participants of the blessings of the covenant of the second Adam, in like manner?

For if Christ, the second Adam, has come to redeem us from the curse, and bring an antidote to the evils entailed by the first Adam on his posterity, and *unconscious infants* are made partakers of those evils, why may they not, in the same *unconscious state*, be made partakers of the antidote procured by the second Adam? and for this end be engrafted by Baptism into that "one body" (1 Cor. xii. 13), of which He is the head, and those who have been baptized are the members, and are "all made to drink into one spirit?" As Baptism is the *initiatory rite* into this kingdom of Grace, and Christ took up little children into his arms and blessed them, and said "of such is the kingdom," why refuse them entrance into it?

3. It is sometimes brought forward as an objection to Infant Baptism, that Christ was not baptized until adult age. But we should remember He was circumcised when eight days old, brought to the temple and dedicated at forty days — was a strict observer of the ritual law of the Jews — and attended the synagogue worship until his death. He was baptized with John's Baptism soon after it commenced, to "fulfil all righteousness," in recognition of the authority of his mission. And if we are to follow his example in all outward acts, we must either submit to all these just as He did, or else so far as they are types of ordinances in the Gospel Church. And if the latter, then we have another argument in behalf of Infant Baptism, rather than against it; for as He was brought into covenant, made a member of the Church, and dedicated to God in infancy, so ought we to be. And as He submitted to the ordinance of Baptism at the earliest opportunity, so ought we to submit. John's Baptism was not instituted in the time of *his* infancy, but He submitted to it the first opportunity after it was instituted, and hence has given no room to plead delay from his example. John's Baptism was not the Christian Baptism, because Christ did not manifest Himself as the Son of

God until after his Baptism, neither did John baptize in the name of the "Holy Ghost." His Baptism was "unto repentance," saying to the people, "they should believe on Him who should come after him." Christ's Baptism was in the name of the Father, Son, and Holy Ghost. And we read of those who had been baptized unto John's Baptism, that afterwards received Christian Baptism (Acts xix.), acknowledging that they had "not so much as heard whether there be any Holy Ghost."

So far, then, as Christ's early life is concerned, his example is altogether on the side of the Church membership of infants; and so far as his acts and words are concerned in regard to "little children," they all tend to the same point. We nowhere read that He himself baptized any infant or adult. "Jesus Himself baptized not, but his disciples."[1] But we read of his being displeased at those who attempted to prevent children from being brought to Him to receive his blessing; and of "his putting his hands on them and praying," or "taking them up in his arms and blessing them," exhorting others to become like unto them, and saying that "of such is the kingdom of heaven." Observing all the different circumstances which have been noticed by the Evangelists, we have it as follows: —

§ 23. Matt. xix. 13; Luke xviii. 15; Mark x. 13, 16. — "*And they brought young children, infants, to Him, that He should touch them, put his hands on them, and pray; and his disciples rebuked those that brought them. But when Jesus saw it, he was much displeased, and called them unto Him and said, Suffer little children to come unto me and forbid them not,*

[1] St. John iv. 2.

for of such is the kingdom of God. Verily I say unto you, whosoever shall not receive the kingdom of God, as a little child, shall not enter therein. And He took them up in his arms, put his hands upon them, and blessed them."[1]

Does anything here indicate that Christ intended to exclude young children from his kingdom? Does He not, on the contrary, say, "of *such* is the kingdom of God?" — every action and word of his own going to show that He recognized little children, not as strangers and foreigners, but fellow-citizens with the saints and of the household of God.[2] He was "much displeased" at those who would keep them from being brought to Him to receive his blessing; rebuked them, and called for the children to be brought, giving as a reason why they should be permitted to come, that "of such was the kingdom of God," and adding that ALL must become as little children to enter into his kingdom. He then took them up, put his hands upon them, and blessed them. And not only did He exhort others to become like unto them — not only did He take them up in his arms, thus manifesting his friendship towards them, but He performed the significant act of laying his hands upon them, to impart a religious or spiritual blessing, thereby recognizing them as belonging to the kingdom of God, and not as "foreigners and strangers."

1. It has been objected that the phrase, "kingdom of God, or of Heaven," does not necessarily refer to God's visible kingdom on earth, but often refers to his kingdom in glory. Whichever construction you give, the result is the same, so far as little children

[1] See Hay's *Treatise on Baptism*. [2] Eph. ii. 19.

are concerned. If fit for the Church in glory, they are certainly fit for it on earth.

"Kingdom of God" is used in both of these senses in the New Testament, but generally refers more directly to the reign of Christ and the visible portion of the Church on earth, and frequently includes both its preparatory state here and its perfect state hereafter. "Repent ye, for the kingdom of heaven is at hand,"[1] refers more directly to the reign of Christ and the ushering in of the New Dispensation. "The kingdom of heaven is like unto a net, that was cast into the sea, and gathered of every kind,"[2] — evidently refers to the visible Church on earth. "Now this I say, brethren, that flesh and blood cannot inherit the kingdom of God."[3] This of course looks to the kingdom in glory. "But seek ye first the kingdom of God and his righteousness,"[4] includes the reign of Christ within and without, on earth and in heaven.

In short, every one who will examine the question thoroughly, will find that the phrase "kingdom of God and of heaven," is used sometimes for the visible state of things on earth, sometimes for them in heaven, and sometimes for the inward work of the Spirit on the hearts of individuals, as, "the kingdom of God is within you;" but it generally includes the perfect as well as imperfect state of Christ's kingdom, even when applied more directly to the Church militant. And in this sense no doubt our Saviour used it with reference to the little children when he said, "Of such is the kingdom of God."

He was preparing the Church, or people of God, for a more spiritual dispensation on earth. They had

[1] Matt. iii. 2. [2] Matt. xiii. 47. [3] 1 Cor. xv. 50. [4] Matt. vi. 33.

been for a long period under a dispensation that was adapted to an age then passed away; and many abuses and corruptions that had sprung up must now be reformed, and a more spiritual reign commence. To be members of this reformed Church, they must forsake and repent of those sins which they had allowed, and seek after righteousness and purity of life, which would prepare them for that perfect state of his kingdom in glory, of which this on earth is the beginning. Hence the penitent, seeking after purity of heart, and governed by his teaching, He regarded as worthy of true membership in that kingdom. And therefore little children, who had no actual sins of their own, and whose tender minds could be taught and trained in the right way, by faithful leaders, were, *par excellence*, members of it.

2. That such was the meaning of Christ when He said, "Of such is the kingdom of God," is the more obvious from the fact that He held them up as models for the imitation of those who, in their unfeeling self-confidence, ordered them to be taken away. He was offended at the manifestation of such temper. And hence He added, "Whosoever shall not receive the kingdom of God as a little child, he shall not enter therein."[1] That is, whosoever shall not humble himself to be taught of Christ, and follow his instruction as a little child, can never be a true member of his kingdom or enter into its perfect state in glory. Men may enter into it on earth, and become members, as those had done who would now send the little children away; but unless they imitate these models, which they were so ready to reject, and follow after their innocency and teachable tempers, they will

[1] Mark x. 15.

never enter into the Church triumphant. As yet they were all in the Old Testament Church — the little children as well as those to whom the Saviour addressed Himself. The day of Pentecost had not come. But Christ was preparing them for it. He was reforming abuses and pointing out duties; and when He said of the little children, "Of such is the kingdom of God," He was pointing out who were the true worthy members that were fitted for it under the more spiritual dispensation on earth about to take place, and its final state in glory.

And who, we ask now, is better fitted for such a kingdom than the little children for whom Christ died? And what could be a more suitable model for men of an overweening self-confidence, whose need of humility and tenderness would drive the lambs away from their shepherd, than the gentleness and innocency of the lambs themselves? But there are those in the present day who reject the little children from the kingdom, even though Christ rebuked others for driving them from Him, and informed them that such were models for imitation to all who would become truly the members of that kingdom! They reject the pattern, but accept the imitation! Is not this strange, when the pattern is part and parcel of the same material? Little children are human beings, have souls, and are susceptible of pleasure and pain. They need and can receive religious blessings, or why did our Saviour pray for and bless them? And why should He afterwards reject them from his kingdom, and receive only those who copied their innocency, humility, and teachable temper?

Could a man utter sophistry more untenable than that of Dr. Carson, when he says, "'Of such is the kingdom,' cannot mean the persons themselves spoken of, but others like them? For the term 'such' *does not signify identity, cannot signify identity*, but likeness."[1] And therefore it cannot include the little children, but those like them!

Where did he learn this construction of language? from Scripture usage? When St. Paul described certain persons as "corrupt and destitute of the truth, supposing that gain is godliness," and warned Timothy "from *such* withdraw thyself,"[2] did he mean that he should withdraw from these persons *themselves*, or only from *others* who were like them?

Again, when the same Apostle tells us that (Gal. v. 21) "they which do *such* things shall not inherit the kingdom of God," does he not mean the very things themselves, as well as other things of like character?

And yet again, when St. John commends the charity of Gaius, and says of certain persons (iii. John 8) "We ought therefore to receive *such*, that we might be fellow helpers to the truth," does he intend that the persons themselves spoken of must be rejected, and others like them be received? How strange that one of such high pretensions should manifest such ignorance of the use of language. Our Saviour did not select *models of wood*, or *patterns of paper*, to be used and then laid aside; He selected *living souls*, for whose redemption He had suffered and died, and for whose benefit, as well as the benefit of all his people, He was about to establish a kingdom on earth in which to train and fit them for his kingdom in glory; To those who would keep little chil-

[1] Carson *On Baptism*, p. 200.

[2] 1 Tim. vi. 5.

dren from him, He said, "Suffer little children to come unto me, and forbid them not, for of such is the kingdom of God. Verily I say unto you, whosoever shall not receive the kingdom of God, as a little child, shall not enter therein." Thus declaring their fitness for his kingdom, and the *necessity* for others to follow their *teachable*, *submissive* spirit to enter in. "He also took them up in his arms, put his hands upon them, and blessed them." Thereby exhibiting his *great love for them*, and showing that HERMAS, a cotemporary of the Apostles, did not say without authority, "*All infants are valued by the Lord and esteemed* FIRST OF ALL."[1]

The objection that the Saviour did not baptize little children, is scarcely worthy of notice in this place, as all know "Jesus Himself did not baptize, but his disciples." He nevertheless taught and prepared the way for the new Dispensation of Grace in its fulness — and by words and signs testified that little children were included with their parents in his atonement for sin, and the covenant of their Redemption.

§ 24. In the opening sermon of the new organization of the Christian Dispensation, on the day of Pentecost, St. Peter informed the multitude astonished at the wonderful manifestations of the Holy Ghost — "This is that which was spoken by the prophet Joel[2] — 'And it shall come to pass in the last days (saith God) I will pour out of my spirit upon all flesh: and your sons and your daughters shall prophesy, and your young men shall see visions, and your old men shall dream dreams: and on (my) servants and on (my)

[1] Simil. 9, c. 29.

[2] Acts ii. 17, 18; Joel ii. 28, 29. See also Is. xliv. 3.

handmaidens I will pour out, in those days, of my Spirit (and they shall prophesy).' "[1]

He then went on to explain that this same Jesus whom ye have taken by wicked hands and have crucified and slain, God hath raised up and exalted on his own right hand; being made both LORD and CHRIST, and having received of the Father the promise of the Holy Ghost, hath shed forth this which ye now see and hear.

And to his conscience-stricken hearers, inquiring "Men and brethren, what shall we do?" he said: —

"*Repent, and be baptized every one of you in the name of Jesus Christ, for the remission of sins, and ye shall receive the gift of the Holy Ghost. For the promise is unto you, and to your children, and to all that are afar off, even as many as the Lord our God shall call.*" (Acts ii. 38, 39.)

In the same prophecy which he had cited, it is added that of those on whom God's displeasure rested on account of their sins, "Whosoever shall call on the name of the Lord shall be delivered, for in Mount Zion and in Jerusalem shall be deliverance," etc.,[2] which the Apostle Paul explains to mean — *all who shall give themselves up to the Lord Jesus Christ;* and that *Gentiles as well as Jews are included.*[3] The whole prophecy is referred to the times of the Messias and his reign by the best Jewish commentators.[4] Hence St. Peter's reply: "Repent and be baptized every one of you in the name of Jesus Christ [the Messias] for the remission of sins, and ye shall receive the gift of the Holy Ghost, *for the promise is to you and*

[1] St. Peter quotes from the Septuagint, not the Hebrew text which omits all in ( ).

[2] Joel ii. 32; Is. ii. 3. [3] Rom. x. 9–13.

[4] See Lowth, Arnold, and their authorities.

to your children and to all that are afar off;" it is made to your whole nation — to all who repent of sin and accept the Messias — no age, sex, or condition excepted, but on every rank, class, and degree among men shall it be poured out, and its wonderful gifts made manifest to all.

But some suppose *little children* are excepted because they cannot exhibit the miraculous gifts of the Holy Ghost,— they cannot " speak with tongues and prophesy." We cannot suppose that *every individual* among the classes enumerated *spake with tongues and prophesied*, but only such a representation of each class as to convince all that no grade or condition of the people had been passed over. Of the thousands baptized on the day of Pentecost and soon after, to whom Peter recited the promise, we do not suppose a hundredth portion spake with tongues and prophesied. But they received of the abundant blessing of the Holy Ghost. The little children needed its blessed influences as well as others, and why should they be slighted!

The promise is, " *I will pour out of my Spirit upon all flesh:* " which would be known and witnessed by its miraculous powers in *every class* and *grade* of men — but *not in every individual.* If so, it is not verified by the facts that followed. This was a very suitable time to make known any radical change to be made by change of dispensation. It was the introduction of the opening in full of the New Organization of Grace, and if little children were not to be received into its membership as under the Old, now, it would seem, was the time to proclaim such change. But no such proclamation was made. On the contrary he tells them that the promises made under the *Old*, *apply to them and to their children under the New, without specification* as to *age*, or to *any other qualification*, leading one to suppose that any such change was to take place. The natural and legitimate inferences, therefore, from the manner in which "you and your children are used by St. Peter, is that he meant the Jews and their children without regard to *age*. That he included the Jewish nation and their posterity from the oldest to the youngest — according to Jewish usage.[1]

1. It is not at all wonderful that persons who have been brought up under Antipædobaptist influence, should at first be disposed to refer the words of St. Peter in this passage, to only posterity grown up; because they read it with entirely different feelings and different views from a Jew. They are disposed to construe everything according to the principles already instilled into their minds. They look through a different medium from that through which a Jew from education must look. And so it is in all cases where children are referred to in the New Testament. Such persons require some specification for any departure from the order under which they themselves have been brought up, or which from other causes they have adopted; whereas the true state of the case is, as every unprejudiced mind can see, that some specification is required wherever there is a departure from the established prinples and known feelings of those to whom the words were at the time addressed. It is well known to every

[1] "The promise to you and to your children and to all that are afar off"— is supposed by many to refer to the promise which God included in his Covenant with Abraham (Gen. xvii. 7). "And I will establish my Covenant between me and thee, and thy seed after thee, in their generations, for an everlasting Covenant; to be a God unto thee, and to thy seed after thee." This, all will agree, embraced little children *eight days* old, and onward of all ages.

Biblical scholar that the Jews, and all connected with them, considered their young children entitled to the same covenant privileges to which they themselves were entitled: and hence must, as a thing of course, construe everything said in relation to children according to such views, unless some specification be made to the contrary. What then could they suppose St. Peter meant, other than to include their young children at that present time? Or how could he, who was himself a Jew, expect them to understand him otherwise, without some specification to the contrary?[1] The fact is, Infant church-membership is taken for granted throughout the New Testament, just as the being of a God is taken for granted in the Old Testament Scriptures; and any attentive student who will read the New Testament, with this truth before his mind, will see how exactly every part corresponds with it. But as soon as one begins to read it with the opposite opinion in his mind, he will find himself constantly reduced to the necessity of giving up broad, plain principles of interpretation, and looking for some hole to escape. And so it is with the passage before us. Such readers take for granted that Infant Baptism is not taught in the Scriptures. Wherefore, when the Apostle declares to the penitent multitude, "the promise is to you and to your children"—they cannot receive it in its full, natural sense, but give the passage a limited application, which *excludes* a portion of their children. So likewise, in the passage just

[1] Verses 41 and 42 are sometimes referred to as explanatory of St. Peter's meaning. But they only refer to the acts of responsible agents. Possibly very few children were present on the day of Pentecost, but if *many*, St. Luke's custom was to speak only of the acts of responsible persons and heads of families, as in the case of Lydia and the Jailer, for neither the names nor deeds of any of their children at their Baptism are recorded by him.

disposed of, where the Saviour says in regard to the little children whom he took up in his arms, "Of such is the kingdom of God"— they set to work and exclude the children themselves (the very subjects of the conversation), and limit the passage to such only as resemble them in certain particulars. Again, the commission given the Apostles "to disciple all nations, baptizing them,"— they, instead of receiving it in its broad, general sense, limit it to believers only. And from the same cause are unconsciously influenced in construing every passage bearing on the church-membership of infants.

Now this is precisely the reverse of the order that ought to be observed in regard to those passages referring to children. We must remember that the writers of the New Testament were all Jews, and of course to a great extent under the influence of previous education, and that all departures from established principles, rather than the continuation of them, would be marked by *specifications.*

2. It has also been argued that the Apostle limits Baptism in this place by repentance, saying, "Repent and be baptized, every one of you."

The irrelevancy of this objection will be seen by simply calling to remembrance the fact that the Apostle replied to persons who had committed actual sins of their own, and who had asked what they must do? and said to them, "Repent and be baptized, every one of you." Just as any Pædobaptist would in the same circumstances, at the present day. Not one word is said as to the repentance of their children, who had not committed actual sin, but who *were affected by original sin*; yet he tells them the promise is to their children, as well as to themselves.

And why not include the little children as well as those of older growth? Cannot children receive grace as well as others? Do they not need it to counteract fallen nature as well as others? If they are capable of moral defilement *through Adam*, why not of counteracting *grace through Christ?* Or why pray for their spiritual benefit, if they be not susceptible of such a thing? If children cannot receive the Holy Ghost, how is it St. John is said to have been filled with "the Holy Ghost even from his mother's womb?" (Luke i. 15; Is. xlix.) Herein lies the error of such — they assume that no benefit can be conferred on children at their Baptism, which they ought first to prove. It is not our object at present to say to what extent, or in what way, spiritual benefit is conferred, whether by the Holy Spirit through the act of Baptism itself, or through the prayers of God's people offered up for the child, or in consequence of covenanted associations, helps, and privileges, or through all these separately and conjointly. Certain it is, from Scripture testimony, that young children may receive the influence of the Holy Ghost,[1] and spiritual graces, as well as blessings of an external nature.

3. Lastly, it has been objected that this promise is limited by the latter clause to "as many as the Lord our God shall call." That is, "to such as can believe, and are effectually called unto salvation." This objection needs only a passing notice, since it is now generally conceded by the most eminent commentators of all shades of doctrine that the call here referred to, means the call made through the Gospel. Namely, that the "promise" extends to all who shall be invited to embrace it — that salvation is offered to as many as by that Gospel are called to repentance —

[1] Luke i. 15; Is. xlix.; Ps. xxii. 9.

"that the promise is to the Jews, and to their descendants, however widely separated by land — and now extends to Gentiles as well as Jews."[1]

Let us see next how some of the other Apostles appeared to have construed the commission under which they acted. We read that Paul, Silas, and others, in travelling and preaching the Gospel, visited a certain town called Philippi, in Macedonia, and that during their stay there they baptized two families; and these are the only Baptisms mentioned whilst there — both of them *whole families*. The first was the family of a certain woman named Lydia.

§ 25. ACTS XVI. 13, 19. "*And on the Sabbath day we went out of the city by a river side, where prayer was wont to be made, and we sat down and spake to the women which resorted thither. And a certain woman named Lydia, a seller of purple, of the city of Thyatira, which worshipped God, heard us, whose heart the Lord opened, that she attended unto the things which were spoken of Paul. And when she was baptized, and her* HOUSEHOLD, *she besought us, saying, If ye have judged me faithful to the Lord, come into my house and abide there, and she constrained us.*"

In this account nothing is said of the faith, names, or acts of any other member of the household, but of the head of it. The Baptism of the other members of the family is referred to, as if a thing of course, when the head of it believed. The whole affair is recorded,

1 Ephesians ii. 13, 17. That this promise extends to the Gentiles under the Gospel Dispensation *we know*, whether embraced at the time in the mind of Peter or not.

NOTE. — The reader will observe that these arguments, though corroborative of each other, are yet distinct and separate, and that he may reject any one of them if unsatisfactory to himself, without affecting the authority of the others.

just as if the privileges enjoyed by the head of the family, in matters of this kind, were the same under the Christian Dispensation that they had been under the Jewish. All of which is in perfect harmony with the views we have already advanced.

Shortly afterwards, Paul and Silas are apprehended and cast into prison. The jailer is charged to keep them safely, who thrusts them into the inner prison, and makes their feet fast in the stocks. At midnight an earthquake throws open the prison doors, looses the prisoners from the stocks, and awakes the jailer; who seeing the prison doors open, supposes the prisoners have fled, and is about to kill himself. But Paul calls to him to do himself no harm, for the prisoners were all there — none had escaped. The jailer called for a light, sprang in and fell down at the Apostles' feet; and having "brought them out, said, Sirs, what must I do to be saved?"[1]

§ 26. Acts xvi. 31–33. "*And they said, Believe on the Lord Jesus Christ and thou shalt be saved, and thy house. And they spake unto him the word of the Lord, and to all that were in his house. And he took them the same hour of the night, and washed their stripes; and was baptized, he and all his straightway.*"

Here is another case, in which no name or act of any member of the family is recorded but that of the head of it. And yet every member of it was baptized the same hour of the night, the jailer and *all his straightway*. No surprise or unusual joy is manifested at the Baptism of the whole family, but all is related as if a thing to be expected, that when the jailer believed and was baptized, "all of his" would be baptized likewise. Precisely such an account as we

[1] Acts xvi. 23, 30.

should expect a Jew to give, when, like pious Joshua, he could say for himself and all his, "As for me and my house we will serve the Lord." Hence, he would take all belonging to him, and bring them with himself into the Christian covenant, as soon as he believed.

So was the reply of the Apostles to the inquiry What shall I do to be saved? of the same character. The answer was, "Believe on the Lord Jesus Christ, and thou shalt be saved, and thy house;" that is, thou and thy house [family] shall be placed in a state of salvation. Faith in Christ is the way to attain safety, and by it you may bring yourself and family into a state of covenanted grace.

These Apostles, like St. Peter, remembered the blessings that would redound to their children with their parents. Believe, and thou and *thy house* shall be saved; brought into a state of salvation covenanted in Christ Jesus.

The Apostle Paul introduces the Baptism of the household of Stephanas in exactly the same manner. He mentions it in connection with the Baptism of two other individuals, without any restriction as to age or sex.

1. 1 Cor. i. 14–16. "*I thank God that I baptized none of you but Crispus and Gaius, lest any should say that I baptized in my own name. And I baptized also the household of Stephanas; besides I know not that I baptized any other.*"

Having heard that there were contentions in the Church of Corinth, and that the disciples were calling themselves by the names of the different ministers who had baptized them, he congratulates himself that there were but few there, who could call themselves by his name. He only remembered two, Crispus and Gaius, besides the family of Stephanas.

The *manner* in which family Baptisms are alluded to in the Scriptures, must ever strike the mind of the attentive reader, as opposed to those who advocate only believers' Baptism. If only believers were baptized, why (one is led to ask) is no restriction màde in regard to young children in these cases? Or if no young children belonged to them, why are we not informed that *all* believed, or that *all* repented, as well as that *all* were baptized? Why are they recorded as if everything depended on the heads of these families? Do not these things go far to show, that no radical change had been made in regard to the principle of receiving young children with their parents into covenanted privileges? For if a change had been made on this point, we might certainly expect to see something corresponding in the record — instead of which, every case is recorded in precisely the manner they would have been under the old dispensation, in the event Baptism had been merely added to it.

Suppose we were to meet in the records of some missionary station of the present day, such cases as these to which we have just referred — say, for instance, one records a visit to some town where he baptized two families, and these the only Baptisms performed by him whilst there; he says nothing of the faith or acts of any one, but the *head* of each family, and speaks of their family Baptisms in a manner that indicates no more surprise than individual Baptism? And suppose we find a few pages further on, in a letter to a church in another city, mention made of another family and two individuals, and that these were all that he baptized there also, and as you continue your research you find as many as five other cases of family Baptisms alluded to or implied, with no special remark, as if more unusual than individual Baptism; would you not conclude that these missionaries belong to a Church that ordered the Baptism of the young children with their parents? Can we come to any other conclusion, unless it can be made to appear that there were no children in those families?

But where is the evidence to that effect? It has been said that the 40th verse of the chapter recording the Baptism of Lydia and her family, shows that there were no children in it. Let us examine it. Acts xvi. 40. "*And they went out of the prison and entered into the house of Lydia; and when they had seen the brethren, they comforted them and departed.*" Now what does this verse mean, but simply that when Paul and Silas were let out of prison, they went to the house of Lydia, at which they met the brethren, and when they had comforted them, both by their presence and words, they departed. Some have endeavored to make this verse support the opinion, that the "brethren comforted," were only the members of Lydia's family, and hence they must all have reached the years of discretion, to be able to receive comfort. Such objectors must have paid very little attention to the whole narrative, or else they would have seen that Timotheus and Luke were fellow-travellers with Paul and Silas, and were at the time lodging at Lydia's house. Acts xvi. 3: "Him (Timotheus) Paul would have to go forth with him." (11, 12 verses.) Loosing from Troas, *we* (Luke the writer, with the others) came with a straight course to Samothracia, and the next day to Neapolis, and from thence to Philippi, which is the chief city of that part of Macedonia, and a colony, and *we* were in that city abiding certain days." Verse 15, "And when she (Lydia) was baptized and her household, she besought *us*, saying, if ye have judged me to be faithful to the Lord, come into my house, and abide there: and she constrained us." Who were these (*we* and *us*) constrained to abide at her house? Evidently Paul, Silas, Timothy, and Luke. The whole company lodged at Lydia's. "And it came to pass as *we* went to prayer, a certain damsel, possessed with the spirit of divination, met us, which brought her master much gain by soothsaying: the same followed Paul and *us*. And when her master saw that the hope of their gain was gone, they caught Paul and Silas and drew them into the market-place," verse 19. They were afterwards thrown into prison and remained there one night, but Luke and Timothy were not with them.

The next day Paul and Silas were released, and came to the house of Lydia, and met there Timothy, Luke, Lydia, and perhaps the "damsel" out of whom was cast the Pythonic spirit. To which number may have been added also the jailer and others. So that these, beyond a doubt, were the brethren whom Paul and Silas "comforted." For so far as Lydia is concerned, there is not a word going to show that one of her family was able to believe. On the contrary, everything connected with the Baptism of her family is put in the singular number, as if all depended on her alone.[1] "Her heart was open to attend to the things spoken. *She* besought us, if ye have judged *me* faithful, come into my house." Nothing is said of any one of her family in conjunction with herself. It does not read *our house*, or if you

[1] See *Apostolic Baptism*, by C. Taylor.

have judged *us* faithful, or that the members of her family attended. Nor should we have known that she had a family, had they not been mentioned as baptized at the same time with her,—"when she was baptized and her family." Instead of circumstances showing that her children were grown up, everything in the narrative goes to prove they were minors. Lydia was a native of Thyatira, residing at this time in Philippi; she could afford accommodations to Paul and his three companions, and constrained them to abide at her house. The Baptism of her (οἶκος) "house," is, strictly speaking, an *example* of *family Baptism* without restriction of age or sex. And we are bound to receive it as a case of promiscuous family Baptism. Just as if informed at the present time that a "certain lady and her family were baptized on a particular day, and no specification made as to age or numbers."

2. In the case of the jailer, it has been argued that there were no young children in his family, because we are informed the Apostles "spake unto him the word of the Lord and to *all* that were in his house." (Acts xvi. 32.) Why, says the objector, did they speak the word of the Lord to *all*, if all were not able to understand it? We might as well ask, Why does a minister of the present day speak the word of the Lord to all his congregation when a part of them are children? The earthquake and the alarm of the jailer, we may well suppose, awoke all in the house, and that they assembled in the same room, guards and assistants probably assembled with his family. And the Apostles preached or explained the Christian religion to all present, to the (οἰκία.) "household"— and "the jailer and all *his* were

baptized straightway;" *i. e.*, all his own immediate family (οἶκος), his house-seed — but not (οἰκία), "the household." We will show the difference presently. Nothing is said or done but what might have occurred, had all his own been young children.

Again it is sometimes affirmed that all the jailer's family were believers, because, after their Baptism, it is written in the 34th verse, "He set meat before them (Apostles) and rejoiced, believing in God with all his house." The word "believing" is made to apply to all his house, as if all believed in God, and rejoiced with him. But the error of this interpretation becomes manifest by merely referring to the original Greek, which shows that "*rejoiced* and *believing* are both in the singular number, only apply properly to the jailer himself." Καὶ ἠγαλλιάσατο πανοικὶ πεπιστευκὼς τῷ Θεῷ "and he rejoiced with all his house (at the head of his family), he having believed in God." The jailer having believed, rejoiced with, among, or in the midst of his family. Compare Acts xviii. 8.

This is the literal rendering of the sentence, "He rejoiced," "*he* having believed in God." Not *they* rejoiced, or *they* believed. The whole is recorded as if everything depended on the father's agency. And had it been otherwise, no doubt it would have been written, He and his house, or *they* all rejoiced, and *they* believed; or some allusion would have been made to the faith and acts of others.

Of the same character is the answer to the inquiry of the jailer. "Sirs, what must I do to be saved?" "Believe on the Lord Jesus Christ, and thou shalt be saved, and *thy house*"— *his faith* only pointed to, as the medium of the blessings to be received by himself and his children — *his acts* only recorded when the blessing was given *to them all.*

3. The Apostles always make a distinction between (οἶκος) "house," and (οἰκία) "household."[1] By "house" they mean *family — children*. And by "household" they include the domestics, or servants, and all connected with the establishment. The term οἶκος means literally "house," or "dwelling," but, metaphorically, the seed, descendants, immediate family — as when we speak of the "house of David," or "house of Israel." But οἰκία, "household," is a different word, of different gender, and embraces those received into the family — servants, attendants, and appendages, making up all in any way identified with the house. And the Apostles always observed this distinction, but our translators seem to have overlooked it in some places. The address, or sermon, was delivered before the οἰκία, "household,"— all who belonged to the establishment, — but only the jailer and family, or children, were baptized.

And so it was only Lydia and her οἶκος, "house," not "household," as it is translated, but "*Lydia and her children, the jailer and all his* [*children*], *and the children of Stephanas were baptized.*" The jailer could not have been a very old man, for his acts are such as we should ascribe to the rashness and vigor of early manhood. His first thought was to kill himself! Age is more deliberate. Next he "sprang in" with the vigor and activity, as indicated in the original, of one in the *prime of life* — *not* of *old age*, and the father of a *grown up family*. Wherefore everything connected with these cases harmonizes with the doctrine of family Baptism, including young children; and as soon as you adopt the opposite opinion, every incident needs explanation.

[1] See Taylor's *Apos. Bap.*, p. 88, 89.

So the Apostle Paul tells us he baptized the (οἶκον) family of Stephanas, but afterwards refers to the (οἰκία) "household" of Stephanas as having "addicted themselves to the ministry of the saints;" that is, the care of attending to the wants of poor saints, and the duties of hospitality. In the first place, he speaks of the Baptism of his children—for οἶκος applies to one's own children, while οἰκία includes servants and all others living in the family. And because, some eight or ten years after the Baptism of the family, he tells us the "household" were active in a certain duty, some have inferred that there were no little children in that family when they were all baptized. But there is no proof that there were none among them when the Baptism took place, or even at this last point of time. The "household," or several of its members, may have done much for the poor saints, and yet some of the children still be too young to act as responsible moral agents. It is the *manner* in which these and all family Baptisms are expressed or implied in the Holy Scriptures, that demands our particular attention.

The Baptism of several families in the New Testament is to be learned also merely by implication—no *special* notice being taken of the event. We have sufficient reason for the belief that the families of Crispus and of Onesiphorus, of Aristobulus and Narcissus, and also of Cornelius, were baptized; but so usual were family Baptisms that the Holy Spirit deemed it sufficient merely to *imply* the fact, as in numerous cases of individual Baptisms. And had the usual course of admitting their little children into covenant with God been departed from, and only *heads* of families, and those capable of self-responsibility admitted to Baptism, doubtless the character of these records would have been different, and family Baptisms less common?

"Being myself convinced," writes the remarkable author of "Apostolic Baptism," after a learned and laborious examination of the subject, "that the Apostles practised Infant Baptism, and that the Evangelists meant to tell us so, I affirm that the natural import of the term οἶκος, "family," includes children of all ages. In proof, I offer fifty examples; and if fifty are not sufficient, I offer a hundred; and if a hundred are not sufficient, I offer two hundred; and if two hundred are not sufficient, four hundred."[1]

Now in questions that do not allow of absolute demonstration, we are bound to follow the stronger probability. Neither party can be required to prove the presence or absence of little children in these families; but which is the *more probable* under all the circumstances noted, that there were no little children in any of them, or that there were, at least in some, if not in all?

When called upon to answer this question, can there be a doubt as to the *stronger probability?* Visit eight families promiscuously in this city, and is it probable that you will find no young children belonging to even *one* of them all, or to *half* of them? Visit three families — representing the jailer's, Lydia's, and that of Stephanas — and take them promiscuously, and which is the more probable, that you will find no children in one out of the three, or that you will find them in two of the three, or in all three? Yes, we may take the families or houses on any street, or through any district of country, and we shall find

[1] C. Taylor's *Apos. Bap.*, p. 89.

little children in a large majority of them all, instead of not in one out of three. Therefore, as a question of *probabilities*, the answer admits of no doubt. No man can hesitate for a moment to determine on which side lies the stronger probability; and when he takes in the number of families, the manner in which they are recorded, the universal custom of the Jewish nation, and all the circumstances connected with these cases of family Baptisms, recorded in the Holy Scriptures, the probabilities multiply to an infinite extent. Then to which shall we give allegiance — to a doctrine which started up in the Dark Ages, or to the practice of Christians from the beginning? If, in duties where demonstration cannot be given, we are morally bound to follow the greater probability, how must we act in this case? Shall we, can we, lay aside the ancient universal custom of the Church, the strongest visible tie between Christ and our children, the faithful constant monitor of our duty to our little ones, and substitute a *conjecture!* brooded and hatched when gloom and ignorance had spread over the earth? What law in morals or in religion will authorize such a course?

4. We have seen that the first generation after the Apostles did beyond all doubt baptize their little children. We have seen that it has been continued by the great body of Christians ever since. We have seen that family religion, including the young children as well as the older ones, was the universal privilege of the people of God up to the coming of Christ; and that his commission to open the Gospel dispensation, instead of curtailing the privileges enjoyed under the *Old*, is clothed in language that *extends* the limits and makes more comprehensive the *New* — embracing all

nations, without regard to age or sex. And, with this construction, his words and deeds concerning little children accord, the preaching of the Apostles correspond, and the frequent Baptisms of whole families, and their mode of record all unite — thus combining doctrine, practice, and incidental circumstances, into one harmonious whole.

And yet we have been told that we ought to give up this time-honored, blessed privilege, and adopt the cold, calculating, unfeeling alternative of leaving our little ones to the uncovenanted mercies of God, till they can work for themselves! Although they have never sinned after the similitude of Adam's transgression, yet they must remain under its bondage (visibly at least), till they can of themselves apply for the Seal of the Covenant of their Redemption!

CHAPTER VIII.

TESTIMONY OF THE HOLY SCRIPTURES CONCLUDED.

Laws of Marriage among the Jews. — The Holy Seed not allowed to mingle with Heathen Nations. — Such Marriages dissolved in Times of Reformation. — Heathen Wives and Children put away. — Difficulties suggested in regard to "believing and unbelieving" Husbands and Wives under the New Dispensation. — Ceremonial Law not applicable. — Sanctifying Influence of Believers on Unbelievers justifies their Continuance in Wedlock lawfully formed, hence their Children are Holy and not Unclean. — Holy and Unclean always used in a Ceremonial or Religious Sense. — Children numbered among the Holy and Saints by St. Paul. — Their Parents instructed how to train them. — St. John divides the Members of the Church into Three Classes, Fathers, Young Men, and Little Children. — Summary of Testimony. — Earnest Exhortation to the Faithful Training of our Little Ones for Christ's Spiritual Kingdom.

§ 27. WE come next to a passage in the first Epistle to the Corinthians, which shows how much the Jewish Christians were under the influence of early education, while it also proves, that the young children of Christians are qualified for church membership.

The Jews, as the people of God, were called "holy," a "holy people" unto the Lord, "a special people," "a holy seed" (Deut. vii., xxvi.; Ezra ix.); just as Christians are called "Saints," a holy nation, "peculiar people," "chosen generation" (Acts ix.; Titus ii.); and pagan nations were called "unclean," "uncircumcised."

The Jews as a "holy people" were forbidden to intermarry with Pagan nations: "Neither shalt thou make marriages with them; thy daughter thou shalt not give unto his son, nor his daughter shalt thou take unto thy son." (Deut. vii. 3.) And further, when such marriages had been contracted, it was deemed essential to a thorough reformation that they be dissolved.

In the time of Ezra, many had broken through this law and taken to themselves Pagan wives. The princes came to Ezra and complained that the "holy seed" had mingled themselves with surrounding nations, having taken their daughters for themselves, and for their sons. (Ezra ix. 3.) This was the cause of much lamentation, and the people were assembled and "wept very sore." "And Shechaniah the son of Jehiel, one of the sons of Elam, answered and said unto Ezra, we have transgressed against our God, and have taken strange wives of the people of the land; yet now there is hope in Israel concerning this thing. Now therefore let us make a covenant with our God, to put away all the wives and such as are born of them, according to the counsel of my lord, and of those that tremble at the commandment of our God; and let it be done according to the law." (x. 2, 3.) Ezra arose and made all the people swear that they would do according to this word. "And they sware." (5th verse.) And accordingly all such marriages were then dissolved.[1]

Certain Jewish believers at Corinth, as it appears, thought the same law, or principle, ought to be observed under the new dispensation. For when it was found that there were some among them, whose husbands or wives were unbelievers, and yet both continued to dwell together in wedlock, the question was raised, whether the believer in such cases ought not to separate from the unbelieving partner? They referred

[1] See Ezra x., *passim*.

the matter to the Apostle Paul, who replied as follows: —

1. 1 COR. vii. 12–14. "*If any brother hath a wife that believeth not, and if she be pleased to dwell with him, let him not put her away — and the woman which hath a husband that believeth not, and if he be pleased to dwell with her, let her not leave him. For the unbelieving husband is sanctified by the wife, and the unbelieving wife is sanctified by the husband: else were your children unclean, but now are they holy.*"

This reply of the Apostle shows that the believer is not required, under the Gospel, which leans to mercy, to separate from an unbelieving partner; and that instead of the believer being polluted by the unbeliever, the latter is in a certain sense sanctified by the former, in virtue of which their children are "holy" — to be treated as the "holy seed," not as "unclean" Pagan children. Now, as the "holy seed," and all persons called "holy" (ἅγιοι) were received into covenant with God, and numbered with his people — and "unclean" and "uncircumcised," were terms used to distinguish those not received into covenant among God's people; this passage teaches, that though only one parent be a believer, their children are numbered among the holy seed, and hence are qualified for the Christian covenant, therefore for Baptism; because they must be baptized to enter into that covenant.

"Holy" (ἅγιοι) is used everywhere in the Septuagint for a Hebrew word which means "pure," "clean," and is used in the New Testament for saints, (ἅγιοι) "holy ones." (Acts ix. 13, 32, 41.) St.

Paul confessed that he had "shut up many of the saints (τῶν ἁγίων) 'holy ones' in prison." (Acts xxvi. 10.) "I go to Jerusalem to minister to the saints" (τοῖς ἁγίοις), "holy ones." (Romans xv. 25.) He frequently addressed the churches under the same title — τοῖς ἁγίοις — "saints or holy ones." "To the saints (τοῖς ἁγίοις, 'holy ones') which are at Ephesus."[1] "To all the saints (τοῖς ἁγίοις, 'holy ones') in Christ Jesus which are at Philippi."[2] "To the saints (τοῖς ἁγίοις, 'holy ones') and faithful brethren in Christ which are at Colosse."[3] This title is given in a multitude of places to the members of the Church, and the "fact is indisputable (says Taylor) that the appellative 'holy,' is not bestowed in the New Testament on any person not a member of the Church of Christ."[4]

But in the passage under consideration, it is expressly applied to young children. Shall we then receive it in the same sense in this as in other passages, or shall we give it a different meaning from all the other places in which the sacred writers use it? "This appellation being never given in the Scriptures (says Hay) to any but to those who are of the Church and in covenant with God, we must understand it here in the same sense; and therefore, the children of one believing parent, and more conclusively, if both be believers, are of the Church, and entitled to be admitted therein by Baptism, for the children of one believer are called 'holy' in the same sense as the Israelites are called a 'holy people,' and the members of Gospel churches are called 'saints' or holy persons, 'a holy nation,' a 'peculiar people:' not because they are all truly pious and sanctified,

[1] Eph. i. 1. [2] Phil. i. 1. [3] Col. i. 2. [4] *Apostolic Baptism*, page 97.

but because they are visibly the people of God, and have been received into his covenant." [1]

Now as the question proposed to the Apostle must have originated in Jewish scruples, so the reasoning in his answer is exactly adapted to the nature of such an origin. If the believer must put away an unbelieving partner, he must, according to the same law and practice, put away the children of such a marriage likewise: for those "born of them" are unclean by the same authority, and must be excluded from the community of God's people and covenanted privileges. But the unbelieving partner, in consequence of his union by marriage before the other believed, is sanctified by her faith for the relationship of husband, and hence their children must not be treated as "unclean" Pagan children, but as "the holy seed."

The whole argument seems to be this: To the question asked (by Jewish believers), "ought not a believer to separate from an unbelieving partner, and their marriage be dissolved?" The Apostle replies — No. If the unbeliever be pleased to continue with the believer, let them continue together, "for the unbeliever is sanctified by the believer," *i. e.*, both being "one flesh" [2] by lawful marriage before the conversion of the believer, the unbeliever in virtue of this union, is raised to a holier relationship, which so

[1] Hay *On Baptism*.

[2] There is a difference between the marriages here alluded to, and those formed by the Jews with Pagan nations. The marriage of a Jew with a Pagan, was contrary to law in the first instance, but a marriage between *two heathens* was according to law, and both consequently regarded as one flesh. The conversion of one afterwards may be supposed to pass an influence on the other, or at least entitle him to such privileges as the connection would justify. These privileges or benefits, so far affect his heathen state of uncleanness, that he must not be regarded in the same light with a heathen, but as one in a certain sense sanctified in consequence of the union preëxisting between the pair.

far entitles one to the privileges of the sanctified, that he must not be treated as unclean, but as fitted by this union for his marriage state — else were the children unclean and must be put away also; but now are they holy, for "the root being holy so are the branches also."

"If," says Dr. Whitby, "the *holy seed* among the Jews were circumcised and made federally holy, by receiving the sign of the covenant, and being admitted into the number of God's people, because they were born seminally holy — then by like reason the holy seed of Christians ought to be admitted to Baptism, and receive the sign of the Christian covenant, and so be entered into the society of the Christian Church." [1]

1. Seeing that this interpretation must admit Infant Baptism, some of its opposers have given the passage a different rendering; in doing which, they are compelled to change the meaning of the words "holy" (ἁγία) and "unclean" (ἀκάθαρτα) from that generally received to one nowhere else given to them in the Holy Scriptures! They render the passage in substance as follows: "For the unbelieving partner is sanctified by the believer, else were your children illegitimate, but now are they legitimate." Neither logic nor philology will admit of this interpretation. For if the question be one of a legal character only, in what sense can the believer add to or take from the lawfulness of the marriage, so as to make the children illegitimate? The children of heathen parents are certainly as legitimate in the eye of the law as they would be though one were a believer. And yet, according to the passage, were it not for some favorable influence of the believer, the children would be "unclean." This uncleanness cannot, therefore, be

[1] *Comment.* 1 Cor. vii. 14.

illegitimacy, because it depends on that which cannot affect the legality of the marriage.

But if the reasoning of the Apostle could be reconciled to this interpretation, the meaning of the words ἀκάθαρτα (unclean) and ἁγία (holy) cannot. For notwithstanding the very frequent use of these terms in the Sacred Scriptures, there is not one single place in which they are used in such a sense. Besides there are specific words in the Greek language for "legitimate and illegitimate," which rendered it necessary for the Apostle to use them in such a sense. Had he meant "illegitimate," he would, beyond a doubt, have used the same word νοθός (bastard) which he uses in his Epistle to the Hebrews (chap. xii. 8); and had he meant "legitimate," there was also its proper word γνήσιος. But referring to the Gentile and Christian state, as the whole argument goes to show, he used in their natural sense the proper words to convey what he meant — ἀκάθαρτα (unclean) and ἁγία (holy.) Instead of requiring these terms to be changed from their natural and proper usage, both the nature of the question and the character of the argument require them to be received in the same sense here, in which they are received in all other places in the Sacred Scriptures, and hence we should receive into the fold of Christ all to whom the appellation "holy" is therein applied, though but one of the parents of such children be a believer.

Others, who are opposed to Infant Baptism, but not willing to adopt an interpretation that changes words so entirely from their usual meaning as to render "holy and unclean" by "legitimate and illegitimate," would refer the reasoning of the Apostle to the relation existing between all Christian parents and their children — *i. e.*, the unbeliever is sanctified by the believer, else were the children of all Christian parents unclean to them and must be put away from them.

This interpretation is inconsistent with itself, for it opposes the idea that "holy and unclean" are used in a legal sense, and adopts that of a religious one, yet changes the religious sense of the terms employed, and issue in hand, by a general application of them to the children of all Christians. While the question is evidently confined to the case of an unbeliever living in wedlock with a believer, and the disadvantages that would accrue to the children, by a separation of such parents from each other. The argument being Jewish, the terms used must of course be of the same character, *i. e.*, according to their general acceptation among that people on such questions; and how could the Apostle expect to be understood, unless he used language as it was generally understood by those to whom he addressed himself? And if he does thus use it, what was understood by the term "holy" when applied to children or to persons among the Jews? What did they mean when the complaint was made, that the "holy seed have mingled themselves with the people of other lands?" And what law was that which was violated thereby, and which some of the judaizing Christians in Corinth thought ought to be applied to the case now brought before the Apostle? And in that law, how are the terms "unclean" and "holy," used? There is but one answer — all persons, of whatever age, called "holy," belonged to the community of God's people — were members of his Church. How then, could they imagine the Apostle to mean anything else, than that these children were to be regarded as all others to whom this appellation had been applied? His reasoning is just such as we might expect one Christian Jew to use with another, under such circumstances — employing language familiar to both. And we are, therefore, bound to give these terms their usual acceptation, and to regard the children to whom they are applied, as numbered with the people of God, and hence entitled to Baptism.

It is a common thing to change the address from the third to the second person; several instances of the kind are to be found in the same chapter to which these words belong — but the use of "holy" in any other than a religious sense, is unknown in the Holy Scriptures. Neither do they allow such a perversion of the first principles of reasoning, as that because religious parents are permitted to live with their little children, therefore it follows, believing and unbelieving husbands and wives may live together if they choose; nor that if you dissolve such marriages then you must dissolve the connection between all parents and children. By thus reversing the propositions you see there is no necessary connection between the premises and conclusions, the analogy fails, and such logic could satisfy no inquiring mind. It comes in direct conflict with the very principle that gave rise to the scruple; which, in order to protect the families and rising generation of the people of God from the corrupting influences of surrounding nations, forbade marriages with them, and made it a condition where such marriages had been contracted, that the partner and children must be abandoned before such an one could be received back among the holy seed.

But if Christian parents must all be separated from their children, according to Dr. Dagg's new theory, then the special object of separating the clean from the unclean, in the beginning, in order to preserve the holy seed from the corrupting influence of the unholy, is perverted, and *all children* cast out as alike unclean, and deprived of the training of pious parents, and the benefits of Christian association. Whereas the inference drawn by the Apostle evidently is — if you put away unbelieving husbands or wives, according to the law referred to, you must put away their children also — for on the same principle would they also be "*unclean.*" But under the Gospel it is different. Those marriages being lawful in the first place, and the man and wife being one in a certain sense, the act of the believer after their marriage redounds in part to the benefit of the other, and entitles him and his children to the privilege of remaining among the people of God if he chooses. "For *the unbelieving husband is sanctified by the wife, and the unbelieving wife is sanctified by the husband; else were your children unclean, but now are they holy.*"

It is strange that such a man as the Rev. Dr. Barnes could not see that it was *by or through the believing partner that* a supposed *religious disability* was removed, and not the *infidel state of the parent or separation* that would make the children civilly *illegitimate*, which would be a *non sequitur* in theory as it is in fact. His own references show that the term "unclean" is used in a *religious* and not in a mere *civil* sense. And the only rendering of the passage that *harmonizes the scope of the argument and the natural use of the terms* with a *logical conclusion* is, that which shows that the law against certain marriages in a former dispensation, did not apply in this case, and that the believing and unbelieving partner may continue together, and their children be treated as "holy"— baptized and numbered among God's people.

And this rendering is confirmed by the fact that the same Apostle addresses children as "saints" and "holy," in other places, and recognizes them as belonging to the Church with their parents. In his Epistles to the Church at Ephesus and at Colosse he enumerates under the title of "saints" (ἅγιοι) and "faithful" (πιστοί), *husbands, wives, masters, parents, and children* — evidently intending to include the whole of Christian families.

To the Church of Ephesus he writes: —

2. EPHESIANS i. 1. "Paul an Apostle of Jesus Christ by the will of God, *to the saints which are at Ephesus and to the faithful in Christ Jesus.*"

Now mark, that this Epistle is written to the Church — to the "saints and faithful," or members of a Christian body at Ephesus. It reads in chapter vi. 1, 2, 3, 4, "Children, obey your parents in the Lord, for this is right. Honor thy father and mother (which is the first commandment with promise), that it may be well with thee, and that thou mayest live long on the earth. And ye fathers provoke not your children to wrath: but bring them up in the nurture and admonition of the Lord."

Here are children addressed among the members of a Church, who are so young that they require the pious training and guidance of their parents in the duties of religion. Their parents are instructed how to bring them up — not to be so rigid and severe as to provoke and develop feelings of anger and crossness in their offspring, but to pursue a kind and gentle course of discipline; to exercise the authority and temper of Christian principles towards them; "*to bring them up in the nurture and admonition of the Lord.*" And thus they would enable them to fulfil the expectations of the Church, and prove themselves worthy of their high calling and name. That such is the meaning of the Apostle is clear from the general scope of the Epistle. After explaining certain doctrines, he then gives some advice and admonition of a practical character. And for this end he specifies the duties that are peculiar to every branch of a Christian family. He points out the corresponding duties of husbands and wives, of masters and servants, and of parents and children; all of whom are classed among the SAINTS, and the motives held forth to influence their conduct, such only as were of authority among Christians.

That the Apostle did not intend to confine himself to those children only who were verging into manhood and womanhood, and were capable of making a profession for themselves, is obvious from the fact that his words apply more especially to *young children*, who yet needed to be trained "in the nurture and admonition of the Lord." This was not so necessary to one capable of a profession on his own responsibility, as for younger members of a family.

Besides, who can suppose that one guided by the principles of Him who so loved little children that He was offended with others for attempting to keep them away from Him — would write for the benefit of every other member of a household, and pass over the little children in silence? not say a single word — or intimate that the parent was bound in Christian love to his dependent little ones, who had souls that needed training, and parental supervision, and heavenly instruction as much as the older children, who had grown up and were able to choose for themselves! What — think it important that the corresponding duties of husband and wife, master and servant, parent and older children should be attended to; but the younger children, whose tender minds are so susceptible of good impressions, and on whose early training so much depends, not worthy of mention, and passed over as forming no portion of that race for whom the Saviour died! believe it who can. No — the Apostle had more of his Master's spirit, than to go into a Christian family and give directions for the benefit of every one in it, and not think of the "little ones" — not even give them a kind look, for that would have called forth some remark concerning them. He acted far otherwise — he included *all the children*, and especially the *younger ones* that still needed the watchful care and kind instruction of their parents, and he instructed their parents to train them in the discipline and doctrine of Christ and his religion; as all little children should be trained.

And he calls them all "faithfuls" (πιστοῖς) — members of the Christian Church, and commands that they be instructed as Christians — that they be governed and guided with kindness and tenderness in the doctrines of the Gospel of Christ — not treated with harshness, or ruled with a tyranny that would provoke and discourage them. To the same effect he wrote also to the Church at Colosse.

3. Colossians i. 1, 2. "Paul, an Apostle of Jesus Christ by the will of God and Timotheus our brother, *to the saints and faithful brethren in Christ which are at Colosse.*" iii. 20, 21. "*Children, obey*

your parents in all things; for this is well-pleasing unto the Lord. Fathers, provoke not your children to anger, lest they be discouraged."

The same principles are inculcated in regard to children in this Epistle, that were inculcated in that sent to the Church at Ephesus. Children are addressed and recognized as members of the Church, and duties are laid down for their observance, and that of their parents. They must be trained with the same care and faithfulness as the children of the Ephesian Christians. And the admonition is addressed to them, and penned for all, as soon as capable of understanding it, that the highest Authority requires them to obey and honor their father and mother. Such instruction gave more importance and authority to the teaching of their parents, and hence aided them in their work of training. But only the simplest form of truth is written to the children — not things difficult to understand — not such doctrines as require children to be grown up nearly to manhood to comprehend. On the contrary, they are among the most simple and easy duties that can be taught the infant mind; because they express the natural feelings of an innocent age. The duty to obey its mother is among the first things that a child learns. To love and honor father and mother is a lesson soon felt and understood. So that the children addressed, are called upon to attend to the first, or what ought to be the first duties, that are taught them.

The object the Apostle had in view, was doubtless the due observance of the duties arising from the corresponding relations of the different members of a Christian family — and the great end of making all the children, young and old, Christians in heart as well as in name. All of them should be trained in the way that will promote that end, and therefore much care and caution ought to be exercised, lest they be discouraged by a want of prudence on the part of those to whom this great work is committed.

And as these Epistles were written to *members* of the Church, enforcing duties on only *Christian principles*, and little children included, the membership of little children is therefore recognized by St. Paul.

In conformity to the custom of the sacred writers in applying the terms "saints" and "faithful" to children without regard to age, and as *confirmation* of the above interpretation, we find from the sepulchral inscriptions of the early Christians that they applied the same terms to those who belonged to the Christian Church, whatever might be their age. We select a few of the many that are still preserved. [1]

4. "A 'FAITHFUL,' descended from ancestors who were 'FAITHFULS,' here lies Zosimus: he lived two years, one month, and twenty-five days."

The symbol of a *fish* and *anchor* accompanies this inscription, which marks the age to which it belonged. The fish and anchor as symbols, were in general use among Christians in the second century, and early part of the third, and is approved by Tertullian and Clemens Alexandrinus.

This child was a "faithful," *i. e.*, a church-member at two years of age. Descended from parents who were "faithfuls," and who caused him to be baptized in infancy, which shows how they understood the Apostolic injunction. Again —

"Posthumius Euthenion, a faithful Christian brother, accompanied with the Holy Grace. On the day before his sixth birth-

[1] Taken from Taylor's *Facts and Evidences.*

day, early, he gave back that which he had received — his life. He lived six years, and was buried the fifth of the ides of July on a Thursday, on which day he was born: whose soul is with the Holy One in peace. Erected to a well-deserving son, Posthumius, by order of his grandmother Euthenia Fytista."

This has the word ΙΧΘΥΣ, a "fish," at the top, and forming an acrostic down the side, which was a private mark of Christian sepulchres, to preserve them from violation by the rude hands of the heathen in primitive times. He is called a "faithful Christian brother," yet died before he was six years old.

"Cyriacus, a 'FAITHFUL,' died aged eight days less than three years."

"Eustafia, the mother, places this in commemoration of her son Polichronis, a FAITHFUL, who lived three years."

"To Pisentus, an innocent soul, who lived one year, eight months, and thirteen days. NEWLY BAPTIZED, buried on the ides of September, in peace."

"Achillia, NEWLY BAPTIZED, is buried here; she died at the age of one year and five months."

The figure of a dove accompanies this last inscription, which was also a symbol of the second century, and derived, says Taylor, from an earlier period. She, though only one year and five months old, was baptized.

We might adduce many others of the same kind, all preserved as belonging to the primitive and persecuting days of Christianity, illustrating and testifying to the truth, that the Apostles and their first successors baptized the young children of Christians, and that the terms "holy and faithful," which are applied in the Holy Scriptures to children without regard to age, were continued to be used in the same way for several centuries, and that church-membership and family Baptisms were never limited by age in the primitive Church.

The same use of the term "faithful" applied to the directions of St. Paul to Titus respecting the qualifications of a bishop, would give them an easy, natural interpretation that would harmonize also with similar directions to Timothy, and with what has been the practice of Christians in every age of the Church.

5. TITUS i. 6, 7. "*If any be blameless, the husband of one wife, having faithful children, not accused of riot, not unruly. For a bishop must be blameless as the steward of God.*"

Now the phrase "*faithful children,*" in the language of the Holy Scriptures, literally means "believing children." And if it be a *necessary qualification* for the office of stewards and bishops of the Church that their children be believers, in what sense must they be so? The parent cannot be held directly responsible for the conversion of his children, nor even for the morality of those who are grown up. And if such be the condition on which offices in the Church are to be filled, how many now would have to lay aside their authority and enter into a more humble sphere! And what branch of the Church has ever acted on that principle?

But if the Apostle meant that the children of such had been numbered among the "faithful" by Baptism and Christian nurture, and kept in proper subjection and not allowed to run riot and grow up as heathen children, then there would be a propriety in selecting such an one as fitted to rule the Church. The term "faithful" would be applied in its usual Scriptural sense, and the fitness of the individual inferred from his own acts, not from that which was beyond his control.

And this accords perfectly with what was written to Timothy on the same subject: —

6. 1 TIMOTHY iii. 4, 5. "*One that ruleth well his own house, having his children in subjection with all gravity: (For if a man know not how to rule his own house, how shall he take care of the Church of God.)*"

"To rule well one's own house having his children in subjection with all gravity," is just what every Christian should do, and especially those who undertake to rule or take care of the Church. And to do this they must "bring up their children in the nurture and admonition of the Lord," which is indeed only another form of words to convey the same ideas. Where polygamy had been indulged in before their conversion to Christianity, and the children of such marriages were in part or in whole in the hands of heathen mothers, or on account of other reasons the children were neglected and their religious training not attended to by the parent, such an one was unfit to be a ruler of the Church, both as an exemplar and guide to the flock. Not so with him who had one wife and a Christian family all living in harmony together, governed by Christian doctrine. He was worthy of his position as a husband and father, showed good fidelity as a Christian, did what he could for the salvation of his children, ruled well his own house, and hence so far, his faithfulness was a guarantee and pledge that he would rule well the Church. And although some of his children when grown up might not prove to be "faithful," worthy of such a father; yet in that family one might look for some of each class of such persons as St. John addresses in his General Epistle.

7. 1 JOHN ii. 12, 13. "*I write unto you little children, because your sins are forgiven you for his name's sake. I write unto you fathers, because ye have known*

Him that is from the beginning. I write unto you young men, because ye have overcome the wicked one."

This is a general epistle written for all Christians, and although "little children," is a phrase sometimes used in a metaphorical sense by this Apostle, and in different senses in this same epistle, yet when he divides Christians into such natural divisions, as fathers, young men, and little children, we can see no reason for supposing they are metaphorical divisions. "*I write unto you little children, because your sins are forgiven you for his name's sake.*" "If it be asked, when were their sins forgiven them?" the Ancient Church replies, "I acknowledge ONE *Baptism* for the remission of sins:" and the Ancient Church was right, says Taylor. "These little children were admitted into the Church by Baptism, administered for the remission of sins."[1] (Mark i. 4; Luke iii. 3; Acts ii. 38.)

And if the attentive reader will interpret the Holy Scriptures in a natural way, according to the scope of the writer, in those passages that refer to little children, to families, and to the subjects of Baptism generally, he will find infant membership and family religion particularly *pointed* to, or more indistinctly *implied*, and *taken for granted* throughout. But if he chooses to make exceptions of such passages, and seeks to evade such meaning, and closes his ears against every other kind of evidence, then nothing but an *absolute specific command* or *example* will be received as authority — and he thereby sets himself up as a teacher to the Holy Spirit, and prescribes to Him the manner in which He should communicate the will of Heaven, and the only conditions on which he will receive and

[1] See Taylor *On Apostolic Baptism.*

obey his instructions! On the same principle he may reject the *Trinity* and other important doctrines and duties, because not made known in the specific manner which he demands.[1]

But such as are willing to be taught in God's way, who are ready to receive the truth in any mode that He may choose to convey it, and are ready to use all necessary means to know the truth, we invite to a liberal and impartial examination of the passages to which we have referred. Why should we desire anything beyond the will of God in this matter? If we wish to exclude little children, after they have been received for two thousand years by express law into covenant with God, why not seek for some positive precept or enactment by which that law has been repealed, and their former privileges not allowed under the New Dispensation? And if this you cannot find, why attempt to *limit* the application of passages, to prove in a negative way that they do not *necessarily imply* their former privileges, and therefore they shall not be continued?

The first Christians did not understand the Apostles to teach that their young children must no longer be included in covenanted privileges with the chosen of God; for as already noticed, they continued to circumcise them as they had done before they embraced the Gospel, and under the belief too (at *least many*, if not *all*), that it was absolutely necessary in the new Church state. For when the Gospel was embraced by the Gentiles, "certain Jewish teachers" insisted that cir-

[1] Dr. Carson excludes Infants in the commission to "disciple all nations" because they cannot believe, — then applies this RULE to all passages referring to or implying Infants, and thus easily *disposes* of them. But would it not be more in accordance with the Christian spirit to learn God's will in whatever way He may choose to make it known, and examine every passage on its own merits and thereby *test the correctness* of the RULE to be of such general application.

cumcision must be observed by them also as the indispensable duty of Christians. "Except ye be circumcised after the manner of Moses, ye cannot be saved." (Acts xv. 1.)

Now how could these men continue a religious rite among their little children,[1] which rite they supposed was a necessary part of the Christian system, and binding on every member, if Baptism had ever been denied to their children, and they taught that young children were no longer entitled to church-membership? And if they believed that they were still entitled to membership, can any one suppose that they would continue to circumcise them under the reign of the Messias and not complete their membership by the appointed mode of Baptism into the name of the King of the new and more perfect organization of grace?

8. Let us place this properly before us. The Gospel was first preached to the Jews, and confined to them exclusively (Acts x., xi., xiv.), until after it had been proclaimed and spread throughout the Jews' territory. Canaan, Judæa, Samaria, and Galilee had all heard its joyful sound, and thousands hearkened and believed. The churches for some years, therefore, were composed exclusively of Jewish believers. They believed Jesus to be the true Messiah, and received Him as the promised Saviour of the world. And they entered into the Christian covenant by Baptism; but what became of their young children who were with them under the old covenant? Did they leave them behind? Or did they bring them with themselves into the Christian covenant? Is anything written, as said or done, that would lead them to suppose that their young children were no longer to be regarded as having any connection with

[1] Acts xxi. 21, 22.

the Church? Nothing is recorded to that effect; on the contrary, they continue to circumcise them as they had always done, which shows they still regarded them as entitled to church-membership; for they regarded the Christian Church as a continuation or enlargement of their former Church, and Christian rites as additional ceremonies in this more enlarged and perfect state. Under this belief must they not have baptized all who were circumcised, unless prohibited by the Apostles? And if prohibited from Baptism, why is nothing said about it, and yet so much contention about circumcision? Would it not be marvellous for a Jew, with all his love for the customs and principles of his fathers, to keep perfect silence, if informed that his little children must be excluded from the Gospel covenant? And yet we hear not of a single complaint on this subject from the beginning to the end of the New Testament. Could this have been so had their children been refused Baptism?

Such was the zeal with which certain believers among them contended for the necessity of circumcision to Gentile Christians, that it was made a matter of much disputation, and a Council called to settle it: which decided in the negative, and letters were then sent by messengers to different places informing Gentile Christians that Mosaic ceremonies were not binding upon them; but recommending that they should follow that which will promote the peace of the Church — *i. e.*, "to abstain from meats offered to idols, from blood, and from things strangled, and from fornication."[1] Nothing is said in regard to any rite or duty peculiarly Christian, because there was no disagreement about anything peculiar to the Chris-

[1] Acts xv. 1, 29.

tian system. To this the Gentiles had strictly conformed. Baptism is not mentioned, because this they had received, and there was no disputation about it; nor should we have heard anything about circumcision had they been so unanimous on that point as they were in regard to Baptism. Had the Gentiles hesitated to baptize their children, or the Apostles refused it previously to the children of Jewish Christians, there would have been room or cause for as much controversy about Baptism as about circumcision. But there is not one word on record to show that the Apostles or any one else ever taught them to regard their children as excluded from the Christian covenant.[1] On the contrary, Gospel liberty permitted the Jewish believers to observe the whole law of Moses as long as it was not substituted for Christ, nor made obligatory on the Gentile Christians. When, however, they began to substitute works for grace, and place Moses before Christ, a warning voice was quickly raised, and the evils pointed out.

If any one doubts the adherence of Jewish believers to circumcision, even after the decision of the Council (Acts xv.) that forbade them to *impose it* on the Gentiles, let him turn to the 21st chapter of the Acts and read what St. James and the Elders say to the Apostle Paul touching this point (verses 21, 22). "Thou seest, brother, how many thousands[2] [tens of thousands] of the Jews there are which believe, and they are all zealous of the law; and they are informed of thee that thou teachest all the Jews which are

[1] The fact that they urged circumcision on the Gentile converts, proves they regarded circumcision as necessary to all Christians and young children as members, because circumcision was as binding on children as on adults.

[2] μυριάδες, "myriads."

among the Gentiles to forsake Moses — saying that they ought not to circumcise their children, neither walk after the customs. What is it, therefore? the multitude must needs come together, for they will hear that thou art come." See how soon an excitement is produced by the rumor that the Apostle taught, their children need not be circumcised.

This visit to Jerusalem was made by St. Paul, according to the best chronologers,[1] about twenty-five years after the first preaching of St. Peter, and the conversion of the three thousand. The Jewish converts had now, as we learn, increased to many thousands, and were "all zealous of the law" of Moses. A report that the Apostle Paul had been teaching their brethren scattered among the Gentiles, that "they ought not to circumcise their children, nor observe their customs," had caused much excitement; to allay which, the Apostle, by advice, conforms publicly to a certain Jewish rite (verses 23, 27), to satisfy the Jews that he was not an enemy to Moses rightly understood. For if he could observe the ritual law *himself*, it ought to convince them that he would not forbid others to do the same under proper instructions, and that he himself lived according to the real requirements of Moses — according to the very thing *shadowed* forth by him.

By this act, we learn there is nothing in the ritual of Moses that a conscientious Christian might not observe, provided he in no way substituted it for the Gospel. It was of course *unnecessary* to the Christian, because the ritual law was merely the shadow of the more substantial things to come under Christ. And this he did not hesitate to declare (Col. ii.,

[1] Horne, Whitby, Townsend, and others.

Heb. x.) and to show that justification was by faith, and not by the deeds of the law. "By the deeds of the law shall no flesh be justified" (Rom. iii. 20), was the tenor of his language. "A man is justified by faith without the deeds of the law." (28th verse.) He proved to them also from the case of Abraham that "Christ is the end of the law for righteousness, to every one that believeth." (Rom. x. 4.) And in all suitable ways did he labor to show the use of the law, moral and ceremonial, and to discourage too strong an attachment for the law of ceremonies, forbidding even its observance, if looked to for justification. (Gal. v. 4.) "Christ is become of no effect unto you whosoever of you are justified by the law; ye are fallen from grace." . . . . "For in Christ Jesus neither circumcision availeth anything nor uncircumcision, but faith which worketh by love."

Can any one suppose that an Apostle who was so constant and unwearied in his efforts to teach, and to keep the minds of Christians rightly informed as to the nature and uses of the law, would permit the Jewish Christians to circumcise their children under a belief that infants still stood in the same relation to the Church they always had done, and never correct their delusion, if this had been one? Can we suppose that such a man as the Apostle Paul, and all the Apostles would so dissemble with the first Christians as to indulge them in an erroneous belief of this kind, and never correct it? It is impossible. Common honesty—their course in regard to every other error, to say nothing of piety, forbids the supposition. Yet where do we find a single sentence, in all the disputes about circumcision, or in all the instructions given in regard to the law, its uses, and the reasons for its discontinuance, or in Christ's commission to his Apostles, or his remarks about *little children*, that even *intimates* that there is to be any change in their case under the Gospel dispensation? Nowhere. Such an intimation is not to be found in the sacred record. Therefore Christians are bound by *testimony*, *positive* and *negative* in its character — *historical*, *circumstantial*, and *inspired* —to *continue infant membership and family religion in the Church of God.*

1. IT IS A FACT, that Infant Baptism was the acknowledged doctrine and common practice of the Christian Church in the next age after the Apostles.

2. IT IS A FACT, that Infant Baptism was the received doctrine and usage of Christians before the books of the New Testament had *all* been received among the various Churches, and the question of their inspiration settled.

3. IT IS A FACT, that Christian contemporaries of the Apostles, and the Primitive Fathers generally, taught that "all ages, young and old, were corrupt through the infection of original sin, and therefore Baptism was (in a ritual sense) necessary to all."

4. IT IS A FACT, that Infant Baptism had the consentient testimony of all antiquity to its validity; that this was believed "everywhere, always, by all," in the Primitive Church, so far as anything to the contrary has been found on record.

5. IT IS A FACT, that the most noted of the early Christian Fathers taught that Baptism had superseded circumcision — that it held the same place under the New Dispensation which circumcision held under the Old, and hence they called Baptism "Christian circumcision."

6. IT IS A FACT, that the first Christians (Jews) did for some time keep both the old Sabbath and the Lord's day, and practised both Baptism and circumcision; and that circumcision and the Jewish Sabbath gradually ceased to be observed in the Church, leaving only Baptism and the Lord's day remaining. Therefore, as an initiatory rite, Baptism has superseded circumcision; and as a day of rest, the Lord's day has superseded the old Sabbath. And, —

7. IT HAS BEEN SHOWN, that the Christian Church is the continuation of the Abrahamic Covenant of Grace in things spiritual (Gal. iii. 15, 17; Matt. xxi. 43; Rom. xi. 17, 18, and others), enlarged in its application to subjects, but more exclusively spiritual in its discipline. Hence, Baptism holds the *same place* in the *same Church*, and fulfils the *same spiritual ends* of circumcision, and by virtue of the right of little children to circumcision, they have an *unquestionable legal right to Baptism.*

8. IT HAS BEEN SHOWN, that the first Christians received the Gospel as the fulfilment of the promises made to their fathers, and the continuation and development of that which was already begun, and hence they continued the circumcision of their little children and other rites of the Jewish Church, which proves that they still regarded little children as members, which they would not have done if Baptism had been denied them. And,

9. IT HAS BEEN SHOWN, that the mistake of Hebrew Christians in supposing that with the continuation of the Abrahamic Covenant of Grace, its types and the Mosaic economy were also to be continued under the Gospel Dispensation; would have been corrected in the beginning, if when they passed into the Gospel Dispensation by Baptism, their little children

were not allowed to pass with them — refused entrance with simply the remark, " They cannot be baptized." A thing so contrary to the feelings, education, and practice of a Jew, must have called up discussion in regard to circumcision and the Baptism of little children in the very commencement of the New Dispensation. Instead of which, the circumcision of little children by Jewish members was quietly continued for some years, and when Gentile converts were brought into the Church, the same was urged upon them also, as a necessary Christian duty.[1] Had Baptism been denied to all the little children circumcised up to that time, how could the strict adherent to Moses suppose that the two rights, so long separated, must now be united? Admit, however, that their little ones had also been baptized, then silence on the subject to that time, and the union of the two rites on Gentile converts, would be natural. And, —

10. WE HAVE SEEN, that instead of closing the door of his kingdom against little children, the Saviour Himself rebuked those who attempted to keep the little ones from Him when on earth, and took them up in his arms and blessed them, saying, " Of such is the kingdom of God." (St. Mark x. 13–16; also Sts. Matt. and Luke.)

11. WE HAVE SEEN, that instead of limiting their privileges, and excluding them from his covenant under the Gospel Dispensation, the Saviour issued his commission to the Apostles in terms of the *widest possible comprehension, embracing all nations;* and when construed according to the established laws of interpreting ancient writings, apply to little children as strictly as to adults. (Matt. xxviii. 19, 20), etc.

12. WE HAVE SEEN, that in the first sermon

[1] Acts xv. 5–29.

preached under the Gospel Dispensation, the promise made to *children* with their parents, was referred to by St. Peter. To the inquiring multitude, he said, " The promise is to you and to your children." (Acts. ii. 38, 39.)

13. WE HAVE SEEN, that the Apostles baptized whole families, without respect to age, so far as the record shows ; for family Baptisms are recorded as if a usual thing, and only the names of the heads of them mentioned, as if they alone were the responsible agents. (Acts xvi. 13–19, 31–33 ; 1 Cor. i. 14–16, etc.)

14. WE HAVE SEEN, that children are included in the Epistles written to the Churches, and instructions given them, and to their parents concerning them ; and that the same appellations of "faithfuls" and "holy" are applied to them that are applied to other members of the Church. (1 Cor. vii. 12–14 ; Eph. i. 1 ; Col. i. 2 ; Phil. i. 1.)

FINALLY, the faithfulness of the parent in "bringing up his children in the nurture and admonition of the Lord," was regarded by St. Paul as a necessary qualification for the appointment to the office of a ruler in the Church. (1 Timothy iii. 4, 5 ; Titus i. 6, 7 ; 1 John ii. 12, 13.)

Who, therefore, can be surprised at finding the Baptism of little children continuing to be the common practice of the next generation after the Apostles ?

§ 28. Whether we go up the stream from the present to the Apostolic age, we shall find young children received into the Church during every stage of our ascent,— or whether we start from the days of Abraham and come down it, we shall find them made members of the Church at every succeeding step. And on reaching the days of the Saviour, instead of the slightest intimation that a change is then to take place, everything is of the opposite character. His own words and acts, and the words and acts of the Apostles, rightly construed, show that young children are still to be received and doubtless *were received.* And in passing into the next age, we find their Baptism common — and not one calling in question the authority for it.

Now were we to admit that the Holy Scriptures are silent on the subject (which they certainly are not, when rightly construed), how shall we account for the fact that in following the stream of time, we find little children in the Church until we reach the Apostolic age, and then again as soon as we leave it? Suppose, in ascending a river, we were to find in its waters certain peculiar qualities till we reach a certain place through which we could not pass, and were compelled to travel by land some miles before we came to the river again, but at the point at which we entered, find its waters possessing the same peculiar qualities that we marked in them at the time we left it, should we not conclude that they possessed the same peculiar qualities between these two points? Could we doubt it?

Now apply this to the case in hand. The opposers of Infant Baptism must admit that from the time of Abraham to that of Christ, young children were received into covenant with God — and again, that from the first age after the Apostles down to the present time, they have been received into the Church. What then may we infer was probably the case during the time the Apostles lived? Were the qualities of the waters the same while passing over that short space, that they were just before, and just afterwards; or were they different between these points and precisely the same again at them? Were little children made members of the Church just before, and again, just after the Apostolic age, but excluded during that century, and not one word left on record to inform us of the fact? Nay, the language of the record rightly construed, informs us in various places, that little children were received into the Church during that century as well as every other, that they have always been precious in the sight of God, and ever permitted to form a part of his peculiar people. "*That of such is the kingdom of God.*" (Mark x. 14.)

1. And why not? If he who adds sins of his own to his original sin, shall on repentance have all his sins washed away, both actual and original, may not he who has committed no sin of his own have his original sin washed away? Is it necessary to add to original sin actual sins, to repent of, before one can have the remission of any sin? Think for a moment — we are all born in sin, inheritors of Adam's fallen nature, "shapen in iniquity," and "by nature the children of wrath;"— every child, therefore, born into the world has *original or birth sin*, and this, which is the root and foundation of *actual sin*, needs a remedy and the appliances of Gospel grace, as much as do the effects flowing from it; and Baptism having been ordained by Christ as the means or visible sign of the washing away of all sin, why withhold it from those involved in original sin, because they have not superadded actual sins?

If to every unconscious babe of Adam's descendants a sin stained nature has been transmitted, and Baptism is the ordained means of washing away only *actual sins*, what becomes of all who die before they commit actual sins? Do they die in a polluted, unforgiven state? and are all infants lost? If not, and Christ has atoned for their original sin, why withhold the cleansing ordinance of Gospel grace and the blessings vouchsafed to his redeemed ones? If repentance and faith after actual sin, entitle one to the seal of the forgiveness of all sin actual and original, certainly they who have been redeemed and committed no actual sin of their own of which to repent, ought to be entitled to the seal of the forgiveness of original sin, and to all the blessings conveyed thereby.

2. Christ died to redeem little children as well as adults. The sin of the first Adam passed upon all, and the provision made in the second Adam is commensurate with the evils of the first. "As by the offence of one, judgment came upon all men to condemnation; even so by the righteousness of one, the free gift came upon all men unto justification of life. For as by one man's disobedience many were made sinners, so by the obedience of one shall many be made righteous. . . . Where sin abounded grace did much more abound." (Rom. v. 18, 19, 20.) Hence the remedy provided is coëxtensive with the evil entailed, and offered as a free gift to all. And little children being involved in the sin of the first Adam, are therefore included in the provision made by the second. And,—

For the more effectual application of the remedy, God instituted his church as a nursery or school, and ordained means whereby the graces and gifts of the Holy Spirit are nurtured and made more effective in enlivening and invigorating the spiritual powers of the soul, to fit it for his spiritual kingdom. Into this nursery all are brought by Baptism, and none can need its protecting care and aid more than little children, and the sooner they are taken into it, and the more faithfully they are nurtured and instructed in the ways of godliness, the more certainly will they become fitted for that spiritual Church for which this on earth was founded. Had half the time and labor consumed in discussions and theorizing about the *effects* of Baptism, been devoted to the duties implied and the faithful discharge of the obligations imposed, a thousand-fold greater would have been the benefits conferred on the Church.

3. The great end, doubtless, of all the institutions of our blessed Redeemer, is to save the souls of fallen men. For this He came to earth and died; for this He founded a church and ordained means of grace; and the more faithfully we adhere to the order that He has authorized, and use the means that He has appointed, the more successful will every one be in fitting himself and his children for the kingdom of heaven. The more diligently we instruct our children, and the more tenderly we lead them on in the duties of religion; the more cautiously we preserve them from evil, and the more thoroughly we imbue them with the principles and practices of his Church; the more certain will be our success in making them truly Christians, not by trusting to the letter and opus operatum of ordinances, but looking to and invoking the accompanying influence of the Holy Spirit on our efforts.

To affirm that children can be trained in the ways of religion as well out of the Church as in it, is the same as to affirm that men can be saved as well without a church as with one. It is virtually impeaching the wisdom of God in organizing a Church at all. And to ask, as some ignorantly do, "What good can Baptism do little children?" is to ask, what good can it do an adult? For there is no reason why it may not do as much for one age as another. Hence the implied objection would make it unnecessary *to any one*. And yet our Saviour says, "Except a man," *any one* (ἐὰν μή τις) "be born of water and of the Spirit, he cannot enter into the kingdom of God."

4. Now which shall rule us, the words of Christ, or of heedless objectors? He certainly regarded Baptism as of great importance, or He would not have made it necessary "to enter into his kingdom." And whether He meant his kingdom on earth or in heaven, or included both, does not affect the *authority* of his words, nor the *obligations* which they impose upon every one. Neither can difference of opinion on the *effects* of Baptism, affect its *necessity* and importance where it can be had. Whether it regenerates men in a lower or higher sense — in a moral, or spiritual sense only: whether it is both the outward visible *sign* and *means* of inward spiritual grace, as well as a *pledge* to assure us thereof — whether it washes away original sin in infants and applies to them the redemption of Christ, thus transferring them from under the condemnation of the first Adam into the liberty and blessings of the second — or whether it is only the sign and outward recognition of the washing away of sin, and of the application of Christ's atonement, certifying to them their redemption, and placing them in new relations to God; *the authority is the same, and being Divine, no man may lay it aside.* Even upon the lowest theory in regard to its office, it may possess an importance in the economy of grace far beyond our highest conceptions.

Because one "believes the child baptized is washed from the guilt of original sin, and grafted into the mystical body of Christ and made partaker of the Spirit," — and he calls this "regeneration and the new birth," — and when a penitent soul turns with all his heart from sin and Satan to God and holiness, this he calls "conversion," which, he says, "may take place before or after regeneration;" and another believes regeneration includes conversion; it does not follow that there is no regeneration or conversion. Nor does it follow, because there are differences of opinion in regard to the *effects* of Baptism on adult age, that there is no authority for the Baptism of that age. On the same principle, differences of opinion in regard to the *effects* of Infant Baptism, constitute no valid objection to the authority of the practice itself. All agree that Baptism puts the child into a new state — removes it from its birth-state of bondage, into the liberty of the children of grace — makes it a member of Christ's church — surrounds it with all the means of grace — secures to it the covenant seal and pledge of forgiveness of all sin; and that if the conditions of this covenant or engagement be fulfilled, it will finally be admitted into the upper kingdom of God.

Here is enough to fill every heart with the deepest solicitude for the Baptism of little ones; and if greater blessings still, as some suppose, accompany the ordinance, then greater, if possible, ought to be that solicitude. And if so much interest be justly felt, in regard to bringing them into covenant relations with God, deeper and greater still should be our anxiety for the fulfilment of every condition expressed or implied in that covenant. An estate may be made over to a minor on conditions and promises made for him by his guardian, and the covenant be signed and sealed, and the estate called by his name, and spoken of as his, yet if he violates the conditions, he forfeits the possession! which may be owing chiefly to the neglect of the guardian in instructing him, and impressing his mind with the importance of what was involved, and the nature of the conditions to be fulfilled.

So, when parents bring their little children to Baptism, they should remember that it is to make them members of Christ's Church and heirs of the kingdom of heaven; that for them and in their names they promise to fulfil all the duties of a member of his Church: to wit, "bring them up in the nurture and admonition of the Lord." So train and instruct them in the doctrines and practices of his religion, that by the blessings of the Holy Spirit, they shall never depart from them, but fulfil all the conditions of their heirship. For this end, let the first impressions made upon their tender minds be heavenly in their nature. Preserve them from evil influences without, and bring the appliances of gospel grace with its quickening and sanctifying power through the spirit to bear upon their impressible hearts from infancy to manhood. Lead them on from one degree of knowledge to another. Instruct them in first principles and then in higher branches. Show them the privileges and advantages of being a member of Christ's Church. Appeal to them as members, and gradually prepare them to understand and rightly appreciate the responsibility of their membership.

It does not follow that because one is a member of Christ's Church, he is therefore qualified for all its duties, or can enjoy all the privileges of membership, any more than because one is a citizen of our country, therefore he enjoys all the privileges of citizenship. A child enjoys all the *essential rights* of a citizen; has a claim to the protection and all the privileges common to the citizens of his country, but he has not the right to vote in the election of the rulers of his country before he is twenty-one years of age, nor to exercise other functions dependent on conditions which he cannot or has not fulfilled. So infant members of the Church enjoy all the essential rights of its covenanted blessings — its seal and promises, the right of instruction, means of grace, and fostering care. But they are not qualified for the higher privileges of adult members, to vote in the councils of the Church, and to partake of the Lord's supper profitably — not being able to "discern the Lord's body" by faith (1 Cor. xi. 29); which is an important privilege, and for which all diligence should be used to prepare them as soon as possible.

It has been supposed by some, that because infants partook of the Passover at its first institution, which was to be a commemorative rite, therefore the sacrament of the Supper might be given to them. But it does not appear that the children of the Jews partook of the Passover after they were settled in Canaan till after twelve years of age. Such was the custom in our Saviour's time.[1] The Passover, however, was a part of the Mosaic covenant, not of the Abrahamic, and therefore does not stand on the same ground with circumcision.

From the nature of things, the Church on earth must be composed of various classes of members, consisting not only of different degrees of growth in grace, but of some absolutely bad as well as good.

[1] St. Luke ii. 41, 42.

This our Saviour told us would be the case, and compared his Church to a "net that was cast into the sea and gathered of every kind, which when it was full they drew to shore, and sat down and gathered the good into vessels, but cast the bad away." (St. Matt. xiii. 47, 48.) And the proportion of the good to the bad of every family gathered into this net, will depend, doubtless, more upon the *faithfulness* of the parents in training up their children than upon any other earthly means. Nothing human has so much influence on the formation of character in after life as faithful training in childhood and early youth. The future man is generally formed and fashioned in the nursery. The moral and religious sentiments there instilled into the minds of our children accompany them through life. If shaken off at any time, they will return, unless thrown under contrary influence and teaching before their characters are formed. It sometimes happens that they are sent from under the parental roof, and exposed to infidel and immoral influences so young, that all that had been done for them in earlier years is lost.

But this is like leaving any other important work unfinished. If we would *establish* them in the doctrines and habits of morality and religion, we must *train them up* to manhood and womanhood; not *begin* to train them and *stop* before their *habits* are *half formed*, but *continue* the good work till it is completed; until they are confirmed in the ways of truth. To train a child a few years and give it up unto its own heart's desires, or expose it to evil influences, is like rolling a stone half up the mountain side, and leaving it to itself to roll down again to the base. Fallen nature needs training *up to manhood*, as the stone should be rolled onward till it reaches the mountain top and rests on the plain above where we would have it placed, if we would crown our efforts with success. How many are ruined because taken from under the pious nurture of the mother, or catechetical class of the minister, before confirmed in the doctrines and duties of religion!

All experience testifies to the importance of training children in the principles and practices which we would have them to continue through life. But to have them baptized, and then neglect to train them in the principles and according to the conditions stipulated, is virtually to renounce their Baptism. It is like making a minor an heir to an estate, as already referred to, and then refusing the aid necessary to enable him to comply with the conditions of its final possession. And it is for this reason that the Church of God in every age has required some security for the faithful training in the ways of the Lord the little ones brought to it for Baptism; that the members of the Church who bring their infant children to dedicate them to God in his Church, and make them members of the same, shall pledge themselves to train them as such members ought to be trained. The Protestant Episcopal Church in this country requires, where it can be had, additional security to that of the parents, for every male child two male securities and one female, and for every female child two female securities and one male; which are called "God-fathers and God-mothers," or "sureties." So important does she hold the proper training of her infant members, that she provides a substitute and aid to the parents, in the case of their death or neglect of this great duty. And all necessary instructions and care beyond this, devolve immediately upon her authorized ministers.

Were it not that Baptism is only the beginning — the initiative of a great and glorious inheritance, requiring future corresponding action, we might baptize every child we meet in the street, if permitted, for all have been redeemed by Christ; but where there is no reason to hope they will ever comply with the conditions of the covenant, it is better to await more favorable indications of Divine Providence. Why encourage an abuse, and bring into disrepute things sacred, that may be even trampled upon and cast away by those to whom they are given? In cases of danger, where death, instead of a long life and the prospect of a better state of things, seems to be the only alternative, we baptize without sureties, if necessary, because we would not withhold from the dying any benefit conferred by the sacrament itself. And if the child live, we use all diligence to secure for it afterwards the necessary nurture and instruction of a child of the Church.

But in all cases where there is the ordinary prospect of continued life in the child, it should be presented for Baptism by pious sponsors, who conscientiously intend to fulfil the duties required at their hands by the Church. If the parents are not such themselves, and wish their children to be baptized, they should procure responsible persons, and pledge themselves to give up these children to the religious training of them who shall consent to act in their places, and fulfil the corresponding duties; which is a serious undertaking, and ought to be well weighed by every sponsor before such responsibility is assumed.

Alas! how often do we find that even members of the Church dedicate their children to God in infancy, and promise to His Church in His presence, to train them in the duties and doctrines of the Church ; but afterwards give up these same children to the care and teaching of those whom they know to hold doctrines contrary to those which they pledged themselves to teach them! For the sake of some vain accomplishment, or some supposed worldly gain, the immortal soul of the child dedicated to God, is subjected to influences of dangerous tendency, and its religious principles budding into life, rooted up and supplanted with the briars and thorns of this world, or the corrupt theory of a corrupt Church! How a parent, conscious of the responsibility of his position, having dedicated his child to God in Baptism, and made it a member of the Church of his faith, and promised to bring it up in the doctrines and principles of that Church, can then send it away to be trained by those who denounce that Church, and teach doctrines contrary to and subversive of those which he is pledged before God and man to instil into its mind, we cannot reconcile with Christian principles. Yet there are Protestants, who have renounced the errors of Popery, and freed themselves from its galling yoke of bondage, who nevertheless send their children to its schools, where they may be instructed in the same errors and imbued with the same principles which they have renounced and hold to be dangerous to the souls and bodies of men!

This is one of the strange things in this strange age of moral and religious culture. The Roman Church is making converts almost daily by means of its schools ; and these schools, as every one knows who has had the opportunity to examine their pupils, are inferior, in point of *thorough literary instruction*, to the best grade of Protestant schools. Yet parents and guardians of

Protestant children persist in patronizing them, and leaving our own schools to languish! And for this we have never heard but two reasons assigned.

The first is, that Roman Catholic schools are something cheaper than other schools. But shall a Christian man endanger the soul of his child, for such a consideration as this? Will he sell the soul of his child, or run the risk of its being sold for so small an exchange of filthy lucre? Is the body worth so much more than the soul that we can risk the sacrifice of the eternal interests of the latter for some slight benefit to the former? Doubtless the chief reason for making these schools cheaper, is to tempt the cupidity of men and draw in Protestant children for the purpose of proselyting them. And to all such as are likely to be caught by such bait as this, we would say, first make the estimate of how much you may save on the one hand, and what will be the loss to yourself and children at the bar of judgment on the other hand.

The other reason is, that their children will be more secluded from company and more closely watched. If this be an object, why not keep them at home, and employ a governess? or send them to some boarding or family school in the country, and make the request of the teacher to keep them from society? We know many such schools, in which they will learn as little evil and more good than in a Roman Convent. They will undoubtedly hear fewer legends and become less superstitious, and have their respect for their parents and confidence in their religion less shaken than in a Roman Catholic school. But if you wish your child to become alienated from you, and to practise deception, to turn Romanist or cast off all religion as a fable, send it to the Convent, and you will attain your end!

But do not make it first a member of a purer body, and violate your vows to God and his Church to use all diligence to bring it up in the faith and doctrines of that Church, and to make it a worthy member of the same. For in so doing you will add to the sin of subjecting it to evil influences willingly, that of violating an implied pledge to the contrary! Consider, we pray you, dear reader, what constitutes faithfulness to the souls of your little children. To you is committed the responsible charge of shaping their course for time and eternity! Not only the care of their bodies, but of their souls, rests upon you, and unfaithfulness in either, may involve *them in irreparable* loss, and you in grievous sin! Their souls are immortal, and to them must be given attention not second even to your own salvation. The welfare of their bodies should be made equal to your own also. But in both cases, the importance of the life to come, so far exceeds the things of this life, that to endanger the soul for any supposed benefit to the body, is reversing the order and setting at naught the command of God; and involves unfaithfulness and disobedience of the most serious kind. For to us and our children the command is, "Seek ye first the kingdom of God and his righteousness; and all these things shall be added unto you." (Matt. vi. 33.)

Subjecting unnecessarily the impressible souls of our dear little children to erroneous teaching, or evil influences of any kind, that may ruin them forever, must be a sin of a much higher grade than is generally supposed. And in most cases, it has been followed by consequences, even in this life, of the most painful character. A great change must yet come over the minds of the vast majority of those who have the charge of little children, before they will rightly appreciate their responsibility, and do justice to the rising generation.

It is not, however, because God and his Church have not placed this subject rightly before the minds of men, that it is not better understood. It has been earnestly inculcated, and pressed upon their attention in every age. It was because of Abraham's faithfulness in this very duty that God commended him and showed him special favors. "And the Lord said, shall I hide from Abraham that thing which I do; seeing that Abraham shall surely become a great nation, and all the nations of the earth shall be blessed in him? *For I know him that he will command his children and his household after him, and they shall keep the way of the Lord, to do justice and judgment; that the Lord may bring upon Abraham that which he hath spoken of him.*" (Gen. xviii. 17, 19.) To Israel, through Moses, he said, "And these words which I command thee this day, shall be in thine heart: And thou shalt *teach them diligently to thy children, and shalt talk of them when thou sittest in thine house, and when thou walkest by the way, and when thou liest down, and when thou risest up.* And thou shalt bind them for a sign upon thine hand, and they shall be as frontlets between thine eyes. And thou shalt write them upon the posts of thy house, and on thy gates." (Deut. vi. 6–9.) Again, through Solomon, "*Train up a child in the way he should go, and when he is old he will not depart from it.*" (Prov. xxii. 6.) And yet again by St. Paul, "And ye fathers, provoke not your children to wrath: but *bring them up in the nurture and admonition of the Lord*" (Eph. vi. 4), is worthy of repetition.

Thus we see there is want neither of authority nor of instruction on this important duty.

And if all Christians would take heed to their instructions and faithfully perform this duty, who can estimate the result? If they would only set their children, first, the worthy example of a Christian life and spirit, as well as teach them the doctrines of Christ, how soon would disobedient children be melted down into submission, the younger ones kindly taken by the hand of the elder, and led on in the ways of peace and holiness instead of mischief and iniquity — the discordant family become united in bonds of Christian love; and this influence spread from house to house, till the wilderness would rejoice and blossom as the rose.

If parents would only use the same diligence to make their children Christians and ornaments to the Church, which they do to make them honest and worthy members of society, what a change would soon take place! What father is as anxious that his son should shine in the Church as in the world? and takes the same pains to impress his mind with the truth, that sin against God should be as much deprecated as sin against men? that he should as anxiously avoid the disgrace of lying to God, as that of being called a liar among men? that to rob God is as great a sin as to rob men? What mother is so earnest and constant to make her daughter feel the importance of piety to God as to be respected in the society in which she moves? to infuse into her heart the principle of making the world and the accomplishment of person secondary to the duties of religion? We do not say that she does not teach this doctrine at times, but we ask, Where are the mothers and the fathers that show at all times the same interest in religion, and are as constant in their efforts, and as anxious to impress their children with the belief that it is even more important to "seek the kingdom of God and his righteousness," than to seek the things that are needful to the body and to their fair reputation in the world? When parents shall act consistently in these things, and make their children see and feel that such is their faith and the object of their efforts, we may expect a great change to take place in the spirit and feelings of their children, and "the word of the Lord to have free course and be glorified."

But very many of the children baptized into the Church at the present day, do but little more than to learn their Catechism as a task, and attend upon the imperfect instruction imparted in the Sunday-school! And as soon as old enough to be sent away from home to school, the great question is not concerning the welfare of their souls, but, simply, where can they get the best education at the cheapest rate? or in what way can they be prepared to shine most in the world? Their immortal interest is lost sight of, or made a question of minor importance! Better for such parents they never had a child, and better for such children if given up to others, who would do them more justice. Education for this world is very important, but for the next, more so. Nor will they ever conflict, when rightly understood and appreciated.

The child should be taught to repeat its little prayers, night and morning, as soon as able to lisp the name of Jesus. His love should be the theme of conversation, when rising up and lying down, when sitting in the house, and by the wayside. The Catechism should be taught as a thing most precious and cheering, the Sunday-school made a mere auxiliary to aid the parent in the good work of his weekly instruction. It can never be made a substitute for parental duty. It is too imperfect; falls far too short of the warm, gentle and full flow of love and sentiment that should be poured out from the parental bosom. Sunday-schools were designed at first for the poor and neglected children of this world, to supply in part the loss such sustained for the want of worthy parents to do justice to their souls and bodies. They were afterwards adopted as means to aid others, and farther than this they cannot or ought not to go. The custom of some, in leaving to the Sunday-school teacher to do what they ought to do themselves, and after sending their children to the Sunday-school in the morning, then permitting them to return home and spend the hours for Divine service in the streets or in their dwellings, is an abuse of the Sunday-school institution, and a dangerous perversion of its objects. Above all things, take your children to church as soon as they are old enough to remain in comfort throughout the services. Let no institution or custom interfere with this duty; better keep them from the school than from public worship with God's people. The evil they may learn in your absence, and the ruinous habit formed, of absenting themselves from Divine worship, more than counterbalance, by a thousand fold, what they gain at the Sunday-school, if such is to be the case. But there need not be, and ought not to be, any conflict between the Sunday-school and regular attendance at church. Both may be attended with great benefit where there is the will and proper arrangement.

God works by means, and has committed to earthen vessels the glorious light of the Gospel and the great work of bringing men to Christ for salvation. Let parents and others be *faithful* in the use of those means, and the Holy Spirit will bless their efforts and grant them success. If we are faithful in our part, God will certainly be faithful in his. The means granted for the spread and effectual working of the Gospel of Christ are doubtless abundantly successful to the end for which they were ordained. If our children are not saved, it will not be because no provision has been made for them in the Redemption of Christ, or insufficient means granted to us for its application; but because we have been unfaithful in their use, and to the trust committed to us.

And when men shall realize their responsibility, and improve the means given them for the salvation of themselves and others, then shall they realize the promises of God to their own souls and to the souls of their children; then shall they see the Gospel of Christ begin to work in the fulness of its power, and to move onward in the majesty of its strength conquering and to conquer, till "the kingdoms of this world shall become the kingdoms of our Lord and his Christ," and the glorious prediction be fulfilled, "The earth shall be full of the knowledge of the Lord as the waters cover the sea," and all know HIM, "from the least to the greatest;" whom to know is life eternal.

CHAPTER IX.

MODE OR MODES OF BAPTISM.

Meaning of words. — Language of the New Testament. — Septuagint, and Jewish Customs. — Divers Baptisms. — Water of Separation. — Ritual Purifications. — Oriental Washing. — Baptism a Generic Term. — John's Baptism. — Prophecies of Isaiah. — Ezekiel. — Malachi. — Baptism of the Holy Ghost, poured out, shed forth, or fell upon, descended. — Baptism applied to the various Ablutions of the Ritual Law. — No English Word will supply its Place. — Immersion not its True Meaning. — No Mode implied in the Term. — No specific Directions in regard to it. — Circumstances of each Case must be examined.

§ 29. THE mode or modes of Baptism is a *secondary* question, which we did not design, in the commencement of this work, to treat of at all. But so much have Baptists magnified its importance, and so remarkable are some of their more recent movements in regard to it, that some notice of it here may not be out of place. They have formed themselves into a society for the translation and circulation of the Bible among different nations of the earth, and in these translations they render the words "baptize" and "baptism," into terms which mean "immerse" and "immersion!" And they openly avow, in their public meetings, that "the nations of the earth must now look to the Baptist denomination ALONE for faithful translations of the word of God."[1] Out of this movement has grown the "Bible Union," formed for the purpose of casting discredit upon our venerable English Bible — so long the source of light and com-

[1] Bible Society Anniversary, April 28th, 1840.

fort to Christians, and by which so many thousands have been guided on their way to glory; and to substitute in its place another version, in which, among other changes, "baptize" and "Baptism" shall be rendered "immerse" and "immersion!" The inevitable tendency of such things must be to undermine the public faith in the truth of our Holy religion!

They contend that the Greek words βαπτίζω, BAPTIZE, and βαπτισμὸς, BAPTISM, mean "immerse" and "immersion," and nothing more nor less; that "baptize" *carries the mode in the name — that it is a specific term, always signifies to dip;* NEVER EXPRESSING ANYTHING BUT MODE.[1] On this simple *issue*, that to "baptize" means only to "dip or immerse" (which they say is the same thing, and is a *specific term* expressing the *mode*), is based the whole superstructure of the high claims and weighty responsibilities which they have assumed.

The whole question turns on βαπτίζω, — BAPTIZE — whether it be a *specific* term confined to one mode of action, or a *generic* term like washing and *purifying*, which implies an end that may be attained in more ways than one?

In order to settle this question we should, of course, first examine the word BAPTISM wherever it occurs in the New Testament: trace its connections, compare passage with passage, and note its references and objects. And if necessary, we may then examine its usage by contemporary writers, and those immediately preceding and succeeding the apostolic age. [2]

The *usage* or meaning of a word may be entirely

[1] See Carson *On Baptism*, p. 55 *et passim*, American edition.

[2] See rules of interpretation in the beginning of this volume.

different in one age from what it is in another. Its application gradually extends from object to object, until a much wider range of subjects is embraced; and to its *primary* is added a *secondary* meaning; then a *metaphorical*, and through means of these still wider applications are suggested — and if frequently applied to *sacred* things, a *sacred* as well as *secular* usage obtains, and finally *a word may* so *enlarge its meaning as to lose sight of its origin.* For instance, take the English word PREVENT — it now means to "hinder," to "stop;" but what did it mean a hundred years ago? Answer, "to lead, to go before, to aid." Shall we then go back several hundred years to ascertain in what sense a writer of the present century uses the word PREVENT? If we do, we shall give the very opposite of its present meaning, and say, PREVENT means "to go before and open the way," when the writer means "to hinder and stop up the way."

Again, look at the use of the word PROVISIONS, at different times? It means now, generally, "food," "victuals," "something to eat;" but what did it mean in the time of Edward III.? Sir William Blackstone cites the following illustration of the principles on which laws are to be interpreted: "A law of Edward III. forbids all ecclesiastics to purchase *provisions* at Rome. The law (continues he) might seem to prohibit the buying of grain and other victuals; but when we consider that the statute was made to suppress the usurpations of the Papal See, and that the 'nominations to benefices by the Pope' were called 'provisions,' we shall see that the restraint is intended to be laid on *such provisions* only." [1]

[1] Blackstone, Introduction, Sec. ii., iii.

Provisions, under the "canon law" of that age, meant "benefices from the Pope;" now they mean "food and sustenance for the body." Shall we go back to Edward's time to learn the meaning of *provisions* at the present time? or for the present use of *prevent*, and many other like terms? And is such the rule by which we are to settle the meaning of words in the Holy Scriptures?

Further, words often obtain a *sacred* as well as *profane* or secular use. For instance, the word ECCLESIA, in secular classical use means an "assembly," however disorderly it may be; but in its *sacred* use it means CHURCH. The word PRESBYTER (πρεσβύτερος) means elder, or old man, in secular use; but in *sacred* use, an officer, or ruler in the Church. In classical Greek, the word Ἄγγελος, *Angel*, means a messenger; has no reference to the spiritual being, to which the Sacred Scriptures apply it.[1]

Therefore, endeavoring to ascertain the meaning of BAPTIZE and BAPTISM, in the New Testament, we must not only compare passage with passage, and examine their use at the time in which the sacred writers wrote, but especially their *sacred use*, or application to sacred things by other writers of the same period. This every Biblical student, and every other scholar must admit. Why then go to the *ancient Greek classics*, as some propose, to learn how Christ and his Apostles used the root or original word for Baptism?

The New Testament is not written in "classic Greek." It is in what is denominated *Hellenistic* Greek; sometimes called the Greek of the Synagogue — having classical Greek for its basis, but into which

[1] See Trench *On the Study of Words*.

idioms and words of other tongues, Eastern and Western, have been introduced; and modes of thought and forms of speech peculiar to the Hebrew and Chaldee languages interwoven into it. Hence one of the ablest of Biblical scholars has remarked — "Classical use in Greek and Latin is not only sometimes unavailing, but may often mislead in the critical study of the Holy Scriptures."[1]

The New Testament was written by men who thought and spoke the Chaldaic and Syriac tongues, and who read and heard in their schools and synagogues the weekly lessons and law of the Prophets. They were, therefore, familiar with the language into which the Old Testament had been translated; which translation was in constant use whilst Christ and his Apostles were on earth, and no doubt influenced their use of words and style of composition. We might as well go to Edward III. for the meaning of "provisions," or to the ancient Greeks for a definition of "angel," as to the Greek classics for the *right use* of the language of the New Testament.

1. Nevertheless Dr. Carson in his work on Baptism, which has been republished in this country by the American Baptist Publication Society, and received as a standard work by the great body of that denomination, goes back to ancient Greek authors who wrote hundreds of years before Christ came to our earth — even to the days of Homer — to ascertain the meaning of BAPTISM in the apostolic age. And yet he admits that a "word may so enlarge its meaning as to lose sight of its origin."[2] He first takes up *βάπτω*, the root of *βαπτίζω* (to baptize); and after citing various authors of classic Greek to prove that

[1] Campbell *On the New Testament*. [2] Carson *On Baptism*, p. 45.

βάπτω means to DIP, — which no one denies, except that it is not its only meaning; and *he admits* that it has the secondary meaning of *to dye*, — and though *dyeing* (he says) is generally performed by *dipping*, he finds in Hippocrates, βάπτω used for dyeing by dropping the dyeing fluid on the thing dyed. In Æschylus he finds a *similar use of* βάπτω. At a later date he finds also in Arrian's "Expedition of Alexander the Great," that "Nearchus (one of his officers) relates that the Indians dye their beard." And though βάπτω is the word used for that purpose, he admits it could not have been by immersion. Coming to a still later period, he finds that Ælian applies the same term to *dyeing the hair* of an old coxcomb, and to the lady's *yellow locks* "*not colored by art*, *but by nature;*"[1] which of course were not dipped or immersed in the dyeing fluid.

2. In tracing the *modal* of the *primary* meaning of βάπτω, by his wonderful perception of the beauty and meaning of figurative language, his appreciation of an enlivened style and facility in supplying elipses, he could see the *modal of dip retained* in the *beach covered by the rising tide*, in the *man drenched by the pouring rain*, *Nebuchadnezzar wet by the gentle descending dew*, *and the dripping hand of the offender*, *scourged before the Tribunal*, *who caught the blood trickling down his body to sprinkle on the judgment seat.*

Now if *dip* means Baptism by the *swelling tide running over the beach*, by *the pouring rain*, *the distilling dew*, and *the blood trickling down the body into the hand*, or the hand wet by it in any other way — then *dip* is as *generic* as any one contends for Baptism ; and

[1] *Ibidem*, pp. 44, 45.

if used for that, we need have no further controversy on the question before us. But Dr. Carson himself, (notwithstanding all his labor on βάπτω) tells us that *it is never used for Baptism in the New Testament;* that it is merely the *root* from which βαπτίζω is derived. And that ζω,[1] added to the root βάπτω, in some sense modifies its meaning — is not introduced merely to vary sound. But he does not consent to it being *frequentative* or *diminutive* in its effect on the root, as some suppose; and criticises Dr. Gale, (whose general views on Baptism he seems to approve highly, and to whom he acknowledges himself much indebted, for his authorities in the Greek classics), for advancing the opinion "that ζω points to a state or condition in the water, rather than to the action of putting one into the water." And adopts a "*causal*" influence, which brings about an end — "making the *action* of the verb to be performed."[2]

3. He proceeds in the same way with βαπτίζω that he had done with βάπτω, to prove that it *always signifies to dip; never expressing anything but mode;* and adds that "βαπτίζω only, to the exclusion of the root, is applicable to the Christian rite."[3] His classical authors are less numerous — indeed, comparatively few. He therefore soon comes to the Septuagint, and introduces the case of Elisha the prophet and Naaman the leper, captain of the host of Syria. (2 Kings v. 10–14.) On the application of Naaman to Elisha to heal his leprosy, Elisha sent a messenger to tell him to go and wash (λούω) in Jordan seven

[1] We do not follow his order, and although his name will be frequently used in this chapter, it will be as the representative of a body holding the same sentiments, rather than the sentiments of one, individually considered.

[2] p. 20. [3] p. 55.

times. And Naaman went down and dipped (ἐβαπτίσατο) himself seven times in Jordan, according to the saying of the man of God. The term used in this place for wash is λούω, which is used for washing in a general sense, and that rendered dip is βαρτίζω. They are, therefore, construed by Naaman as meaning the same thing; and rightly, for he was healed according to promise.

He cites also several passages from Josephus, but only one in which βαπτίζω is used in a religious sense; and this in connection with the funeral of Miriam, sister of Moses. After they had mourned for her thirty days, Moses *purified* the people as prescribed in Numbers xixth chapter, for touching a dead body, and defilement from any cause connected with the dead. This was done by sprinkling running (spring) water and ashes on the people.

Josephus describes the manner in which these ashes were obtained and preserved, and says: "When therefore, any persons are defiled by a dead body, they put a little of these ashes in spring water, with hyssop, and dipping (baptizing) part of these ashes in it, they sprinkle them with it both on the third and on the seventh day, and after that they are clean."[1] The original institution in Numbers xix. 17, reads, "And for an unclean person, they shall take of the ashes of the burnt heifer of purification for sin, and running water shall be put thereto in a vessel." Here Moses directs the *water to be put to the ashes*, that is, poured in upon them; and Josephus puts the ashes to the water (if Whiston does not mistranslate him — we have not the original), and calls it *baptizing* them. In either case there is a *pouring* and a *mingling* of

[1] *Antiquities*, book iv. ch. 4, translated by Whiston.

the ashes and water, and their purifying power no doubt the same; but whether Josephus calls the *pouring*, or the *mingling together* the Baptism, who is to decide?

4. Again, in order to prove that Baptism never denotes purification by sprinkling, Dr. Carson cites Ecclesiasticus xxxiv. 30: "He that washeth (βαπτιζόμενος) himself after the touching of a dead body, if he touch it again what availeth his washing (λουτρόν αὐτοῦ)?" The literal rendering of which in the Septuagint, is: "He being baptized (purified) from a dead body, and again touched by it, what availeth his (τῷ λουτρῷ αὐτοῦ) washing (purification)?" Here the *same sprinkling of water and ashes*, which we have just considered, is referred to, and called a "*baptism;*" and this "baptism" and λουτρόν are used in the same sense. Dr. Carson *himself* refers it to Numbers xix. 19—"which (he says) shows that sprinkling was but a part of *that purification*, and that the unclean person was also bathed in water. It is this bathing that is effected by Baptism." [1]

But unfortunately for the Doctor he has mistaken entirely the person who was required to "wash his clothes and bathe himself in water." He was not the person sprinkled; it was the *clean person* who had sprinkled the *unclean*, that must wash his clothes and bathe in water, to protect and cleanse himself from any defilement that he might have contracted by the touch of the unclean, or otherwise, whilst sprinkling the water of separation—and he would be clean at even the same day. But those to be purified by the *ashes and water*, must be sprinkled the third and seventh day, and after that they were clean.[2]

[1] p. 66. [2] See Numbers xix. 19-21.

For defilements that affected the habits and comforts of society at large, *washing clothes and bathing the body* in water were imposed.[1] For very slight defilements, such as touching an unclean animal, or removing any part of it when dead, or eating ignorantly of flesh that had died not properly slain — *washing clothes only*, was the rite of purification.[2]

For leprosy, issues of certain kinds in males and females, and purification after child-birth, *sacrifices* were required to be offered, in addition to various ceremonies of cleansing.[3]

For such defilement as a priest would acquire in the routine of daily life, *the washing of his hands and feet* before going into the sanctuary was required, to purify him for the duties of his office.[4] While these ritual purifications had a happy influence upon the habits and lives of the Israelites, they also inspired love and admiration of the purity of that Being whose sanctuary could not be entered until purified of all uncleanness; and, likewise, reverence for the sanctuary itself and its services.

But the moral pollution of sin and the expiation of its guilt, were more clearly symbolized by the ashes and water, called the "water of separation," and "purification for sin." These were twofold, combining both *sacrifice* and *purification*. The ashes were from a victim without spot or blemish; slain without the camp; under the supervision of a priest; her blood sprinkled seven times before the Tabernacle; her body burnt — every part of it in the presence of a priest; her ashes gathered by a clean or purified person, and kept in a clean place for permanent and ready

[1] Levit. xv.
[2] Levit. xi. 25-40.
[3] Levit. xiv. 2-32; xii., xv.
[4] Exod. xxx. 18-21.

use. They were the ashes of a sacrifice whose blood had been offered, and doubtless emblematical of the expiatory sacrifice of that *spotless One whose blood cleanses from all sin.* Of all the ritual services under Moses this was most highly prized, because the application of the ashes and water was regarded as evidence of participation in that which expiated the guilt of sin, as well as purified them from its pollution.

Now, when Dr. Carson cites Ecclesiasticus, referred to above, he tells us this "purification for sin" has two parts — "sprinkling," and "washing the clothes and bathing the body;" and that the "baptism" or purification alludes to the latter — "washing the clothes and bathing the body,"— and not to the "sprinkling." But what says the Divine record? Numbers xix. 19-21. "And the clean person shall sprinkle upon the unclean on the third day, and on the seventh day; and on the seventh day, he (the sprinkler) shall purify himself and wash his clothes and bathe himself in water, and he shall be clean at even. But he that shall be unclean and shall not purify himself, that soul shall be cut off from among the congregation, because he hath defiled the sanctuary of the Lord: the water of separation hath not been sprinkled upon him, he is unclean. And it shall be a perpetual statute unto them, that he that sprinkleth the water of separation shall wash his clothes; and he that toucheth the water of separation shall be unclean until even." So *great* was the particularity that every one connected with this purifying rite should be clean (for unless they were clean, the ordinance would be defiled and therefore of no avail), that the priest who supervised the burning of the heifer, and the clean person who gathered the ashes and put them in a clean place, must each afterwards wash his clothes and bathe himself in water and remain until the setting of the sun, to purify himself from any defilement with which he might be infected during the operation.

It was to preserve the *purity* of those who were engaged in the preparation and administration of the ordinance, that washing and bathing were imposed. When the " water of separation " had been sprinkled the third and seventh day, the unclean were purified ritually, and the service ended. This service was sometimes connected with others, as in the case of the Levites who were first purified by the sprinkling of the " water of separation ; " and then followed services special to setting them apart for their office. But the institution " of the purification for sin " was always the *same in itself*; and ended with the sprinkling on the seventh day. Dr. Carson is, therefore, convicted by his own witness. The Baptism he refers to in Ecclesiasticus, is only " *sprinkling water and ashes* on the unclean."

5. Turn again to the Divine record. In the Epistle to the Hebrews the Apostle Paul having shown the superiority of the Priesthood of Christ over that of Aaron, proceeds to show that he is also the " Mediator of a better covenant, established on better promises : " that the sacrifices, offerings, and external purifications under the Mosaic dispensation could not expiate the guilt of sin, nor make him that did the service perfect, as pertaining to the conscience; but were merely a symbol of what was to be effected under the new dispensation of the Gospel; and were appointed to be continued only " until the time of reformation," or change to be made by the introduction of the new and spiritual Priesthood of Christ.

In comparing *the ritual* of the Levitical Priesthood under Moses with that which it shadowed forth, the Apostle writes: —

HEBREWS IX. 9, 10. "Which was a figure for the time then present, in which were offered both gifts and sacrifices, that could not make them that did the service perfect, as pertaining to the conscience, which stood only in meats and drinks, and divers washings, (Baptisms) and carnal ordinances, imposed on them until the time of reformation."

What does the Apostle mean by "divers washings," in the last verse? In the original Greek the word translated "washings" is βαπτισμοῖς — BAPTISMS. And that these "divers baptisms" refer to the various ablutions of the Levitical law must be obvious to every intelligent reader. "Most evidently (writes Professor Stuart of Andover) βαπτισμοῖς (Baptisms) refers to the ceremonial ablutions of the Jews, which were concerned with external purification." With which Bloomfield coincides. And the Professor goes on to show that the *tenth* verse as above is a continuation of the *ninth*, adding new matter, instead of explanatory of what is meant by "gifts and sacrifices" immediately preceding. In order to make this more intelligible to his readers, he retranslates and points out the connection of "gifts and sacrifices" with what follows in the next verse: "Oblations and sacrifices were offered, which cannot fully accomplish what is needed for the conscience of him who performeth the services, being imposed (together with meats and drinks, and divers washings, ordinances of the flesh) only until the time of reformation."[1]

This is clear and satisfactory, and in perfect accord-

[1] *Commentary on Hebrews*, p. 430.

ance with what appears to be the object and reasoning of the author. But whether adopted or not, will not affect the meaning of the phrase "divers Baptisms." This refers to the *ablutions* of the Jewish ritual which we have been considering. All of which were connected with the Tabernacle service, and necessary to enter therein, or participate in the worship of the holy sanctuary. First, as we have seen, the priests must *daily wash their feet and hands.* Another class of defilements must be purified by *washing clothes and bathing in water the body.* Another by *washing their clothes only.* Another still, by the *sprinkling* the water and blood — every one according to the kind and degree of his uncleanness — and above all must the *ashes of the heifer and water* be sprinkled on those defiled by touching the dead, and such things as were the manifest effects of sin.

Now if the Apostle embraces all these modes of purifying under the head of "*divers baptisms*" as his language clearly teaches, who has ever claimed for βαπτίζω a *wider application?* and *what better evidence that it is a* GENERIC *term?*

But the exponent of the views of our Baptist brethren would limit these "*divers washings*" to such purifications only as were performed by dipping or immersion! By what *authority?* The original Greek does not thus limit them. And of all the ablutions of the Mosaic ritual, we do not know of an *instance* of one person literally washing another, except that of Moses' washing Aaron and his sons when he inducted them into the office of Priesthood. And this a *special service*, not applicable to the people at large. For certain defilements the unclean were directed to wash themselves and their clothes; but does the

Apostle refer to only one kind of purifications when he calls them "*divers baptisms?*" He cannot mean the multiplication of only *one kind*, for the word he uses, "διαφόροις," means (unless overstrained) *difference* in *kind* and *difference* in *degree* — diverse, various baptisms. This is made manifest by what immediately follows. Continuing the comparison of the Tabernacle service and Priesthood of Aaron with the spiritual service and Priesthood of Christ, the Apostle adds: —

Verses 11–14. "But Christ being come a high-priest of good things to come, by a *greater and more perfect tabernacle*, not made with hands, that is to say, not of this building. Neither by the *blood of goats and calves*, but by *his own blood*, he entered in *once into the holy place*, having obtained *eternal redemption for us*. For if the blood of bulls, and of goats, *and the ashes of a heifer sprinkling the unclean* sanctifieth to the *purifying of the flesh*, *how much more shall the blood of Christ, who through the eternal spirit offered himself without spot to God, purge your conscience from dead works to serve the living God.*"

The superiority of the priesthood of Christ and his new dispensation over the priesthood and ritual of the old, is here continued: and the "*sprinkling of ashes and water*" *specified* as *one* of those rites that shadowed forth more spiritual things under the new. So the Apostle reasons: If the blood of bulls and of goats sprinkled by the high-priest before the mercy-seat on the great day of atonement each year, shadowing forth the expiation for sin, first for himself, and then for the people, and the *ashes of a heifer sprinkling the unclean*, sanctifieth to the purifying of the flesh, how much more shall the blood of Christ, who, without spot, offered up Himself to God as an expiatory sacrifice, cleanse your conscience (or soul) from the guilt of sin, and through its application by the Holy Spirit, purge your heart from the love of sin and its works of death, to the love and service of God *in sincerity and truth;* of which *this* legal purification is a symbol. Do we need evidence more decisive and full to prove that St. Paul includes the "*sprinkling of ashes and water*" among the purifications of the ritual of the Tabernacle and Temple, and hence included it in his summary — "divers baptisms?" The Temple succeeded the Tabernacle, and its services were regarded as the same — its sacred utensils were the same. It was built after the same model, but on a much larger scale. Its courts were much enlarged and their number increased. Hence under the name of "Tabernacle" the Apostle speaks of services that were to be continued until superseded by the Gospel Dispensation, which shows he includes the Temple with the Tabernacle. And it must also be remembered, that these services were performed chiefly in the courts and near the door of the Tabernacle, to purify and fit the worshippers to enter the sanctuary and participate in its worship. Uncleanness in many cases, especially when ignorantly contracted, was not in itself a sin; but it was sin, and of a serious kind, *not to be cleansed*, or to *defile the sanctuary!* Such were cut off from intercourse with the congregation and from the privileges of worship in the Holy Place. If a priest officiated in a state to defile the sanctuary, he was cut off from its privileges, and from the people of God forever; and would afterwards, as was generally believed, be visited by death from the hand of God.

Now the services of the "Tabernacle," to which the Apostle refers, he classes under four heads: 1. Gifts, or thank offerings. 2. Expiatory sacrifices. 3. Meats and drinks, lawful and unlawful. 4. Divers washings (baptisms) "imposed till the time of reformation." This embraces, as before remarked, the whole Jewish ritual.

To provide for its observance, an altar for offering sacrifice was placed in the court, between the gate of entrance and the Tabernacle; still nearer to the door of the Tabernacle, was placed a *laver* filled with water, for cleansing or purifying the unclean; and in the women's court on the right side of the Temple, was a room provided for the purifying of lepers after they were healed; and various provisions made for other purposes. But as we are concerned for the present with only the *fourth division*, — purifying by water or "*divers baptisms*," — let us turn our attention more particularly to the LAVER erected for such purifications.

EXODUS XXX. 17–21. "And the Lord spake unto Moses, saying, Thou shalt make a laver of brass, and *his foot also of brass*, to wash withal: and thou shalt put it between the tabernacle of the congregation and the altar, and thou shalt put water therein. For *Aaron and his sons shall wash their hands and their feet thereat:* When they go into the tabernacle of the congregation, they shall wash with water, that they die not: or when they come near to the altar to minister, to burn offering made by fire unto the Lord: *So shall they wash their hands and their feet, that they die not:*[1] and it shall be a statute forever

[1] The italics are our own, to draw the attention of the reader to such parts.

to them, even to him and his seed throughout all generations."

This *laver* was placed near the door of the Tabernacle as we see, and filled with water; and its basis or "FOOT" for which special directions are given, was so constructed as to receive the water running from the spouts or cocks placed around the side (the laver being circular in form), for washing the hands and feet of the priests, before they entered upon their ministrations in the sanctuary. Had they put their hands and feet into the laver, the water in it would have been defiled by the first man that washed therein.

Now this washing was confessedly one of the *daily purifications of the Tabernacle*, and must come under the head of the fourth division, called by St. Paul "*divers baptisms.*" Aaron and his sons must daily wash or purify themselves at the laver before going into the sanctuary, the water running therefrom through the spouts or cocks on their hands and feet at the base to receive it.[1] This was the most frequent and constant ritual purification of the Tabernacle service, and cannot be excluded from its place among "*divers baptisms.*" When the Levites were set apart for their office in and about the Tabernacle, God commanded Moses to cleanse them by *sprinkling the water of purifying upon them*; and then they must shave all their flesh, and wash their clothes, and make themselves clean.[2] This ritual service can be placed under no head of the Apostle's summary but that of "*divers baptisms.*" Therefore, if as we have now seen under the head of "divers baptisms," that βαπτίζω is applied

[1] The Talmudists tell us that there were twelve of these cocks around this laver, to accommodate the *twelve priests of the daily sacrifices at the same time.*

[2] Numbers viii. 7.

to the different modes of purification expressed by λούω, to wash the body, — πλύνω, to wash clothes, — νίπτω, to wash the hands and feet, — and περιῤῥαίνω, to sprinkle the water of purifying, — is it not beyond all question a GENERIC TERM, embracing the application of water in as many various modes as could be claimed for any term? What then becomes of the assumption — "it is a specific term, and always signifies to dip: never expressing anything but mode?"

6. Turn next to another inspired writer of the New Testament. St. Mark writes: —

CHAP. VII. 1–4. "Then came together unto him the Pharisees, and certain of the Scribes which came from Jerusalem. And when they saw certain of his disciples eat bread with defiled (that is to say, with unwashen) hands, they found fault. For the Pharisees, and all the Jews, except they wash their hands oft (carefully), eat not, holding the tradition of the elders. And when they come from the market, except they wash (baptize [1]), they eat not. And many other things there be, which they have received to hold, as the washing (baptizing [1]) of cups, and pots, and brazen vessels, and tables."

The first point to which we should direct our attention here is, whether the washing (βαπτίζω) after returning from market, is the same kind of washing (νίπτω) before meals, in the preceding verse, as the translators of our version seem to have supposed. Or does St. Mark mean the washing of the *whole body*, after returning from market?

They both mean, evidently, a ritual purification before meals from any defilement contracted by the

[1] "Wash" and "washing" in our English version, but *baptize* and *baptizing* in the original Greek.

touch of things that were unclean; and the Pharisees found fault because this religious ceremony handed down by the elders was not observed by the disciples of Jesus. Comparing with these passages of St. Mark what another Evangelist writes on the same subject, will aid the reader, perhaps, in making up his decision.

ST. MARK VII. 2, 3, 4.

"And when they saw certain of his disciples eat bread with defiled (that is to say, with unwashen) hands, they found fault. For the Pharisees and all the Jews, except they wash their hands oft (carefully), eat not, holding the tradition of the elders. And when they come from the market except they wash (baptize [1]), eat not."

ST. LUKE XI. 37, 38

"And as he spake a certain Pharisee besought him to dine with him, and he went in and sat down to meat. And when the Pharisee saw it, he marvelled that he had not first washed (baptized [1]), before dinner."

Now both of these Evangelists specify washing before meals to be the custom of the Pharisees. And St. Luke applies βαπτίζω to the case of the Saviour going from the people whom he had addressed, into the house of the Pharisee by invitation, to dine with him; which St. Mark applies to persons after returning from market. And if applicable to one going from a crowd to dinner, why not to those who in their daily avocations mingle with people in the crowded streets, and all who for any other purpose go into society or hold intercourse with their fellow men? This purification before meals, no doubt originated in the fact that knives, forks, and spoons were not known, and that the touching of things unclean with the hands defiled them, and then dipping the fingers into the

[1] Translated in our version "wash," but the same word βαπτίζω that denotes Baptism.

dish or dishes out of which they ate, defiled the food, and thereby the whole body became virtually unclean. Then St. Mark *specifies* the *washing of hands* before meals — "except they wash their hands (carefully, or up to the wrists), eat not;" ("oft," is rejected by nearly all commentators, and the above or similar renderings substituted.)

But how were their hands washed? So invariably was the mode of washing hands by *pouring of water* on them by a servant in the days of Elisha the son of Shaphat, that the office of servant or of ministering to another, was designated by the phrase "*he that poureth water on the hands*." (2 Kings iii. 11). But we will give to the question its widest application, and answer — sometimes in a basin, sometimes by water running from the spout of the pump, and sometimes by water poured on them by another person. The advocates of immersion contend that washing the hands in a basin is an immersion of them. But such an immersion or dip, is not the "*modal*" of thing to be done, nor the object in the mind of the doer. The dipping was merely preparatory to the washing. This "tradition of the elders" was doubtless twofold in its object, a *literal* as well as a *ritual* purification. Hence, to wash "carefully" as our best commentators construe it. *Cleansing* was *the object* of the washing, both literal and ritual. And the *washing of the hands*, for which the water is supplied, is performed by rubbing with the palms of the hands the water, on every part of them. When one commands another *to wash his hands* or to do anything else that can be done in different ways, if he has any choice as to the mode of doing it, he *specifies that mode*, otherwise the thing is done according to the choice of the performer. Now, no one will contend there is but *one mode of washing hands*; nor that hands cannot be washed in either mode which we have specified; nor that washing by pouring the water on them, is immersion. And to one going into the house of a stranger unexpectedly to his family, it would be much more convenient to himself and to his hosts, to wash only his hands, than his whole body.

Therefore, if the washing before meals, referred to by St. Luke, be performed in the same way as those spoken of by St. Mark, then βαπτίζω and νίπτω are used in the same sense. But if not so used, and βαπτίζω means only to dip or immerse, how can it be applied in the latter part of the last verse of the extract from St. Mark?

CHAP. VII. 4. "And when they come from the market, except they wash (baptize), they eat not. And many other things there be, which they have received to hold, as the washing (baptizing) of cups, and pots, and brazen vessels and tables" (couches).

How can it be applied to these tables or couches on which the people reclined at meals? If it applies to tables, as some choose to have it; these were from three to four feet high, four feet broad, and varying from six to twelve and twenty feet in length; how could they be taken to a bath or pool of water (if one deep enough be near at hand), and plunged under the water by the members of an ordinary family? If they were couches such as were reclined upon during meals at the table, they were long enough for people to recline at full length of body, broad enough to accommodate from three to five persons, and not a great deal below the height of the tables proper; and not unfrequently fastened to the wall. At night they were used for beds, mattresses and coverlets being spread on them, which were removed in the morning to a place provided for such things, and these κλιναί during the day used as seats and such purposes as we now employ chairs and sofas (such articles not being known at that period in the East[1]).

Could cumbrous articles like these be plunged under the water of an ordinary bath of a private family? Or carried to a public cistern at a considerable distance from houses without a male member, or composed of aged and infirm persons, or of a widow and little children? We cannot suppose the common people among the Jews had private baths large enough for such a purpose, or that the public baths were so abundant that they were to be found near at hand to every family in sparsely populated districts.

Under such circumstances we repeat the inquiry — Is it probable that such cumbrous articles were ritually purified by plunging them under the water? They could have been easily washed in the usual way of washing "cups and pots, brazen vessels and tables" — as the Pharisees washed their hands before meals, in obedience to the same authority.

And it should be remembered that during the sojourn of our Lord on earth, purifications were performed from pots and pitchers, by the Jews, especially on festive occasions. St. John ii. 6: "And there were set there six water-pots of stone, *after the manner of the purifying of the Jews*, containing two or three firkins apiece." These water-pots (ὑδρίαι) were the same brought by the woman of Samaria to Jacob's well for water (St. John iv. 28) — the same, according to the Septuagint, which Rebecca carried on her

[1] See Calmet, Jahns, and others.

shoulders, out of which Abraham's servant drank (Gen. xxiv. 15–18); and which Gideon put into the hands of his army to be broken in pieces with the blasts of trumpets, to dismay the Midianites (Judges vii. 15–19); and which in our English version of the Bible are called "PITCHERS." They could be carried "on the shoulder" or "in the hand." These were the *baths*, used for purifying in houses and families of the Jews in our Lord's day. Did they plunge their brazen vessels and couches into them?

Admit that those used at the wedding in Cana were of the largest size of such pots or pitchers, and that they held, as some have estimated, half or two thirds of a barrel of water; were they of the proper form, or did any of them hold water enough to allow of plunging a man or a couch under? No, but they contained enough for all the purposes of a large wedding, and for any ritual services that were required to be performed in the usual way on such occasions, and no doubt, enough when filled again, for the purification of all the cups, pots, brazen vessels, and couches made unclean on such occasions.

But Dr. Carson declines to enter into a rigid examination of the case, on the ground, as he tells us, that having proved the meaning of the Greek word (Baptism) by the authority of the whole consent of Greek literature, he is under no obligation, beyond the proof of the mere *possibility* of existence, "*to prove that any of the possible ways of solution did actually exist.*"[1] Not so fast, Dr. C. You have *not proved* the meaning of BAPTISM in the age and writings of the New Testament, *which is the thing to be done — the great question at issue.* You have shown from

[1] pp. 66, 73.

passages cited from Greek writers, who lived hundreds of years before the New Testament was written, that βαπτίζω was used by them, as *a general rule*, in the sense of immersion, but as you advanced towards the times of the Apostles, *exceptions multiplied*, and having entered upon an investigation of its *use* in the New Testament, we find that an inspired Apostle calls the *ritual ablutions of the Mosaic dispensation* "DIVERS BAPTISMS"; and both the term employed and ablutions referred to, as we have shown, imply *different kinds* — *various ablutions*, and not only the multiplication of one kind.

Again, we find two other inspired writers using the term BAPTISM in connection with washing of hands and purifications before meals; and by one of them applied to the washing of "couches" — articles too large and unwieldy to be put under the water of the ordinary baths of private families, or to be carried to a public cistern or bath by the members of most of them — even should not the water of such be regarded as *unclean* by frequent use in that way. [1]

You cannot escape the duty of a critical examination of the *usage of Baptism* in any passage of the New Testament, by throwing the "burden of proof" on others. For you admit that a "word may come to enlarge its meanings, so as to lose sight of its origin;" and that "USE *is the sole arbiter of language*." [1] Therefore your own principles, if there was no higher law, will not allow you to go to past ages for the meaning of a word, and then withdraw from the labor of investigating its USAGE at a later period, when truth and duty are at stake.

But relying still on his supposed *established usage*, and that he is no longer bound to do more than prove

[1] pp. 45, 46.

its application *not impossible*, — a petitio principii — begging the question in hand, — Dr. Carson tells us that there were two kinds of beds among the Jews, and that St. Mark perhaps refers to such as that carried by the paralytic, whom Jesus commanded after healing him, "to take up his bed, and go to his own house," recorded by St Matthew. [1]

To that kind of bed St. Mark also refers in another place, and calls it by its proper name κράββατος, not κλίνη. These beds were carried about by invalids not too infirm to bear a small burden, and were composed of two cotton quilts, one to double and lie on, the other to throw over the body, — sometimes only a thin cotton mattress and coverlet, — these could be rolled up, and carried on the back or under the arm. They *are sometimes* referred to, as in the case of St. Matthew, under the general head of *bed* (κλίνη), as the *single blanket* on which one may have slept, is called "*his bed*;" or a very *small hut* in a general way may be called a *house*. But St. John, and St. Mark referring to them in a less general way, call them by their proper name κράββατοι. [2] St. Mark is led to speak of both kinds of beds, κλίνη and κράββατος, and hence to draw the proper distinction. He calls the bed of the impotent man healed by the Saviour, at the pool of Bethesda, κρὰββατος — which means a "little or mean bed" in the Jewish sense.[3] But when he refers to beds in the houses of another class of people, as in the case before us, he calls them κλιναί, such as we have before described. The same that our Saviour alluded to, when he asked whether a candle is brought to be put *under a bed*, or on a candlestick ?" [4]

[1] Chap. ix. 6.
[2] John v. 11, 12 ; Mark ii. 10, 12.
[3] See Calmet.
[4] Mark iv. 21.

Instead of the quilt or mattress on the floor, St. Mark specifies the washing or Baptism of κλιναί, "couches" connected with the dining-room, and associated with cups, and vessels for different kinds of liquids on the table. We need not dwell longer on the *kind of couches* under consideration, for the connection in which they are introduced, and the distinction of names made by St. Mark himself, must settle that point; for certainly an author will be allowed to explain the meaning of his own words.

One more "*possibility*" has been suggested, that is, "these couches might have been so constructed as to be conveniently taken to pieces for the purpose of purification."[1] Could any one *without a purpose* suppose such a thing! Has any Talmudist or rabbi ever taught or hinted such a tradition? So might they have been washed with water and soap for the double purpose of a *literal* and *ritual* purification. Furniture constructed to be taken to pieces for the expressed object of carrying it to the bath every time touched by an unclean person, or anything else that may defile, or as often as required to be purified by the traditions of the elders! Credat Judæus Apella. One must be driven to the last degree of "*possibility*" to seek refuge under such a shelter!

We would advise the followers of Dr. Carson to adopt no scheme for holding aloof when duty calls to action — meet faithfully your responsibility; labor to *know the truth* and to *follow the truth.* Instead of attempting to throw the "burden of proof" on others, or trusting to past efforts, examine afresh the word of God for the USAGE of Baptism, and for *the whole truth as it is in Jesus.* If one prefers *immersion*,

[1] Carson, p. 76.

certainly he has the right to follow his choice, but should take heed that under a dispensation of GRACE, he does not limit the privileges and blessings of GRACE to the infirm, helpless, and dying, without the authority of the Giver.

3. And let us examine, in the next place, if PURIFICATION is not in fact the *leading idea*, attached to the Baptism of both John and Christ in the New Testament, rather than that of immersion? When John the Baptist entered upon his mission, he proclaimed himself one going before to prepare the way for another. He called upon the people to make ready for the coming of the kingdom of God — to repent, for it was at hand. And to all who gave ear to his preaching, he administered Baptism, as an outward sign of their preparation — emblematical of the cleansing of their hearts and lives, to prepare them for the reception of the promised Messiah. He at the same time called upon those who came to his Baptism to "bring forth fruits meet for repentance:" saying, "Now also the axe is laid unto the root of the trees; therefore, every tree that bringeth not forth good fruit is hewn down and cast into the fire. I indeed baptize with water unto repentance; but he that cometh after me is mightier than I, whose shoes I am not worthy to bear; he shall baptize you with the Holy Ghost and with fire." (St. Matt. iii. 8, 11.) His Baptism shadowed forth the Baptism of the Holy Ghost, the Divine Sanctifier, whose enlightening influence would act "as purifying water, to wash away any internal pollutions; and as a refining fire, to consume all their dross and the remains of corrupt nature."[1] To which he added, "Whose fan is in his hand; he will thor-

[1] Thomas Scott.

oughly purge his floor" — cleanse or purify it — "and gather his wheat into the garner." (Ver. 12.) Precisely what the prophet had foretold. "He shall sit as a refiner or purifier of silver; and he shall purify the sons of Levi, and purge [purify] them as gold and silver, that they may offer unto the Lord an offering in righteousness." (Malachi iii. 3.)

That such was John's meaning, and that he and his followers regarded his Baptism as a *ceremonial purification* is confirmed by the fact that when a question about "PURIFYING" had arisen between his disciples and the Jews, he treated it as synonymous with Baptism, and called upon them to bear him witness that he had from the beginning claimed only to be one sent before the Christ, to prepare his way; and that Christ must increase whilst he must decrease. The followers of the Saviour were now baptizing greater numbers than John, which had evidently given rise to the question. See the connection, St. John iii. 22–30: "After these things came Jesus and his disciples into the land of Judea; and there he tarried with them and BAPTIZED; and John was also BAPTIZING in Ænon, near to Salim, because there was much water there; and they came and were BAPTIZED. For John was not yet cast into prison. *Then there arose a question between some of John's disciples and the Jews about* PURIFYING. And they came unto John and said unto him: Rabbi, he that was with thee beyond Jordan, to whom thou barest witness, behold, the same BAPTIZETH, and all men come unto him. John answered and said: A man can receive nothing, except it be given him from heaven. Ye yourselves bear me witness that I said, I am not the Christ; but that I am sent before him. He that hath the bride is the bridegroom; but the friend of the bridegroom, which standeth and heareth him, rejoiceth greatly because of the bridegroom's voice; this my joy therefore is fulfilled. He must increase, but I must decrease."

It must be obvious to the intelligent reader, that St. John, the writer, the disciples who came, and the reply of John the Baptist, all refer to "Baptism and purifying" as synonymous terms: for "John's Baptism" was doubtless the "*purifying*" under discussion. St. Mark calls it "the *Baptism* of repentance for the remission of sins" (chap. i. 4); *i. e.*, a washing or purification from sin. St. Luke likewise calls it "the *Baptism* of repentance for the remission of sins" (chap. iii. 3), emblematical of the same cleansing or *purifying*.

The Jews evidently expected some ritual lustration or purification when their Messiah or his forerunner should come — at least, showed that such a thing did not surprise them. For instead of inquiring into the nature and meaning of John's Baptism, they first ask him if he was the *Christ*, or one of their predicted prophets? and then why he *baptized*, if not one of them? (St. John i. 19–25.) "And this is the record of John, when the Jews sent priests and Levites from Jerusalem, to ask him, Who art thou? And he confessed, and denied not; but confessed, I am not the Christ. And they asked him, What then? Art thou Elias? And he saith, I am not. Art thou that prophet? And he answered, No. Then said they unto him, Who art thou? that we may give an answer to them that sent us. What sayest thou of thyself? He said, I am the voice of one crying in the wilderness, Make straight the way of the Lord, as said the prophet Esaias. And they which were sent were of the Pharisees. And they asked him, *Why baptizest thou then*, if thou be not that Christ, nor Elias, neither that Prophet?"

The *Baptism* itself caused no surprise, but that John should baptize did, if he were not one of such *note* as would authorize this extra *purification*. John was the promised Elias, and forerunner of Christ, but not Elijah himself, whom they expected. The prophecies on which they based their hopes of a Saviour, and the blessings that would follow, had induced the expectation of some ritual preparation, or extra purification of the people, for his reception. Isaiah, pointing to Christ and his reign, had said, in the name of Jehovah (chap. lii. 13–15), "Behold, my servant shall deal prudently; he shall be exalted and extolled very high . . . . so shall he sprinkle many nations; the kings shall shut their mouths at him; for that which hath not been told them shall they see; and that which they had not heard shall they consider." Ezekiel, shadowing forth the blessings of Christ's reign, and its influence upon the hearts of his people, had, in the same name foretold them (chap. xxxvi. 25–29), "Then I will sprinkle clean water upon you, and you shall be *clean;* from all your filthiness and from all your idols will I cleanse you. A new heart also will I give you: and a new spirit will I put within you; and I will take away the stony heart out of your flesh, and I will give you a heart of flesh. And I will put my spirit within you, and cause you to walk in my statutes, and ye shall keep my judgments and do them. And ye shall dwell in the land that I gave your fathers, and ye shall be my people, and I will be your God." Malachi had pointed out how their Saviour and his reign would be introduced (chap. iii. 1–3), "Behold, I will send my messenger, and he shall prepare the way before me: and the Lord, whom ye seek, shall suddenly come to his temple, even the messenger of the covenant, whom ye delight in: behold, he shall come, saith the Lord of hosts. But who shall abide the day of his coming? and who shall stand when he appeareth? for he is like a refiner's fire, and like fullers' soap. And he shall sit as a refiner and purifier of silver: and he shall *purify* the sons of Levi, and purge them as gold and silver."

With such prophecies familiar to them, and the Levitical and traditional *purifications* constantly practised among them, we need not wonder that John made no further explanation of his Baptism than its shadowing forth the *refining and purifying* influence of the Holy Ghost. (St. Mark i. 8.) "I indeed baptize you with water, but He shall baptize you with the Holy Ghost." By which he clearly indicates the relation of the two, and that his Baptism was emblematical of the Baptism of the Holy Ghost. And if so, it was necessarily a rite of purification, signifying the washing away of sin on repentance and reformation, preparatory for the Messiah. John's Baptism was not Christian Baptism — because not in the name of the Holy Trinity, and particularly of Christ. It was not an initiatory rite into any church, because he did not found, or pretend to be a founder of a church. It was simply the work of the predicted Messenger sent to prepare the way for the coming and reception of Christ. That it was not Christian Baptism is farther made known by the fact that when St. Paul found certain persons at Ephesus who had received John's Baptism, he re-baptized them in the name of the Trinity (Acts xix. 1–5). Although "Jerusalem and all Judea, and all the region round about Jordan," received John's Baptism, and the disciples of Christ before his crucifixion baptized at one time even greater numbers than John, we find that on the day of Pentecost, the whole number of the New Dispensation was only one hundred and twenty. (Acts i. 5.)

Until his crucifixion, Jesus, as well as John, acted under, and recognized the authority of the law of Moses; he was circumcised on the eighth day, brought to the temple and presented to the Lord, after his mother's purification; attended the public worship of the temple, and drove from its hallowed courts the money-changers, who would change his Father's house of prayer into a den of thieves. When he cleansed a leper, he bade him "Go and show thyself unto the priest, and offer for thy cleansing, according as Moses commanded, for a testimony unto them." (Luke v. 14.) And in his *public* teaching to the multitude, said to them, "The scribes and Pharisees sit in Moses' seat: All, therefore, whatsoever they bid you observe, that observe and do; but do not ye after their works; for they say and do not." (Matt. xxiii. 2. 3.) Almost the last thing that he did before He suffered, was in obedience to Moses, to observe the "passover." (Matt. xxvi. 17–25.) But here ended the Old Dispensation.

He had united with John in preparing the people for the New. He had submitted to his Baptism, not because he needed repentance, but as recognizing John's mission and appointment from Heaven, and his ritual purification for the introduction of the New Dispensation, and as submitting himself also to all Heaven's regulations "under the law" — "to fulfil all righteousness" (Matt. iii. 15); and, it may be, to set him apart for his priestly office, as was Aaron. For John's Baptism, as a preparation for the Gospel of Christ, was certainly very similar to the purification of the Israelites, to prepare them for the reception of the law at Mount Sinai. (See Exodus xix.)

It was necessary that Christ should become subject to "*the law in all things*, to redeem them that were under the law." He therefore fulfilled all that was required under the first Dispensation, even submitted to and aided in the mission of John the Baptist in preparing the people, especially his chosen Apostles, for the New Dispensation. But from the moment he rose from the grave, a new order of things commenced, and his submission to the Old ended. His public declaration now is, "*All power is given unto me in Heaven and in Earth.* Go ye, therefore, and teach all nations, *baptizing them in the name of the Father, and of the Son, and of the Holy Ghost.*" (Matt. xxviii. 18, 19.) Up to this time all was under Moses; henceforth all shall be under Christ. The *Baptism of John was therefore for the remission of sins*[1] *and purification* under the Dispensation of Moses to those purposing reformation of life, *preparatory* to the ushering in of the New Dispensation under Christ. It implied uncleanness through sin, and symbolized the purifying and renewing influences of the Holy Ghost. And the Saviour directed his Apostles to tarry at Jerusalem after his departure, for the special gift of the Holy Ghost to qualify them for their work.

4. Now did "purifying," under the Mosaic Dispensation, imply only one mode of action? And is the *Baptism of the Holy Ghost represented under the figure of dipping?* The various modes of "purifying,"

[1] St. Mark i. 4; St. Luke iii. 3.

under the ritual law, we have already considered. And if because of the omnipresence of the Holy Spirit, we are necessarily *immersed* in the Spirit, then it is not by dipping or plunging we get into the Spirit; but we are born in the Spirit, and grow up in the Spirit, and every one has already been baptized in Him. That is not something yet to be done. But if it be an act, or an influence, or gift to men, which any do not yet possess, then it must come of the Spirit, and be applied to them. How this application is made, let us hear what the Holy Scriptures teach? Under what mode or figures do they represent the Baptism of the Holy Ghost? The Saviour, when about to leave his disciples, told them they should be baptized with the Holy Ghost not many days hence, and to tarry at Jerusalem till this was accomplished.

Acts iii. 1–4. "And when the day of Pentecost was fully come, they were all with one accord in one place. And suddenly there came a sound from heaven, as of a mighty rushing wind, and it filled all the house where they were sitting. And there appeared unto them cloven tongues, like as of fire, and it sat upon each of them. And they were all filled with the Holy Ghost, and began to speak with other tongues, as the Spirit gave them utterance."

St. Peter informed the multitude that came together, that this Baptism was the fulfilment of the prophecy of Joel.

Verses 16, 17, 18. "But this is that which was spoken by the prophet Joel, And it shall come to pass in the last days, saith God, I will POUR OUT of my Spirit upon all flesh, and your sons and your daughters shall prophesy, and your young men shall see visions, and your old men shall dream dreams:

And on my servants and on my handmaidens, I will POUR OUT, in those days, of my Spirit; and they shall prophesy."

Here the figure used expressive of the mode is that of POURING, not DIPPING. "I will POUR OUT OF my Spirit." When the actual Baptism took place, a sound came from heaven as of a mighty rushing wind, and "cloven tongues of fire sat upon them," which was the fulfilment of the prophecy, "*I will pour out of my Spirit.*" And the Apostle goes on further to explain (verses 32, 33), "This Jesus hath God raised up, whereof we are all witnesses. Therefore, being by the right hand of God exalted, and having received of the Father the promise of the Holy Ghost, he hath SHED FORTH this which ye now see and hear."

He uses in this place the figure of "SHEDDING FORTH," as expressive of the same thing, which is closely allied to "pouring."

Again, when St. Peter was preaching to Cornelius and his company, St. Luke informs us (Acts x. 44-46), "While Peter yet spake these words, the Holy Ghost 'FELL' on all them which heard the word. And they of the circumcision which believed were astonished, as many as came with Peter, because that on the Gentiles also was POURED out the gift of the Holy Ghost. For they heard them speak with tongues and magnify God." So, St. Luke applies both "*shed*" and "*pour*" to those same gifts of the Holy Ghost received on the day of Pentecost. St. Peter, relating this event on his return to Jerusalem, says (Acts xi. 15, 16), "And as I began to speak, the Holy Ghost FELL on them, as on us at the beginning [day of Pentecost.] Then I remembered the word of the Lord, how that he said, John indeed baptized with water; but ye shall be baptized with the Holy Ghost." (Acts i. 5.) Hence he regarded this as another fulfilment of our Lord's promise of the Holy Ghost, and uses the figure of St. Luke — "the Holy Ghost FELL on them."

In another place he speaks of "the Holy Ghost SENT DOWN from Heaven" (1 Peter i. 13.)

St. John says, "I saw the Spirit DESCENDING FROM HEAVEN like a dove, and it abode upon him." (John i. 32.)

Thus we see the Baptism of the Holy Ghost is described as "*poured out*," "*shed forth*," "*fell upon*," "*sent down*," "*descending*," and "*abiding upon;*" and yet we are told that *baptize* "has but one signification — it always signifies to dip — never expressing anything but mode;" and that "*baptism* always implies immersion!" And with this idea, the "Bible Union," as they call themselves, are making a new translation of our English Bible, in which *immerse* and *immersion* are to be substituted for "baptize" and "baptism!"

Besides *pouring*, *shedding forth*, *falling upon*, *sent down*, *descending* and abiding upon, we have seen that Baptism is applied in the New Testament to washing of hands and feet, cups, pots, brazen vessels, tables (couches), and to the *various purifications* of the ritual law of Moses.

Dr. Carson is very averse to calling "*Baptism*" a "*purification:*" for although it be administered for that purpose, he says, "purification is the *consequence*, not *the Baptism* itself." This he repeats oftener than once. But it is a *distinction without a difference*, as he applies it. For though purification be not attained until the Baptism is performed, the Baptism is not complete until its work is done. It is no more a *Bap-*

tism in its initiative and progressive stages towards completion, than it is a *purification.* They both begin and end together. They are *practically and really one* and *the same thing.* Therefore, in all such cases, *Baptism* is ipso facto *Purification.* What is there in the act of the purification not in the act of the Baptism? As a ritual service the same act is called by both names. Independent of the Baptism the purification has no existence; and whatever is a *necessary part* of the Baptism, as to time or mode of existence, is a *necessary part* of the purification.

No other word in the English language would convey, perhaps, so well the full meaning of βαπτίζω as — PURIFY. We would, therefore, adopt in full the words of another, who has written an excellent book on this branch of our subject since the publication of our first edition: "If we reject our English word baptize — for baptize has become truly and properly an English word — and attempt to translate the Greek βαπτίζω, we should translate it by the word PURIFY, and not IMMERSE. At the same time we remark, that the word *purify*, as used in the Old Testament, is used in a sense different from that in which it is used in common conversation and in the English classics. The English word baptize, in its common acceptation, more nearly expresses the exact idea of the Greek βαπτίζω than the English word *purify* would. And on this account, we would greatly prefer to see our venerable English stand 'as of old.' To translate the Greek βαπτίζω in the Word of God, by the English word *dip* or *immerse*, or into any other language by words corresponding to our English words *dip* and *immerse*, is to mistranslate the Word of God; not simply to make an allowable variation in a version of the Bible, but to *mistranslate the Word of God.*"[1]

It being now evident to every attentive reader of these pages that BAPTIZE *and* BAPTISM are *not specific* terms, confined to *one mode* of action in the Holy Scriptures, but *generic*, and express *various modes*, it is unnecessary to dwell any longer on this branch of the subject.

We might have referred to the Baptism of the Israelites — "unto Moses in the cloud and in the sea" (1 Cor. x. 1, 2), — concerning which strange perversions of a plain case have been attempted to twist it into immersion! But, after all, the idea of immersion in water on "dry ground," is difficult of comprehension — especially when the water had been removed out of the way for them to pass on "dry ground through the midst of the sea." That they were sprinkled by a mist from the cloud and sea, and therefore baptized by aspersion, is easily comprehended. The Psalmist explains it clearly enough (Ps. lxxvii. 16, 20), "The waters saw thee, O God, the waters saw thee; they were afraid; the depths also were troubled. The clouds poured out water. . . . Thou leddest thy people like a flock by the hand of Moses and Aaron." The rain which fell from the clouds while they were crossing the sea, in advance it may be of a storm that accompanied the closing up of the waters on the Egyptians, was the Baptism which the Israelites received; while the rushing together of the waters, covering the Egyptians, literally *immersed them*, for *they were buried* in the Red Sea. We might also have enlarged on the washing of Naaman, the leper, in the river Jordan (2 Kings v. 14), at the command of Elisha. And we

[1] Armstrong *On the Doctrine of Baptisms.*

might likewise have examined more *critically* the Baptism of Nebuchadnezzar by the dews of Heaven, in his deranged state (Dan. v. 21): for the term applied to him in the Septuagint is *the root* from which βαπτίζω is derived, and *more intensive* in its meaning. Yet it is used to express the wetting or baptizing of one by the settling down of the dew upon him at night. We should hardly conclude, in such a case, that he was dipped or immersed in the dew. We might further have referred to Christ's allusion to his own sufferings under the figure of Baptism (St. Mark x. 38, 39). These would have given additional illustrations of the various applications and modes of Baptism, but why multiply cases to establish what must be already proved to the satisfaction of every attentive reader? that BAPTIZE and BAPTISM, as used in the Holy Scriptures, are not specific terms *signifying only one mode*, but are applied to *various modes*. If Christian Baptism, then, was administered in one particular way, and that way designed to be binding on all generations, we must look to the *circumstances* under which it was administered in the cases recorded in the New Testament;—for the *term itself* implies *no particular mode*, nor have we any *specific directions* from Christ or his Apostles on that point.

CHAPTER X.

EXAMINATION OF THE MEANING AND MODES OF BAPTISM CONTINUED.

John's Baptism. — Prepositions "in," "into," and "out of," determine nothing. — Ænon or Springs. — Apostles baptized without Regard to Circumstances. — Baptism of Three Thousand — of the Samaritans — of the Eunuch — of Saul — of Cornelius — of the Jailer — of the Disciples at Ephesus. — Mode indicated only by the Spirit. — End or Object of Baptism. — Christ the Second Adam. — Circumcision of Christ. — Figurative Allusions. — Explanations. — Summary of Scriptural Testimony. — Concluded with Historical Proof of Baptism by Different Modes in every Age of the Church since the Death of the Apostles. — No Prevailing Mode without Exceptions.

§ 30. WE now proceed to examine the *circumstances* under which the various cases of Baptism recorded in the New Testament occurred. And in order to make our work thorough, we will take up every passage that can throw any light on the mode, from the beginning of John's Baptism to the end of the Divine Record.

But we must first premise that the Greek prepositions translated "in," "into," and "out of," prove nothing of themselves; because, as every Greek scholar knows, they as often mean "unto," "to," "at," "near by," "with," and "from," and are so translated in various places in the New Testament. They weigh nothing, therefore, as *proof* for one side or the other, independently of the verbs and other things with which they stand connected. We shall find that in every passage rendered "he went down *into* the water," and came up "*out of the water*," the same terms would be used for "going down *to* the water," and "coming up *from* the water." So that something more than such forms of speech must be found to justify any one in confining Baptism to the mode of *dipping*.

1. The first passages recorded in the New Testament, on which Baptists rely for proof of immersion, are found in Matt. iii. 1, 5, 6: "In those days came John the Baptist, preaching in the wilderness of Judea. . . . . And there went out to him Jerusalem and all Judea, and all the region round about Jordan, and were baptized of him in Jordan, confessing their sins." They lay much stress on "baptized of him in the Jordan;" but the Greek ἐν translated "in," means also *at*, *on*, *by*, *near*, and might have been rendered "*at* the Jordan," or "by the Jordan;" and, therefore, can determine nothing by itself. St. Luke uses the same preposition to point out the position of the tower *at* (ἐν) or *near* the fountain of Siloam. (Luke xiii. 4.) St. Paul uses the same frequently in describing the relation of one (ἐν) *at* or *near* the right hand of another. (Heb. i. 3; viii. 1; Rom. viii. 34.) St. John uses it to describe the light shining (ἐν) *on* one's path. (St. John xi. 10.) And others, in like manner. Therefore, we must have something more than the translation of ἐν into *in*, to prove anything in regard to *the mode* in such cases.

Besides, even admitting the translation to be correct, the language used in such cases, would apply equally well to persons who, with wooden sandals and short, loose robes, in a sultry climate, would as soon walk a short distance into the water, as to stop at its edge, even for the purpose of pouring the water on their heads, or of sprinkling it over them. In the heat and dust produced by crowds under such circumstances, it would refresh them, and wash the dust from their feet and sandals, to go a few paces into the stream: whilst John could accompany them into the water, or baptize them whilst standing himself on the bank or a rock near by, as we often see their Baptism represented in ancient engravings. Nothing, therefore, is to be inferred from the rendering, "were baptized in Jordan."

2. Additional stress, however, has been laid on the following verses (13 and 14): "Then cometh Jesus from Galilee to Jordan unto John, to be baptized of him. And Jesus, when he was baptized, went up straightway out of the water." Here, it is often said, "went up out of the water" shows that John immersed him. But not so; the preposition ἀπό, translated "out of," is more generally rendered "from" than "out of." And so far as that is concerned, the reading would be equally correct if translated "went up *from* the water." St. Matthew so uses it in the same chapter to describe fleeing from the wrath to come (verse 7): "O generation of vipers! who hath warned you to flee (ἀπό) *from* the wrath to come?" not "out of" the wrath to come. Again, he applies it to coming down *from* the cross of Christ (chap. xxvii. 40): "If thou be the son of God, come down (ἀπό) *from* the cross,"— not "out of" the cross. St. Luke applies it to the act of one person leaving another: "And it came to pass as they departed (ἀπό) *from him*,"— not "*out of* him." (St. Luke ix. 33.) Such is its frequent and most common use in the New Testament; therefore it is of no force as proof that Christ was immersed by John.

3. St Mark's account of John's baptizing in or at Jordan, is as follows (Mark i. 4, 5, 9, 10): "John did baptize in the wilderness, and preach the Baptism of repentance for the remission of sins. And there went out unto him all the land of Judea, and they of Jerusalem, and were baptized of him in the river Jordan, confessing their sins. . . . And it came to pass in those days, that Jesus came from Nazareth to Galilee, and was baptized of John in Jordan. And straightway coming up out of the water, he saw the heavens opened, and the Spirit like a dove, descending upon him."

Here we have precisely the same terms applied to the act of baptizing, that are used by St. Matthew, except in the Baptism of Christ, where εἰς is used instead of ἐν, and is used perhaps in a hundred places in the New Testament to express proximity or nearness to a place — for *at*, *to*, *by*, *on*, *upon*, and *near to*. For instance, "his fellow servant fell down (εἰς) *at* his feet,"— not in his feet. (St. Matt. xviii. 17.) Again, "Seeing the multitudes, he went up (εἰς) *on* the mountain,"— not *in* the mountain. (St. Matt. v. 1.) Again, "He gave commandment to depart (εἰς) *unto* the other side,"— not *in* the other side. (St. Matt. viii. 18.) Once more: "So they ran both together, and that other disciple did outrun Peter, and came first (εἰς) to the sepulchre," — not *in* or *into* the sepulchre, for we are told that the "other disciple" did not go into the sepulchre at all. (St. John xx.)

Thus St. Mark records nothing that throws any additional light on the account given by St. Matthew, or on the *mode* of Baptism by John.

4. We come next to St. Luke. All that he says on the subject is, "And he (John) came into all the

country about Jordan, preaching the Baptism of repentance for the remission of sins. . . . Now when the people were baptized, it came to pass that Jesus also being baptized, and praying, the heaven was opened, and the Holy Ghost descended in a bodily shape, like a dove upon him." (St. Luke iii. 3–22.)

He says nothing about *going into* or coming "out of" the water, but simply informs us that all the people in the country about Jordan were baptized of John, and that Jesus also being baptized, while in prayer, the Holy Ghost, in the bodily shape of a dove, descended upon him.

5. St. John is the only remaining witness whose testimony can throw any light on this question. He, after recording the answer of John to the Pharisees who were sent to inquire who John was, and by what authority he baptized, tells us, "These things were done in Bethabara beyond Jordan, where John was baptizing." (St. John i. 28.) Again, "And John also was baptizing in (or at) Ænon, near to Salim, because there was much water [many waters] there." (Chap iii. 23.) "And he [Jesus] went away again beyond Jordan, into the place where John at first baptized." (Chap. x. 40.)

The advocates of immersion have drawn largely from the clause, "because there was much water there," urging that immersion required much water, and for that especial reason John sojourned at Ænon, a place of several springs or fountains of water. But abundance of water, for drinking, washing, and culinary purposes, is as necessary to crowds and large assemblies in a wilderness, or uninhabited portions of the country, as it would be for their Baptism by immersion. When our Methodist brethren purpose holding a large camp-meeting, abundance of good spring water is regarded as a very important item. And they are influenced in their selection of a place for such an assemblage more perhaps by a good supply of water than any other one thing — not because of immersion, but for the necessary use and comfort of their assembly. Ænon, being the plural of fountain, or spring, probably took its name from the many springs or fountains there. And this agrees with the Greek ὕδατα πολλὰ, "*many waters*," many springs or fountains, instead of much water in one body. And the passage would be more literally translated if rendered, "And John also was baptizing at Ænon (the Springs), near to Salim, because there were many waters there," — springs and streams, to supply *all the wants* of the multitudes that flocked to his Baptism. He would hardly have left the JORDAN for ÆNON, if water for immersion had been his object. Yet he might have done so for the sake of purer and cooler water to slake the thirst of the people, and for other necessary uses.

The question has been triumphantly asked, "Why did John baptize in the river? Why did he go down to the water at all — even to the edge of the water — if Baptism was performed by pouring or sprinkling? Why not bring the water from the river to the people to baptize them?" Such questions would not arise if the circumstances of the case were rightly pondered. Crowds of people collected to see and hear something new outside the city limits, and in retired places, do not often take with them vessels for carrying water. John did not select the city for his operations; had he done so, the multitudes must have blocked up the streets, and excited the civil authorities against his mission. He made choice of more open and retired places, under the groves and along the banks of the Jordan. It was, therefore, an easy matter to step down to the edge of the water; it would even be more convenient for taking up the water in his hand to pour upon the heads of his numerous converts. For it must be remembered that *many thousands* were baptized by him; while we have no right to suppose that articles for such purposes would be very abundant in assemblages of like character in "the wilderness." (Judges vii. 5, 6.) We are informed that "all Jerusalem and all Judea, and all the region round about Jordan," received his Baptism. And if one twentieth of this population, according to the estimate of Josephus, was baptized by immersion, John must have remained in the water a large portion of each day during his whole mission.

Such interrogations, therefore, have no force as arguments against Baptism by aspersion or otherwise. Place and circumstances show that stepping down *to* or *into* the river, would be a natural and easy way to obtain the water even for sprinkling so many; preëminently so, since John's Baptism was a *Jewish purification* for the reception of Christ; and such purifications required "*running water*," as opposed to stagnant or unclean water. Hence the propriety of selecting the river Jordan, and the running fountains or streams of Ænon, as suitable places for both the *rite* and the necessary comfort of the people.

It must now be clear to the reader that nothing definite in regard to the *mode* can be learned from John's Baptism. We have examined this point, not because it could decide the mode of Christian Baptism (for we have already shown that John's Baptism was not Christian Baptism), but because it is supposed that whatever mode was practised by John, was adopted by the Apostles. This, however, does not necessarily follow, and might conflict with the theory that John sought places of *much water* for the object of immersion; for it is certain no such intimation is to be found in the sacred record, for the purpose of *Christian Baptism.* On the contrary, in every case where the message of the Apostles was received, *there* and *then* they were baptized. The three thousand on the day of Pentecost, in the city of Jerusalem — men and women by Philip in Samaria, the eunuch by the wayside, Paul in Damascus, and probably in the room where the scales fell from his eyes, Cornelius at his own house, Lydia near the river side, the jailer within the prison walls, the disciples at Ephesus, and others besides, without one word in regard to inconvenience or delay, or removal to another place for water for the Sacrament.

1. We will now proceed to examine every instance of CHRISTIAN BAPTISM in the New Testament from which an *inference* in any possible way can be made to bear on the mode in which it was administered. We begin with the *three thousand* on the day of Pentecost. Having received the Baptism of the Holy Ghost, the Apostles entered forthwith upon the great work for which they had been set apart. The people collected in large numbers to hear them, and many were made to cry out, " Men and brethren, what shall we do? "

Acts ii. 38, 39, 41. " Then Peter said unto them, Repent and be baptized every one of you, in the name of Jesus Christ, for the remission of sins, and ye shall receive the gift of the Holy Ghost. For the promise is unto you, and to your children, and to all that are afar off, even as many as the Lord our God shall call. . . . Then they that gladly received his word were baptized; and the same day there were added unto them about three thousand souls."

This was the first day's work of the Apostles under the New Dispensation. They were baptized themselves by the Holy Ghost, and three thousand souls converted by their preaching, were then baptized by them. But nothing is said or done, so far as the record shows, to indicate in the slightest degree that they were baptized by immersion. Not a word about their going to river or pool for Baptism; the whole transaction is recorded as if they were baptized as soon as convinced by the preaching of the Apostles, and they ready to receive them. And the Baptism might easily have been performed in a short time from the contents of the watering pots kept for purifying; but if by immersion, it must have been laborious work for the remainder of that day.

Further, it was at a season of the year when the little brook Cedron was generally dry; the public baths, if any, we may suppose were in the hands of those in authority; and the supposition that they were scattered through the city to find private baths for such a number, would hardly correspond with the time allowed them, and with the purport of the record. The only *mode* intimated is that of the Baptism of the Holy Spirit, under the figure of "POURED OUT," (ἐξέχεε.) Therefore, so far as *allusions* indicate mode they are decidedly in favor of pouring, or aspersion, rather than immersion. So much for the Baptism of the three thousand.

2. We come next to the Baptism of the people of Samaria.

Acts viii. 12, 13. "But when they believed Philip, preaching the things concerning the kingdom of God, and the name of Jesus Christ, they were baptized, both men and women. Then Simon himself believed also; and when he was baptized, he continued with Philip, and wondered, beholding the miracles and signs which were done."

We have no allusion to MODE here — consequently, nothing to favor the idea of IMMERSION.

3. The next in order is the Baptism of the eunuch by Philip. The eunuch, while riding in his carriage, was reading the prophecy of Isaiah, and invited Philip, who drew near to him, to take a seat with him. That portion upon which he was engaged, treated of the vicarious sufferings of Christ, which is embraced in the 52d and 53d chapters of Isaiah (divisions into chapters had not then been made), and he asked Philip "of whom speaketh the prophet this? of himself, or of some other man?"

Acts viii. 35, 39. "Then Philip opened his mouth, and began at the same Scripture, and preached unto him Jesus. And as they went on their way, they came to a certain water; and the eunuch said, See, here is water; what doth hinder me to be baptized? And Philip saith, If thou believest with all thine heart, thou mayest. And he answered and said, I believe that Jesus Christ is the Son of God. And he commanded the chariot to stand still; and they went down both into the water, both Philip and the eunuch, and he baptized him. And when they were come up out of the water, the Spirit of the Lord caught away

Philip, that the eunuch saw him no more; and he went on his way rejoicing."

This passage has been regarded by some persons as proof positive of immersion. But the very same reasoning applies to it that applies to the Baptism in the river Jordan. The Greek words rendered "into" and "out of," as often mean "unto" and "from." And if translated, "they went down both *to* the water," and were "come up *from* the water," it would be in perfect accordance with the Greek; and hence proof resting upon the mere translation of such words amounts to nothing. St. Matthew uses the same Greek word which is rendered "into," in this place, when he says: "Go thou (εἰς) *to* the sea," — not *into* the sea. (Chap. xvii. 27.) He used it also for "unto," in the passage, "I am not sent but (εἰς) *unto* the lost sheep of the house of Israel," — not *into* the lost sheep. (Chap. xv. 24.) Again: "All things are ready, come (εἰς) *unto* the marriage," — not *into* the marriage. (Chap. xxii. 4.)

Thus it will be perceived how uncertain is the meaning of the phrase "went down into the water." And equally uncertain is its corresponding one, "come up out of the water." St. Matthew uses the same word for separating the wicked from the righteous. "Sever the wicked (ἐκ) *from* among the just," — not *out of*. (Chap. xiii. 49.) Again: "The tree is known (ἐκ) *from* or *by* its fruit," — not *out of*. (Chap. xii. 23.) St. John uses it in like manner: "Many good works have I shown you (ἐκ) *from* my Father," — not *out of* my Father.

Now what is an argument worth in any cause, resting on such a basis as this? The *verbs* with which these prepositions stand connected, accord as well with descending from the chariot *to* the water, and going up *from* the water to the chariot, as descending into the water, and going up out of it. And even admitting that they went into it, would not prove any particular *mode* of the Baptism, as we have before shown. Besides which, there are other circumstances that seem to conflict with the idea of immersion. There is no river or water-course of any note between Jerusalem and Gaza, where they were travelling — St. Luke calls it a way that is "desert." He also calls the place of the Baptism, "a certain water," as if so inconsiderable as not to deserve the name of river or pool or lake, and hence it was probably one of those *way-side wells*, which travellers inform us are to be found sometimes in desert countries, provided for the accommodation and lodging places of those who travel through that way. And such being the case, one might be washed or sprinkled, when plunging him under the water would be impracticable. It must be remembered also that travelling on foot as Philip was, wet clothes after an immersion would be rather inconvenient to carry; or, if the operation was performed *nude*, we hope that we shall be excused in this age if we depart from the letter in that particular.

We should further inquire what suggested Baptism to the mind of the eunuch, that he should propound to Philip the question, "What doth hinder me to be baptized?" as soon as he saw water. By turning to that portion of Isaiah which the eunuch was reading, we shall see that the prophet, among the first things after introducing the vicarious sufferings of Christ, says, "So shall he sprinkle many nations." (lii. 15.) If Philip preached to him Baptism from these words, he could hardly have preached Baptism by immersion. Therefore, in either case, the probabilities are against, rather than in favor of immersion.

All the circumstances considered, the condition of travellers, scarcity of water, and language of Isaiah — this passage, on which so much reliance has been placed for immersion, and which Dr. Carson thinks, under the "most violent persuasion it could sustain on the rack, would still cry out, *immersion*, *immersion*,"[1]— really proves as much for any other *mode* as for immersion. No logician can admit that it proves the eunuch was plunged under the water. And this is all that we are now to settle concerning it. We have no objection to immersion in itself, unless made exclusive without authority; our object is to ascertain whether it was the *mode* practised by the Apostles, and whether we can find any authority that will justify one in confining Baptism to that *one mode*, and forbidding all others. This we have certainly failed to do thus far.

4. Next follows the Baptism of St. Paul: while on his way to Damascus as a persecutor of Christians, he was struck with blindness, and removed to the house of a friend, where he remained "three days without sight, and neither did eat nor drink." At the end of which time Ananias was sent to him to open his eyes and baptize him.

Acts ix. 17, 18. "And Ananias went his way, and entered into the house: and putting his hands on him, said, Brother Saul, the Lord (even Jesus that appeared unto thee in the way as thou camest) hath sent me, that thou mightest receive thy sight, and be filled with the Holy Ghost. And immediately there

[1] *Baptism*, p. 128.

fell from his eyes, as it had been scales: and he received sight forthwith, and arose and was BAPTIZED."

The following is St. Paul's own account of the same: Acts xxii. 12, 16. "And one Ananias, a devout man according to the law, having a good report of all the Jews which dwelt there, came unto me, and stood, and said unto me, Brother Saul, receive thy sight. And the same hour, I looked up upon him. And he said, the God of our fathers hath chosen thee, that thon shouldest know his will, and see that Just One, and shouldest hear the voice of his mouth. For thou shalt be his witness unto all men, of what thou hast seen and heard. And now why tarriest thou? arise and be baptized and wash away thy sins, calling on the name of the Lord."

These two narratives are essentially the same. Saul had been struck with blindness, and after three days' praying and fasting in the house of Judah, Ananias is sent to him by the Lord, who finds him engaged in prayer, lays his hands upon him, saying, "Receive thy sight," — scales of blindness fall from his eyes — he looks up, and Ananias bids him "arise and be baptized," — and he arose and was baptized. Literally, "standing up, he was baptized." [1]

[1] "At the time of our Lord's sojourn upon earth, the Syriac seems to have been the general medium of colloquial intercourse, and consequently was the vernacular of CHRIST and his Apostles. And the Syriac New Testament uniformly translates the Greek word *to baptize*, by the Syriac Amad, which in Hebrew, Chaldee, and the kindred dialects, signifies (1) *to stand*, (2) *to cause to stand*, to which the Syriac adds the special usage (3) *to wash*, (4) *to baptize*.

"Now in Hebrew and Arabic, *to stand*, i. e., before one, implied *servitude* or *ministry*. In Latin a derivation from a kindred root (*sto, stare*) *to stand*, denotes *to make a set speech*. What, then, ought we to conclude, was that peculiarity of Baptism which led our Lord and his Apostles to call *Baptism* a *stand* or *standing*. Neither the element by which it was per-

Now what do we find here pointing out the exclusive mode of immersion? So far as the narrative and circumstances indicate anything, it is that of baptism in the *room* and on the *spot* where Ananias found him; which suggest pouring or sprinkling rather than immersion. "Standing up, he was baptized." Imagination can take him out to a river or pool and make a great display — but as faithful interpreters of God's word, we must confine ourselves to the laws of interpretation — we must be governed by the record and circumstances of the case. We cannot, therefore, infer immersion, or confine Baptism to that *particular mode*, from such an account as this. But rather the reverse.

5. We come now to the first Baptism of one outside of the pale of the Jewish Church. Cornelius, a Gentile and Roman officer, but truly a devout man, was commanded by an angel to send for Peter, who

formed, nor the person administering it, nor the mode of its application, were prominent considerations, but the receiver received a *standing* or else *took a stand*, in the Church, and on the side of the Gospel. It should also be added, that the Syriac words denoting *Ordination* and *Confirmation*, are from a root (*Kom*) which signifies *to stand*. From what point of view, therefore, are we to conclude the Sacrament was looked at, when it received the name *stand?*

"The early Britons, before the advent of the Saxons in that island, translated *to baptize* by *bedyz*, or *bedydd*, which seems to have for their primary meaning to *give*, to *consecrate*. And the Anglo-Saxon itself, when that people came to translate the New Testament, denoted *Baptism* by Fullian, *to cleanse*, *to purify*. From what point, or under what aspect, must those have regarded the Sacrament of Baptism, who employed this word?

"The Ethiopian translation has Tamaka, *to tinge*, *dye*, *color;* also, *to baptize*. The ancient Celtic, both Scotch and Irish, rendered the word BAIST, *to pour*, *to sprinkle*, *to baptize;* while the Coptic employed OMS, *to stand in the water*, *to baptize*.

"We should be glad to see a satisfactory account of the probable causes which led to this diversity in the use of language, by the early Christians. Especially should we be glad to see what account our Baptist brethren can give of the matter." — CALENDAR.

received also instructions by a vision, not to despise the Gentiles, and went to the house of Cornelius, and there preached Jesus to him and his assembled friends.

Acts x. 44, 48. "While Peter yet spake these words, the Holy Ghost fell[1] on all them which heard the word. And they of the circumcision which believed were astonished, as many as came with Peter, because that on the Gentiles also was poured out[2] the gift of the Holy Ghost. For they heard them speak with tongues and magnify God. Then said Peter, Can any man forbid water, that these should not be baptized, which have received the Holy Ghost as well as we? And he commanded them to be baptized in the name of the Lord."

This, though the first Baptism among uninitiated Gentiles, is accompanied with no prescribed mode — nothing about going to a pool or to a bath; simply a command at the time and place that they be baptized. And when it was heard at Jerusalem that "the Gentiles had received the word of God," it caused much commotion among the "circumcision." And St. Peter thus rehearsed the matter: —

Acts xi. 15, 17. "And as I began to speak, the Holy Ghost fell[3] on them, as on us at the beginning. Then remembered I the word of the Lord, how that he said, John indeed baptized with water; but ye shall be baptized with the Holy Ghost. Forasmuch then as God gave them the like gift, as He did unto us, who believed on the Lord Jesus Christ, what was I, that I could withstand God?

There is nothing to suggest the *mode* of their Baptism in this case, unless it be the Baptism of the Holy Ghost, which "FELL UPON" or was "POURED

1 'Επέπεσε. 2 'Εκκέχυται. 3 'Επέπεσε.

OUT;" and which St. Peter himself says was the fulfilment of the promise of the Lord — "ye shall be baptized with the Holy Ghost." And seeing these were baptized with the Holy Ghost, Baptism by water was suggested to his mind; and he asked, "Can any man forbid water, that these should not be baptized, who have received the Holy Ghost as well as we?" When an *invisible operation* is likened to something *visible*, we may presume it is because of some resemblance between the things thus associated. Between POURING OUT OF THE SPIRIT and DIPPING OF THE BODY UNDER WATER, there is certainly very little; but *pouring the water on the head*, and *pouring out of the Spirit on men*, very strikingly resemble each other; while *Baptism* by the Holy Ghost and *Baptism* by water, have both the same leading object in view — the PURIFICATION and RENEWAL of the heart.[1] And both were intimately associated in the minds of John the Baptist, the Saviour, and his Apostles.[2]

POURING being the only MODE alluded to in the case of Cornelius and his friends, it is consequently the MODE suggested by the narrative of *their* Baptism, and *not* immersion. Therefore, from this case, instead of finding authority for confining Baptism to immersion, we are led to the opposite conclusion.

6. The next case from which anything can be inferred from the circumstances, under which it was administered, is that of the jailer. Paul and Silas had been apprehended, beaten, and thrown into prison! An earthquake the same night threw open *the prison* doors, and the jailer being aroused *from*

[1] John iii. 5; Acts ii. 38; Titus iii. 5.
[2] John iii. 5; Matt. iii. 11; Acts i. 5; xi. 16; Titus iii. 5.

sleep and finding them open, supposed the prisoners had escaped, and was about to kill himself. Paul called to him to do himself no harm; saying, "We are all here."

The jailer called for a light, sprang in, and fell down at the Apostles' feet, and then "brought them out (of the inner prison), and said, 'Sirs, what must I do to be saved?'"

Acts xvi. 31–34. "And they said, Believe on the Lord Jesus Christ, and thou shalt be saved, and thy house. And they spake unto him the word of the Lord, and to all that were in his house. And he took them the same hour of the night, and washed their stripes, and was BAPTIZED, *he, and all his straightway.* And when he had brought them into his house, he set meat before them, and rejoiced, believing in God with all his house."

Here the Baptism, like that of Cornelius and others, was administered forthwith, the same hour of the night, even before they went into the apartment where the jailer lived, as it appears. The earthquake having aroused all in and about the prison, they had collected, probably in the outer court, where the Apostles addressed them. The jailer first washed the lacerated bodies of the Apostles, and was then baptized, he and all his, straightway. After which he took them into his own apartment and set meat before them. The Apostles preached to all present, the (οἰκία) "household," which includes the domestics and attendants of an establishment — but only the jailer and his own immediate family (οἱ αὐτοῦ πάντες) were baptized.

There is nothing written in this place to indicate the mode of this Baptism; but the late hour of the night, within prison walls, and without any apparent delay, all taken together, suggest the probability of any *other* mode, rather than that of immersion. We are not informed that prisons, in those days, were fitted up with *baths* and conveniences of like nature. And no allusion being made to such things, or to immersion, we have no right to assume them. Consequently this, like all the other cases examined, fails to prove the practice of immersion, or to show any authority for confining Baptism to that mode.

7. The only remaining instance of Baptism, from which the slightest inference as to mode could be drawn, is that at Ephesus. The Apostle Paul meeting with certain disciples there, said unto them: —

Acts xix. 2, 6. "Have ye received the Holy Ghost, since ye believed? And they said unto him, we have not so much as heard whether there be any Holy Ghost. And he said unto them, unto what then were ye baptized? And they said, unto John's Baptism. Then, said Paul, John verily baptized with the Baptism of repentance, saying unto the people, that they should believe on Him which should come after him, that is, on Christ Jesus. *When they heard this, they were baptized in the name of the Lord Jesus. And when Paul had laid his hands on them, the Holy Ghost came upon them;* and they spake with tongues and prophesied."

We certainly do not find any intimation of immersion in this place. If any inference affecting the mode can be drawn from it, it is that the narrative *would* intimate more delay between the Baptism and *laying on of the Apostles' hands* in the case of immersion, than the record indicates. Its natural interpretation leads one to infer that the imposition of hands followed immediately after the Baptism, and without any such delay as the immersions of the present day require.

We have now examined every case of Christian Baptism in the New Testament that can throw any light on the *mode*. Some other cases of the *mere fact* of Baptism, without any reference to the circumstances, are mentioned — as the Baptism of Lydia and her family, of Stephanas and his family, and of Crispus and Gaius, but *only* the *fact* is recorded. We have considered all in which the *language* or *circumstances* give any intimation as to how they were probably performed.

Have we then found a single case of *unequivocal immersion?* or *anything* that can authorize any man, or any set of men, to confine Baptism to immersion, and pronounce all other modes invalid? The first that occurred under the Christian dispensation, that of three thousand in Jerusalem, was under circumstances *highly unfavorable*, instead of favorable to immersion. And all that we have heard about baths and cisterns in Jerusalem (for which we have never yet seen credible authority), does not meet the difficulties. Besides, what could the cisterns in Jerusalem do for other places? Paul was baptized in Damascus, Cornelius in Cæsarea, the jailer at Philippi, and others at Ephesus; not one of which was even in Judea. And in every case there is not the slightest intimation to lead one to suppose they were immersed; but on the contrary, under *circumstances* and *recorded in terms*, that suggest *affusion* or *aspersion* as the most probable.

The only case, the narrative of which could suggest the idea of immersion, is that of the eunuch, and this to such as are governed entirely by our English translation; for the original Greek, as we have shown, is susceptible not only of a different rendering, but of one that excludes even the *possibility* of immersion. The present translation in our English version does not teach immersion, nor could any rendering of which the passage is susceptible, teach it. Laying aside the circumstances, and placing everything in the most favorable light, neither immersion nor any other particular mode can be inferred from it; therefore, it gives no authority for any exclusive mode. Shall we then base an *invariable law* on such a passage, and make immersion the only valid Baptism?

The only mode of Baptism which we have seen clearly indicated, is that of the Baptism of the Holy Ghost. And this, under the figures of "*poured out*," "*shed forth*," and "*descending*." And this Baptism was intimately associated with the Baptism of water in the minds of the Apostles, as St. Peter's own words prove. Therefore, if we are guided in our practice of Baptism by the teaching of the Holy Scriptures, in connection with the recorded instances therein, *pouring* and *sprinkling* have both stronger claims to our election than immersion.

8. Great reliance, however, is placed on certain *figurative allusions* to Baptism by the Apostle Paul. First, in his Epistle to the Romans, after explaining the system of salvation by grace, and having shown that *where sin abounded*, grace *did superabound*, he then meets the question that might be raised: "Shall we continue in sin that grace may abound?" and shows that this would be contrary to the *means* and *end* of

grace; that Christ died to deliver us from sin, and in his death were buried all the sins of his people; for as many as were baptized into Jesus Christ, were baptized *into his death;* through which they obtain deliverance from sin, that they may walk in newness of life. (Romans vi. 2, 7.) "How shall we that are dead to sin, live any longer therein? Know ye not that so many of us as were baptized into Jesus Christ, were baptized into his death? Therefore we are buried with him by Baptism into death: that like as Christ was raised up from the dead by the glory of the Father, even so we also should walk in newness of life. For if we have been planted together in the likeness of his death, we shall be also in the likeness of his resurrection. Knowing this, that our old man is crucified with Him, that the body of sin might be destroyed, that henceforth we should not serve sin. For he that is dead is freed from sin."

Now it is supposed by many that the words "buried with Him by Baptism into death," refer to the *mode* of Baptism by immersion. But before we interpret figurative language, we should examine the subject-matter in hand, and also the connection in which it is found. The author was not discussing the *mode* of Baptism, nor the *authority* of Baptism. *Our deliverance from sin through Christ was his theme.* And we being delivered from its condemnation, must strive to be delivered from its practice also; for if we recognize Christ as our deliverer, who suffered in our room and stead — "by whose stripes we are healed," — we must reckon ourselves to have been represented by Him, and participants in his sufferings. In his death we died with Him, and in his resurrection we rose, to walk with him in newness of life. All the sins of his people *were buried in his death*, because all truly united to Him in Baptism must be regarded *as one with Him in his sufferings for them; and should "reckon themselves to be dead indeed unto sin*, but alive unto God through Jesus Christ." (Verse 11.) Grace, therefore, instead of encouraging sin, is in direct opposition to it; it provides a cure for its wounds, and demands that it be put away from all who would be saved by grace. Baptism ritually connects us with Christ — it is the *sacramental rite* by which we are grafted into Him, our second Adam, and through Him into his death; hence "we are by virtue of this union buried with Him by Baptism into death" — death to sin; and death to the bondage of our first Adam. But in saying "we are buried with Him by Baptism into death," in virtue of our connection with Him through Baptism, the Apostle makes no necessary allusion to the *mode* of Baptism. He could not make any unless whilst earnestly unfolding a great principle, and the duties which it involved, he turned aside to *an incidental resemblance*, if there be one, which he did not explain. For he does not say that Baptism symbolizes a burial, therefore we are buried with Christ in our Baptism; but that "we were baptized into his death," — united with Him in his death by Baptism, and therefore buried with Him. The words "*into death*" are evidently connected with *Baptism*. "Know you not that so many of us as were baptized into Jesus Christ, were baptized into his death? *Therefore we are buried with Him* (for this reason) because "*we were baptized into his death.*" Not because of the *mode* by which we were baptized, or of a Baptism *emblematical* of a burial; but because of the *object* for which we were baptized. "The point of comparison (as Professor

Hodge of Princeton very justly remarks) is not between our *Baptism and the resurrection of Christ;* but *between our death to sin and rising to holiness, and the death and resurrection of our Redeemer.* As Paul had expressed in verse 2, the idea of the freedom of believers from sin, by the figurative phrase "dead to sin," he carries the figure consistently through; and says, that by our reception of Christ we become united to Him in such a way as to die as He died, and to rise as He rose. As He died unto sin (for its destruction), so do we; and as He rose unto newness of life, so do we."[1]

The *antithesis* between burial and resurrection, shows that it is not a *physical* burial under water to which the Apostle refers, because the resurrection, the corresponding part of the comparison, is *spiritual* and *moral.* "That like as Christ was raised up from the dead by the glory (power) of the Father, even so we also should walk in newness of life."

You perceive that the *resurrection* here spoken of is entirely *moral* and *spiritual;* and, therefore, the burial must be of like nature.

To place this question beyond all doubt, turn to a parallel passage in Colossians ii. 12. "Buried with Him in (or by) Baptism: wherein[2] also ye are

1 *Commentary on Romans,* chap. vi. 1–11.

2 *Wherein,* is from ἐν ᾧ, and may be rendered *in,* or *by whom,* referring to Christ; or, *in* or *by which,* referring to the ordinance. The older MSS. unite the clause "*buried with Him by Baptism,*" to the preceding verse, by placing a colon after Baptism; which is followed by Bloomfield. The verse thus arranged stands—"In whom also ye are circumcised with the circumcision made without hands, in putting off the body of the sins of the flesh by the circumcision of Christ, buried with Him in Baptism:" This exhibits more clearly the correspondence between Baptism and circumcision, and leaves the next verse to begin precisely as the preceding —ἐν ᾧ καί, "*In whom* (Christ) *also*" *ye are risen through faith;* which follows naturally the two preceding verses—the first of which tells us *we*

risen with Him *through the faith of the operation of God*, who hath raised Him from the dead." Here we read beyond all dispute, that those *buried* with Christ in or by Baptism, arise with Him through *faith*. Their resurrection from *this burial* is "through the faith of the operation of God," or *by faith wrought by the power of God*, "who hath raised Him [Christ] from the dead." And do we rise from a *physical burial* under water "*through the faith of the operation of God?*" Are men plunged under water by mortal hands, and then left to rise from the "liquid grave" *by faith?* Manifestly the burial from which such a resurrection takes place is a *moral one*, and the Apostle intended to teach in these passages that by Baptism we are so united to Christ *our substitute for sin* and *federal head*, that in his death we died, and in his resurrection we rose to a life of holiness. Consequently there is no necessary allusion to the *mode* of Baptism, and all that we have heard and read about "burial under water," and the "duty of immersion," as taught in these passages, is based on a false interpretation; which has gained ascendency over the minds of many through the familiar association of *burial* with *death*.

9. Much stress has been laid on the sentence, "For if we have been planted together in the likeness of his death, we shall be also in the likeness of his resurrection" (Rom. vi. 5).

Now, whilst this verse confirms what we have said in regard to the antithesis above, by showing if united

***are complete in Christ*, the next that in Christ all the blessings of circumcision are secured by Baptism into his death, and in this we are risen with Him through faith. But whether we refer these words to Christ, to the preceding sentence, or to the ordinance of Baptism, nothing is implied that can indicate the *mode* of Baptism.**

to Christ in his death, we shall be united to him in his resurrection, it affords no evidence of Baptism by immersion. For the figure *planted together in the likeness of his death*, is not supported by the original Greek. The word translated "*planted together*," σύμφυτοι, means literally *homogeneous*, *cognate*. And "must be so explained," says the learned Moses Stuart, "if philology be our guide." He also tells us this sentence may be rendered — "*If we have become connected or homogeneous by a likeness in respect to his death*, τοῦ θανάτου being the gen. objecti, *i. e.*, the object in respect to which we have become like Christ; or we may translate — *if we have become cognate in the likeness of his death*, the latter clause showing that in respect to which we have become cognate. The meaning is, 'If we have become dead to sin, as he died for sin; then shall we in like manner live a new life, when risen from our [moral] death, as he lived after his resurrection.' There is no good foundation for the translation '*planted*,' as φύω does not mean *to plant*, but *to grow*, *spring up*, *become nascent*, etc. Besides the nature of the imagery here employed is obscured by such a version."[1]

Let us also hear the views of this learned author on the other passages which we have just considered :—

"Most commentators," he writes, "have maintained that συνετάφημεν, *we have been buried* (*with Him*), has here a necessary reference to the mode of *literal* Baptism, which, they say, was by immersion; and this, they think, affords ground for the employment of the image used by the Apostle, because immersion under water may be compared to *burial* under the earth. It is difficult, perhaps, to procure a patient rehearing for

[1] *Commentary on Romans*, vi. 5, 6.

this subject, so long regarded by some as being out of fair dispute. Nevertheless, as my own conviction is not, after protracted and repeated examinations, accordant with that of commentators in general, I feel constrained briefly to state my reasons for it.

"The first is, that in the verse before us (4th) there is a plain *antithesis;* one so plain that it is impossible to overlook it. If now συνετάφημεν, *we have been buried*, is to be interpreted in a *physical* way, *i. e.*, as meaning *burial* in the water in a physical sense, where is the corresponding *physical* resurrection in the opposite part of the antithesis or comparison? Plainly there is no such *physical* idea or reference in this other part. The *resurrection* here spoken of is entirely *moral* and *spiritual*, for it is one which Christians have already experienced during this present life; as may be fully seen by comparing verses 5–11 following. . . . If we turn to the passage in Col. ii. 12 (which is altogether parallel with the verse under examination, and has very often been agitated by polemic writers on the subject of Baptism), we shall there find more conclusive reason still, to argue as above respecting the nature of the antithesis presented. 'We have been buried with Him (Christ) by Baptism.' What now is the opposite of this? What is the kind of *resurrection* from this grave in which Christians have been buried? The Apostle tells us: 'We have risen with Him (Christ) by faith wrought by the power of God [τῆς ἐνεργείας τοῦ Θεοῦ] who raised Him (Christ) from the dead.' Here, then, there is a *resurrection by faith*, *i. e.*, a *spiritual and moral one*. Why then should we look for a *physical* meaning in the antithesis? If one part of the antithesis is to be construed in a manner entirely *moral* and *spiritual*, why should we not construe the other in like manner, provided it is susceptible of such an interpretation? To understand *burial here*, as designating a *literal burial under water*, is to understand it in a manner which the laws of interpretation seem to forbid."[1]

After discussing various points connected with these passages, he tells us that he further objects to this figure of *immersion Baptism*, because he can find no such symbol of burial in the grave anywhere else in the Holy Scriptures. "Nor can I," he says, "think that it is a very natural symbol. The obvious import of washing with water or immersing in water is, that it is symbolical of *purity*, *cleansing*, *purification*. But how will this aptly signify *burying* in the grave, the place of corruption, loathsomeness, and destruction."

In his concluding remarks on this passage, he informs his readers that he can find nothing in it that can be used with confidence in a contest respecting the *mode* of Baptism. And that in this view the commentator Reiche concurs with him.[2]

Therefore these passages, so often referred to in support of the mode of Baptism by immersion, teach absolutely nothing on the subject. They make no *necessary* allusion to any mode whatever. The Apostle had a different object in view, and neither from his words, nor the general scope of his discourse, can we legitimately infer that he intended the most distant allusion to Baptism by immersion. He teaches that by Baptism we have been made *homogeneous with Christ* in his sufferings and death, and risen with

[1] See *Commentary on Romans*, vi. 4, second edition, corrected and enlarged.

[2] *Ibidem*. p. 275.

Him in his resurrection to a new life. "Knowing this," he adds, "that our old man is *crucified* with Him, that the body of sin might be destroyed, that henceforth we should not serve sin. For he that is dead is freed from sin (verses 6, 7). But in saying "our old man is crucified with Him," he does not teach that we have hung upon the cross as a symbol of crucifixion. For he likewise says, "As many as have been baptized into Christ have put on Christ;" but he does not mean that putting on clothes is a symbol of the mode of Baptism. He designs to teach that by Baptism as the appointed rite, we put on Christ as a garment — were crucified with Him in our affections — died with Him on his cross — and were buried with Him in his death. We were, therefore, baptized into his death for the death of our sins — henceforth to live a new life.

Which also affords an explanation of what the Apostle means when he asks, "Else what shall they do which are baptized for the dead, if the dead rise not at all? Why are they then baptized for the dead?" (1 Cor. xv. 29.) They had been baptized into the death of Christ, for death to their sins, and regeneration in their second Adam. If he had not risen, "then their faith was vain," and they were yet in their sins. For on his resurrection depended the validity of his atonement, and in it was involved the earnest of their own resurrection.

The Apostle is here reasoning with those who denied the resurrection of the body. This, he argued, involved the truth of Christ's resurrection. And if Christ had not risen, then his death, into which they had been baptized for death to their sins, had not accomplished for them what they sought, and they were all yet in their sins.

Now had Baptism been received among them as the symbol of a burial under the water, and resurrection from the "liquid grave," how could the Corinthians have rejected the doctrine of the resurrection of the body? If every Baptism was to them a symbol of death and resurrection, they would hardly have adopted the idea that there was "no resurrection." But regarding Baptism as the symbol of cleansing and seal of their covenant relations with Christ, the question is different. Their connection with his death is seen in another form, and their Baptism into his death is for the death of their sins. And the Apostle may well ask, why are they then baptized for the dead — the death of Christ, and their own death to their sins — if Christ has not risen to accomplish this end for them? These objects are sufficient for "the dead" to be put in the plural, whether for the "plural of dignity," or of numbers.

10. By the same principle we understand what the Apostle means in his Epistle to Titus, when he says: —

Titus iii. 5, 6: "Not by works of righteousness which we have done, but according to his mercy He saved us, by the *washing of regeneration* and the renewing of the Holy Ghost; which He shed on us abundantly through Jesus Christ our Saviour."

He uses the common word λουτρόν, *washing*, for *Baptism*, and includes with the outward sign the thing signified; by which we are regenerated in Christ, the second Adam.

The same great principle also explains the meaning of the Apostle Peter, when he tells us the saving of Noah and his family in the ark by water, was a type of Baptism.

1 Peter iii. 20–22: "When once the long suffer-

ing of God waited in the days of Noah, while the ark was a preparing, wherein few, that is, eight souls, were saved by water. The like figure whereunto, *even Baptism*, doth also now save us (not the putting away of the filth of the flesh, but the answer of a good conscience towards God), by the resurrection of Jesus Christ: who is gone into Heaven, and is on the right hand of God, angels and authorities and powers being made subject unto Him."

The resemblance is in the *instrumentality of water floating the ark* wherein Noah was saved, *and of Baptism* bringing us into the Church of Christ as the ark of our salvation. As the waters of the flood, which destroyed the old world, were made instrumental in saving Noah and his family in the ark, so the waters of Baptism, by which we are initiated into the Church and thereby connected with Christ, are made ritually instrumental in saving us. But lest we might from such language infer that the mere outward application of the water saves, he explains, it is the thing symbolized — to wit, the internal purification, corresponding to the emblem — "not the putting away of the filth of the flesh, but the answer of a good conscience toward God" — the possession and fulfilling, through the Spirit, what Baptism implies: which saves, through the resurrection of Jesus Christ.

In this, as in the other cases just examined, the symbol is of Baptism as the *instrument*, *ritually* grafting us into Christ, and not the mode of baptizing. To suppose there is an allusion to the mode of immersion in saving Noah in the ark, is to suppose it to be found in every place where water is alluded to. Those who were lost in the flood, were literally immersed — were *buried;* but *not those* who were "saved."

There is an allusion to purification, as "the putting away of the filth of the flesh" by washing of water, clearly indicates. And such is the emblem wherever water Baptism is used. It symbolizes *purity* — the *washing away of sin*. Its *Office* is to graft us ritually into Christ — its *Emblem* is *purity* of heart — *Cleansing*, not a *Burial*.

St. Paul says, "Let us draw near with a true heart, in full assurance of faith, having our hearts sprinkled from an evil conscience, and our bodies washed with pure water."[1] Ananias said to Saul, "Arise, and be baptized, and wash away[2] thy sins." All of which shows that the emblem of Baptism, as pointed out in the Holy Scriptures, is CLEANSING — not a burial. The imagnation may make it the emblem of many things, and so make it a burial; but we do not understand Christ or his Apostles so to teach. John the Baptist could not refer to a burial; yet it is contended that his mode probably became the mode of Christ. Nor did Christ command Baptism to be administered as an emblem of his death; but he did institute the Supper, and say that the bread represented his broken body, and the cup or wine his shed blood, which He commanded us to eat and drink in commemoration of his death. But Baptism He commanded simply to be given in his name, in union with the name of the Father and of the Holy Ghost.

11. We have now examined all the figurative allusions made to Baptism in the New Testament that can aid us in our inquiries. But not a single unequivocal allusion to immersion has yet passed under our *review*. The two on which most reliance is placed

[1] Heb. x. 22. λελουμένοι — common word for wash, used for Baptism.

[2] Acts xxii. 26. ἀπόλουσαι — wash or cleanse from, by Baptism.

(Romans vi. and Colossians ii.) instead of being undoubted symbols of the mode of Baptism, are required by the context to refer to Baptism as *the instrumental rite*, uniting us to the death of Christ as the branch to the vine; and hence, *with his crucifixion and resurrection as well as his burial;* and therefore have no necessary reference to the modal act at all; for Baptism in any mode could be applied to the same end. We have seen also that the resemblance is not so apt for immersion in a "liquid grave" as some suppose: the end for which we are baptized, as the Apostle tells us, being a death unto sin, and a new birth unto righteousness. Wherefore, "we are buried with him, by Baptism *into* [or *unto*] *death*." Not in a "liquid grave," in imitation of death, but with Christ in HIS DEATH, as our representative head. Those baptized into Him, were made one with Him, united to Him as their head,— hence represented in all his sufferings, so that when He was buried, they were buried in or with Him. Thus a principle is brought out, before which immersion as a symbol of the mere mode of burial, fades away as the shadow in the light of the sun.

Further, in the judgment of many able and learned divines, the Baptism referred to in these two passages is altogether spiritual Baptism; and therefore could have had no reference to the Baptism of water. And this view certainly accords well with what is said in regard to the resurrection, in the passage to the Colossians: "Buried with Him in [or by] Baptism, wherein also ye are risen with Him." How? "Through the faith of the operation of God, who hath raised Him from the dead." Not risen from the "liquid grave," by mortal power, in resemblance of his resurrection, but by a spiritual power, through faith in the operation of God.

We must therefore have something more certain than a very improbable allusion, to bind our faith, or to authorize us to bind the faith of others. Even if there was no other obvious and probable meaning, we cannot establish a principle of doctrine on a mere allusion. Much less, when that allusion cannot be proved to have any reference to the supposed object.

Thus, we have failed to find in the symbols and figurative language of the New Testament, any authority for immersion as the Apostolic mode of Baptism!

12. We have, first, examined the meaning of the word baptize (*βαπτίζω*), and found that the writers of the New Testament apply it to the use of water in different ways for ritual purification, and that instead of being a specific term, "signifying always to dip," it is generic in its character, and used in the New Testament in the general sense of PURIFYING. Therefore, from the meaning of the word alone, no particular mode of baptizing can be inferred.

In the second place we took up the practice of John the Baptist, and passed under review every recorded instance of Baptism by him, to ascertain what mode or modes he adopted; and especially with reference to the mode of dipping or immersion; but could find no particular mode defined or brought out from a single case, or from them all united. The use of water and its object are recorded in specific terms, but the manner of applying it is treated as a matter of indifference, and left undefined.

In the third place, we examined the practice of the

Apostles, and investigated every case of Christian Baptism, with all the circumstances connected therewith, and instead of "dipping," found the circumstances more favorable to a less inconvenient mode, and that the only mode, in fact, clearly pointed out, is that of the Baptism of the Holy Spirit, under the figures of "pouring out, shed forth, and descending upon." Neither from the *words* of Christ nor the *example* of his Apostles, have we *precept* or *example* for immersion.

Lastly. We examined the *symbols* and *figurative language* applied to Christian Baptism in the New Testament, and still found no certain allusion to the mode of dipping.

Therefore, after *a rigid investigation* of all that the New Testament contains or the subject, we *affirm*, that there is not a PRECEPT, EXAMPLE, or ALLUSION, from which an *undoubted inference for immersion* as the mode of Christian Baptism can be deduced. NOT ONE that any impartial or legal mind will admit, *can* be made the basis of an *invariable law* to bind the judgment and consciences of men.

CHAPTER XI.

BAPTISM BY DIFFERENT MODES VALID IN EVERY AGE OF THE CHURCH.

At the Time of the Reformation. — Church of Geneva. — At Mentz. — Council of Cologne. — English Church. — Lynwood's Constitution. — Wickliffe. — Langres. — Synod of Angiers. — Thomas Aquinas. — Bonaventur. — Strabo. — Gennadius. — Augustine. — Chrysostom. — Jerome. — Athanasius. — Gregory Nazianzen. — Basil. — Baptism of Constantine. Washing before Pouring. — Cyprian. — Lawrence and Romanus. — Novatian. — Basilides. — Origen. — Tertullian. — Clemens Alexandrinus. — Justin Martyr. — Baptism of Christ. — Catacomb of Pontianus. — Reasons for no prescribed Mode. — Essence and Incidents. — Supper and Baptism. — Greek Church. — Mar Yohannan. — Examination of Principles. — Summary.

§ 31. As we are unwilling to shut out any light that can aid us in the attainment of truth, even in a question of secondary importance, we will now examine the testimony of history so far as shall be necessary to show that Baptism by different modes has been allowed and regarded as valid in every age of the Church. For although Baptist writers profess to ignore history, they are in the habit of making very broad assertions in regard to the history of immersion, such as, "that it was the universal practice of the Church for fifteen hundred years."

We will pass to the time of the Reformation, and see what the learned men of that age said and did on this subject.

In A. D. 1536, Calvin drew up a formula for the administration of the sacraments in the church at Geneva. In which, for the order of Baptism, it was written—"*Then the Minister of Baptism pours water on the infant*, saying, I baptize thee in the name of the Father, and of the Son, and of the Holy Ghost."[1] In his "Institutes" he tells us—"The difference is of no moment, whether he that is baptized be dipped all over, and if so, whether thrice or once, or whether he be only *wetted with the water poured on him*."[2]

In A. D. 1551, the Agenda of the Church of Mentz, in Germany, as published by Sebastian, directs,—"Then let the Priest take the child in his arms, and holding him over the Font, let him with his right hand, three several times, take water out of the Font and pour it on the child's head, so that the water may wet its head and shoulders."[3] A note of explanation is added, which informs the reader, that immersion or pouring is equally valid, and that a man will do ill to break the custom of his church for either. But gives several reasons why *pouring* is better where the church will allow it.

In A. D. 1536, a Council of Cologne refers to it as a matter of indifference, whether "the child is thrice dipped or wetted with water."[4]

And in A. D. 1422, one hundred years before the Reformation openly commenced, Lynwood, the Dean of Arches under Henry V., in his account of the English Constitution, speaks of Baptism by POURING and SPRINKLING as alike valid with DIPPING. Referring to the more common mode at that time of dipping, he adds in a note: "*But this is not to be accounted to be of necessity to Baptism; it may be given also by pour-*

1 *Tractat. Theolog. Catechismus*, p. 57. Ed. Beza.
2 *Inst.*, lib. 4, ch. 15.
3 See Wall's *Hist. Baptism*, vol. ii. p. 361.
4 *Ibidem.*

ing or sprinkling. And this holds especially where the Church allows it."[1]

It seems that in some places the practice was altogether by dipping, and in others altogether by affusion, and in others again both modes were allowed.

Wickliffe, the first to preach the doctrines of the Reformation in England, writing a half century before Lynwood, A. D. 1380, says: "*Nor is it material whether they be dipped once or thrice, or water be poured on their heads:* but it must be done according to the custom of the place where one dwells."[2]

About the same time, a Synod of Langres, in France, A. D. 1404, on the subject of Baptism, speaks only of the *mode of pouring* — "Let the Priest make three *pourings* or *sprinklings* of water on the infant's head."[3]

Advancing onward another century towards the Apostles, we come to a Synod held in Angiers, A. D. 1275, which on the subject of Baptism, directs that, "The infant be *dipped thrice*, or the water *poured on three times*, according to the general custom of the Church."[4]

Some quarter of a century before, Thomas Aquinas, in Italy, A. D. 1255, writes: "Water is used in the sacrament of Baptism for the purpose of corporeal ablution, by which the *interior ablution from sins is signified: and ablution with water can be made, not only by immersion, but by aspersion or affusion.*"[5]

Bonaventur, about the same time, in France, re-

[1] *Constit.*, lib. 3, c. De Bapt., — cited by Wall.
[2] *Trialog.*, lib. 4, c. 11, — cited by Wall.
[3] See Wall's *Hist. Baptism*, vol. ii., pp. 360–362.
[4] *Ibidem.*
[5] § 3, art. vii. quest. 66. Cited by Bishop Kenrick, *Treatise on Baptism*, p. 159.

cords: "The way of Affusion is common in France and other places, and was probably used by the Apostles: but the way of dipping is more general."[1]

1. As sculpture, carving, and paintings, cannot be affected by translations, but speak the same language to every age and every nation, instead of detaining our readers with dry repetitions, we shall let the artists of several centuries teach us what was recognized in their times. The following representation is the work of Greek artists, and was common in the ninth and tenth centuries.

I. NINTH AND TENTH CENTURIES.

BAPTISM OUTSIDE OF THE CHURCH.

"The boy is unclothed, and the ordinance is administered by *pouring*. This representation shows that the present Abyssinian mode of Baptism, first washing the whole body and then pouring water, was anciently extant among the Greeks as well as among the Romans: for, although this plate is at Rome, yet it is the work of Greek artists of the ninth and tenth centuries."[2]

[1] L. 4, Dis. 3, art. 2, cited by Wall.
[2] C. Taylor, Editor of Calmet's *Bible Dictionary*.

Mr. Salt, a modern English traveller, describes the Baptism of a Mussulman boy which took place in his presence while in Abyssinia. The boy was first washed all over in a large basin of water, after which a smaller basin called *metemar* was brought, the water in which was consecrated by prayer, and waving the incense over it, dropping into it a portion of the *meiron* in the shape of a cross. The boy then repeated his belief, and answered certain questions; and the priest dipped his own hand in the water and crossed him on the forehead, saying, "George, I baptize thee in the name of the Father, Son, and Holy Ghost."

The Abyssinian Church is in East Ethiopia, the country of the eunuch who was baptized by Philip. It was at a very early period connected with the Church at Alexandria, Egypt, which was founded by St. Mark, and between which there still exists a very kind relationship. We shall notice this washing before Baptism in another place.

The prevailing custom varied at this time in different countries; at one, trine immersion was the general rule, but in cases of weakness and danger, the less inconvenient mode of pouring and sprinkling was allowed; in others, pouring or affusion was the general mode.

In England an effort was made in the early part of the ninth century to confine it to immersion *only*, except in cases of necessity. A canon was passed in A. D. 816, requiring the priests, when they administered Baptism, not to pour the water on the head of the infant, but always to dip it in the font, as the Son of God was thrice dipped in the waters of the Jordan. We do not wonder that a canon attempted to be enforced on such reasoning, availed but little. But it explains the reason why Erasmus, in pointing to the *national* peculiarities or prevailing customs in regard to Baptism, says, "With us (the Dutch) they have water poured on them; in England they are dipped." That is, dipping was the prominent mode, for we know that pouring was very common in England at the time Erasmus wrote.

2. The following plate illustrates an earlier period than the last, and such representations were common in the seventh and eighth centuries, and had their origin in the sixth.

II. SEVENTH AND EIGHTH CENTURIES.

ADMINISTRATION OF BAPTISM.

"This depicts two points of time. First, the candidate is seen kneeling down and praying near the bath of water; and a hand issues from a cloud above him, to denote the acquiescence of heaven in his petitions. Second; Baptism is administered by *pouring water* out of a pitcher on persons who are kneeling on the ground, and *not immersed* at all. Either then, Baptism was administered *without immersion* by *pouring only;* notwithstanding the convenience of the bath, or those persons had previously been washed and afterwards received Baptism as a distinct, subsequent, and separate act."[1]

We shall not dwell on this period, but pass on to the practice of the church nearer to Apostolic times, which is of much more importance to us.

Gennadius, who wrote at the close of the fifth and in the beginning of the sixth century, shows that in that period Baptism was administered in the French Church by both modes, affusion and immersion. And at a time, too, when it was regarded necessary to salvation: the only exception being martyrdom, in which it was supposed all the essentials of Baptism were embraced. And in support of which, he pointed out the analogy of the catechumen receiving Baptism, to that of the ordeal of the martyr receiving his martyrdom. "We believe," he says, "the way of salvation to be open only to baptized persons; and that no catechumen, though he die in good works, has eternal life . . . . except in the case of martyrdom, in which all the sacraments of Baptism are completed. The person to be baptized owns his faith before the priest; and, when the interrogatories are put to him, he makes his answer. The same does a martyr before a heathen judge: he also owns his faith; and when the question is put to him, makes his answer. The one after his confession is either *wetted with water* or else *plunged into it:* and the other is either *wetted*

[1] C. Taylor, Ed. C. B. D.

with his blood, or else *plunged into* (or overwhelmed with) *fire*."[1]

In this passage Baptism is plainly pointed out as performed with little or much water: by only *wetting with the water*, as the *martyr with his blood*, or by *plunging* into the water, as the martyr is plunged into or overwhelmed with fire.

III. FIFTH AND SIXTH CENTURIES.

BAPTISM OF A HEATHEN KING AND QUEEN.

3. This picture represents the King and Queen in a family bath, and the Baptizer pouring water on their heads from a pitcher. In the preceding illustration the bath or laver not being large enough to accommodate the candidates for Baptism in like manner, their ablutions were performed at or partially in the

[1] *De Eccl. Dogma*, c. 74, Wall's *Hist. Bap.*, vol. ii. p. 357.

laver, and *the pouring* received whilst on their knees outside.

This monument of sculpture is found on a tomb at Chiaia, near Naples, and represents the Baptism of Argilulfus and Theolinda, the King and Queen of the Longobardi, who occupied Beneventum in the sixth century. The original has a much larger number of attendants than are here delineated.

Augustine writing in the earlier part of the fifth century, and speaking of the virtue of the Baptism through the power of the Spirit, teaches that however small be the quantity of water applied to the infant, it cleanses it *wholly* from the condemnation (not the stain) of original sin. "This is the word of faith which we preach, whereby Baptism also is doubtless consecrated that it may cleanse. For Christ loved his Church and delivered Himself up for her. Read the Apostle and see what he adds: 'That He might sanctify her, cleansing her with the laver of water in the word.' This purification would by no means be attributed to the liquid and transient element, were it not added, 'in the word.' This word of faith is so powerful in the Church of God, that by means of her believing, offering, blessing, tinging even in a slight degree, it cleanses the infant."[1]

Thus in Augustine's day it was held by the Church in Africa, that the smallest quantity of water in Baptism cleansed not partially, but as entirely as a large quantity would: if touched by it in the slightest degree, we are cleansed.

Indeed Baptism of the sick, which was confessedly by affusion or aspersion, is constantly spoken of by the Fathers of the Church as conferring no less grace than that of immersion.

[1] Tract lxxx. in Joan., cited by Kenrick, p. 170.

In the latter part of the fourth century, and only two hundred and eighty years from the Apostolic times, Chrysostom, Bishop of Constantinople, praising those who seek Baptism in health, instead of putting it off till the hour of sickness and danger; remarks, "Although the same gift of grace is bestowed on you, and on those who are initiated at the close of life, your free choice and preparation are different; for *they receive it in their bed*, you in the *bosom of the Church*, the common mother of us all; they sorrowing and weeping, you rejoicing and exulting; they sighing, and you giving thanks; they in a lethargy from fever, you full of much spiritual delight."[1]

They could not plunge people under water "in their beds."

Jerome of Palestine, about the same period, applies the prediction of Ezekiel, "I will sprinkle clean water upon you," to Baptism.

4. A few years nearer to the Apostolic age, A. A. 274, Ambrose, Bishop of Milan, addressing the neophytes, says: "You took afterwards the white garments to indicate that you cast away the cloak of sin and put on the spotless robes of innocence; whereof the prophet said: 'Thou shalt sprinkle me with hyssop, and I shall be cleansed; thou shalt wash me, and I shall be made whiter than snow.' For he that is baptized seems to be cleansed both according to the law and the Gospel: according to the law, since Moses with a bunch of hyssop sprinkled the blood of the lamb: according to the Gospel, because the garments of Christ were white as snow, when in the Gospel he

[1] *Ad Illuminandos Catech.* 1, Kenrick *On Baptism*, p. 167.

showed the glory of his resurrection. He whose sins are forgiven is made whiter than snow." [1]

265 after the Apostles, Athanasius reckons up eight Baptisms, and the sixth in his enumeration is that of "tears." [2]

260 A. A., Gregory Nazianzen uses similar language, saying, "I know of a fourth Baptism — that of martyrdom and blood; and I know of a fifth — that of tears." [3] He refers also to Baptism at the point of death, when immersion could not be often, if ever, practicable.

260 A. A., Basil, bishop of Cæsarea, warning his hearers against delay in their Baptism, points them to a time when fever, and weakness of body and mind, may render them unconscious of what is going on, or death may come upon them in the night, when there is no one to give them Baptism. He says: "If you utter something in a faint and faltering manner, it may not be understood: everything you say will be disregarded as the ravings of a dying man. Who will give you Baptism then? Who will remind you of it, when you will be sunk in deep lethargy? Relatives are in affliction: strangers take no interest: friends are loath to alarm you by warning. Perhaps even the physician deceives you; and you do not know your situation, being blinded by the love of life. It is night, and there is no one to succor: there is no one at hand to baptize you." [3]

Such language clearly teaches that Baptism may be administered on the dying bed, and at any moment, which we know could not be done where only plunging under water is allowed.

[1] L. *de Initiandos*, c. 7, Kenrick *On Baptism*, p. 170.
[2] Pond, cited by Hall, pp. 71, 72. [3] Ibid.
[3] Hom. 13, in S. Bap. n. 7. Cited by Kenrick, p. 169.

5. The following plate shows that even where immersion, or washing of the body was practised, *pouring* was made a part of the Baptism.

IV. FOURTH CENTURY.

BAPTISM OF THE EMPEROR CONSTANTINE.

This is a representation of the Baptism of Constantine the Great. The Emperor receiving Baptism is partially *immersed* in a " laver," and Eusebius *pouring water* on his head.

These ancient representations of both Greek and Roman origin, taken in connection with other facts, have led many to suppose that pouring was the essential part of Baptism, and that the immersion or washing was a preparatory rite for receiving it. As under the Levitical law, the washing of the body, and sprinkling of blood and water, were united to cleanse the leper:[1] so for the leprosy of sin, to the washing of the body must be united pouring or sprinkling of water in the name of the Father, Son, and Holy Ghost, to complete the washing away of sin under

[1] Levit. xiv. 2–22.

the Gospel. Therefore, first there was a washing, and then pouring, as represented in the Baptism of Constantine, in the preceding plate, and as in the case of the Abyssinian Church.

Whatever credit may be due to this theory, it is certain that even in those periods when immersion was most general, it was never regarded as essential to Baptism. Magnus, living in a retired part of the country, where immersion was the usual practice, wrote to Cyprian, bishop of Carthage, to learn whether those who put off their Baptism by culpable delay, and received it on a bed of sickness by aspersion only, ought to share equal privileges with their more diligent brethren.

150 A. A. Cyprian, in reply, writes in that modest strain which characterizes great minds, and after giving his opinion, adds: "The contagion of sin is not, in the sacrament of salvation, washed off by the same measures whereby the dirt of the skin and of the body is washed off in an ordinary secular bath: so that there should be necessity of soap and other helps, and a large pool or fish-pond by which that body is washed or cleansed. It is in another way that the breast of the believer is washed — after another manner that the mind of a man is by faith cleansed. In the sacrament of salvation, where necessity compels, the shortest ways of transacting Divine matters, do, by God's gracious Dispensation, confer the whole benefit.

"And no man need, therefore, think otherwise, because these sick people, when they receive the grace of our Lord, have nothing but an affusion or sprinkling: whereas the Holy Scripture by the Prophet Ezekiel says: 'I will sprinkle clean water upon you, and you shall be clean.'" He further adds: —

"The Holy Spirit is not given by several measures, [as if the degree of the gift depended on the quantity of water] but is wholly poured on them that believe."[1]

6. The following plate represents the Baptism of Romanus by Lawrence, who suffered martyrdom not long after the above letter was written.

V. THIRD CENTURY.

LAURENTIUS BAPTIZING ROMANUS.

"This representation is in the Church of St. Lawrence, extra muros, at Rome," says Taylor, "and the jugs or vases are remarkable, being the same as in other pictures of far remoter antiquity." The martyr-preacher is represented to us as baptizing by POURING, in the vestibule of the church or some other building.

158 A. A. "A little while before his death, he also baptized one Lucillus with a *pitcher of water*."[2] The

[1] *Cypriani Epist.* lxix. "It is a pedantic Jewish literalism (says Schaff) to limit the operation of the Holy Ghost by the quantity or the quality of the water." — *Ch. Hist.*, p. 123.

[2] *Acta Laurenti*, cited by Bingham.

"Acts" of Lawrence were interpolated in after ages, but the above is taken from Strabo, who lived before the times when the forgeries and additions are said to have been made.[1]

120 A. A. Early in this century, Novatian was baptized by affusion as *he lay sick on his bed.* This was not noted as anything unusual at the time, nor would it have been handed down to succeeding generations, but for the fact that he afterwards attempted to supplant Cornelius as the Bishop of Rome, who, among other things, upbraided him with having delayed his Baptism till terrified by the approach of death, and then of neglecting to receive confirmation by imposition of hands on his recovery. It had become a rule among Christians of that age, and was afterwards enacted into a canon, that those who delayed Baptism till sickness, and were baptized under the fear of approaching death, ought not to be promoted to the ministry. An exception was made in cases of great fervency of spirit. Cornelius, in his letter to Fabius, bishop of Antioch, accuses Novatian of having obtained the order of Priesthood unlawfully in the first place; and that, therefore, he was ineligible to the office of Bishop; for all the clergy and a majority of the laity were against his being ordained Presbyter, because it was not lawful for "any one baptized in bed, *in time of sickness*" (*τὴ ἐν κλίνη διὰ νόσον περιχυθέντα*), "as he had been, to be admitted to any office of clergy." In another place, he says: "Baptized by affusion in bed as he lay" (*ἐν αὐτή τῆ χλίνὴ ᾗ ἔχειτο περιχυθεὶ.*)[2] No objection was made to

[1] See *Hist. Bapt.*, by Wall, vol. ii. p. 356.

[2] Baptism on a sick bed was called "Clinic Baptism,"—and *affusion* was allowed in such cases to sick and feeble infants, as well as to adults, even in times when trine immersion was the prevailing mode.

the validity of his Baptism ; that not allowed, would have cut off all his pretensions at once. The objection was to his criminal delay in receiving it, and to the manner in which he rose to the office of Presbyter, and afterwards aspired to the bishoprick.[1]

About the same time Callistus, bishop of Rome, as recorded in the Martyrology of Ado, after enjoining fasting, and catechizing a candidate, *water having been brought*, he *baptized him.*[2]

It is also recorded in the "Acts of Cornelius" that Sallustia, having been converted, *presented to the bishop of Rome a vessel with water, wherewith he might baptize her.*[3]

100 A. A. About the close of the first century after the Apostles, or a little later, Eusebius informs us that "Basilides was baptized in prison by some brethren, and the next day after receiving the seal, he was beheaded."[4] We can hardly suppose facilities would be afforded by those in authority to baptize him by immersion, and thus aid in the very thing for which he was imprisoned, when they would not allow him the common necessaries of life.

120 A. A. Origen represents the wood on the altar, over which water was poured at the command of Elijah (1 Kings xviii. 33), as having been "baptized," and speaks of each pouring as a Baptism.[5]

100 A. A. Tertullian associates the "sprinkling" of water with the act of Baptism, when he asks the negligent candidate, "Who will vouchsafe to you so faithless a penitent, a single *sprinkle* of water?" He further alludes to a fact, which shows that *others* at

[1] Cornelius to Fabius, bishop of Antioch. Euseb., *Eccl. Hist.*, lib. 6, c. 43.

[2] Cited by Bishop Kenrick, p. 166.

[3] *Ibidem.*

[4] Euseb. *Eccl. Hist.*, lib. 6, c. 6.

[5] *Facts and Evidences*, p. 132.

that time supposed *wetting* or *sprinkling* was enough for a Baptism. Referring to the Baptism of the Apostles, about which there was some speculation then as now, he says: "Some suggested they were sufficiently baptized when they were sprinkled (*adspersi*) and wet by the waves: and that Peter himself was sufficiently immersed when walking on the sea."[1] Now if nothing less than plunging under the water constituted Baptism, primitive Christians would hardly have associated *sprinkling* with it, or have supposed that a partial wetting in the boat, or Peter's beginning to sink, was Baptism.

60 A. A. Clemens Alexandrinus, who lived still nearer to the Apostles, calls wetting with tears Baptism. Referring to a backslider, whom John was the means of reclaiming, he says: "He was baptized a second time with tears." He also uses the words βαπτίζω and λούω interchangeably.[2]

40 A. A. Justin Martyr, born in the Apostolic age, writing to the Roman emperor in behalf of Christians, invariably describes Baptism by the terms λούω, to wash, and λοῦτρον, washing. These words apply to no particular mode of washing — least of all, to an indispensable immersion.

Further, when Justin writes to the Jews (in his dialogue with Trypho), he uses the words βαπτίζω and λούω interchangeably. Which shows he did not use it as a specific term, but rather as Christians generally use it at the present day.

Thus, Apostolic men, and the Apostles, used the word BAPTIZE in a *generic sense*, which admits Bap-

[1] *De Penitentia*, c. 6, *De Bapt.* n. 4, cited by Kenrick.
[2] Pond 33, cited by Hall, p. 96.

tism in different modes, and which has been practically exemplified by the Church in every age since.

Therefore, examination of the use of the word BAPTIZE by the Apostles, and by their successors — the figurative language associated with it — the doctrine and practice of the Church in every age since the Apostles — instead of leading to the exclusive mode of immersion, all unite in testifying to the liberty of baptizing by different modes.

7. What was the most *usual mode* practised by the Apostles themselves and their immediate successors, is involved in much obscurity. The error of looking for outward *correspondences* and rendering *literally* the *figurative* language of the Apostles, commenced ere the last of them had left the stage of action. And nothing connected with our Holy religion was more magnified than the office and effects of Baptism. Anointing the baptized with oil was practised immediately after, if not before, the death of St. John,[1] making literal the words of the Apostle, "He who hath anointed us is God." (2 Cor. i. 21). It was accompanied with the sign of the cross on the forehead, as crucified with Christ. (Gal. ii. 20.) Next, the tongues of the baptized were touched with milk and honey, in token of their new birth,[2] as the food of "new born babes" (1 Peter ii. 2); and also in token of "refusing the evil and choosing the good." (Isaiah vii. 15.) And *putting off their clothes* to be baptized,[3] which was to represent putting off the "old man" of sin; and putting on white linen after

[1] *Const Apost.*, lib. 7, cap. 47.
[2] Tertul., *De Coron. Mil.*, c. 3.
[3] See Bingham and Wall, and their various authorities.

Baptism, as the emblem of the "new man" in Christ. (Eph. iv. 22–24).

And so Baptism by trine immersion, was practised as the symbol of a burial (Rom. vi. 4), and in honor of the three persons in the Trinity. All of these customs were in vogue at an early period, and in origin followed each other in quick succession.[1]

At a period when to every figure was given a literal correspondence, it was natural to look for one in the Apostle's allusion to a BURIAL in connection with the Baptism of all grafted thereby into his death; and hence are *represented* as *one with him* in his death and resurrection, as the scion becomes *partaker* and *one* with the stock into which it is grafted. And all these additions and changes in connection with the *ceremonial* of Baptism opens abundant room for conjecture in regard to the changes made in the *mode* or *modes* practised by the Apostles. They certainly teach us to distinguish between the *essentials* and *non-essentials* of a valid Baptism.

8. It is remarkable, that during a period when trine immersion with all these addenda, prevailed more generally than at any other, the artists of that time should represent the Baptism of our Saviour as STANDING in the river nearly to his waist in water, and John POURING the water on his head from a shell.

[1] See Bingham and Wall, and their various authorities.

VI. BAPTISM OF JESUS IN JORDAN.

This picture of the Baptism of Jesus in the river Jordan is the centre-piece of the dome of the Baptistry of Ravenna, erected A. D. 454.

John the Baptist is drawn standing on the bank of the river, holding an oblong cross in his left hand, and pouring water from a shell on the head of the Saviour, who is standing in the river in water to his waist. The Saviour's head is surrounded with a glory, and the figure of a dove symbolizing the Holy Spirit descending upon him. The Baptism is a partial immersion and aspersion at the same time.

Writes the Baptist historian Robinson: "This representation at Ravenna *is not singular, for most artists of those ancient times describe the Baptism of Jesus in the same manner.* The doors of the very ancient Church of St. Paul in the suburbs of Rome, are plated with brass; the whole is divided into six circular segments. Each segment is divided into nine parts, and each part contains one or more figures relating to the history of Jesus," and "Much in the same manner he is described in the Greek Church."[1]

Be it remarked, that at the very time when trine immersion ruled with its greatest sway, both Greek and Roman artists represent the primitive mode of Baptism to be that of *pouring water* on one standing in water. Now, whether the subjects of Baptism first washed their bodies in the river and then came up to John to receive *the pouring* from him, or whether the twofold ablution by a *partial immersion* of the body, and *the pouring* of water on the remaining part constituted the Baptism, or whether the washing was only *a preparation* for the *true Baptism* which symbolized the Baptism of the Holy Spirit, are questions of deep interest to earnest inquirers after truth.

9. We introduce another representation of the Baptism of Jesus in Mosaic, of somewhat earlier date, very similar in outline, preserved in the Church in Cosmedin at Ravenna, by which the artist teaches us how Christ was baptized, and what was the mode of Baptism in the primitive days of Christianity. Not what was the mode at the time the Church of Cosmedin was erected, but at the time the Saviour received what was to be the sign and seal of his new and better covenant,— which should be the badge of his people and the mode of bringing them into a sacred nearness to himself.

[1] R. Robinson, *History of Baptism*, p. 86.

VII. VERY ANCIENT.

CHRIST BAPTIZED IN JORDAN.

"In the centre is Christ our Saviour, in the river Jordan. On a rock stands John the Baptist; in his left hand is a bent rod, and his right hand holds a *patera*, shell, from which he pours water on the head of the Redeemer, over whom descends the dove, the symbol of the Holy Ghost, with expanded wings, and emitting rays of Grace." [1]

Taylor is of the opinion that such representations in the midst of a different practice, and at a time when "the administration of Baptism had departed greatly from its original simplicity," give stronger evidence for affusion than if made at an earlier period. They speak the language of a practice of a former age handed down, but nearly overrun by a more imposing ceremonial.

[1] C. Taylor, Editor *C. B. D.*

He further tells us that "the antiquary, Cimpiana, reasons in regard to them to the following effect: 'In these pictures we see Christ immersed in water, and John also pouring water on his head. This raises a doubt whether Baptism shall be performed by *immersion* or *aspersion*, or by both.'"

10. There has been also found in the Catacomb of Pontianus, outside the Portese Gate, at Rome, which was a burial place of the Martyrs, under the persecutions of the Roman emperors, a Baptistry, in which primitive Christians baptized their converts, when hunted after as wild beasts for confessing Christ! In this subterranean recess was discovered a spring of water, for which a basin two feet deep, and wide, was cut out at the side of a high rock, to receive its waters, and a room some six feet square excavated for the purposes of a Baptistry. On the side of the rock above the basin of water is rudely sketched the Baptism of Jesus in the river of Jordan, and just under it an ornamented cross with the symbolic letters A (alpha), and Ω (omega), suspended on its transverse beam.

This representation of the Baptism of Jesus is in perfect accordance with the two immediately preceding, and confirms what Robinson, the Baptist historian, says on the subject: "*Most artists of those ancient times, describe the Baptism of Jesus in the same manner.*" That is, by pouring water on his head while standing in the water. And he had as well have included ALL of the *earliest artists*, for none of them in the times to which he refers, have left any other description so far as we have seen, and so zealous are our Baptist friends to produce whatever will strengthen their cause, it is not very probable they would have omitted such a fact.

VIII.—JESUS CHRIST BAPTIZED IN THE JORDAN BY JOHN THE BAPTIST.

The Saviour is here, as in the other representations of his Baptism, standing in the river up to his waist in water, and John at his side, in a small recess made in the rock, *pouring* water on his head. A lamb is also introduced, in allusion to the "lamb of God."

This is in a place that was undoubtedly one of refuge for Christians during the persecutions of the Roman emperors in the first ages of Christianity! Which began under Nero in A. D. 64, and ended under Diocletian in A. D. 305, and raged with more or less severity, according to the state of public opinion and the character of different Emperors.

It was first a place of Baptism, and as the persecutions relaxed became a burial place of Christians. We need not delay our readers with the proof.

The Baptisms administered in this place could not have been by submerging the whole body under the water; because the font or basin was too small, and the arrangement for the Priest such, that he could only baptize as represented in the picture. This, however, would not exclude an ablution of the candidate first by his own hands, or even by the application of water to his body by another, and then to receive *the pouring;* as in the case of those baptized outside of the smaller fonts which we have already considered.

The reader will also bear in mind that this Baptism corresponds with all the others introduced, in the *fact*, that *the administrator did not enter the water.* And one can easily conceive that he could not dip another *under* the water in the river whilst standing *above it* on a rock or on the bank.

11. If then we adopt "*immersion*" as the only mode of Baptism, we shall not only find it inapplicable to various conditions of our race and of climate, but we shall find it *involved in difficulties* in its connection with historical facts, of which only those who have examined them are aware.

As a historical question, with *immersion* we must take NAKED SUBJECTS — the immersion of people entirely NUDE. This the Baptist historian, Robinson, himself acknowledges, and says: "There is no ancient historical fact better authenticated than this. The evidence doth not go on the meaning of the single word NAKED: for then a reader might suspect allegory: but in many facts reported, and many reasons assigned for the practice." [1]

The fact therefore being admitted by the advo-

[1] R. Robinson, *History of Baptism*, p. 85.

cates of IMMERSION — that Baptism by immersion in the primitive Church was administered to persons *naked; the proof not dependent on the meaning of the single word* NAKED, *but on many facts reported, and many reasons assigned; no ancient historical fact better authenticated than this* — we need not dwell on the *proof*, but may pass on to the introduction of the rite itself as a Christian ordinance. And as it is generally conceded, on both sides, that the Baptism of John and that of the Apostles were the same as to mode and manner, we will begin with the first.

Now, that John baptized in public assemblages of both sexes, *men and women naked*, does not comport with our ideas of the *chaste manners and decency* inculcated by the founders of our holy religion. Yet, according to the narrative given us of his Baptisms in Jordan, we do not see how the thousands who received his Baptism in the Wilderness were accommodated with extra garments for immersion, coming, as we suppose most of them did, without any expectation of being baptized when they left their homes; but rather to see and hear what the babbler in the Wilderness had to say; they brought with them only their necessary apparel for the day, and we can hardly presume that they returned home in wet clothes. Did they, then, disrobe themselves in public on the bank of the river, and march into the water stark naked, and after being dipped return back as they went? Such is the natural inference, if the multitudes baptized by John in the Wilderness were baptized in a *nude* state.

Is it not more rational to suppose they sought the protection of the banks of the river, and the shrubbery growing on it a short distance below, to unclothe themselves, and there went into the water, and after washing or bathing walked up the stream to John (the depth being known) and received the *pouring*, as the artists represent the Baptism of Christ by him? This could be done in water of a certain depth without offending the most delicate sense of propriety. It would accord with the usual modes of purification under the Levitical law, when to aspersion was added the washing or bathing of the body. The person to be cleansed or purified was always required [if able] to wash himself.[1]

It also corresponds with the representation of the baptizer standing on a rock on the bank of the river, near the proper depth of the water for such a purpose, instead of remaining *successive hours*, *day after day*, *in water to his waist*, to *dip* or submerge the multitudes that came to him.

John came to prepare the way for the coming of the promised Messiah. His Baptism was a rite of purification on the part of the people for the reception of their promised deliverer; administered on the pledge of reformation of life, and their recognized obligation to "bring forth fruits meet for repentance."[2] John acted under a dispensation that did not require the washing of naked bodies in public.

But the advocates of immersion seem to ignore the idea of any *indelicacy* in the Baptism of *naked subjects* in the times of primitive Christianity. Even the exposure of the *naked body* "without a wrapper around the middle," many of them contend, would be no more offensive to the taste of a *rude age* than the

[1] The consecration to the Priesthood the only exception.

[2] Matt. iii. 8.

public exhibition of statuary without a veil at the present day; that our ideas of indecency and vulgarity depend chiefly on our familiarity with objects and customs. "If (say they) in countries where statuary abounds, the two sexes can examine together *nude figures* without a blush on the cheek, why not the living bodies which these figures resemble?"

Usages of society and *familiarity* of objects, beyond a doubt have their influence, but *stone* and *painting* are not *living objects*, and we opine that never since "Adam and Eve sewed fig leaves together and made themselves aprons" to hide their nakedness, has it been regarded otherwise than *indelicate* in man or woman to present themselves naked to public gaze. The Apostle Paul did not look upon such things with indifference, when he instructed Timothy to teach the "women to adorn themselves in *modest apparel, with shame-facedness and sobriety;*"[1] thereby reproving any unnecessary exposure of the body, or mode of dressing, which would excite lustful feelings in others, or appear inconsistent with modesty and sobriety in themselves.

12. After *trine immersion* gained the ascendency, we know that for a long time people were baptized naked, but much care and prudence were brought to bear to prevent unnecessary exposure of the body. BAPTISTRIES were erected in many places, and different apartments provided in them for the privacy of the two sexes in undressing and preparing themselves for their Baptism. Deaconesses were also appointed to supervise the apartments of women and children, and to notify the Minister when the candidates were

[1] Tim. ii. 9.

ready for his services. This shows an appreciative sense of female decorum and decency as early, at least, as the third century.

Sozomen relates an incident of the fourth century, of an outrage of certain soldiers committed in the baptistry of the Church of Chrysostom, in Constantinople, on Easter Eve, in which he says: "There was a great tumult at the font, the women shrieking in affright, and the children crying; the priests and deacons were beaten and forced to run away with their vestments on."[1]

Chrysostom, complaining of the same thing to Innocent, Bishop of Rome, says: "The women, who had undressed themselves to be baptized, were forced by fright of this violence to run away naked; not being permitted in their amazement to provide for the modesty and credit of their sex."[2]

This confirms the fact that not only *men, women, and children* were then baptized naked, but that there was also a delicacy of sentiment among the people that caused every necessary effort to be made to prevent exposure of person on such occasions. For we are further informed by the same authority, that none but women came near or in sight of a female candidate preparing herself for Baptism until she was placed in the font, and then the Priest, being notified, came and bowed her head in the water as he repeated each name of the Trinity, according to his formula for Baptism. After which he left her in the font to be taken charge of by her female attendants.[3]

But those who practised *trine immersion did not themselves* claim for it *Scriptural authority.* "*Tradition* was its ground, and *custom* its confirmer."[4]

[1] Cited by Wall, vol. ii., p. 380. [2] Ibidem.
[3] Ibidem. [4] See Tertullian, *De Corona Militis.*

What USAGE preceded it, and what the groundwork of the first illustrations and pictures of primitive Baptism by the artists, are questions still open to inquiry.

We can easily conceive in what way *many* of the *changes* could have been made as time rolled on. As, for instance, how the language of the Apostle Paul, "*buried with Him (Christ) by Baptism into death,*"[1] could have suggested the immersion of the body under water, as representing "a burial in a liquid grave;" and then how the adoption of such a *modal of Baptism* for the purpose of representing *Christ's death and burial,* should call forth the canon called Apostolic — "*Jesus did not say baptize in my death,*" *but* "*Go, teach all nations, baptizing them in the name of the Father, and of the Son, and of the Holy Ghost.*"[2] The canon, although not of Apostolic origin, is of *very early date,* and no doubt framed to correct an error that was gaining ground by the misconstruction of the Apostle's words, supposing they referred to the *mode* of Baptism, instead of the *end* for which it was given. And *immersion being adopted,* the change of *one* immersion into *three names,* was easily made into *one for each name of the Trinity* — and hence *trine immersion.*

Further, the words of the Apostle Paul: "*That ye put off concerning the former conversation, the old man, which is corrupt according to the deceitful lusts. . . . . . And that ye put on the new man which, after God, is created in righteousness and true holiness,*"[3] might easily suggest *the putting off old clothes at Baptism, and putting on white garments after it.*"

[1] Rom. vi. 4.
[2] *Canon Apos.* I., cited by Kenrick.
[3] Eph. iv. 22, 24.

And so the use of *private baths* or *lavers* to accommodate the rich, as in the case of Constantine, and the King and Queen, of Longobardi referred to in plates III. and IV., on whom water was *poured while in the family bath.* And so afterwards, to accommodate persons less opulent, when the family lavers were smaller, and not large enough to receive the whole body of the candidate, they washed themselves at the side of the laver, and received the *pouring* a short distance from it, whilst kneeling in the attitude of prayer, as represented in plate II., illustrating a usage common in the seventh and eighth centuries. When we come to the ninth and tenth we find, according to the illustration of plate I., the candidate for Baptism is first washed in one place, and brought to another to receive the *pouring.* In *cases of emergency*, as in the Baptism of Romanus by Lawrence, in the third century, the water was only *poured* on him whilst standing *nude*, or nearly so, in the porch of the church, as in plate V. Or of Lucillus, at a still earlier period, who was baptized by *pouring water from a pitcher only.*[1] Or of Novatian, who was baptized on his sick bed, by *aspersion* alone.[2] The same privilege was allowed to sick and delicate children and feeble infants as to adults, and all accepted by the Church as *valid Baptisms.*

13. Thus *changes* in the *mode* and *ceremonies* of Baptism were made during the first thousand years of Christianity, as circumstances seemed to render expedient. After that time *bathing, or washing* and *pouring* were less generally united together, and the former became much the most *usual*, down to the

[1] Page 349. [2] Page 350.

time of the great Reformation in the sixteenth century. Since which, pouring and aspersion have become the *most usual.*

As a sacrament and seal of the new covenant, Christian Baptism grafts us into the death of Christ, and secures to us all the privileges of the Christian Covenant; but as a symbol of purification, which it also signifies, the *quality* of the water rather than the *quantity* is its leading feature. "*Running water*," which means *pure water*, as if running from a spring or fountain, in opposition to stagnant or defiled water, by use, is prescribed *throughout the Jewish ritual* for purification from defilements by cleansing or washing with water. And the same idea was continued into the Christian ritual — as, for instance, "Let us draw near with a true heart in full assurance of faith, having our hearts sprinkled from an evil conscience, and *our bodies washed with pure water*" (Heb. x. 22). "Arise and be baptized and *wash away thy sins*, calling on the name of the Lord" (Acts xxii. 16). The "*ritual-bathing*" of the Jews was, applying the water to their person with their hands while in the bath, not simply dipping themselves or remaining in an *inactive* state in the water. Even in the case of Naaman (which was not a ritual of the law) his frequent dipping in the "running water" amounted to an application of the water to his body by his own hands. The prevailing mode of bathing in Oriental countries at the present day, as we are informed by travellers, is not by immersing the body in the water, but by applying the water to the body, and generally by an attendant.

D'Ohsson, speaking of women's baths in the East, says: "They *scarcely ever immerse their bodies in water;* the large marble urns, which are in the form of bathing tubs, *are for invalids.* The strictest decency is observed."[1] Denon, describing the bath of men in Egypt, writes: "The bather . . . . . is inundated with water, which the attendants take out with a small basin and pour over his body."[2] The Abyssinians, a very large body of Christians, much more numerous than the Greek Church, still unite *washing* and *pouring* in Baptism; or rather first wash the body in a large *urn*, and then remove the candidate to a smaller one, to confess his faith and receive the *pouring.* They baptize young children, as do also Copts and all Eastern Christians.

A careful examination of the history of Baptism, must lead the intelligent reader to distinguish between the *essence* and the *incidental circumstances* connected with it. The *essence* of Baptism does not consist in the *quantity* of the water, nor the *mode* of applying it to the person. These are only *incidental matters;* things *extraneous* in their nature. *Water* applied in the name of the *Holy Trinity*, by a *properly qualified agent*, are the essential ingredients to a valid Christian Baptism. "Pure water" should be used when it can be obtained. Tertullian writes: "The bishop has the right of giving Baptism; in the next place, the presbyters and deacons, yet not without the bishop's authority, on account of the honor of the Church, which being preserved, peace is preserved."[3] He further says that *laymen* have also the right, in the absence of their superiors, and should certainly exercise it, and baptize in cases of necessity; "inasmuch as one will be guilty of a human creature's loss

1 *Facts and Evidences Ap. s. Bap.*, p. 130.
2 Ibidem.
3 *De Baptizo*, c. xvii.

if he shall refrain from bestowing what he had free liberty to bestow." *Circumstances*, therefore, will justify a *different agent*, as well as a *different mode* from what may be the common USAGE. Hence the *essence* of Baptism may be defined *water* in the *right name* by *proper authority*. To *immersion* we have no objection, as before remarked, where it can be administered with convenience; but to make it an *exclusive* mode without Divine authority, and thereby cut off *one soul* from Baptism by applying a rule which neither the Word of God nor any branch of his Church ever applied till the rise of the Anabaptists in the sixteenth century, we can never assent to.

To limit Baptism to immersion only, as Baptist writers propose, would restrict the application of an ordinance designed for God's people in all ages and under all circumstances; and thereby cut off *many* for whom it was provided! In frozen regions, where everything is bound up in ice for a large portion of the year, and in hot, sandy countries, where water can scarcely be obtained to sustain life during certain seasons, immersion would be impracticable for long periods. So, in cases of sickness, dying women and men, and gasping infants, under such a law, would go into eternity unbaptized, however much the former might desire it for themselves, or for their little ones!

Our Saviour, therefore, in this, as in other things, acted with his accustomed benevolence in leaving to circumstances that which circumstances ought to control. And we confess that we have no sympathy with those who *define* what God has *not* defined, and then boast of standing by and seeing persons fit and desirous for Baptism die without it, because they could not be immersed all over in water,[1] and who further take delight in "cutting holes in the ice, while the weather is so cold as to keep several men stirring the water with poles to keep it from freezing, while they are baptizing delicate women."[2] We have not so learned Christ, nor can we ever yield to such "the liberty wherewith Christ has made us free."

EXAMINATION OF PRINCIPLES.

We must look to the *end* for which things are done, in order to determine what is *essential* to them, rather than to the mode. If corporeal washing was the end of Baptism, then much water, and even soap, as Cyprian remarks, would be essential to it. But the end of Baptism is *an inward spiritual grace;*[3] and all the outward symbolism as to sign and instrument is given for internal spiritual blessing. Therefore, a *small quantity* of pure water would as clearly signify spiritual purification and grace to an enlightened age and country, as would a *larger quantity* to a rude and uncultivated people. And this suggests to us again the wisdom of our Saviour in prescribing no particular mode for the initiatory rite of grafting into things spiritual, provided for creatures who are subject to time, place, and circumstances. Wherefore, if it could be proved (which it cannot) that the Apostles usually *immersed* in Baptism, inasmuch as no *command* to Baptize by that mode, or in any other particular way is given, it does not follow that we should confine ourselves to that mode, when a less inconvenient one would have all the influence upon a refined and enlightened age, that plunging

[1] Hinton's *Hist. Bap.*, cited by Kenrick.

[2] See Hall, p. 115.

[3] Catechism of Epis. Ch.

and washing of the whole body would have on a ruder age.

Further, if we are to imitate in this age the example of those ages in which immersion was generally practised, we must be baptized NAKED. Is that necessary in this age? will any one insist that we follow out the mode of Baptism in this particular? If thus we have the discretion allowed us to omit *washing the naked body*, why not the same discretion in breaking through the ice and plunging under the freezing water the feeble and delicate body? And if we have the discretion even to *postpone* such Baptisms, and the persons die unbaptized, which involves the greater responsibility, to baptize such by *pouring* or *aspersion*, or permit them to die *unbaptized?* What says the Lord? "*I will have mercy and not sacrifice.*"

"But," says Mr. Booth (assuming that immersion alone is true Baptism), "positive institutions admit of no degrees, no supplements, and no commutation. It is the will of God for the trial of our obedience; nor will He allow us to inquire why or how? Compliance MUST be so, and NO MORE, and NO LESS, and NO OTHERWISE. What we call little things, trifling deviations, are the pins and screws which hold the sacred tabernacle together; take these away, the whole edifice falls. The same rash hand that makes one alteration, may make twenty; if in small things, why not in greater? till at length the foundation is destroyed; Christianity is superseded; superstition takes its place, and all is death, desolation, and darkness."

How dare you then, Mr. Booth, change the order of immersing "people naked," and now clothe them?

This change will authorize other changes, and thus you take away *one* by *one*, the "screws" and "pins," and "the whole edifice falls."

The holy Scriptures teach NO mode of baptizing, and by parity of such reasoning, you can adopt *no mode;* hence you cannot baptize at all! Reductio ad absurdum.

Apply to the other sacrament the rule which this writer designed to be applied to Baptism.

The Lord's supper was instituted, as before remarked, at night, in an upper room; received in a reclining posture; after a meal, and no female present. We are told: "Compliance MUST be so, and NO MORE, and NO LESS, and NO OTHERWISE." If you neglect these "pins and screws, the tabernacle will fall." Has he neglected not *one* of them, and done everything just *so*, *no more*, *no less*, *no otherwise*? Alas! how easily does poor human nature deceive itself! In the Sacrament of the Supper, the Baptists as well as others, have departed from *every one* of these particulars, and regard no part of the *mode* or *manner* in which the last supper was received as essential to the sacrament, beyond the elements lawfully administered. And why not apply the same principle to Baptism, and distinguish between things essential and not essential?

Three men may wash their hands at the same time and for the same *object*, one at the pump, another in the river, and the third in basin, and all three attain one and the same end, to wit, the cleansing of their hands. And so we may baptize in three ways for the same end. If different degrees and phases constitute the *essence* of a thing, then we have many more faiths than we have Baptisms; for no two

Christians, perhaps, have precisely the same degrees and shades of belief in all the doctrines of the Gospel.

It is the *end* and *unity of design* that make our Baptism one, and our faith one, and our Lord one; for without these we may even have different Lords under the same name. *Unity of mode* would not make *one Baptism*, for we may give different baptisms by the same mode. When the disciples at Ephesus, who had been baptized unto John's Baptism, were again baptized by St. Paul[1] (if in the same mode), they received two Baptisms, and yet by one mode. Therefore, *mode* cannot constitute *oneness*. But Baptism once administered in *unity of name* and *design* into the great body of Christ's people, is *one Baptism*, in whatever way given.

Herein seems to be the cause of much of the error of immersionists: they lose sight of the GREAT END of the Institutions of the Gospel, and magnify incidental matters into undue importance, thereby destroying the proportions of the grand system of Christianity!

Again; they deceive themselves by the sound of words; they often boast: "We take the Bible alone for our guide;" but put their *own interpretation* upon it. This interpretation is opposed by greater numbers of equal learning; and what is the result? They reject the light of history and testimony of facts, and attempt to force upon others *their opinions*. But here they deceive themselves, for they always act on the testimony of history, when it helps a peculiar view, without seeming to be aware of it. They cannot find an *undoubted example of immersion*, or *precept* for it, in the Holy Scriptures; and yet they

[1] Acts xix.

say it was practised for many centuries. But ought not *candor* to require the admission, that, according to the same authority, other modes have for many centuries existed too, and that Infant Baptism has been the practice of the Christian Church in every age since the Apostles?

Bear in mind the proper distinction between the *essence* of Baptism and what is merely *incidental*. *Water*, in the *right name*, by *proper authority*, is all that is of the essence of Baptism; as it is acknowledged even by Baptists, that *bread* and *wine*, with like authority, are all that is of the essence of the Supper — objectively considered. If we think it is no longer necessary to apply water to the *naked* body, and, therefore, baptize it *clothed*, may we not omit also the inconvenient and often inappropriate mode of *submerging?* In this age, it does not require much water to suggest its property of cleansing; and the Lord's Supper frequently received, impresses us much more seriously with the crucifixion and death of our Saviour, than Baptism by immersion can do. And it was for that *especial end* the Eucharist was instituted; for the remembrance of *that very thing*, we are commanded to observe it; whilst Baptism was commanded to be given in the name of the Trinity — not of the death of the Son.

Shall we then hold to the liberty handed down through every age of the Church, and baptize as circumstances may direct, and take our *little ones* into Christian covenant with ourselves, or shall we adopt immersion as the only Baptism and *naked subjects* in the beginning, and refuse to our *little ones* the privileges and blessings of the Gospel covenant? Such is the doctrine of Antipædobaptists; and yet the liberty of other modes, and Infant Baptism, have always been allowed. History cannot therefore be brought to sustain the authority of one and not the other. This certain writers clearly see, and hence the attempt to throw aside history altogether. But this cannot be done, unless we intend to remain in ignorance on important points, and surrender the Divine authority of our holy religion. And in appealing to the Greek Church for immersion, as is often done, we can appeal to it also for Infant Baptism, and the liberty to baptize by *aspersion, in cases of necessity.* But what is the immersion of the Greek Church? "The infant is placed in the baptismal font, with its head above water, and face downward, supported by the left arm of the priest, who, with his right hand, pours water on it."[1] Such is the immersion of the Greeks. It is part pouring, applied to infants; and the *pouring* alone required, if *necessity* demands it.

What is the immersion of all the East? A few years ago, when the Bishop of Ooroomiah, in Media, Asia — Mar Yohannan, visited this country, he was asked particularly how he baptized? His reply was, "We baptize children by putting them in the font, in a *sitting posture, up to the breast in water*, facing the East — then pouring water on them, in the name of the Father, Son, and Holy Ghost."[2] And he further added, "Such is the kind of immersion practised all over the East, at all periods." What shall we say,

[1] *Euchologium*, with Goar's Notes, cited by Kenrick.

Some dip the head under the water as they repeat the names of the Trinity. — THE AUTHOR.

[2] NOTE. The author is indebted for the above to the Rev. H. W. Ducachet, D. D., of Philadelphia, to whom the Bishop of Ooroomiah also remarked that he had never seen an adult baptized. So long had Infant Baptism been universal.

then, to the noise we hear about "Greek immersion, and immersion in the far-off East?" Is it immersion, or is it pouring? would it be complete if there was no pouring? Is it immersion according to the Baptist sense and mode of plunging people entirely under water? And, worst of all, *infants* are the chief *subjects!* Will it satisfy our Baptist brethren if we place our little ones in a font, up to the breast in water, and then pour water on them, in the name of the Father, and of the Son, and of the Holy Ghost? Oh no. This would be no better than "baby sprinkling" after all! It would not be a burial. And their own good sense would further teach them that, if they were nicely washed by their mothers at home before they were brought to the font, and the water there devoutly poured on them, in the name of the Trinity, it could not make much difference whether they were set down in the font or held in the arms.

1. We have now seen Baptism administered by day and by night, in sickness and in health — the subject standing by the font, and kneeling by the font — standing in the water, and kneeling in the water — sitting in the water, and held in the arm of the minister in the water, and out of the water — in prison, and on his bed — by aspersion, and by immersion; and all recognized by the Christian Church as valid Baptism. What does all this teach, but the non-essential character of *modes*, and *liberty* allowed in such things.

2. We have also seen that the word BAPTIZE is applied to different modes of ablution in the New Testament — that neither Christ nor his Apostles *pre-*

scribed any particular mode of Baptism, and that in this respect their example was followed in the next and succeeding ages of the Church. Hence no man is authorized by the teaching of the word of God, and practice of primitive Christians, to say to his fellow man, "*thou hast not been baptized unless thou hast been immersed.*"

We should "stand fast, therefore, in the liberty wherewith Christ hath made us free." Taking the Bible as our guide, and supported and sustained in our interpretation by the practice of the Church in every age, we cannot go far wrong. With this authority, we may bring all our little ones into covenant with God, and seal it by baptizing them in that *mode* which we believe will comport most with the dignity of the sacrament, and the glory of God through Christ.

CHAPTER XII.

THE ORIGIN OF ANTIPÆDOBAPTISM AND THE CLAIMS OF BAPTISTS EXAMINED.

Modern Organization. — Waldenses and their Faith. — Albigenses. — Pierre De Bruys. — Cathari. — Paterini. — Paulicians. — Bulgari. — Donatists. — Novatians. — Bede. — Pelagius. — Ancient Church of Britain. — Rome. — Greece. — Alexandria. — Palestine. — Coast of Malabar. — Rise of Antipædobaptists in Twelfth Century. — Collected together in 1521. — Munster taken in 1533. — Retaken next Year. — Anabaptists scattered. — Rallied under Menno, 1536. — Confession of Faith published, 1636. — First Church in England, 1638. — In America, 1639. — Present Position. — High Standard of Family Religion needed. — Concluding Remarks.

HAVING considered the subjects and modes of Christian Baptism, and particularly the claims of Infant Baptism, we will now examine the claims of those who oppose us. They do not claim for themselves great antiquity as an organized body, but contend that their principles have been entertained in the Church of God in every age.

And some of them profess to be able to trace them through different sects, or through branches of the Church to an early period. They tell us the Waldenses held similar views, and that they were also advocated among the Cathari in Germany, the Paterines in Italy, and Paulicians in Greece. And before them by the Donatists in Africa, and even the Novatians at Rome.[1]

Let us examine the facts in the case. The Waldenses were a body of Christians inhabiting the valleys of the Alps, brought to light in the twelfth cen-

[1] See Fessenden, *Encyclopædia, R. K.*, Jones' *Hist. Ch.*, and others.

tury. They were an exemplary people for the age in which they lived, and advocated some of the principles of the English Reformation. They were called the "VAUDOIS, VALLENSES, WALDENSES, and *the people of the valleys*."[1] They had been in existence as a religious sect, as it appears, several centuries before the preaching of Peter Waldo commenced. He visited Piedmont about the year 1160, and there found churches holding sentiments similar to those he had preached at Lyons, and became renowned among them as a friend and ally. Some have supposed they were called after his name (Waldo) Waldenses. But it has of later years been shown to be the more probable that they were called after the place they inhabited. And after their union with the disciples of the Lyonese reformer, they obtained for themselves also the name of Lionist, thereby blending with. them the Christians of Lyons.[2]

The Waldenses were opposed to many of the doctrines of the Church of Rome; but did they oppose Infant Baptism, or denounce all Baptisms besides immersion? These are the points that distinguish Baptists from other Christians. But who is to give us a better account of the faith of the Waldenses than themselves? When their adversaries and persecutors, the Romish priests, falsely accused them, among other things, of refusing Baptism to children, they denied the charge. They acknowledged, however, that some of their children went longer without Baptism than they desired, because their own pastors or Barbs were abroad in the service of the Church, and they detested the human inventions added to the

[1] Dr. Allix's *History of the Church of Piedmont.*
[2] Waddington's *Church History.*

sacrament by the Romish priests, and hence deferred the Baptism of their children oftentimes longer than was desirable, awaiting the return of their own Barbs.[1] In an ancient record among them, called the "Spiritual Almanac," they acquit themselves of this accusation as follows: —

"Neither is the time or place appointed for those who must be baptized; but charity and the edification of the Church and congregation ought to be the rule in this matter; yet, notwithstanding, we bring our children to be baptized, which they ought to do to whom they are most nearly related, as their parents, or those whom God has inspired with such a charity."

In this they declare they bring their children to Baptism, and point out the persons who ought to bring them.

In their articles of rules of faith and practice, adopted by *all the Waldenses* assembled at Angrogne, September 12th, 1535, their seventeenth article reads as follows: —

ART. XVII. "As to the *sacraments*, it has been determined by the Holy Scriptures, that we have but two sacramental signs or symbols, which Christ Jesus hath left unto us: the one is BAPTISM, the other the EUCHARIST, or Lord's Supper, which we receive to demonstrate our perseverance in the faith, according to the promise we made in our Baptism in our INFANCY; as also in remembrance of that great benefit which Jesus Christ hath conferred upon us, when He laid down his life for our redemption, cleansing us with his most precious blood."[2]

[1] See Perrin's *History of the Waldenses.*

[2] Perrin and Du Pin.

This article shows that so *general* was the *practice of Infant Baptism* among them and their forefathers, that their whole assembly had been baptized in infancy ; or at least so nearly all, that they speak of their Baptism as received only at that time. "According to the promise we made in our Baptism in our infancy." All their descendants practise Infant Baptism to this day. Nor is there a single word in their *whole history* that indicates they ever denied it to young children, if we will distinguish properly when different names are used.

The name Waldenses was first applied only to the Christians in the valleys between the Alps, who opposed the Romish Church. The name Albigenses was applied to those in the southern parts of France, who (about the same time) opposed also the Church of Rome. But some of these Christian bodies, though united against Rome, differed widely among themselves on other points.[1]

"Albi, a city of Languedoc, in France," says Waddington, "was peculiarly prolific in heresies about that time." All those sects known by the name of Albigenses, and also others in the northern parts of Italy, are frequently, by writers in later and succeeding ages, included under the general name of Waldenses, though widely differing in various particulars —just as the name Protestant is now frequently applied to all who do not belong to the Church of Rome; or of Presbyterian to all who adopt their kind of Church government; or Arminian to all that oppose Calvinism. But who in this day would charge all the erroneous doctrines among Protestants to any of the respectable bodies of Christians that come

[1] Ibid.

under that name? Or charge Presbyterians proper with all the errors of many others who adopt the same kind of church government? Owing to this loose way of writing, — not distinguishing between the Waldenses proper, and other sects incorrectly embraced under the term, — many have been led into the erroneous opinion that the Waldenses denied Infant Baptism! Their own works, however, prove the contrary.[1]

"It is a well known fact," says Dr. Murdock, in a note on Mosheim, vol. iii. p. 228, "that in the sixteenth century, the genuine descendants of the old Waldenses, Wickliffites, and Hussites, who were numerous in France, England, and other places, readily united with the Lutheran and the reformed communities, and at length became *absorbed in them;* and that very few, if any of them, ever manifested a preference for the Mennonite, or for any of the Antipædobaptist[2] sects of that age." . . . "And if we endeavor to trace the history of that grand peculiarity of all Mennonites, their confining Baptism to adult believers, and rejecting Infant Baptism altogether, we shall find, that at the time Menno first embraced it, it existed among the numerous German Anabaptists, but not among the Waldenses of France or Bohemia, who were then universally believers in Infant Baptism." . . . "These Waldensian Pædobaptists, moreover, declared that they held the same belief which their fathers had maintained for several centuries; and they appealed to their old books to make good their assertions. There were, indeed, various mystical sects, tinctured more or less with Manichæism, in the

[1] Compare Du Pin, Perrin, Wall, and Waddington.

[2] Meaning Baptists.

twelfth and following centuries, who rejected all water Baptism on much the same grounds that the Quakers still do, and some of them assailed Infant Baptism especially, as being peculiarly unsuitable and absurd."

Were we to enter into a full examination of this subject, it would swell this chapter beyond its prescribed limits, and be a matter of small moment to our present inquiry, when ended, — because too far removed from the days of the Apostles to affect the main point at issue.

Pierre de Bruys, in the beginning of the twelfth century, as has already been remarked, is the first public teacher *on record*, who preached against Infant Baptism, and whose followers entirely rejected it whilst they retained adult Baptism. He was a native of Languedoc, and of the town of Albi. And, of course, belonged to one of the sects of Albigenses. He has, by some writers, been classed under the more general name of Waldenses. He differed, however, from the Waldenses proper on Infant Baptism and several other points. Some short time after his death we read of several sects who rejected it, but all of them appear to be branches of the same, although called by other names, and generally after the places in which they flourished, or after their leaders. For instance, the Henricians were called after the name of Henry, who was a disciple of De Bruys, and an Italian by birth. He was zealous and active, and spread his doctrines through various parts of France. His followers were called in some places Henricians, and in others after the names of the places in which they were known. Arnold, of Brescia, returned to Italy about the year 1135 from Paris, assumed the monastic garb, and began to preach the same doctrines advocated by the Henricians in France. His followers were called Arnoldists.

A display is sometimes made of all these names; and readers who are not aware of their origin, are induced to think they weigh something against Infant Baptism.[1]

Decretal Epistles and Councils are also referred to. But we need only examine the dates and circumstances with which they stand connected, to see how little bearing all of them have on the subject.

The Lateran Council, under Pope Innocent the Second, which condemned Pierre de Bruys and Arnold, was held Anno Domini, 1139, some thirty years after the rise of the Petrobrussians.

The Lateran Council, under Pope Innocent the Third, was in 1215, some seventy-six years later than the former, and only shows that the doctrines of Peter was still spreading.

In the Decretal Epistle of Innocent the Second, is found a letter, in answer to one from the Bishop of Arles, in Provence, the country of Bruys, written about the beginning of the twelfth century, which shows that that country gave birth to the first Antipædobaptists, and that they first agitated, for a short time in a more private way, what De Bruys soon after proclaimed publicly.

A Synod held at Arras, in the year 1025, which has been already referred to, has often been adduced in this controversy. This was first brought forward by Stennet, from Dr. Allix's work. Stennet only gave a part of the facts there recorded. We there find that Gundulphus and his followers denied that Baptism could do good to ANY ONE — that their doc-

[1] Jones' *Hist. Ch.* *Encyclopædia of Religious Knowledge.*

trines were very similar to the Quakers of the present day.[1]

The Cathari of Germany, Paterines in Italy, and the Paulicians of Greece, are next appealed to as the line of descent in which Antipædobaptism can be traced. These were all branches of the same under different names in different countries, and were semi-Manichæans, and objected to all Baptism, likewise to the sacrament of the Lord's Supper.[2]

The Paulicians, in Greece, from whom all the others sprang, took their name from one Paulus, who commenced his career in Armenia, about the beginning of the seventh century. He rejected both of the sacraments, Baptism and the Lord's Supper — denied the authority of the Old Testament — interpreted the New allegorically — and taught that the Supreme Being created neither the world nor the human body — and that this was the work of some inferior being. They were branded as heretics and persecuted by the Greek Church, but persisted in their doctrines. When banished from their own country they sought refuge in others, continuing to inculcate their principles wherever they went.[3] "In different countries," says Mosheim (in which he is followed by Baptist writers), "they were known by different names. In Greece, they were called Paulicians — in Italy, Paterines — in Germany, Cathari, or rather Gazari — in France, Bulgarians, because they came from Bulgaria, the country in which the head of the sect had resided — also, Publicans, probably a corrupt pronunciation of Paulicians. They were also called 'good men,' with several other titles."[4]

[1] Wall.

[2] Waddington and Mosheim.

[3] See Fessenden's *Encyclopædia of Religious Knowledge*, Mosheim and Waddington.

[4] See also Waddington.

Whether these were all different names given to the same sect, at different times and in different countries, or not, certain it is, they differed very little from each other in their doctrines. And there can be but little doubt in regard to the fact, that the influence of these doctrines on the minds of the people of Albi among whom they lived, gave rise to that particular sect of the Albigenses who objected particularly to Infant Baptism. The Catholics on the one hand, baptized both infants and adults — the Paulicians, on the other, rejected all Baptism and the sacrament of the Supper. The inhabitants of Albi being pleased with many of their doctrines, were not prepared to leap across the whole ground from the Catholics to the Paulicians, and so took a middle position between them, blending together what they most highly approved of each, and rejecting the remainder. They were disgusted with the lives of the Roman Catholic priests and with useless ceremonies, but were not willing to give up the sacrament of the Supper — and hence retained Baptism so far as it could be made a preparatory step to the Supper, but rejected the Baptism of Infants.

Or, it may be, that the Paulicians, coming among a people where the Gnostic philosophy of the East was little known, and gradually losing its influence over their own minds, began to decline from the doctrines of their forefathers, and to adopt in part the doctrines of the Christians around them. Their first step was probably to administer the sacrament of the Supper, which required Baptism, as a preparatory rite to its observance — but they refused it to infants, because, among other reasons, they said, " since they cannot *believe*, they cannot be *saved*, and it is therefore *useless* to them." This was, at least, the chief reason given for refusing it to them after De Bruys began to preach in public what they had canvassed among themselves more privately.

The probabilities in favor of this conjecture are increased by the fact, that Alanus, a writer towards the close of that century, 1192, reckoning up the opinions of the Paulicians, or Cathari, as they were then called, says, they "differ among themselves as to Baptism; some rejecting all water Baptism, others refusing it only to infants." This was in the same century in which Pierre de Bruys lived, but some time after his death. Before this century, all writers, who give their doctrines on this point, unite in testifying that they rejected water Baptism and the Lord's Supper altogether.

This, after much labor in examining and comparing the accounts given by various authors, is, according to our most careful and deliberate judgment, the most probable of all the conjectures that we have yet seen in regard to the *origin* of Antipædobaptism, or rejection of Infant Baptism. If it originated before this time, evidence of the fact has not been brought forward by any writer yet known to us on the subject. And why certain Baptist writers should profess to trace their Church through these sects, we are at a loss to conjecture, unless it be, because they objected to the cross, to the worship of the Virgin Mary, and to some other popish rites. For certainly there is nothing in their history to show they held the peculiar doctrine of Antipædobaptism before the twelfth century. And had they opposed it even from their origin as a sect, that was too late a date to avail anything on the question before us.

The next step is to the Donatists. Through these, it has been pretended by some, the principles of Antipædobaptism can be traced. This sect arose A. D. 311. The Bishop of Carthage, Mensurius, died that year, and Cecilianus was elected and consecrated in his place. The Numidian bishops, who belonged to a subordinate province, were not present, and objected both to the person elected, and to the manner of procedure; and determined to consecrate Majorinus in opposition to him, declaring Cecilianus was not properly put into office, and alleging against him and also against one of his consecrators, viciousness of life. Two parties were now formed, and several successive councils assembled to decide the controversy. The Numidian party lost their cause in every Council. A schism was finally produced, and a schismatic body formed, called Donatists, after the name of Donatus, their principal leader in the controversy.[1]

Between the Donatists and Church Catholic, from which they separated, there was no difference as to Church organization, except that the Donatists afterwards re-baptized such as happened to come over to them from the Church, alleging as their reason for this, that Baptism was not valid in a church in which such officers as Cecilianus and some others of his party were permitted to administer it. As to Infant Baptism, they continued to practise it, as they had done before their separation. This has been before shown from the acts of Councils passed, when the Donatists began to come back into the great body of the Church from which they had separated. In two Councils in the Church of Africa, as cited in the first part of this work, resolutions were passed concerning those bap-

[1] Mosheim, Waddington, and Church historians generally.

tized in infancy among the Donatists, in regard to the promotion to Church offices. In the first, it was resolved, that it should be made a question of consultation with neighboring bishops, whether those baptized in infancy among the Donatists might not be promoted, because they were too young to know the error that was committed, and, therefore, less guilty than those capable of judging for themselves.[1]

In a following Council it was resolved, that such as turned to the Church as soon as capable of understanding the error, might hold office in it; but those who continued with the Donatists, and became teachers, before correcting what had been done, must be deferred for longer consideration.[2]

Again: Optatus, bishop of Milevis, persuading the Donatists to union with the Church, tells them, "The ecclesiastical organization is one and the same with us and you. Though men's minds are at variance, the sacraments are at none. And we may say we believe alike, and are sealed with one and the same seal: not otherwise baptized than you, nor otherwise ordained than you."[3]

Cresconius, who was himself a Donatist, anxious to unite the two parties, uses also these words: "There is between us and you one religion, the same sacraments, nothing in Christian ceremonies different. It is a schism that is between us — not a heresy."[4]

Now, as no one can doubt whether the Church baptized infants at that time, what plainer testimony need we that the Donatists practised the same? there

[1] Concil. Carthag. tertii. can. 48

[2] Codex Canonum Eccl. Africanæ, can. 57.

[3] Lib. 3 de Schis. Donatist.

[4] Apud Augustinum lib. 2, contra Cresconium. See Wall, vol. i. p. 105.

was "no difference in the sacraments," and "Christian ceremonies," say both parties; and Councils passed laws for such as were baptized in infancy by the Donatists. What need we more to prove that the Donatists baptized infants? Surely this is enough to convince any reasonable man. Nor does any writer, in plain terms, deny this fact. Yet some will insinuate and imply as much, even passing on to the Novatians, professing to see signs of Antipædobaptism in that sect also! We must, therefore, inquire who the Novatians were, and what they taught.

The Novatians were a sect called after Novatian,[1] a Presbyter in the Church of Rome, who was a man, says Mosheim, "of uncommon learning and eloquence, but of an austere and rigid character, entertaining the most unfavorable sentiments of those who had been separated from the communion of the Church. He indulged his severity so far as to deny that any who had fallen into the commission of grievous transgressions, especially those who had apostatized from the faith under the persecution set on foot by Decius, should ever be again received into the bosom of the Church. The greater part of his brother Presbyters were of a different opinion in this matter, especially Cornelius, whose credit and influence were raised to the highest pitch by the esteem and admiration which his eminent virtues so naturally excited. Hence it happened that when a bishop was to be chosen, in A. D. 250, to succeed Fabius in the see of Rome, Novatian opposed the election of Cornelius with the greatest activity and bitterness. His opposition, however, was in vain, for Cornelius was chosen to the office, of

[1] See Mosheim, Lardner, Milner, Waddington, and historians generally.

which his distinguished merit rendered him so highly worthy. Novatian, from this time, separated himself from the jurisdiction of Cornelius, who, in his turn, called a Council at Rome, A. D. 251, and cut him off and his partisans from the communion of the Church. This turbulent man erected a new society, of which he was the first bishop." [1]

From this extract, we see that Novatian and Cornelius entertained the same doctrinal views, belonged to the same Church, but differed in regard to the disposition of those who had fallen away from fear of persecution. But this is not all. Novatian was an aspirant to the office of bishop in the same Church, and a rival of Cornelius. And the success of Cornelius was, no doubt, the chief cause of his forming a new society, over which he could be bishop, while laxity of discipline was made the ostensible reason.[2]

As they were ministers in the same Church, and rivals for the same office, they must have entertained the same general views in doctrine. And when Novatian separated, the only reason pretended for it was *laxity of discipline*. Nothing was said about Baptism.

On the other hand, Cornelius charged him with want of moral courage and unfitness for the office of bishop, because he had been baptized under the influence of fear on his sick bed, instead of receiving it of his own free will, uninfluenced by external causes.

On what ground, then, can he be claimed as the advocate of Baptist principles? A man baptized by aspersion himself, and the baptizer of infants! Nor are we anywhere informed that Novatian or any of his followers ever afterwards changed on these points.

[1] Mosheim, vol. i. p. 96.
[2] Milner, Waddington, and Lardner.

No, neither Augustine, nor any others who give an account of the various sects of that age and their doctrines, intimate that they held peculiar views as to *mode*, or refused Baptism to infants. Cyprian, who lived and wrote at the time this schism was made, and Eusebius and Optatus whilst the Novatians flourished, say nothing in their accounts of the differences between them and the Church to that effect. Mosheim, on the contrary, expressly states that "there was no difference in point of doctrine between the Novatians and the great body of Christians. What peculiarly distinguished them was their refusing to re-admit to the communion of the Church, however penitent, those who, after Baptism, had fallen into the commission of sins; yet they did not pretend that such were excluded from all possibility of salvation."[1]

What then, it may be asked, ever suggested the thought that the Novatians rejected Infant Baptism? Nothing, so far as we can learn, except it be the misapprehension of a *single word*. The Novatians, like the Donatists, required those who had been baptized in the Church Catholic to be re-baptized when they united with them, on the ground that a Church so lax in its government vitiated and rendered null the holy rite of Baptism; and, for re-baptizing in such cases, they were sometimes called Anabaptists, which simply means those who baptize anew.[2] Certain Dutch writers of later years, finding this term applied to the Novatians, inferred from it that they rejected Infant Baptism; and others have handed down what *they supposed*.[3] "The Novatians assumed to them-

1 Vol. i. p. 96.
2 'Ανά, "anew." Βαπτίζω, "to baptize."
3 See Wall, vol. ii.

selves," says Mosheim, "the title CATHARI — *i. e., pure ;* and what shows a still more extravagant degree of vanity and arrogance, they obliged such as came over to them from the great body of Christians to be baptized a second time, as a necessary preparation for entering into their society." [1]

It was some half century before this schism, that Origen declared "Infant Baptism was the usage of the Church handed down from the Apostles." It was before this and before the name of "Cathari," as a sect, was heard of, that a Council at Carthage had legislated against the delay of Baptism till the eighth day after birth, as a rule. Hence, had the Novatians rejected Infant Baptism, it would have been an innovation on the established order of the Universal Church. This, however, they did not do, nor did any other sect branching from or uniting with them in that century. For in addition to the united testimony of historians, that "there was no difference in point of doctrine between them," *the same is confirmed by the incidental testimony* of writers against these various schismatical sects. These writers trace their origin, describe their tenets, and point out their peculiarities, and show wherein they differed from the Church; but in no instance is Baptism of Infants specified as a point of difference; whilst Infant Baptism was the universal practice of the Church at the time they wrote. Four of these writers, Epiphanius, Philastrius, Augustine, and Theodoret,[2] lived about the time, and wrote two of them, after the Novatian schism arose; and had the Novatians opposed Infant Baptism, they would most assuredly have mentioned it. But since

[1] Vol. i. p. 96.

[2] See ch. iii. of this volume.

they say nothing about it, their silence accords with the general testimony that they baptized Infants also.

Baptists, therefore, will find no authority from the practice of the Novatians to justify them in excluding little children from the fold of Christ; nor can they find any traces of their Church in the sects that arose before the Novatians.

The writings of the early Christians have been ransacked also to find testimony of *another kind*, to disprove the infant's claim to church-membership. Much labor has been spent to find cases of the *children of Christians* who were baptized at adult age, in order to prove that it was not the universal custom of Christian parents to have their children baptized in infancy. And could any such cases be found, they would only show that some Christians in that age may have neglected this duty whilst they acknowledged its authority, as many do in this age. It seems, however, that there was great unanimity of action among ancient Christians on this point; for out of fourteen cases, produced from first to last, it has been found, on strict examination, that all of them were either baptized in infancy, or were born before their parents became Christians, with the exception of one single case, in the fourth century. That was Gregory Nazianzen, concerning whom it is doubtful whether his father was a Christian or not, when he was born.

Not many years since, the editor of a public journal having made a flourish of *modern names* favorable to Antipædobaptism, was called upon to give some *ancient authorities*, or produce a *single passage* from any writer during the first thousand years of Christianity, that would show Infant Baptism was not the practice of the Church during that period. He, in reply, cited a passage from Fabian's "Chronicle of English History," written in the fifteenth century, in which the author professed to be indebted to the "Venerable Bede" for his account of the ancient affairs of the Britons; but, unfortunately, as it appears, he quoted from a *defective edition* of Fabian — the passage not being sustained by another edition of the same author, nor by the text of Bede.

In the early part of the eighth century, the "Venerable Bede," as he is called, wrote an "Ecclesiastical History of England," in which is recorded the efforts of Augustin, the monk, to plant the Roman Church among the Ancient Britons in the early part of the seventh century. He found the Christian Church already established among them, but in some respects different in ceremonial and customs from the Roman Church; the latter having *added* to the ceremonial of primitive Baptism. Augustin proposed to the Britons to unite with him, and to adopt his customs wherein they differed from their own. And for the purpose of perfecting such an arrangement a conference was held at a place long since known as "Augustin's Ac" — [Oak].

But failing to persuade the bishops of Britain to change their customs, another conference was appointed, and attended by a larger number of bishops and learned men among the Britons; many of whom had been advised by a sagacious Eremite, renowned for his practical wisdom, not to give up their traditions and follow Augustin, unless "he was a man of God — meek and lowly in spirit" — like HIM who said, "Take my yoke upon you." And to the question, "How is this to be known?" he advised them to delay their arrival at the place appointed until Augustin had reached it, and then, if on their approach he *rose up* to meet them, to hear submissively what he had to say; but if he *rose not up* when they approached him, to act towards him accordingly.

On their arrival they found Augustin "sitting on a chair," who, without rising, said to them: "You act in many particulars contrary to our custom, or rather the custom of the Universal Church, and yet, if you will comply with me in these three points, namely, to keep Easter at the due time, to administer Baptism (by which we are again born to God) according to the custom of the Holy Roman Apostolic Church, and jointly with us preach the word of God to the English nation, we will readily tolerate all the other things you do, though contrary to our customs."

They answered they would do none of those things, nor receive him as their archbishop. "For (they said among themselves) if he will not rise up to us, how much more will he contemn us as of no worth, if we shall begin to be under his subjection."[1] Fabian, in his chronicle, quotes this passage (perhaps from memory), and changes the words of the sentence "To administer Baptism . . . *according to the custom of the Holy Roman Catholic Church*" into "*Ye give Christendom to the children in the manner that is used in the Church of Rome:* which is substantially of the same import with Bede; but he specifies *children*, which Bede only implies, and if he means "*little children*," he teaches that it was the custom of both the Roman Church and the Church of Britain to baptize little children, rather than that the Church of Britain had omit-

[1] Bede's *Eccl. Hist.*, lib. ii. ch. 2, edited by J. A. Giles, D. C. L. Third London edition.

ted it. In the copy of Fabian, however, from which this Antipædobaptist made his extract, the clause "IN THE MANNER *that it is used in the Church of Rome*," is left out, and simply reads "*Ye give Christendom to the children*" — as if the Church of Britain had omitted or refused to give Baptism to the children. Even if this is not an omission of the transcriber, it is contradicted by another edition of the same author, and also by the authority to which it is professedly indebted; consequently can avail nothing on either side.

But as to the question of *Fact*, whether Infant Baptism was then the doctrine and practice of the Church in both countries represented in that assemblage? Nearly two centuries before Augustin landed on the shores of Britain, Pelagius, as we have seen, born and bred in Britain, and who had lived in Rome, declared that "*he had never heard of even an impious heretic that denied Baptism to infants*." And Celestius, born in Ireland, and who had visited the most notable churches in Asia and Africa, as well as in Europe, in regard to the same question said, "IT IS THE RULE OF THE UNIVERSAL CHURCH TO GIVE BAPTISM TO INFANTS."

The same has been found to be the RULE of the Church on the coast of Malabar, which had been separated from other Christians more than thirteen hundred years. When first discovered, after this long period, and brought to the knowledge of other portions of the Christian world, they had the custom of Infant Baptism, and still continue it, claiming as the founder of their Church and doctrine the Apostle St. Thomas.[1]

[1] Buchanan's *Researches*.

To whatever point we turn, we find evidence accumulating on evidence, that Infant Baptism was the practice of the Primitive Church. And beyond doubt, it must surprise the reader as it has the writer, that any who have examined the evidence, can resist it. But it is stranger still, that Christian men should ransack all history to find testimony on the other side, and then turn round, and try to cast discredit upon all Church history, and make an array of the corruptions in the Church to invalidate the authority of a rite known to exist before such corruptions were made! And shall we discard a doctrine merely because of abuse? Ought we not rather to discriminate between the abuse and the thing itself? "Prove all things, hold fast that which is good," is the Apostolic injunction.

Shall we discard the Lord's Supper because some have vainly supposed the bread and wine were changed into the natural body and blood of Christ? The fact that Infant Baptism was the practice of every Church, extending over thousands of miles, from the first knowledge of them on that point, and no one ever called its lawfulness in question, is of itself sufficient to dispel the *mere surmise* that it is an innovation. Again, the fact that there was much conjecture and discussion among early Christian writers, as to its *effects* and the *reasons* why it was commanded, shows that it was not instituted by men. For had it been of human origin, the reason and grounds of necessity would have been given in the first place. But, like adult Baptism, being ordered by Divine wisdom, men are left to conjecture as to its grounds, effects, and other particulars, which the Master did not think proper to reveal.

The evidence that has been adduced, be it observed, is not merely the *opinions* or *conjectures* of men; but *their testimony* to that which was the *object of their senses*, and is intended as corroborative evidence of the correctness of the interpretation which we give the holy Scriptures — as a tree, showing by its leaves and fruit what is the *nature of the scion*, about which there had been much difference of opinion.

Ancient records and passages that speak of Infant Baptism, are referred to, just as we refer to passages of the same writings, that speak of the different books of the New Testament, when our object is to prove that any one of those books was received among the early Christians as of Divine authority. How then can one under any pretence whatever, gainsay this testimony, so long as he appeals to it in support of the genuineness of the different books of the New Testament, and to which *we must* appeal, or open the way to the rejection of the Holy Scriptures?

By such appeal and tests, we can find no Christian body that admitted the necessity of Baptism to adults and refused it to infants, until the beginning of the twelfth century, when, in the midst of the darkness that overspread Europe, Pierre de Bruys, of Languedoc, and some others connected with him, began to promulge the doctrine, that it was unnecessary to baptize infants, because they could not believe, and therefore could not be saved.[1] Peter, Abbot of Clugni, writing about A. D. 1146, says: "It might have seemed there was no need to confute such a doctrine as this, were it not that it had now continued twenty years. The first seeds of which were sown by Pierre de Bruys."

[1] See Milner, Mosheim, Waddington.

This sect opposed the building of churches, and said that singing "was mocking God." In regard to Infant Baptism, this author thus writes: "They say, 'Christ sending his disciples out to preach, says in the gospel: *Go ye out into all the world and preach the Gospel to every creature — he that believeth and is baptized shall be saved, but he that believeth not shall be damned.* From these words of our Saviour it is plain that none can be saved, unless he believes and is baptized: that is, have both Christian faith and Baptism. For not one of these, but both together, do save! So that infants, though they be by you baptized, yet since by reason of their age they *cannot believe, are not saved.*'" [1]

This is the first public and open avowal against Infant Baptism as a Christian rite (so far as we can learn) on record. [2] The followers of Gundulphus, who were condemned in a Synod, at Arras, in the preceding century, have been cited as the first. But they held all Baptism to be of no use — that a moral life was sufficient.

"This," said they, "is our doctrine, to renounce the world, to bridle the lusts of the flesh, to maintain ourselves by the labor of our own hands, to do violence to no man, to love the brethren. If this plan of righteousness be observed, there is no need of Baptism; if it be neglected, Baptism is of no avail." [3] They are said to have regarded the Lord's Supper and dignitaries in the Church, in the same light. And in their opposition to Baptism, they gave as a

[1] Cited by Wall, vol. ii. pp. 235, 236.

[2] If any writer will produce an *undoubted passage* to that effect of an earlier date, it shall be *inserted* in the next edition of this book, if it shall ever reach another, and acknowledged in other ways.

[3] See Wall, vol. ii. c. 7.

particular reason for the case of infants, that they could not understand and confess the truth. They may be regarded, therefore, as esteeming Infant Baptism even more unreasonable than adult, but both alike unnecessary.

In this sense, it may be said, the first opposers of Infant Baptism were brought to light in the beginning of the eleventh century. But the Petrobrussians, in the following century, took a very different ground, and opposed Infant Baptism, whilst they received adult Baptism. They contended that infants could not be saved, though they were baptized, because they could not believe. And they certainly interpreted that passage of Scripture, on which the opponents of Infant Baptism lay so much stress in this age, more consistently than is now done: "He that believeth and is baptized shall be saved — he that believeth not shall be damned." (Mark xvi. 16.) If, according to this reading, faith be in all cases necessary to Baptism, consistency in all its parts requires faith as necessary in all cases to salvation. So that if it be applicable to infants in the one case, it must be in both; therefore, the Petrobrussians were more consistent than the Antipædobaptists of the present day, on this point.

The doctrine of Pierre de Bruys was adopted afterwards by several sects, or rather advocated by those called by other names, but they were few in number, and but little known till after the dawn of the Reformation under Luther; when it appears, that about A. D. 1521, they collected together in considerable numbers, chiefly from Saxony and the adjacent countries, headed by Munzer, Stubner, and Storck, and are described by various writers as very fanatical, turbulent, and seditious; — who, says Mosheim, "declared war against all laws, government and magistrates of every kind. . . . But this seditious crowd was routed and dispersed without much difficulty, by the Elector of Saxony and other princes; Munzer was put to death, and his factious counsellors were scattered abroad in different places."[1] They were afterwards more timid, but still continued to spread their principles, and were called Anabaptists. About A. D. 1533, a portion of them, perhaps more fanatical and seditious than others, headed by John Matthison, John Bockhold, a tailor, and one Gerard, took the city of Munster, deposed the magistrates, and proclaimed John Bockhold king and legislator of their new hierarchy. Munster was retaken in A. D. 1536, after a long siege, and their New Jerusalem as they called it, destroyed, and its mock monarch punished with a most painful and ignominious death.[2]

Their doctrine of a new and perfect Church, guided by visions and revelations from Heaven, which set aside the necessity for civil government; and the abolishing of ranks and titles, and the equal distribution of goods, making a common stock for all alike; together with polygamy and other liberties, brought upon them the dislike and persecution of civil rulers. In A. D. 1536 Menno Simonis, who had been a Roman Catholic priest, was chosen their leader, who modified many of their tenets, rejected polygamy, visions, and other more objectionable features, and reduced their system to more consistency and order.

Their intolerance when in possession of Munster, and open avowal of intention to bring all the nations

1 Vol. ii. page 129.

2 Idem 131. See historians generally.

of the earth under their dominion, had spread far and wide, which excited unkindness and intolerance toward them in return. And not until the publication of their faith in A. D. 1626, in a form still more improved, did they obtain the confidence of public rulers, and the liberty to inculcate generally their doctrines unmolested.

They were first introduced into England through emigrants from Holland. Fuller in his "Church History," recites from Stow — "In 1538 four Anabaptists, three men and one woman, *all* Dutch, bore fagots at Paul's Cross: And that three days after, a man and woman of their sect were burnt in Smithfield. And says, *This year the name of this Sect first appears in our English Chronicles*." [1]

Again, he tells us that — "In 1572, about the 16th year of Queen Elizabeth, a congregation of Dutch Antipædobaptists was discovered without *Aldgate* in London: whereof twenty-seven (27) were taken and imprisoned." [2] Some of these it seems were punished with death, and the congregation broken up.

In 1610, the Rev. John Smith, an Englishman, returned from Holland with some other Puritans who had embraced the faith of the Anabaptists, and set up public worship. But after his death they dispersed, and a portion of them went back to Holland. [3]

In 1638, the first permanent congregation of Anabaptists, or Baptists as they are now called, was organized in England under the pastoral care of the Rev. Mr. Jesse. "They sent over one of their number, Mr. Blunt, to be immersed by one of the Dutch

[1] Fuller's *Ch. Hist.*, lib. 5, sec. 5.
[2] Idem, lib. 9, sec. 3, — cited by Wall.
[3] Murdock on Mosheim.

Anabaptists of Amsterdam, that he might be qualified to baptize his friends in England after the same manner. A strange and unaccountable conduct," says Neal, "for unless the Dutch Anabaptists could derive their pedigree in an uninterrupted line from the Apostles, the first reviver of this usage must have been unbaptized, and consequently not capable of communicating the ordinance to others." [1]

The first Baptist Church in America was formed in A. D. 1639, in Providence, Rhode Island, by Roger Williams; who not being able to obtain immersion at the hands of one who had been immersed, first immersed Mr. Ezekiel Hopkins, who afterwards immersed Mr. Williams.

But Mr. Williams afterwards, having come to the conclusion that *the succession of believer's immersion had been lost*, left the Baptist and turned SEEKER, *i. e.*, one who believes that the *true Church Ministry and ordinances are lost*, and for which he is seeking.[2]

We cannot find that *immersion* was made essential to Baptism by the Anabaptists before the *sixteenth* century; nor that Infant Baptism was rejected by any sect, branch of the Christian Church, or writer, before the twelfth. After its rejection by the Petrobrussians, their views were adopted by some of the sects that were in existence before the time of Pierre de Bruys, but that any one of them rejected it before, we challenge the opposers of Infant Baptism to prove, and pledge ourselves, if a single case can be produced, to acknowledge it as publicly as we here declare our belief to the contrary.

1 Neal's *History* — cited by Summers, p. 56.

2 Hildreth's *History* — also *Memoirs of Roger Williams*, by J. D. Knowles.

And we call upon those who are accustomed to repeat the broad assertions to which we have alluded, to examine the ground on which they stand. The unqualified, dogmatic manner, in which many speak of the mode and subjects of Baptism, is unwarranted by Christian charity and the facts in the case. How often do we hear Infant Baptism denounced as unscriptural and a great evil, with as little qualification as when they condemn a gross sin!

If such persons will examine the whole question, as they should do, and do not afterwards teach the opposite doctrine, they will at least learn to speak of such things with more modesty. It cannot be that these men realize how much is implied in the doctrines which they teach. They assume not only that the Church, against which Christ promised "the gates of hell should not prevail," became corrupt in *essentials*, in the first age after the Apostles, but continued so until the sixteenth century, thereby destroying its "tens of thousands," hence for a long period there was no Church, because all, with here and there exceptions, who were baptized in the missionary fields, were baptized in infancy, which they do not admit is Baptism; and as Baptism is the only initiatory rite by which they could become members of the Church, therefore, God had no Church at the time of the great Reformation. And none who were engaged in reforming the Church were members of the Church, because they had all been baptized in their infancy![1]

[1] And these missionaries having been baptized themselves in *infancy*, were not baptized at all according to the Baptist theory, hence could not give lawful Baptism, and therefore Baptism was lost; and the Church had come to an end long before the Reformation, and the "Gates of Hell" *had prevailed against it!* although our Saviour expressly declared the contrary. So the Baptist theory is wrong, or our Saviour was a false prophet. Read and see: Roger Williams in a few years saw this dilemma, and left

Is not this a serious thought to a believer in the Bible, and member of the Christian Church, that none of our Reformers, the translators of the Bible, and the long galaxy of great and good men who have written commentaries, and handed down so many learned and pious works on the doctrines of our religion, and workings of the Holy Spirit — not one of them baptized and a member of Christ's Church? No, not one — if the doctrine of the Baptists be true — none of them were baptized, unless perchance a rebaptized one by the Anabaptists! What better argument needs the infidel?

But this is not all; none of us are now members of Christ's visible Church, who have not been immersed in water on a profession of faith. The whole question of membership is made to depend upon the *manner* of performing one of the rites of the Church! They carry out this principle, and allow no one to commune with them in the sacrament of the Supper, who has not been baptized according to their particular mode. He cannot enjoy this great and essential privilege of God's people — this distinctive right of the members of Christ's body is not to be granted him, because he has not been immersed! Therefore, on *the mode* of performing a rite, depends not only our membership in the Church of Christ, but the existence of the Church itself! There is no Church where there is no believer's immersion!

To what a condition does this bring the Church of God on earth, and where does it place all the great

them [the Baptists], admitting that Baptism had been lost on their theory, and could not be restored unless an angel should be sent from heaven with a new commission! Which shall we adopt, Infant Baptism and the continuance of Christ's Church on earth, or a theory that excludes little children, destroys the Church, and makes the Saviour a false prophet?

and good men, whose names we so much reverence, and to whose teaching we are so much indebted for our Christian instruction? On the same principle, where was the Church when no believers were baptized? And when the Church was lost, how was it recovered? If when that was lost the Church became extinct, who but God could begin it again? Roger Williams afterwards saw the dilemma into which this theory of the Baptists must bring the Church, and came to the conclusion that "Baptism was lost, and could not be restored unless an angel from Heaven was sent to give it to the world again," and left them. And if Baptism was lost, so was the Church also, as the existence of the latter depended on the former!

So much for the assumptions and theories of men. If the continuance of the Church has depended on the succession of Baptism, then it must have been the succession of Infant Baptism. Every historian will admit that.

A modern teacher of the Antipædobaptist school after making Infant Baptism responsible for nearly all the evils that ever afflicted the Church of God, [1] congratulated his own Church, as less liable to corruptions and divisions than others. Is he really not aware of the fact, that many more divisions and corruptions have sprung up among Antipædobaptists since their origin, than among all others? In the very beginning, their creed was mingled with Manichæism and Socinianism, and a motley crowd of undigested principles, that required a long time to be reduced to a consistent system. And scarcely were they organized under their present name, before they

[1] Dr. Howell.

were divided into General and Particular Baptists; then Open Communion and Close Communion Baptists; Seventh Day Baptists, to which a long train has followed, such as Seven Principle Baptists; Free Will Baptists; Church of God Baptists; Hard Shell Baptists; Soft Shell Baptists; Little Children Baptists; Christian Baptists; Ironside Baptists; Scotch Baptists; Campbellite Baptists, or Reformers; Dunkers; Mormons, and a host of others, all of whom are Antipædobaptists. Some of these may be the same bodies, called by different names, but there are many more, and no two hold precisely the same doctrines. The author of the "Biographia Britannica Literaria," informs us there are some *Eighty sects*, that have sprung from the Anabaptists of the sixteenth century, spread through Europe and America. And yet the Baptist Church is based on a system that cannot be corrupted!

Our Baptist brethren claim also to be the true friends of Christian liberty; and boast of being the first advocates of true religious toleration; but the signs of the times do not augur that power in their hands will be any less liable to abuse than in the hands of others. Their proceedings in their Bible society, the productions of some of their later writers, and their manner of teaching in public and in private, cause us to fear the *scenes of Munster* might be acted over again, power and opportunity being afforded them.

And while we claim the liberty to defend our own principles and our own firesides, we grant them the same. And though we may have written earnestly and plainly, we have endeavored to do so in a Christian spirit, certainly as much so as our opponents. Nor do we intend that difference of opinion where we have the right to differ, shall affect our social intercourse.

We now close this work by earnestly requesting our readers to weigh well the facts and principles herein contained. The principle involved is of more importance than is generally supposed. Our children will never be trained and instructed as they ought to be, till we learn the responsibility resting upon us, in regard to them — until we dedicate them to God in good faith, train them as his children, as Christians from childhood, pledged and bound to the service of their Redeemer.

A high standard of family religion, is a special need at the present time, and always necessary to a healthful state of the Church and the rapid spread of the Christian religion. The want of this causes trouble and divisions in the family circle, and is the fruitful source of schism and inactivity in the Church of God. Unity of purpose and of effort is necessary to the success of every kind of organization among men. This Christ and his Apostles taught, and prayed should be the rule of the Christian Church.

But this union of hand and heart cannot be expected where one half of the house only, and sometimes less, are baptized members of Christ; and the other portion informed that they are not qualified for membership, and must wait until they arrive to a certain age, or attain certain moral qualifications. Consequently they feel more at liberty in the meantime to indulge idle thoughts and wicked suggestions, and are gradually drawn into the habit of supplying omissions of present duty by resolutions of future amendment; while the seeds of evil spring up and take deep root, before the faithful culture of Divine Grace in the heart is begun.

And though the advocates of this system may then teach their children many good things, and explain the love of Christ and his willingness to save all who come to Him; and the duty of every one to accept Him as their Redeemer, and keep his commandments; they cannot apply their teaching with the same force on the consciences of such, as when appealing to those who are baptized. For since these children know they are regarded as yet too young, or not fit for Baptism and to be numbered among the people of God, they hold themselves free from the obligations of church members; and the great enemy of truth avails himself of such opportunities to fill their minds with doubts and evil surmisings that too often follow them through life and keep them from Baptism throughout their sojourn on earth!

But the child baptized in infancy is the recipient of the grace of the sacrament, and the special prayers of God's people accompanying it, and taken into the nursery and training of the Church, before evil principles get fast hold upon the mind. He is taught, as soon as able to learn, the name of Christ and his love for little children; how He redeemed them from the condemnation of the law, and receives them into covenant with Himself; — having paid the penalty due sin, and organized a church into which to bring and train them for the kingdom of heaven. And for the inestimable privilege of being baptized and taken into this nursery of piety and holy living — of being made a member of Christ, the child of God, and an inheritor of the kingdom of heaven, — his gratitude and love are appealed to, and his obligation to follow the precepts and live unto his Redeemer are felt and acknowledged. He knows no period when the blessings of such a Redeemer were not upon him, and he the object of his love and mercy.

And as his mental powers are developed, the teaching of God's word, by the operation of the Holy Spirit, changes his natural love for sin into love for holiness. And through the continued sanctifying influence of the same Spirit on the means of grace, his love of holiness increases, and he day by day is more and more conformed to the Divine image of his Saviour: his piety deepens, its influence is felt by those around him; its sanctifying power passes from him into the family circle, then into the Church, and spreads its transforming power among his fellow men, continuing its work of love on earth after he has been transferred to the kingdom of glory.

THE END.

COMMENDATIONS.

From the Presiding Bishop of the House of Bishops (*P. E. C.*)

"The Rev. Mr. Hodges has succeeded in a very remarkable manner in condensing the substance of many ponderous tomes into one thin volume without impressing you with the dulness of an index. He does indeed give you in a short space the cream of the whole matter. . . . . How familiar does he render what before seemed abstruse; how amusing what was before so very dull; and how charming and sweet-tempered is the manner in which points are treated that have alienated half the Protestant world. And as we go forward we begin to perceive how very instructive he is, how *absolutely exhaustive* indeed in all important points. He methodizes excellently, and modestly adorns most beautifully what he extracts from others. IT IS THE BOOK OF A THOUSAND TO BE PUT INTO THE HANDS OF INQUIRING MYRIADS." — B. B. SMITH.

From the late Bishop BURGESS, *of Maine.*

"It is an exceedingly full, thorough, and satisfactory treatise on a most important subject, and renders a signal service to the cause of Divine truth. The best and most popular work of the kind within my knowledge. It is a work, too, much needed; and I hope will have an extensive circulation and repeated editions, ... for it is desirable that this book shall be, and I think will be, the manual of both clergy and laity on this sacredly interesting subject." — GEORGE BURGESS.

From the Protestant Churchman.

"This book supplies general readers with what has probably never before been presented to the public in one volume. The author informs us that it is the result of many years' thoughtful and laborious research; and we think embodies all that need be said on the questions at issue. It is conclusive both *for* Infant Baptism, and *against* the unwarrantable assumption of confining baptism to any particular mode. The work ought to be widely circulated and read, not only in our own church, but among all pædobaptists. It would not, in our opinion, injure our Baptist brethren, nor dwarf their spirit." — *Protestant Churchman.*

From the Church Journal.

"The Church is indebted to the Rev. William Hodges for an excellent volume — BAPTISM TESTED BY SCRIPTURE AND HISTORY, — in which the witness of the Church on the subjects and modes of Baptism is clearly traced through the Fathers up to the fountain head of Holy Writ; and the proof-texts of Scripture are carefully and minutely analyzed: this testimony being elicited in a way peculiarly satisfactory and convincing. We wish the book were in the hands of every Baptist. Churchmen interested in the controversy with that numerous and plausible denomination, will find in this book more accurate information and sound argument than are to be found in the same space of any book in our knowledge." — *Church Journal.*

From the American Quarterly Church Review.

"In this work Mr. Hodges has done good service to truth and to the Church, showing conclusively, both by positive and negative proofs, that the baptism of infants has the sanction of Gospel authority, and was never called in question by any body of Christians using baptism at all before the twelfth century. The historical investigation of the subject seems to have been conducted with *great impartiality and complete success.* There is no book within our knowledge that we regard as more likely to be useful and satisfactory to persons disturbed with doubts upon the lawfulness of baptizing infants. We would also commend it to the candid examination of our Baptist brethren," etc. — *A. Q. Church Review.*

From the Bishop of Maryland.

"My Dear Doctor, — I am glad to learn that your new edition of the valuable 'Test of Infant Baptism' is about to appear. It is much wanted; for among the many excellent works that we have on the subject I know none that comprises the same range of research and fulness of argument within the same limits. Its clearness of method, too, and facility of style tend to make it preëminently useful to the many who need its information and instruction without having time or ability to grapple with formidable controversial or historical treatises. I feel confident that by its publication, with the improvements on which I know you to have bestowed so much care and labor, you are rendering to the Church a service of great value. Very faithfully," etc. — William R. Whittingham, *Bishop of Maryland.*

From the Assistant Bishop of Maryland.

"My Dear Doctor, — I am rejoiced to hear that there is to be a new edition of Infant Baptism tested by Scripture and History. It is a work of very great value, and ought to be widely circulated. It needs no endorsement. For thoroughness, beauty of order, keen analysis, and cumulative force, it occupies a place that no other book extant can so well supply. I anticipate for it a ready sale. I shall do all in my power to aid in its circulation." — William Pinkney, *Assistant Bishop of Maryland.*

From the Bishop of Virginia.

"Rev. and Dear Brother, — Your volume on Baptism tested by Scripture and History contains all that is necessary to a right understanding of the questions involved in the controversy. And the proofs are so well presented, and the objections so fully and fairly considered, that with your book in hand, a careful and candid inquirer may be left to reach a conclusion without fear as to the result. Yours," etc. — John Johns.

From the Assistant Bishop of Virginia.

"Baptism tested by Scripture and History, by the Rev. William Hodges, D. D., is an admirable book, on a plan well conceived and executed, and in my judgment unanswerable. I trust it may be circulated and read throughout Virginia." — Francis M. Whittle, *Assistant Bishop P. E. Church.*

From the Bishop of Alabama.

"Rev. and Dear Brother, — I am greatly rejoiced to learn that you have a third edition of your admirable book in press. There is scarcely a day that I do not see the use of such a book as yours; and I know no other work equal to it as a substitute. I am sure that its republication will be hailed with joy by the whole Church. I shall see that it is for sale in all points of my Diocese." — Richard A. Wilmer.

From the Bishop of North Carolina.

"Rev. and Dear Sir, — I am glad to learn that another edition of your work on Baptism is about to appear. It is, in my judgment, of *uncommon merit;* learned and yet well adapted to common use; calm and charitable, but at the same time decided and outspoken." — Thomas Atkinson.

COMMENDATIONS.

From the Bishop of Mississippi.

"**Rev. Dr. Hodges**, — Permit me to thank you for your excellent work on Baptism. It is a perfect 'Thesaurus' on a subject which might well be termed *fundamental* in the Christian scheme. The denial and rejection of infant baptism is a latter day heresy which would have convulsed the Primitive Church throughout her borders. In order to secure success to your work, it is only necessary that it be impartially read. Very truly," etc. — W. M. Green.

From the Bishop of Texas.

"**Rev. and Dear Brother**, — It affords me pleasure to add my testimony to your invaluable work, Infant Baptism tested by Scripture and History. It is the most thorough and complete that we have, and in a form adapting it not only to the clergy but to the laity as well. It ought to be introduced as an elementary text-book into our Theological Seminaries; for the subject of which it treats is one that should be mastered by those preparing for the ministry in order that they may be prepared to meet a question of the present day so largely discussed in this sectarian country of ours." — Alex. Gregg.

From R. S. Mason, D. D., *of Raleigh, N. C.*

"**My Dear Dr. Hodges**, — I have learned with great pleasure that you are about to publish a third edition of your excellent book on Infant Baptism. It is so full, and yet so clear and condensed in the arguments you employ, that I have made much use of it in my parish; and not being able to find any copies among the booksellers for some time past, I have been at a loss to supply its place with any book of the same size equally useful. I hope for the cause of truth and your own benefit that it will not be long before you are called upon to issue a fourth and succeeding editions." —Richard S. Mason.

From a long and successful Classical Teacher of Youth.

"I was first a member of the Baptist Church, brought up in the midst of a Baptist community, and many of my dearest relatives and friends are members of that Church. . . . . Consequently I brought up a large family of children without baptism. But last spring I read Hodges carefully and I think candidly. I knew all the Baptist arguments, for I had read Carson as carefully before. I had seen most of the arguments of Hodges too, but never so admirably arranged; never so linked together, with constantly accumulating power; and the result was *the complete removal of all doubt, and the thorough conviction that Infant Baptism is according to the mind of Christ.*" — Pike Powers.

From the Rt. Rev. F. D. Huntington, D. D., *Bishop of Central New York.*

"I join cordially in the strong testimonials to its excellence found at the close of the volume; and I shall place it on the list of books to be examined by candidates for Holy Orders in the Diocese." — F. D. Huntington.

12mo, 421 pages .... Price $2.00.

Sent by mail, postage paid, on receipt of price.

SHILOH; Or, WITHOUT AND WITHIN.

By W. M. L. Jay. Sixth Thousand, 12mo, 488 pages, $2.00.

A Story of Common Life; beautifully written, with quiet Pictures of New England Farm and Parish Life.

"A venerable and beloved brother in the ministry having earnestly commended it to our reading, we now desire not only to thank him most heartily for the pleasure and profit which we have enjoyed in its perusal, but to pass over his commendation to every one of our readers." — *Standard of the Cross.*

"We have many popular books in our parish library, but none doing more solid good every day than 'Shiloh' — a book which people like so much that they often purchase a copy after reading it." — *Gospel Messenger.*

"Its value as a work of fiction has been abundantly established. The struggle of good and evil in us is skillfully drawn. It is one of the few fictions in which the love-story portion is quite unnecessary for the majority of readers." — *Church Journal.*

"No praise of ours can add to the reputation it has already acquired. It is delightful to get hold of a good, bright, thorough *Church* story, such as this, after the dreary trash we are called upon to wade through. It is a permanent addition to our Church literature, and should be in every parish library." — *Pacific Churchman.*

"It is a sweet, simple story of New England country life, showing what one earnest worker for Christ and His Church can do to build up the waste places, and kindle into a flame the smouldering fires of devotion and work. A city girl, from considerations of health, chooses to spend her summer at Shiloh, a country village, rather than at Saratoga, the fashionable watering-place; and this is the history of her life, as written to her distant friend. The story is well told; the characters are well delineated; the pathetic and the humorous are skillfully blended; and we have both laughed and wept in reading it. We look forward with great pleasure to the future products of the author's pen, and are very sure that her place will be an exalted one among the writers of our time." — *Maryland Church Record.*

"'Shiloh' I like more than ever, and I greatly rejoice to see it in a permanent form. It is an achievement — a real one — to write to the times and to write as one should; to write a story (so to speak), and keep up interest without cheap sensation; to write religious fiction, and yet to avoid platitudes; and all this you have done, and I congratulate you. Now give us what Oliver Twist asked for — *more.*" — *Bishop Williams, of Conn.*

"I greatly like the atmospheric *infusion*, instead of the disconnected *intrusion*, of the religious element, and the influence of the Church. There are parts of it I should like to preach, and the whole book is far beyond any story yet written of, or in, the American Church." — *Bishop Doane, of Albany.*

"'Shiloh' is a twofold success. The contention between *Bona* and *Mala* constantly evokes valuable truths which strike us in a quite original light, and the social and natural features of rural life in New England have rarely been more pleasingly presented. The style is really charming, and pays the reader the compliment of care in the choice of epithets and the arrangement of the thoughts. Like a well bred man, the author comes into the reader's presence in his best apparel." — *New York Evening Post.*

"This is a book of decided merit. It is well written, and the authoress gives evidence of unusual descriptive powers. . . . . But 'Shiloh' is also designed, we think, to make apparent that no duty performed, no service offered, is too slight to be acceptable to God. 'Whatever thy hand findeth to do, do it with thy might;' or, to use Mrs. Jay's words, 'The sterling usefulness of doing quiet duties in quiet ways, unobtrusively and uncomplainingly, is one which, though the world may make little account of it, God will surely bless and abundantly reward.'" — *New York Herald.*

"'Shiloh' is a novel with a purpose, and that, too, of the most exalted kind. It deals in a spirit at once earnest and sincere, with some of the deepest problems that can occupy humanity, touching here and there, with a lighter hand, upon social foibles and individual eccentricities. On the whole, 'Shiloh' may be characterized as belonging to the healthiest type of modern fiction, and, though possessing no claims to striking originality in design or execution, as exhibiting a freshness of style and sentiment that will commend it to the mass of reflective readers." — *New York Times.*

"We can award this book — what is, after all, our highest praise — a place among our missionary books." — *New York Mail.*

"The scene is laid in a remote New England town, and the fortunes of a weak parish are described. There is much cleverness in drawing a variety of character, and some sharp contrasts are presented just such as one often sees around him. A quiet, intelligent, and well-founded religious faith influences to a life that abounds in good works, and the story suggests to readers how they may go and do likewise, and benefit those that are around us. Even in the sparsely populated country there is ample field for domestic missionary work, and if 'Shiloh' is read as it should be, it will have a beneficial influence in inciting to these much-needed labors." — *New York Commercial Advertiser.*

"It has decided power and point in it, and we design to make some large extracts from it, to give our readers a taste of its merits." — *New York Observer.*

"Its pictures of New England life and people are singularly faithful. Nothing could well be more affecting than the story of Maggie Warren's death-bed. The author has a fine artist-feeling which displays itself unostentatiously, but with a pervading and delightful presence." — *Christian Union.*

"A more carefully written book we have rarely seen. Its composition has evidently been a labor of love; and every paragraph bears evidence of having been written with the care which only a man of leisure and of earnest thought can command. In many respects it is a remarkable book, and will amply repay the reader. It is to be read; not for the narrative, though that is by no means without interest, but as a storehouse of earnest thought and valuable suggestion." — *The Citizen and Round Table.*

"In order to get back 'the roses' which a gay and tiresome New York winter, together with some hidden heart-sorrow, has taken from her cheeks, the heroine has come to board for the summer at a farm-house in the little village of Shiloh. And we have, in this book, the history of that summer as she writes it out in letters to a friend. After the summer is ended, she says: 'I came to it seeking rest. I got, first work, then peace, finally joy.' And we know, when we have read her letters, that the work was the doing of whatever good she could find to do among the people with whom she was thrown; that the peace was that quietness of soul which came when she had gained the victory over self; and the joy, the blessing of a love which she had thought lost to her forever. In closing our notice, we repeat our conviction of having been brought in contact with a writer of more than ordinary power, with a deep, thoughtful, spiritual nature, which has imparted to 'Shiloh' so much of its own intensity and earnestness as cannot fail to make the events of the story linger long in the memory of the reader, and their many lessons help him very often in his daily living." — *Boston Daily Advertiser.*

"It is a sweet book, and the author has made herself a name by it. We beg her to continue as she has begun. There is a high seat for her in American literature; and if she is wise, she will yet occupy it." — *Providence Press.*

"The style is singularly simple, clear, and graceful, while the interest and variety of situation, incidents, and character, are such as to secure the reader's gratified attention throughout." — *Chicago Interior.*

"We have been very much pleased with 'Shiloh.' It is written with power and sweetness. It breathes throughout, a tender, pure, and Christian spirit, seldom obtruded in the sermonizing fashion; but permeating the whole book, and giving it what may be styled, a moral fragrance. The name of the author is unfamiliar to us, but unless we are much mistaken, it is destined to become the name of a very popular author." — *Sacramento Record.*

www.ingramcontent.com/pod-product-compliance
Lightning Source LLC
LaVergne TN
LVHW021147110826
845150LV00005B/1151

9781425547127